DEATH AND SPIRITUALITY

Kenneth J. Doka with John D. Morgan

Death, Value and Meaning Series
Series Editor: John D. Morgan

Baywood Publishing Company, Inc.
AMITYVILLE, NEW YORK

Library of Congress Catalog Number: 92-31413
ISBN: 0-89503-107-8 (Paper)
ISBN: 0-89503-106-X (Cloth)

Library of Congress Cataloging-in-Publication Data

Death and spirituality / Kenneth J. Doka and John D. Morgan, editors.
     p. cm.   - - (Death, value, and meaning series)
  ISBN 0-89503-106-X (cloth) : $38.95. - - ISBN 0-89503-107-8 (pbk.)
: $28.95
    1. Death- -Religious aspects. 2. Bereavement- -Religious aspects.
3. Spiritual life. 4. Pastoral counseling. I. Doka, Kenneth J.
II.   Morgan, John D., 1933- . III. Series.
BT825.D37 1993
259' .6- -dc20   92-31413
                                          CIP

DEDICATION

To
Johnny Mandala
and
John Turissini
Whose early deaths from Leukemia some 20 years ago
and to
Marcus
Whose successful struggle with cancer
taught me much about
The Human Spirit
and
Life

Table of Contents

ACKNOWLEDGMENTS

One of my favorite tasks is always to acknowledge the help of others who made this volume possible. First and foremost, I would like to thank Dr. John Morgan. This volume acknowledges that it was written *with* John Morgan. At every stage, John Morgan was a guiding force. It was John who suggested this volume, helped select and contact authors, commented on chapters, advised on any problems, and when he became an editor of Baywood, took this volume under his official tutelage.

Dr. Charles Corr also has been a valued colleague and quiet contributor to this work. Over time I have learned I can count on Charles for everything from editorial assistance to thoughtful, gentle criticism. If Dr. Corr permits me to press on his time, he is likely to be acknowledged in any future works.

Anita Field, my graduate assistant, was also a great help. Her writing and editing skills were well used. A number of chapters should note *with* Anita Field. I would also like to thank those who also made this volume a reality. The College of New Rochelle provided a sabbatical and secretarial help. The Graduate School's Dean, Dr. Edward J. Miller not only contributed a chapter but also secretarial assistance. I'd like to thank and acknowledge the help of those secretaries and graduate assistants. I could not have done without Maureen Dillon, Lorin Peritz, Robin Pierce, Denise Hughes, and Sally Pure. My own Program Director, Dr. Marguerite Coke, and departmental secretary, Rosemary Strobel provided valuable support.

Additionally, too, I would like to thank all the authors who contributed chapters. And I would like to thank the staff of Baywood Publishing Company and their reviewers.

But there are a number of people who, while not directly associated with this work, have influenced my thinking about spirituality and death. My colleagues at ADEC, the Association of Death Education and

Counseling, are a continued source of insight, inspiration, support and delight. Dr. Austin Kutscher and the Foundation of Thanatology have provided frequent opportunities to explore these ideas as has Betty Murray at the National Foundation of Funeral Service. Dr. Robert Kastenbaum and Dr. Hannelore Wass have always encouraged my writing. I also would like to thank the IWG and *Death Studies* for permission to reprint a key chapter. Rev. James B. Jeffrey, Supervisor of my 1971 CPE at Sloan Kettering Memorial Hospital and Pastor Thomas Hammond taught me much about spiritual issues in dying and death. And I learned even more from my clients and parishioners. I also thank Thomas M. Quinn and Sons for all that I continue to learn there through my consulting.

Finally I'd like to thank all my family and friends for their constant love, support, and encouragement. They are all truly gifts to the human spirit.

PART I

Introduction

- An elderly Chinese immigrant, hospitalized with terminal disease, requests to burn incense.
- A 30-year-old Roman Catholic gay male, dying of AIDS, is consumed by deepening moral guilt, troubled by beliefs he thought he abandoned years ago.
- A mother whose teenage son died of an aneurism is angry at God over his death yet fearful of expressing that anger lest He 'punish her again.'
- A young widower seemingly has difficulty expressing grief believing it to be a sign of a weak faith.

All of these examples illustrate the kinds of issues that clinicians and counselors constantly encounter. For although North American society has long been characterized as secular, this does not deny the potency of spiritual concerns and religious values on the individual level. Polls affirm that vast majorities of North Americans both believe in God and consider religion important in their lives. This is clearly evident when one faces the crises of dying or bereavement. For, one of the strengths of belief is that it provides support and succor at a time when secular explanations are largely silent.

For these reasons, educators and clinicians have long recognized the significance that religious and spiritual themes have in counseling with the dying and bereaved. Yet, in cultures as religiously diverse as the U.S. and Canada, caregivers and educators may feel inadequate to the task.

This book addresses this need. Specifically it seeks to reach two, perhaps overlapping, audiences. First, it considers the needs of death-related counselors and educators, seeking to provide them with both a sense of the norm of religious tradition and the religious and spiritual issues that might arise in illness and bereavement, as well as suitable interventions, approaches and resources that might be useful in assisting clients in examining and resolving such issues. The book also speaks to the complementary needs of clergy who also may wish to assist parishioners and others as they face the spiritual and psychological crisis of dying and grief.

The book begins with two opening chapters. In the first, John Morgan explores the basis of spirituality. In an earlier essay, Morgan identified spirituality with specialness [1]. To Morgan, the term "spirit" refers to non-material aspects of a person, that which makes the person unique and special. Human thinking, willing and deciding which are distinct from bodily function and sensation are the heart of spirituality to Morgan. In Chapter 1, Morgan expands upon that perspective. As beings that think, feel, and decide, we are engaged in a perpetual quest for meaning, an attempt to make sense out of life. Knowledge, ethics, creativity, and religion all emerge from that struggle for meaning. This quest for meaning engages one in a paradoxical encounter with death. As creatures capable of symbolic thought, we are able to transcend the immediacy of the present. Yet that transcendental ability also compels us to affirm mortality. To paraphrase Becker, we recognize that we have the minds of angels but the finite bodies of worms [2]. To Morgan then, this attempt to understand and give meaning to death underlies that death is much more than a medical, psychological and social event. It is a spiritual crisis as well and spiritual needs too, must be addressed.

This perspective underlies the second Chapter "Assumptions and Principles of Spiritual Care." These principles, developed by the International Work Group (IWG) on Death and Dying and Bereavement note that while death is a spiritual event, often the spiritual needs of patients and clients are neglected. Beginning then with a recognition of that spiritual side, the IWG offers sets of principles that assist caregivers in addressing spiritual needs of patients and clients.

The IWG makes explicit a distinction implicit in Morgan's work and generally followed throughout in this book. "Spirituality" is broadly defined as referring to the non-material aspects of human life. Thus, ethics, art, music, culture, literature and religion, transcend their material aspects and are manifestations of spirituality. "Religion" is more narrowly defined as a given system of beliefs. An underlying assumption is that while individuals may or may not profess a religion, all have spiritual needs and concerns that must be considered.

REFERENCES

1. J. Morgan, Death and Bereavement: Spiritual, Ethical and Pastoral Issues, Death Studies, 12, pp. 85-90, 199.
2. E. Becker, The Denial of Death, Free Press, New York, 1973.

CHAPTER 1

The Existential Quest for Meaning

John D. Morgan

THE UNIQUENESS OF THE PERSON

When Cecily Saunders began St. Christopher's Hospice in London, she stated as one of the aims that there be relief of "total pain," including the physical, emotional, psychological, social, economic and *spiritual* [1]. Since St. Christopher's has an openly Christian orientation, there did not seem to be much question about the spiritual side of human experience. Since early hospices in North America were secular institutions, the stress was on the relief of physical and emotional pain and symptoms. There has been a great deal of literature in recent years dealing with the meaning of spiritual and its place in discussions of care for the dying and the bereaved.

In 1971, the White House Council on Aging defined spiritual *concerns* as "the human need to deal with sociocultural deprivations, anxieties, and fears, death and dying, personality integration, self-image, personal dignity, social alienation, and philosophy of life" [2]. This is such a broad use of the term "spiritual" that it does not help in the discussion of spiritual needs. It is important that the idea of the spiritual not be reducible to "none of the above." I believe that there is a specific content to the word which is important for us to understand. In this chapter, I will explore the basis of human spirituality by looking at the uniqueness of the person and the effect that the knowledge of death has on the person.

The term spiritual is identified with religion, but it is not a term that has its roots in religion. The Hebrew bible does not use the term extensively. The word spirit comes from the Greek word *pneuma* which means breath. As thought emerged, our ancestors identified the word spirit with living things; that is, those who had breath. It was not until Plato that spiritual became identified with the immaterial [3-4].

THE UNIQUENESS OF THE INDIVIDUAL

When the World's Fair was held in New York City in 1960, the Vatican gave the commissioners permission to bring the Pieta, Michelangelo's statue, over to New York. People were worried with good reason. Boats do sink; not very often, but they do. If such an accident had happened the Pieta would have been lost. We are quite concerned over the loss of something precious, and something is precious precisely because it is rare.

The Pieta is a wonderful creation, but it is not by far the most precious thing in existence. The Pieta and similar artifacts are literally set in stone. They do not have the ability to be self-creations. Persons however are self-creations. Each one of us is a one-in-a-lifetime-in-the-universe event. Although our bodies and our instincts are structured by nature, and we are influenced by our parental guidance and our culture, we decide what *person* we shall be. We are unique.

One of the main differences between twentieth century thinking and that of previous generations is this emphasis on the uniqueness of the person [5, p. 192]. While the distinction between an individual (one of several similar things) and person (unique rational being) is at least as old as Boethius [6], the emphasis in prior cultures has been on human nature; that is, the similarities among individuals. It is only in the twentieth century that we have become really conscious of ourselves as unique beings. In our culture we think of ourselves as a unique being [7, p. 10].

Language is fundamentally objective. The structure of our language is to distinguish between subject and object. As a result we grow up thinking of ourselves in an objective manner. We go through an evolution of answers to the question "Who am I?" We start with "Daddy's little boy," and "Mommy's little girl." Then we become "so and so's friend." Then we think of ourselves as a "student at such and such a school," or in "such and such a class." Then we identify ourselves with a few good friends, girlfriends or boyfriends. In each case, we define ourselves in terms of something or someone else. We treat ourselves as objects.

None of us are really happy with being considered merely as objects. What existentialist philosophers such as Ortega y Gasset [8] or Jean-Paul Sartre [9] would have us believe is that our loneliness is a sign of our radical subjectivity [9, p. 37]. An object gets its meaning from something other than itself. We are the kind of being that has meaning in itself rather than takes its meaning from someone else. Subjectivity is the awareness that I am more than the sum total of the categories by which I define myself [9, p. 32]. I am me. That is the most important thing that I can say about myself.

One consequence of this uniqueness is the inability to be truly known by another persons. In moments of depression or sadness we may feel sorry for ourselves. We say to ourselves and to anyone who will listen, that "nobody really understands me." The philosopher Jose Ortega y Gasset would say "You're absolutely right" [7]. At the core of each of us is a solitude; he uses the term radical solitude to describe what it is to be a person [7, p. 5]. There is something about us that others just can not grasp and something about them that we can not grasp.

In the process of growing up we discover ourselves. Our culture tells us how to define ourselves, but being self-creating beings we stop and ask ourselves if our culture is correct in the definition it has provided. We step aside from our culture from time to time. The human condition is to find ourselves on the stage of life knowing we have a role to play but not knowing what that role is or even the plot of the story. No other animal has to live this terrible condition. The other animals have instincts by which they run their lives. Jean-Paul Sartre says "Man is the only animal that can fail" [8, p. 43].

The first conclusion one can draw about human spirituality is that the human quest is a quest for meaning. We are not an instinctual animal. We are the only animal that has to decide from moment to moment, who am I? What do I have to do?

It is in precisely the confrontation with death and loss that we become fully aware of the human situation. We, and every one we love, will die. In spite of our uniqueness, we are still radically contingent and will someday cease to be. Few people have expressed this dilemma better than Ernest Becker [10, p. 26]:

> We might call this existential paradox, which we are the condition of individuality within finitude. Man has a symbolic identity that brings him sharply out of nature. He is a symbolic self, a creature with a name, life history. He is a creator with a mind that sorts out to speculate about atoms or infinity, who can place himself imaginatively as a point in space, and contemplate amusedly his own planet. This immense expansion, dexterity, self confidence, gives to man the status of a small god as the Renaissance thinkers knew. Yet, at the same time the thinkers also knew, Man is a worm and food for worms. This is the paradox, he is out of nature, and hopelessly in it. He is dual, up in the stars, yet housed in a heart pumping, breath grasping body that once belonged to a fish and

still bares the gill marks to prove it. His body is a material fleshly encasing that is alien to him in many ways. The strangest and most repugnant would be that it aches and bleed, one day decay and die.

Human spirituality is to seek an answer to the question "How can you make sense out of a world which does not seem to be intrinsically reasonable?" For Camus, human life is one frustration after another [11, pp. 13-21]. You roll the stone up to the top of the hill, you think you have it all together, then you step back and it all falls apart. The world does not provide ready answers to our search for meaning, thus Camus draws the conclusion that we live in an absurd situation. A situation in which we have a need for meaning because we do not have instincts, but the world is silent.

THE SPIRITUAL NATURE OF THE PERSON

While it is evident that the human person is composed of a material body, the idea that he or she cannot be described adequately in material terms is seemingly as old as the first recognition by a primitive that the human manner of existence differs from that of the other animals. The term *spiritual* has been used to describe this specialness of the human person.

We use the term *spirit* in many ways, referring to the vitality a high school team has, to the content of beverages, as well as to the position that there are conscious beings who are not bodied. However, the term fundamentally means independence from matter: either that the creature is a nonbodied being or that there is something about the being, in this case the human person, that acts in a nonbodied way or at least cannot be fully explained by bodied functions. Other meanings are extensions of ideas of immateriality given to us by our linguistic heritage. Because the language of Greek philosophy was a convenient tool for presenting their message, early Christians adopted the idea of a spiritual soul, a notion not found in quite the same way either in Judaism or in non-Western philosophies. As a consequence, we who live in a Western culture shaped both by the language of the Greek intellectual experience and by the Christian religious experience identify the idea of spirituality with religion. But the spiritual nature of the person is broader than at least organized religion.

There are, as it were, levels of spiritual activity. Thinkers who hold that there is a spiritual dimension to human experience, usually hold that spirituality is a factor found in the very nature of human thinking and human willing. Thinking on a truly human level consists of interpreting our sense data by abstracting common elements from sense data. Thinking is not the same act as sensation. Sensation is the awareness of our experience in a here-and-now way. This color, this smell, this tactile sensation right here and now. Thinking is an awareness of the data of sensation, apart from the here and now characteristics of it. Thus the human mind, as it were, steps away from its sense data, dematerializes and/or *spiritualizes* that data by considering it apart from specific spatial or temporal qualities. We have many sensations of the color white, yet each sensation is of a particular time and place. Our idea of "white" is one which applies to all individual experiences of white things.

One of the most important lessons to be learned from our consideration of human thinking is the fact that the human mind is capable of answering the question "what is a human mind?" The human mind can reflect on itself. We can, for example, give a definition of thinking as "the process by which we are aware of experience in a non-spatial or temporal way." Even if one were to disagree with a particular definition of thinking, the point remains that the human mind (the thinking power) is capable of defining itself, capable of thinking about what thinking is. No other material or animal capacity seems to be able to reflect back upon itself. When we consider that all material things are composed of parts along side of parts, the spirituality of the human knowing capacity is shown in its ability to reflect upon itself [12].

The freedom that we prize is also a spiritual function. By willing, by committing ourselves to a goal or a plan, we determine that something we know only as a future possibility cannot only exist, but can exist as a good thing, as a goal. The goodness of this goal exists only in the human will determining that it shall be and shall be good.

Consequently, those human pursuits that exist primarily at the level of thinking and willing share in the person's spiritual awareness. The meaning that one finds in music, art, and literature, while dependent on the physical characteristics of tones, rhythm, paint, canvas, and words, is not identifiable with these tools of expression. The arts enable people to find meaning in their lives, "to overcome fragmentation in their lives" [13]. Art, as the French philosopher, Jacques Maritain has said, is "the expression of the inexpressible" [14, p. 60]. It is the creation, or at least the awareness of a value that is not found directly in the material make up of the work of art. Our culture—"the ideas by which we live"—exists for us not as a group of physical factors, but as human constructs, as interpretations of fact, and thus is part of our spiritual heritage [15].

The first degree of spirituality is knowledge. We all wish to know, in spite of the schooling we may have had [16]. The second level of spirituality is the quest for feeling good about oneself, being comfortable in the world. There have been two historical trends to answer the question. The one is that we discover answers be seeing what other people are doing. What are the customs of our society? Thus we have "morality," rooted in the Latin word *mos* meaning custom. The second historical trend has been to ask the question, what kind of person do I want to be? The Greek word *ethos,* from which our word "ethics" is derived, means character. Thus ethics is the determination of the character or person we wish to be.

This ability of persons to self-determine his or her life, is perhaps the most fundamental example of the spiritual nature of the person. We are a person who has to make sense out of our life by our decisions and our actions. This is the one chance we have to be the particular person we know that we can be. The philosopher Jean-Paul Sartre has told us that we are the only animal that can fail. We are in his words "condemned to be free" [9, p. 23]. We alone must decide, moment by moment, if we will be, what we will be, and whether we will be the kind of person that we know that we could be. Our spirituality is expressed through our decision making, as we establish a world of values and communicate that world to others [17]. Perhaps, in the long run, maturity in both our personal and professional lives consists in taking seriously the fact that things do not just happen, that each of us has a responsibility to effect what Brodie calls our vision of reality [18].

The spiritual nature of the person encompasses the idea that each of us is a part of a larger whole. We not only find the meaning in our lives in that larger whole but have some obligation to it. This I think is what is meant by religion. In this sense, *religious* applies not only to the usual western or eastern religions, but also includes philosophies and other movements in which persons find meaning in their lives. Each person must ask what it is that gives meaning to life, and whether whatever is chosen will be a defense against those bad times, such as death and bereavement, that come into each life.

We cannot escape from our spirituality. Even Camus' call to live absurdly, as though there were no values, as though life were totally meaningless, is a call to exercise our spirituality [11]. We can live absurdly, reject all values only be becoming conscious of the power to think and the power to will, the root of our spirituality.

REFERENCES

1. F. S. Wald, In Search of the Spiritual Component of Hospice Care, in *In Search of the Spiritual Component of Hospice Care*, F. S. Wald (ed.), Yale, New Haven, 1986.

2. I. B. Corless, Spirituality For Whom?, in *In Search of the Spiritual Component of Hospice Care*, F. S. Wald (ed.), Yale, New Haven, 1986.
3. Plato, The Phaedo, in *Euthyphro, Apology, Crito*, F. C. Church (trans.), Bobbs-Merrill, Indianapolis.
4. M. Stockhammer, *Plato Dictionary*, Littlefield, Adams, Towata, 1965.
5. R. Kastenbaum and R. Aisenberg, *The Psychology of Death*, Springer, New York, 1972.
6. Boethius, Contra Eutychen, in *A History of Philosophy: Volume II: Medieval Philosophy, Augustine to Scotus*, F. J. Coplestone, Newman, Westminster, 1966.
7. J. D. Morgan, Living our Dying, in *Thanatology: A Liberal Arts Approach*, M. A. Morgan and J. D. Morgan (eds.), King's College, London, 1987.
8. J. Ortega y Gasset, *Man and People*, R. Trask (trans.), Norton, New York, 1957.
9. J. P. Sartre, Existentialism, in *Existentialism and Human Emotions*, B. Frechtman (trans.), Philosophical Library, New York, 1957.
10. E. Becker, *The Denial of Death*, Free Press, New York, 1973.
11. A. Camus, The Myth of Sisyphus, in *The Myth of Sisyphus and Other Essays*, J. O'Brien (trans.), Vintage, New York, 1960.
12. T. Aquinas, Summa Theologiae, I, q. 682, a. 2, in *The Basic Writings of St. Thomas Aquinas*, A. Pegis (ed.), Random House, New York, 1945.
13. S. Bailey, The Arts as an Avenue to the Spirit, in *In Search of the Spiritual Component of Hospice Care*, F. S. Wald (ed.), Yale, New Haven, 1986.
14. J. Maritain, *L'intuition creative dans l'art et dans la poesie*. Desclee de Brower, Paris, 1966.
15. J. Ortega y Gasset, *Mission of the University*, Newton, New York, 1944.
16. Aristotle, The Metaphysics, in *The Basic Works of Aristotle*, R. McKeon (ed.), Random House, New York, 1941.
17. I. Kant, Foundations of the Metaphysics of Morals, in *Philosophic Classics: Bacon to Kant*, W. Kaufmann, Prentice Hall, Englewood Cliffs, 1968.
18. G. Brodie, Should a Christian Endorse Suicide in Extreme Cases?, *Death Studies, 12*:2, pp. 147-172, 1988.

CHAPTER 2

Assumptions and Principles
of Spiritual Care*

*Developed by the Spiritual Care Work Group
of the International Work Group on
Death, Dying and Bereavement†*

INTRODUCTION

In those areas of the world where medical care has been shaped by
sophisticated technologies and complicated health care delivery systems, efforts to humanize patient care are essential if the integrity of
the human being is not to be obscured by the system. This is especially
needed for individuals with chronic maladies or those who are in the
process of dying.

Dying is more than a biological occurrence. It is a human, social and
spiritual event. Too often the spiritual dimension of patients is
neglected. The challenge to the health care provider is to recognize the
spiritual component of patient care and to make resources available for
those individuals who wish them and in the form desired.

Spirituality is concerned with the transcendental, inspirational and
existential way to live one's life as well as, in a fundamental and
profound sense, with the person as a human being. The search for

*This chapter is reprinted with the permission of the International Work Group on
Death, Dying, and Bereavement, and *Death Studies*. It was previously published in
Death Studies, 14:75-81, 1990.
†Inge Corless–Chair, Florence Wald–Former Chair, Rev. Canon Norman Autton, Rev.
Sally Bailey, Rev. Roderick Cosh, Ms. Majory Cockburn, Rev. David Head, Dr. Barrie De
Veber, Mrs. Iola De Veber, Dr. Dorothy C. H. Ley, Rev. John Mauritzen, Ms. Jane
Nichols, Ms. Patrice O'Connor, and Rev. Takeshi Saito.

spirituality may be heightened as one confronts death. This uniquely human concern is expressed in a variety of ways both formal and informal. Those who provide care for dying persons must respect each person's spiritual beliefs and preferences and develop the resources necessary to meet the spiritual needs of the patients, family members and staff. These resources and associated support should be offered as necessary throughout the bereavement period.

While the modern hospice movement has arisen within the Western Society with its particular cultural, social and spiritual milieu, the following principles may be applicable in and adapted to other countries and cultures. Ultimately the Assumption and Principles of Spiritual Care should influence other aspects of health care and be integrated into the larger system. Their need and manner of implementation, however, will be shaped by the spiritual life of a given individual and society.

GENERAL ASSUMPTIONS AND PRINCIPLES

1. A. Each person has a spiritual dimension.
   P. In the total care of a person, his or her spiritual nature must be considered along with the mental, emotional, and physical dimensions.
2. A. A spiritual orientation influences mental, emotional, and physical responses to dying and bereavement.
   P. Caregivers working with dying and bereaved persons should be sensitive to this interrelationship.
3. A. Although difficult, facing a terminal illness, death, and bereavement can be a stimulus for spiritual growth.
   P. Persons involved in these circumstances may wish to give spiritual questions time and attention.
4. A. In a multicultural society a person's spiritual nature is expressed in religious and philosophical beliefs and practices which differ widely depending upon one's race, sex, class, religion, ethnic heritage and experience.
   P. No single approach to spiritual care is satisfactory for all in a multicultural society; many kinds of resources are needed.
5. A. Spirituality has many facets. It is expressed and enhanced in a variety of ways both formal and informal, religious and secular, including, but not limited to: symbols, rituals, practices, patterns, and gestures, art forms, prayers and meditation.
   P. A broad range of opportunities for expressing and enhancing one's spirituality should be available and accessible.

6. A. The environment shapes and can enhance or diminish one's spirituality.
   P. Care should be taken to offer settings which will accommodate individual preference as well as communal experience.
7. A. Spiritual concerns often have a low priority in health care systems.
   P. Health care systems presuming to offer total care should plan for and include spiritual care as reflected in a written statement of philosophy, and resources of time, money and staff.
8. A. Spiritual needs can arise at any time of the day or night, any day of the week.
   P. A caring environment should be in place to enhance and promote spiritual work at any time, not just at designated times.
9. A. Joy is part of the human spirit. Humor is a leaven needed even, or especially, in times of adversity or despair.
   P. Caregivers, patients and family members should feel free to express humor and to laugh.

INDIVIDUAL AND FAMILY
ASSUMPTIONS AND PRINCIPLES
(NATURAL AND ACQUIRED)

10. A. Human beings have diverse beliefs, understandings, and levels of development in spiritual matters.
    P. Caregivers should be encouraged to understand various belief systems and their symbols; as well as to seek to understand an individual's particular interpretation of them.
11. A. Individuals and their families may have divergent spiritual insights and beliefs. They may not be aware of these differences.
    P. Caregivers should be aware of differences in spirituality within a family or close relationship and be alert to any difficulties which might ensue.
12. A. The degree to which the patient and family wish to examine and share spiritual matters is highly individual.
    P. Caregivers must be nonintrusive and sensitive to individual desires.
13. A. Health care institutions and professionals may presume they understand, or may ignore, the spiritual needs of dying persons.
    P. Spiritual needs can only be determined through a thoughtful review of spiritual assumptions, beliefs, practices, experiences, goals and perceived needs with the patient, or family and friends.

14. A. People are not always aware of, nor are able, nor wish to articulate spiritual issues.

    P. (1) Caregivers should be aware of individual desires and sensitive to unexpressed spiritual issues.

        (2) Individuals need access to resources and to people who are committed to deepened exploration of and communication about spiritual issues.

15. A. Much healing and spiritual growth can occur in an individual without assistance. Many people do not desire or need professional assistance in their spiritual development.

    P. Acknowledgement and support, listening to and affirming an individual's beliefs or spiritual concerns should be offered and may be all that is needed.

16. A. Patients may have already provided for their spiritual needs in a manner satisfactory to themselves.

    P. The patient's chosen way of meeting spiritual needs should be honored by the caregivers.

17. A. The spiritual needs of dying persons and their families may vary during the course of the illness and fluctuate with changes in physical symptoms.

    P. Caregivers need to be alert to the varying spiritual concerns that may be expressed directly or indirectly during different phases of illness.

18. A. Patients and their families are particularly vulnerable at the time of impending death.

    P. Caregivers should guard against proselytizing for particular types of beliefs and practices.

19. A. As death approaches, spiritual concerns may arise which may be new or still unresolved.

    P. (1) Caregivers should be prepared to work with new concerns and insights, as well as those which are long standing.

        (2) Caregivers must recognize that not all spiritual problems can be resolved.

20. A. The spiritual care of the family may affect the dying person.

    P. Spiritual care of family and friends is an essential component of total care for the dying.

21. A. The family's need for spiritual care does not end with the death of the patient.

    P. Spiritual care may include involvement by caregivers in the funeral and should be available throughout the bereavement period.

CAREGIVERS ASSUMPTIONS AND PRINCIPLES

22. A. Caregivers, like patients, may have or represent different beliefs as well as different spiritual or religious backgrounds and insights.
    P. Caregivers have the right to expect respect for their belief systems.
23. A. Many health care workers may be unprepared or have limited personal development in spiritual matters.
    P. (1) Staff members should be offered skillfully designed opportunities for exploration of values and attitudes about life and death, their meaning and purpose.
    (2) Caregivers need to recognize their limitations and make appropriate referrals when the demands for spiritual care exceed their abilities or resources.
24. A. The clergy is usually seen as having primary responsibility for the spiritual care of the dying.
    P. Caregivers should be aware that they each have the potential for providing spiritual care, as do all human beings, and should be encouraged to offer spiritual care to dying patients and their families as needed.
25. A. Caregivers may set goals for the patient, the family and themselves which are inflexible and unrealistic. This may inhibit spontaneity and impede the development of a sensitive spiritual relationship.
    P. Caregivers and health care institutions should temper spiritual goals with realism.
26. A. Ongoing involvement with dying and bereaved persons may cause a severe drain of energy and uncover old and new spiritual issues for the caregiver.
    P. Ongoing spiritual education, growth, and renewal should be a part of a staff support program, as well as a personal priority for each caregiver.

COMMUNITY COORDINATION
ASSUMPTIONS AND PRINCIPLES

27. A. Spiritual resources are available within the community and can make a valuable contribution to the care of the dying patient.
    P. Spiritual counselors from the community should be integral members of the caregiving team.
28. A. No one caregiver can be expected to understand or address all the spiritual concerns of patients and families.

P. Staff members addressing the needs of patients and families should utilize spiritual resources and caregivers available in the community.

EDUCATION AND RESEARCH
ASSUMPTIONS AND PRINCIPLES

29. A. Contemporary education for health care professionals often lacks reference to the spiritual dimension of care.
    P. Health care curricula should foster an awareness of the spiritual dimension in the clinical setting.
30. A. Education in spiritual care is impeded by a lack of fundamental research.
    P. Research about spiritual care is needed to create a foundation of knowledge which will enhance education and enrich and increase the spiritual aspect of the provision of health care.
31. A. Freedom from bias is a problem in the conduct of research into spiritual care.
    P. Research should be carried out into the development and application of valid and reliable measures of evaluation.

GLOSSARY[1]

Assumption: The act of taking for granted.
Principle: A general or fundamental truth, a governing law of conduct.
Acquired Family: Friends who have a special relationship, share the same household but are not related by blood and/or marriage.[2]
Bereavement: Loss of loved one by death.
Care: To provide for or attend to needs.
Caregiver: One that gives care.
Clergy: A body of religious official of functionaries prepared and authorized to conduct religious services and attend to other religious duties.
Existential: Based on experience of existence; empirical as contrasted with theoretical.
Grief: Emotional suffering as caused by bereavement.

---

[1] It was recommended that an international dictionary be utilized to define the terms contained in the glossary of a document propounded by an international body of scholars and clinicians.

[2] Definition developed by Work Group Members.

Integrity: The quality or state of being complete or undivided: material, spiritual or aesthetic wholeness.

Need: A want of something requisite, desirable or useful.

Proselytize: To (wittingly)[3] convert from one belief, attitude or party to another.

Religion: The personal commitment to and serving of God or a god (transcendental power)[4] with worshipful devotion, conduct in accord with divine commands especially as found in accepted sacred writings or declared by authoritative teachers.

Spiritual: Relating to the nature of the spirit rather than the material.

Spiritual Dimension: Sensitivity or attachment to religious values and things of the spirit rather than material or worldly interests.

---

[3] Modified to incorporate notion of intentionality.

[4] Modified to amplify concept of deity.

PART II

Perspectives on Death

In a recent essay, Bracki, Thibault, Netting, and Ellor emphasize the importance of incorporating spiritual assessment into the counseling process [1]. The authors also suggest that counselors should educate themselves about the traditions, expectations, and resources of the varied religions of their clients. Chapters in this part attempt to facilitate such a process. In very broad strokes they outline the perspectives of major American religious traditions.

Grollman begins this section by reviewing Jewish perspectives on death. To Grollman, Judaism is a life-centered tradition. Death is viewed as a part of life. Grollman reviews the varied interpretations of death that exist within Judaism and he describes the rituals and ceremonies that surround death. Grollman notes that while there are traditions within Judaism that accept life hereafter, the emphasis in both ritual and theology is on life here. Concepts of personal salvation then have less meaning.

Miller's chapter discusses Roman Catholic perspectives on death. Miller explores three roots of Catholic teachings—its Biblical base, its medieval tradition, and its current theological emphasis showing how each contributed to both theology and ritual. Miller implies another critical point. There is often a distinction between popular and official theologies.

Klass offers an overview of Protestantism. Klass both defines some central theses of Protestantism, centering in its individuality, and then goes on to describe the ways that individual spirituality addresses the challenges of death suffering and evil.

While these traditions define three major religious traditions, there are others that should be explored as well. Since 1965 there has been increased migration of Asians into North America. Ryan's chapter does great service by explaining basic theological traditions and rituals in eastern religion. Ryan identifies some basic distinctions between eastern and western religions on both the nature of death and the afterlife. He also implies one other critical point: bearing one's troubles in silence to an Asian expresses human dignity. This may be a salient point for those trying to counsel such clients.

Irion reviews another tradition: reminding counselors and clinicians that there indeed are atheists, secularists, and agnostics in the foxholes, but that they too have spiritual needs that should be addressed. Finally, Meagher and Bell explore Afro-American perspectives on death. This chapter is also a reminder of how history, custom and religion shape spirituality.

A final caveat ought to be offered. It is important to reaffirm the individuality of each person's spirituality. While religious traditions may shape understandings of death, they rarely or solely define it. Thus it is dangerous to assume from a person's singular religion or lack of it what his or her spiritual concerns, understandings and issues are. Understanding religious traditions, at best, helps one ask the right questions. Similarly, it is important to remember that each religious tradition is very broad. Even a tradition's rituals may be diverse. And the theologies of individuals, even those that consider themselves devout, may be very different from their church's religious view. A piece of research illustrates this well. An extensive study of Lutheran clergy and laity found that while Lutheran clergy almost unanimously adhered to the central tenet of Lutheran theology, salvation by grace, a significant proportion of lay people did not [2]. The point is that counselors should use their knowledge of traditions and beliefs to assist their exploration of client's spiritual perspectives. Bracki, Thibault, Netting, and Ellor suggest one additional closing question: "Is there anything else you would want us to know about you that might be unusual?" [1]. In the spiritual quest for meaning, the answer might quite surprise.

REFERENCES

1. M. Bracki, J. Thibault, F. E. Netting, and J. W. Ellor, Principles of Integrating Spiritual Assessment into Counseling with Older Adults, *Generations, 14,* pp. 55-58, 1990.
2. M. Strommer, M. Brekke, R. Inderwager, and A. Johnson, *A Study of Generations,* Aubsburg, Minneapolis, Minnesota, 1972.

CHAPTER 3

Death in Jewish Thought

Rabbi Earl A. Grollman

Yea, though I walk through the valley of the shadow of death, I shall fear no evil for Thou art with me.

Psalms 23:4

To every thing there is its season, a time for every purpose under heaven:
a time to plant, and a time to uproot;
a time to kill, and a time to heal;
a time to pull down, and a time to build up;
a time to mourn, and a time to dance;
a time to scatter stones and a time to gather them up;
a time to embrace, and a time to let go;
a time to keep, and a time to throw away;
a time to tear, and a time to mend;
a time for silence, and a time for speech;
a time for love and a time for hate;
a time for war, and a time for peace;
a time to be born, and a time to die.

Ecclesiastes 3:1

They are like grass which groweth up.
In the morning it flourisheth and groweth up;
In the evening it is cut down and withereth . . .
So teach us to number our days,
That we may get us a heart of wisdom.

Psalms 90:5-6, 12

The Lord hath given, and the Lord hath taken away;
Blessed be the name of the Lord.

Job 1:21

21

Judaism is more than a creed; it is a way of life. And death is a reality of life. Since there are diverse ways in which Jews throughout the ages have viewed life, so there are different approaches by which Jews practice the rites of death.

There are those who believe in a fixed authority derived from supernatural revelation. Others recognize the principle of development in religious life and would affirm the right of the individual to follow the dictates of his or her own conscience.

Over the centuries the rabbis have evolved patterns of practices for the rites of death. Even though Judaism recognizes the value of historical continuity and tradition, there is no single path to the varied rituals and theology of death. For example, traditional Judaism is opposed to cremation as a denial of belief in bodily resurrection. On the other hand, a prominent liberal rabbi in Cleveland writes, "I have no particular faith in physical resurrection. About one in ten funerals in which I officiate involves cremation." Although some rabbis might forbid cornea transplantation, among some of the Orthodox scholars, permission would be granted on the grounds that organ donation would help restore the sight of the living.

Thus, there is no unanimity of acceptance as to the rites of burial and manners of mourning. One can offer only general guidelines. There is but one statement to which all Jewish scholars would agree. Judaism has one major prejudice—a prejudice toward life. This tradition has always said to do everything possible to preserve life. Even the most important practices, for example, the dietary laws of the Sabbath, may be suspended in order to save life. Jews are raised and educated to embrace this view. One does not accept a truce in the battle for life.

Death and sickness are not considered punishment in Judaism. They are not perceived as tests or chances for self-improvement. These events are simply a part of life. The patient or family may ask why this has happened to them. They may reflect on their moral behavior. Of course, they ask questions that often cannot be answered. In Judaism there is no theological base on which to see these unfortunate events as God's recompense for life misspent. Judaism does not see reward in sickness and death.

Judaism is a life-centered tradition. Within its bounds, it offers support for people experiencing a loss. Even that support is life-centered in order to help people go through their grief, to have the support of a community of faith and to readjust to everyday living.

For the Jew, the ceremonies of death are of enormous significance. The Jewish religion suggests rites that play a vital role in the healing work of grief. The bereaved must realize that a loved one is dead and that the void must be filled gradually in a constructive way. He or she should not suppress memories or the disturbing, even guilt-producing recollections which are an inevitable part of all human relationships. Shock and grief are structured by defined solemn procedures. Joshua Liebman in *Peace of Mind* points to the wisdom of the sages in assigning a definite period of mourning participated in by the entire family [1].

One becomes a mourner (Hebrew, *Ovel*) upon the death of seven relatives: father, mother, husband, wife, son or daughter, brother or sister, including half-brother or half-sister. A child less than thirteen years old is not obliged to observe all the rituals of mourning.

From the moment that one learns of the death of a loved one, there are specific religious rites which help to order his or her life. A most striking expression of grief is the rending of the mourner's clothes (*Keriah*). In the Book of Genesis when Jacob believed that his son, Joseph, was killed, the father "rent his garments" (37:34). Today many mourners indicate their anguish by cutting a black ribbon, usually at the funeral chapel or at the cemetery prior to interment. The ceremony is performed standing up to teach the bereaved to "meet all sorrow standing upright."

FUNERAL

The Jewish funeral is a rite of separation. The presence of the casket actualizes the experience. Denial is transformed to the acceptance of reality. The public funeral affords the community an opportunity to offer support and share sorrow. All the emotional reactions that the bereaved are likely to experience—sorrow and loneliness, anger and rejection, guilt, anxiety about the future, and the conviction that nothing is certain or stable anymore—can be lessened by the support of caring friends.

Jewish rites and ceremonies help bear the painful loss. The rabbi recites those prayers which are both expressive of the spirit of Judaism and the memory of the deceased. The most commonly used Psalm XXIII, expresses the faith of the members of the flock in the justice of the Divine Shepherd. From the Psalm, "O Lord, what is man?" is epitomized the thought that although "our days are a passing shadow" there is immortality for those who have "treasured their days with a heart of wisdom." During the recitation of the prayer "*El Molay Rachamim*" the name of the deceased is mentioned. The eulogy of the dead (*Hesped*) is usually included in the service to recognize not only that a death has occurred but that a life has been lived.

The rabbis deem it a most worthy deed not only for the friends to attend the funeral service but to follow the procession to the Jewish cemetery. The *Halvavyat Hamat* is the ultimate demonstration of honor and respect. At the graveside, the burial service is conducted. After the recitation of the *Kaddish,* the prayer of condolence is offered: *"Ha-maw-komY'na-chem Es-chem B'soch Sh'ar A-vay-lay Tzee-von-Vee'roo-shaw-law-yim"*—"May the Eternal comfort you among the other mourners for Zion and Jerusalem." By accepting death as a part of God's order for the world, Jews make death another part of life's plan. When death comes, one does not walk the lonely road alone.

AFTER THE FUNERAL

Shiva (meaning seven), refers to the first seven days of intensive mourning, beginning immediately after the funeral, with the day of burial counted as the first day. Mourning customs are not observed on Sabbaths and Festivals.

The bereaved remain at home receiving a continuous stream of condolence calls. Difficult as this may sometimes be, it helps in keeping the mind active and attentions engaged. Companionship lends the comfort of the loving concern of family and friends.

Even though minors are exempt from many of the mourning rites, youngsters should not be arbitrarily dismissed from the family gathering. They should be afforded the opportunity to face grief and mingle with their loved ones. Some enlightened adults allow their children to share in the family duties such as answering doorbells and telephones, and even in the preparation of the *Seudat Havra-ah,* the meal of consolation. The young person is given the opportunity to help the adults and be helped by the adults.

Immediately upon returning from the cemetery, a light (*Shiva Candle*) is kindled and remains burning for the entire seven days. Before his death, the great sage, Judah Hanasi instructed that a light should be kept aflame in his home for "Light is the symbol of the divine. The Lord is my light and my salvation."

Following the Shiva comes the *Sh-loshim,* the thirty days. The mourners resume normal activity but avoid places of entertainment. At the end of thirty days, ritualistic mourning is over except where the deceased was a parent, when mourning continues for an entire year.

Adults might attend the *Minyan* (daily worship) as well as the Sabbath Services. They read aloud the *Kaddish* prayer, originally not a liturgy for the dead, but a pledge from the living to dedicate one's life to the God of Life, "Magnified and Sanctified." This is the highest approach to commemorate the memory of a loved one. Each time during the year that they recite the *Kaddish* they reinforce both the reality of death and the affirmation of life. They openly display their own needed concern and profound feeling of being a good son or daughter, father or mother, brother or sister, husband or wife. They participate with others who are also suffering the emotional trauma of bereavement. They belong to the largest company in the world—the company of those who have known anguish and death. This great universal sense of sorrow helps to unite human hearts and dissolve all other feelings into those of common sympathy and understanding.

The complete mourning period for those whose parents have died concludes twelve months from the day of the death. For other relatives *Sh-loshim* concludes the bereavement.

The anniversary of the death (*Yahrzeit*) is observed annually on the date of death, commencing on the preceding day and concluded on the anniversary day at sunset. *Kaddish* is recited in the synagogue and the *Yahrzeit* candle is kindled.

The service of commemoration of the tombstone of plaque is called the *Unveiling*. The time of the Unveiling may be anytime after *Sh-loshim* and usually before the first year of mourning is over. Unveilings are not held on the Sabbath or Festivals. Any member of the family or a close friend may intone the appropriate prayers, usually a few psalms, the *El Molay Rachamin* ("God, full of compassion") and the *Kaddish*.

The memorial prayer of *Yizkor*, ("May God *remember* the soul of my revered") is said four times a year during the synagogue worship: *Yom Kippur, Shemini Atzeret,* on *Sukkot, Pesach,* and *Shevuot.*

Judaism is strict in limiting mourning to the given periods and the customary observances. With time, the havoc wrought by death should help to repair itself. Though no one is ever the same after a bereavement, he or she is expected, when mourning is over, to take up existence for the sake of life itself. The garment that the pious mourner rends can be sewn and worn again. The scar is there, but life must resume its course. The approach of Judaism is the climb from the valley of despair to the higher road of affirmative living. The observance of the Jewish laws and customs of mourning helps the mourner face reality, gives honor to the deceased, and guides the bereaved in the reaffirmation of life.

THEOLOGICAL CONCEPTS

In the beginning of the first Christian century, the party of the Sadduces rejected a belief in an afterlife, while at the same time, the Pharisees proclaimed that there was a world-to-come. The bitterest complaint against the doctrine of the hereafter was that by directing minds Heavenward, it diverted people from taking action to correct social evils and encouraged a toleration of unfortunate contemporary conditions.

Judaism has not wholly harmonized or integrated a precept of death and the hereafter. However, in spite of the varied beliefs throughout its circuitous history, there are observed certain central and unifying patterns.

Death is regarded by Jews as both a real and inescapable part of life. It is the completion of life, the rupture of the pleasures of family and friends, the destruction of the possibility of one's enjoying the praise of God.

The development of the religious thought of the Jews showed a marked tendency to fix the center of gravity of religion not in the thought of a world beyond, but rather to foster and establish it in the actual life of people on earth.

The Hebrew expressions for soul in the Bible (*Nefesh, Neshamah, Ruach*) indicate a principle that the human body is the vehicle of all the functions of life. "The soul," says the Midrash, "may be compared to a princess who is married to a commoner. The most precious gift that the husband brings to his princess fails to thrill her. Likewise, if one were to offer the soul all the pleasures of the world, it would remain indifferent to them because it belongs to a higher order of existence." Before the body comes into being, the soul already exists. It is pure and untainted. The exact place of the soul cannot be determined, and this is another of the mysteries of life.

Still another concept of the hereafter is resurrection (*Tehiyyath Hamethem*). The earlier religion of Israel was more concerned with nationhood, and retribution was conceived in national terms. It was later that resurrection was interpreted as the reunion of body and soul together, standing in judgment before God. The dead will rise and then be judged as to whether they will share in the blessings of the messianic era.

Each Jewish tradition has distinct understanding of death and an afterlife. In liberal, reform Judaism, there is generally not a belief in the resurrection of the body. The emphasis is that there is that within us which is immortal and is not bounded by time and space. It is this, the soul, which continues to live after the death of the body. Death is but an incident of life, not a distinct change. Death is not considered an evil. It is universal, natural and inevitable. It comes from God, just as life does. Thus it is not to be feared.

The Orthodox Jew is committed to a belief in recompense, immortality, and resurrection. The scales of cosmic equity will end up in balance, with the body of the dead arising from the grave to be reunited with the soul. In the presence of all the multitudes of all generations, God will pronounce judgment of bliss or damnation.

The Conservative movement has retained some of the liturgy where belief is expressed in resurrection and immortality of the soul. For many, the concepts are not regarded literally, but rather figuratively and poetically.

Even within each of the three Jewish movements there is the widest possible latitude for difference of opinion. There are many thoughts, yet none is declared authoritative and final. The tradition teaches, but at the same time seems to say there is much we do not know and still more we have to learn. And even then, only God can completely discern the mysteries of life and death. Unlike dogmatic theologies which focus only upon individual salvation, Judaism affirms that but adds a different fulfillment within the life of the group as well. Jews hold this world with open arms and attempt to find meaning and love in it. Life is a wonder and whatever lies beyond it will be comprehended only when we get there.

How Does Judaism Help the Living to Find Meaning in Life?

Moses Maimonides, one of the greatest of the Jewish philosophers, wrote: "People complain that life is too short, that man's life ends before he is done preparing himself for it. The truth is that while our life is short, we live as though we had eternity at our disposal; we waste too much of life. The problem is not that we are allotted a *short* life, but rather that we are *extravagant* in spending it."

Death makes life more precious. We want to attach our fragile and fleeting existence to that which is eternal and enduring. The personal tragedy, the waste, lies in what we can do with life—but do not; the love we do not give; the efforts we do not make; the powers we do not use; the happiness we do not earn; the kindnesses we neglect to bestow; the gratitude we have not expressed; the noble thoughts and deeds that could be ours if only we would realize the sanctity of life.

In Judaism, the living must utilize their existence to perpetuate the memory of the deceased. Only then can they ennoble ignoble misfortune. In many a sign is found an insight: in sorrow a jolt out of complacency. The maxim of Jewish philosophy is, "This also for good." Every experience—even death—may be "for good" if the bereaved transforms the value potential into an instrument of spiritual stature, of enlarged sympathy, courageous acceptance, and active determination. Even as the darkness eventually changes into light, so adversity may be converted ultimately into good.

No one can determine how each individual will react to the fact of death. The mystery still walks with our imagination and lurks in our dreams. It is good to remember that courage is not the absence of fear, but the affirmation of life despite fear. For as far as we know, only humankind faces life with the certain knowledge of having to die. This knowledge, this loss of innocence, can lead to the edge of the abyss and threaten all actions with meaninglessness and futility. Or one can seek a bridge that will span the chasm and affirm those things which really give meaning—friendship, honor, a desire for justice, love, dignity, family, friends, country, and humankind.

By facing the meaning of our limits as seen in death, Jews come to accept the limits and possibilities of life realistically. They see the parallel between the acceptance of their biological death and the facing of limit and loss in everyday life. Judaism's concern is more with life in the "here" than in the "hereafter," with this world's opportunities rather than with speculation about the world-to-come.

Judaism helps the adherents to face death and to face away from it. It aids them to accept the reality of death and protects them from destructive fantasy and illusion in the unconscious denial of fact. Most important of all, the Jewish religion offers an abundance of sharing religious resources in the encounter with helplessness, guilt, loneliness, and fear. Though reason cannot answer the *why,* and comforting words cannot wipe away tears, Judaism offers consolation in death by reaffirming life.

Eventually, we all come to the final gate, the final closing. The trail ends, leaving behind only memories of steps taken, leaps tried, grace achieved and shared. How do we mark this final gate? With tears and stories, with memories and love, with food and friends.

And with silence. Silence is the heart of death, and silence alone can do it justice. But silence does not mean passivity, and the Jewish tradition speaks of four virtues which form the core of silence.

The first is hearing: hearing the inner voice of pain and love, rejoicing that nothing, not even the grave, can rob that supreme human emotion.

The second is memory: reclaiming the past by refusing to forget the joys it once held. He or she who once lived among us now lives within us, and there he or she cannot die.

The third is action: we must honor our dead by continuing to live ourselves. Their memory is quickened only in the fullness of our own lives, our own futures; our own ongoing struggles to make sense out of an often senseless world.

The fourth is wisdom: every life is a teaching, every person a guide to truth. We must allow the wisdom that was our loved one to become a part of ourselves, that his or her memory might lead us to an even greater wisdom of our own.

Hearing, memory, action, wisdom . . . may each of these find a place in our silence, our grief, and our moving out again into the world where yet another gate beckons wide.

Finally Some Guidelines in Assisting the Jewish Counselee

Most important, treat the person as a person and not on the basis of some religious group generalization. Though there are unifying characteristics in the methods but which many Jews approach death and dying, there are also significant variations even within Orthodox, Conservative, Reform and Reconstructionist Judaism. The joke that rabbis cite is the one similarity that one Jew has in common with the second Jew: the agreement about what the third Jew should give to charity. In other words, identify the unique orientation of each individual.

As a general rule, unless you are an especially close friend of the mourners, do not disturb the family during the brief period between death and burial. The service usually takes place within a day or two after the death. Thus the bereaved have immediate and pressing concerns in the arrangement of the funeral. It is preferable to pay your respects later by attending the service and *then* by offering your condolences by visiting the family home during the days of mourning, the *Shiva.*

What might you take to the house of bereavement? Sages tell us that material gifts are of small solace to those experiencing personal disorientation. On the other hand, bringing food for the "meal of consolation" is always considered appropriate. An inspirational and informative book on working through one's grief would also be welcome. But know that while your Christological belief may bring you solace, many Jews may feel suspicious that this is a hidden motive of proselytizim.

Sending flowers is not in Jewish tradition. Consult the newspaper obituary if there is a notice requesting that they not be sent. Often in the death notice, other suggestions are offered: "In lieu of flowers donations may be made to the synagogue . . . or hospital . . . medical research. . . ." This is the family's recommendation for remembrance but does not exclude other forms of expression. A contribution to any worthwhile charity is a fitting memorial.

You might express your condolences with a proper sympathy card (again pictures of Jesus and Mary are not within the Jewish context). Better still send an individual letter with your personal memories as a permanent record to be read in the days and years ahead.

Even after the *Shiva*, the bereaved need other people to help them return to the mainstream of life. Don't just offer cliches. Do! Telephone. Visit. Drop by with food. Take their children on outings. Call them on holidays, birthdays, and anniversaries. Tell them about support groups, the sources of help from organizations of people who have suffered similar losses. For sorrowing individuals of *all* faiths, demonstrate that you care, that you have not forgotten them. That is what love and friendship are all about.

A GLOSSARY OF OFTEN-USED WORDS IN JUDAISM RELATIVE TO DEATH

The following explanation of terms may prove helpful:

Alav Hashalom (pronounced Ah-la-hv Ha-shaw-lome) "Peace upon him." Phrase often used after the name of a departed male is mentioned.

Alehaw Hashalom (All-le-haw Ha-shaw-lome) "Peace be upon her." Phrase used after a departed woman is mentioned.

Avelim (Ah-veh-leem) "Mourners." Laws of mourning apply in case of death of one of seven relatives: father, mother, husband, wife, son or daughter, brother or sister.

Chevrah Kaddisha (Chev-rah Ka-dee-shaw) "Holy Brotherhood." Society whose members devote themselves to burial and rites connected with it.

El Moleh Rachamin (Ale-moh-lay Ra-cha-meen) "God full of compassion." Memorial prayer recited at funerals. Dates from the seventeenth century. Popular Yiddish name is "Molay."

Gilgul Hanefesh (Gil-gool Hah-neh-fesh) Transmigration of the soul. According to *Zohar*, "Truly, all souls must undergo transmigration" (III, 99b). Kabbalistic School of Rabbi Luria (1534-1572) believed that a soul which had sinned returned to its earthly existence in order to make amends.

Hesped (Hes-peed) Eulogy delivered by rabbi for the dead. Orations date back to biblical times, and contain an account of life accomplishments of the departed one.

Kabbala (Kah-bah-lah) "Tradition." Applied to important complex of Jewish mystical philosophy and practice. Basic work is *Zohar* ("Splendor"), which appeared at end of thirteenth century.

Kaddish "Holy" or "Sanctification." Aramaic prayer for the dead. Essentially a doxology, praising God, and praying for speedy establishment of God's kingdom upon earth. Recited by mourners for period of eleven months from date of burial.

Keriah (Ka-ree-ah) "Rending." Custom of mourner tearing a section of his garment or a black ribbon as symbol of grief. Rite performed before funeral. Rent made over the left side, over the heart. To be performed standing up, for the mourner is to meet sorrow standing upright.

Matzevah (Mah-tzave-vah) Tombstone that is erected toward the end of the first year of interment.

Midrash "Exposition." Books devoted to biblical interpretations. In form of homiletic expositions, legends, and folklore.

Minyan "Number" or "Quorum." Minimum number of ten Jews above the age of thirteen required for public services. According to Jewish law, *Minyan* is required for community recital of the *Kaddish*.

Mirrors Practice of covering mirrors is not based on explicit Jewish law. Some authorities regard practices as superstitious and discourage use. Others interpret the rite symbolically. "We ought not to gaze upon our reflection in the mirror in the house of mourning. In so doing, we appear to be reflecting upon ourselves."

Rabbi Leader and teacher in the congregation. Conducts the funeral services, answers many ritual questions regarding the ceremony of death, and aids in important approach of *Menachem Avel* (Mine-a-chem Ah-vel), "comforting the bereaved."

Seudat Havra-ah (S-oo-data Chav-vey-rah) Meal of consolation.

Sh-loshim (Sh-lo-sheem) "Thirty." Mourning begins on first day of the funeral and ends on morning of the thirtieth day.

Shiva (Shee-vah) "Seven." Refers to the first seven days of mourning after burial.

Soul Biblical expressions: *Nefesh* (Neh-fesh), *Neshamah* (n'sha-ma), and *Ruach* (Rue-ach), derived from roots meaning "breath," and "wind." Soul is the source without which there can be no life. Maimonides, the philosopher, asserted that only that part of the soul which each develops by his or her intellectual efforts is immortal.

Tachrichim (Ta-ch-re-cheem) "Shroud." Robe in which some dead are buried. Made of white linen cloth.

Tehiyyath Hamathem (Th-chee-yaht Ha-may-teem) "Resurrection of the dead." Belief by some that at the end of time the bodies of the dead will rise from the grave.

Unveiling (Tombstone consecration in which special prayers are recited, such as *El Moleh Rachamin* and the *Mourner's Kaddish*. Customary to cover the tombstone with a veil and during service for one of the mourners to unveil the stone or plaque.

Yahrzeit (Yohr-tzite) Yiddish term for the anniversary of death. Observed by reciting the *Kaddish* in the synagogue and lighting memorial light in the home.

Yahrzeit Light or Candle Well established practice to have candle or special lamp in house of mourning for 24 hours on the anniversary of death.

Yizkor Prayer "May God remember the soul of my revered . . ." Recited on *Yom Kippur, Shemini Atzeret,* last day of *Passover,* and second day of *Shavuot.*

CHAPTER 4

A Roman Catholic View of Death

Edward Jeremy Miller

The most startling Roman Catholic view on death, which is also the view shared by Christians generally, is that God experienced death. Jesus of Nazareth, confessed by Catholics as being fully human and fully divine, actually died. In fact Jesus died a horrible and scandalous death, crucifixion at the hands of Roman soldiers. Although Christians also believe that Jesus rose from the dead and so entered into his glory (Luke 24:26), nevertheless the awesome fact must not be minimized that Jesus really and truly underwent death. This conviction shapes everything that Roman Catholics understand about human death. Moreover, it influences how a Catholic views his or her own impending death and how the Catholic community (e.g., a parish) gathers together on the occasion of the death of one of its members.

This chapter, which is intended for bereavement counselors, will treat three major topics. It is first necessary to consider how Roman Catholics, from a biblical perspective, understand the death of Jesus Christ. A biblical picture is simply fundamental to anything else that can be said about death from a believer's point of view. For this topic a caution is in order. It would be impossible to summarize the various exegetical and theological studies within the Catholic community concerning the death of Jesus Christ. Not only are they seemingly innumerable; they would involve us in nuanced arguments and issues which would deflect from the pastoral and pragmatic intentions of this essay and its usefulness for counselors.[1] Our approach, rather, is to

---

[1] To take but one example, the interested reader is directed to the monumental study of E. Schillebeeckx [1] and to the many reviews of this book in the standard biblical and theological journals.

summarize in a somewhat pastoral manner the biblical teaching on the death of Jesus Christ, much as one would find it in catechetical materials prepared for Catholic laity.

The second major topic deals with the Catholic medieval tradition. Many non-Catholics view Catholic teaching through this prism, as if Catholic thought reached an apex at that period and forever remained frozen. Many of Catholicism's achievements from its medieval legacy remain part of its current teachings, but not all do. To take one example germane to our topic, the medieval teaching on purgatory shaped Catholic devotional practices for centuries, but the situation is changed today. Thus it is instructive to situate the medieval period of Catholicism in a proper prospective.[2]

Finally it remains to consider contemporary developments in Roman Catholicism as these come to expression in liturgical and theological writings. These developments, in large part associated with the Second Vatican Council (1962-1965), reflect understandings and practices of Catholics today. If one were to be at the bedside of a dying Catholic, or to attend a Catholic wake or funeral service, one would encounter these understandings in actual practice.

JESUS CHRIST DIED AND RISEN:
A BIBLICAL PORTRAIT

Concerning the death of Jesus Christ there are two temptations that must be resolutely resisted if one is to appreciate the biblical portrait. First of all, some are tempted to think that Jesus fully and clearly knew he was about to die "into his resurrection" as if it was to be a placid passage form earthly life into heavenly life and without the attendant anxiety of the "unknown." If this were so, not only would this impression be difficult to harmonize with many scriptural texts, it would also make Jesus' experience with impending death so unlike that which his followers would have to face. The Bible describes Jesus' death vigil in the garden as genuine anxiety and fear (Matthew 26:38; Mark 14:33; Luke 22:44), and it describes his experience on the cross as

---

[2] The Protestant theologies of Luther and Calvin react against some aspects of medieval Catholicism, but it is now generally held that the Reformers accepted more of the medieval legacy than the traditional rhetoric allowed, especially in fundamental views of death. For a readable introduction to their views from a Protestant perspective, see [2].

abandonment (Matthew 27:46; Mark 15:34).[3] An early Christian fringe movement, Docetism, was so protective of Jesus' divinity in the face of his death that it "washed out" such fear and anxiety from Jesus' portrait, even to the point of denying that there was any bodily suffering; however, the wider Christian Church branded Docetism a heresy and distanced itself from it. Earliest Christianity thus maintained the "scandalous fact" that its Lord genuinely feared death and actually suffered agony unto death.

The second temptation involves how we think of Jesus' disciples during the events leading up to and including his crucifixion. Some would like to think that the disciples somehow knew all along Jesus was meant to die and meant to rise again. After all, do not the scriptural texts speak of prophecies about such matters, prophecies made by Jesus during his lifetime for his disciples' instruction? We are here involved in the complex question of how the New Testament scriptures came to be written. The Gospels were composed several decades after the disciples experienced the death and resurrection of Jesus. These disciples came to grasp, *after the fact,* that God's hand had been involved in what happened to Jesus; they were able to understand many Old Testament passages in the light of what Jesus experienced in undergoing death. As a result they preached the crucifixion of Jesus with "God's meaning and intention" already embedded into the events, and our scriptures reflect such decades-later preaching. But in their actual experience of their Lord being taken from them and hung on a cross, they were crushed, scandalized, filled with fear, and cast adrift. That is how *they* experienced this particular death at the moment it occurred.

If we resist these two temptations, we are able to establish some very important "Christian experiences" of death, anyone's death. On the part of Jesus himself, dying was a fearful experience. This was natural; it was only human to fear death. But over and above such natural fear, impending death evoked from Jesus the element that will come to characterize, or rather ought to characterize, what a dying person can say in the teeth of death: "Father, into your hands I commit my spirit" (Luke 23:46). Jesus died in faith and in hope, and into the relationship he called His Heavenly Father. It is left to theologians to explain how Jesus, ever remaining divine, nevertheless as human lived in faith and by faith, for Jesus surely was dying in faith and by faith.

---

[3] The Johannine texts remove these elements of fear and abandonment for "theological purposes." Such "redaction theology" of the Fourth Gospel is explained in the standard commentaries. See, for example, [3].

Yet an element of natural apprehension in the face of death must always remain. On the part of Jesus' disciples, his death caused grief, and in their grief they fled that awful crucifixion scene and likely fled Jerusalem itself.[4] Thus if someone were to say that a genuine Christian, a "really believing Christian," ought never to grieve over a death, it is asking an unnatural response and a response that those who "walked with Jesus from the beginning" (Acts 1:21) could not themselves muster.

With these temptations, then, put to the side, how is the death of Jesus biblically understood by Catholics?[5] It is grasped first and foremost as a death that involves them, his followers, in its deepest meanings. To appreciate the personal implications for Christians of Jesus' death, let us briefly consider what is understood to have happened to Jesus.

Although fearful of what was to transpire, Jesus freely and willingly accepted his death in obedience to the mission given to him by God, by the one whom he addressed as *Abba* (Father). This is clear in the accounts of Jesus' last meal with his followers (Matthew 26; Mark 14; Luke 22). There is, furthermore, the sense that this death culminates and brings to fulfillment many Old Testament realities, thus leading the earliest Christian preaching to say it was "in accordance with the Scriptures" (Acts 2:23, 3:18). It is noteworthy that Jesus' death scene echoes Old Testament themes: the offer of wine (Psalm 69), dividing the garments (Psalm 22), the presence of two robbers (Isaiah 53), the mocking words (Psalm 22; Wisdom 2), the vinegar (Psalm 69), the death cry (Psalm 31), and the torn Temple veil (Exodus 26) [8, p. 154].

His is a death that brings forgiveness of human sinfulness (1 Corinthians 15:3) and redemption from all bondages. The very fact that the title "servant" is used to describe the crucified Jesus (Acts 3:13; 4:27; 1 Peter 2:22) alludes to the four redemptive "servant passages" in Isaiah 42, 49, 50, and 52. Jesus' spilled blood becomes another vehicle to depict the significance of this awesome death. The blood describes a new fellowship (of those believing in its power), a new covenant that harkens to the animal blood shed in establishing an older covenant (Exodus 24), and the "description by blood" is recalled whenever Christians repeat Jesus' words at his supper on the eve of his death: "This is my blood which is shed for you" (Matthew 26:28; Mark 14:24). For a

---

[4] The resurrection appearances to the disciples are complex. Did Jesus first appear to the disciples in Jerusalem (Mark, Luke, John 20) or in Galilee (Matthew, John 21)? For a clear account of the problem, see [4, pp. 96-113].

[5] Three catechetical sources of a conservative, moderate, and progressive orientation respectively would be [5-7].

Gentile audience not familiar with Old Testament allusions, early Christian preaching described Jesus' death as a ransoming from bondages (Mark 10:45) and as a liberation (Romans 5, 6). It was not understood as a ransom paid to an avenging God, for God "so loved the world" as to offer his own beloved (John 3:10). Thus in Catholic thinking the death of Jesus is not a divinely inflicted punishment on him in any sense.

Given such biblical teaching on what the death of Jesus involved and meant, Catholics see themselves in solidarity with all humankind both as the sinners who occasioned the tragedy and as the beneficiaries of its forgiveness and liberation. Catholics participate in Jesus' death, that is to say, they come into contact with its significance and benefits through their experience of Baptism and Eucharist (= Lord's Supper = Mass). Of these two sacraments, and of the sacrament called the "Anointing of the Sick," more will be said later, when death and grief are considered in contemporary liturgical and pastoral practice. It suffices now only to situate those sacramental activities in their proper Christological context: the death of Jesus of Nazareth, as its liberating power is made present to Catholics in these sacraments. Furthermore, the understanding of Jesus' death as somehow "foreseen" by God, which is one way of translating "according to the Scriptures," has riveted the conviction in Catholic minds that all deaths, Jesus' included, are part of God's overall providence. Death is not mere fate or happenstance or without deeper meaning. This "providential view" has implications for how Catholics view anyone's death.

The fuller understanding of Jesus' death requires a further consideration. Jesus was raised (or as some texts say, Jesus rose) from the dead.[6] Good Friday lacks meaning without Easter. And Easter cannot be reached without passing through Good Friday, for the palmary symbol of Christians is not the Easter lily but the cross. The New Testament presents Jesus' resurrection as an integral dimension of the death, and this is clearest in John's gospel where the lifting up on the cross is depicted as an exaltation into heavenly glory. Resurrection is not a mere sequel to the death, not simply the thing that happened next in time; nor is it the "award" given to Jesus by his Abba (Father) as if it were a stamp of approval bestowed upon a noble and heroic life's work.

---

[6] The Greek verb *egerthe* normally means "was raised" but such aorist passive forms can also carry an active sense. When St. Jerome translated the Koine Greek into the Latin bible, he rendered this verb into Latin by the active sense *surrexit*, thus the meaning that Jesus raised (himself) from the dead. Still, many New Testament texts state that God the Father raised Jesus from the dead. For the biblical and theological significance, see [4, p. 79].

Rather, his death is the very entry into kingdom life, and in Jesus' case, entry into the Lordship of that kingdom. The earliest texts are clear: through his resurrection Jesus *becomes* both "Lord" and "Christ" [Messiah] (Acts 2:36; Philippians 2:11),[7] and the Greek word used to describe his Lordship, *Kyrios,* was the very word used by the then current Greek rendition of the Old Testament to translate God's hallowed Hebrew name, *Yahweh.* Accordingly, the risen Jesus is to all of creation what the God of Genesis is: creation's sovereign, the Lord of heaven and earth. In entering resurrected life through death, Jesus dominates the power of death (Romans 6:8-14) and extinguishes its apparent finality and meaninglessness for those who, in Paul's words, believe in him. In John's account, Jesus' resurrection returns him to where he had originated (John 6:62), within God's very being.

All these descriptive words reach for the reality of what Jesus became in dying, and of course the words can never render full justice to it. Jesus lives on the other side of death, and the disciples who describe their experience of him as resurrected live on this side. However it is important to realize what they said Jesus is not. He was not a resuscitated corpse, for he passed in and out of their midst by another set of laws, as it were. Nor was he there to be "seen" by everyone but only by those to whom he "revealed" himself, and "insight" was required by them. Such ability to "see into" divine realities is what the New Testament calls *faith.* The disciples' resurrection faith enabled them to "see into death" and to perceive that it was the entry into life with God.

The death-resurrection of Jesus becomes for Catholics, as for all Christians, the pledge (or "first fruits" to use the Biblical term) of their destiny in death. By living through Jesus' power (i.e., by faith, by being baptized, through his grace, by living lovingly, and other such biblical expressions), Christians can die "in Christ" and thus be raised to glory "in Christ." One does not die into emptiness or become nothing; one passes through the "temple veil" into the true Holy of Holies— note the allusion to the Jerusalem Temple—where God lives because Jesus sundered the veil (Hebrews 8-9). Accordingly, the New Testament (Revelations 21:2, 10-14) and later Church tradition calls heaven the New Jerusalem.

I have been stressing that Jesus' resurrection is the immediate implication of his death and not its mere sequel or next-in-succession

---

[7] When the Gospels describe these titles being accorded Jesus even during his lifetime, it is a recognition by the post-resurrection Church, which composed the Scriptures, that Jesus always was what they, in experiencing Jesus as resurrected, came to appreciate and hence call him.

distinct action. The Gospels, however, describe it as if later, i.e., "on the third day," both for the reasons of what that biblical phrase means [9, p. 41] and because gospels are a story, a narrative (Luke 1:1); narratives require "before and after" segments. The narrative genre, however, has led many Catholics, indeed many Christians, to insert "time" between death and resurrected life with God on the other side of death. In subsequent centuries this led to conceptions of purgatory as a kind of "waiting time" between death and kingdom life. Let us consider some such developments, which came to full expression by the time of the Middle Ages.

MEDIEVAL VIEWS ON
DEATH AND DYING

Contrary to many popular depictions of it as well as the current connotation of the word itself, the "medieval" Christian world was heterogeneous and insightful, though it had its myopias and exaggerations. Even when the Protestant Reformation, at the epoch's end, called for a "return to the Bible," those reformers were medievalists; their agendas were shaped by the period, and the *return,* as now recognized by scholars, never fully left the environment. Medieval Christianity, willy-nilly, has shaped the present views of all Christians, especially on death.

Popular medieval piety was preoccupied with the "state of one's soul," that is to say, there was rigorous self-examination of one's moral condition against the background of God's Final Judgment.[8] Whether conditioned by millennial movements expecting Jesus' Second Coming at any moment or by the harshness of social life (e.g., the recurring plagues) or from other factors too complex to identify, many were possessed by a fear of death and hell. Dante Alighieri's *Divine Comedy* (cir. 1313) with its vivid cantos depicting Inferno and Purgatorio, the frequent medieval penitential processions, the emphasis on gaining indulgences, even Martin Luther's "Tower experience,"[9] were expressions of the general anxiety about one's eternal salvation.

The funeral liturgy of the period, the Requiem Mass, fostered this anxiety. The liturgical vestments were black and somber. The prayers called on God to have mercy on the sinner. The famous hymn, "Dies

---

[8] For one of the best sources on the topic, see [10].

[9] Luther's *Turmerlebnis* became for him a personal revelation that faith in the word of Jesus Christ removed the anxiety of one's possible condemnation.

Irae,"[10] its Gregorian melody mournful and searching, its words sober and fearful, reminded worshippers of their accountability before God's judgment throne. The liturgy reminded everyone that in death their bodies "return to dust."

Prior to the individual's death, the ancient Christian sacrament of anointing the sick had, by the Middle Ages, become restricted to "the Last Rites"; the anointing was offered only to those in danger of death. Thus the visit by the priest with the anointing oils harbingered one's exit from life; it did not auger bodily and spiritual renewal. The priest also brought final communion, called Viaticum, which was the sacramental body of Jesus to aid passage into death. These sacramental supports, to be sure, assuaged anxieties about the fear of death, but the emotional context was that of the sinner departing this world to face one's demanding Judge. In the concluding section I will report on recent liturgical renewals which place these sacramental actions in a wholly different context and emotional tone.

The *theological* enterprise of the Middle Ages could be characterized as a systematizing of the theological writers of all preceding centuries (e.g., the Latin and Greek Fathers of the early Church, various Church synods, more recent writers, etc.)[11] along with an effort to frame questions from multiple aspects. Let us take one such theological development, the doctrine on purgatory, since it relates to our theme.

In its treatment of sin, medieval theology distinguished those sins which were so heinous as to separate one completely from God's love (mortal sin) from those lesser sins which only weakened one's relationship with God (venial sin). To die with unforgiven mortal sin brought eternal damnation. Regarding any sin, furthermore, medieval theologians distinguished the sin's debt of *guilt* from its debt of *punishment*. God's forgiveness removed guilt but a debt of punishment could remain, and acts of reparation in this life amortized the owed punishment. Prayer, fasting, almsgiving, conversion of life style, etc., are such acts of reparation. Even though all analogies limp in describing spiritual realities, a useful analogy for guilt/residual punishment might be a viral illness. When the *virus* of chicken pox is fully eradicated (= God's forgiveness of guilt), vesicles remain temporarily on the

---

[10]This "Day of Wrath" hymn was composed in the XIII Century and was part of Requiem Masses by the end of the following century.

[11]The personal and original insights of the systematizers must not be overlooked, e.g., Peter Lombard, Thomas Aquinas, Bonaventure, Duns Scotus.

skin awaiting a full reparation of the disease's *remnants* (= sin's debt of punishment).[12]

Medieval Christianity, furthermore, was extremely sensitive to the teaching, grounded in the Scriptures and developed by early Church writers, that only the "pure of heart," only the completely sinless who have fully reparated for past transgressions, could see the face of God. If a Christian died who had received forgiveness of all (mortal) sins, it was still possible that his or her already forgiven past sins carried a debt of punishment that had not been fully expiated in this life. Thus in death it would have to be so reparated before one could enter God's all holy presence. Purgatory is the situation on the other side of death, but before entry into the Kingdom, in which the "soul" undergoes final purification.[13] For those in purgatory, who were known only to God, the Church prayed and commended them to God's loving mercy. Without entering the debate whether purgatory is scripturally warranted, this view certainly answered to a Christian instinct from the very beginning—see Paul's prayer for Onesiphorus (in 2 Timothy 1:18)—to pray for the dead.[14]

Thus construed, purgatory shaped Catholic attitudes toward death and grief which have endured until recent times. In its best features the thought of purgatory chastened moral behavior (conversion) and kept one's eyes focused on death's ultimate issue: the possibility of kingdom life with God. In its worst features it extended suffering beyond this life and drove people to "gain indulgences" with a passion. (Indulgences are spiritual actions that remitted some or all of the punishment owed to forgiven sins; thus indulgences could shorten or eliminate purgatory.)[15] Not only was death terrifying but those who grieved for the dead had also to cope with the thought that the deceased was in a "purifying" torment.

---

[12]In explaining spiritual realities, it is important to note where analogies "break down." Sin is not a virus except by a stretch of the imagination. Another analogy for understanding sin would be the civil crime of embezzlement. A governor or president could issue a pardon to the felon, thereby eradicating the felony from the record, yet an obligation of monetary restitution remains.

[13]For an English account of Purgatory, see [11]. The fullest account remains the French dictionary article [12].

[14]In post-exilic Judaism, Judas Maccabeus prayed for the forgiveness of his dead soldiers (2 Macc. 12:39-45). The instinct to pray for the dead, to effect their betterment, crosses religious lines.

[15]It has always been Catholic teaching that the seeker of an indulgence required a contrite and "converted" heart. Yet indulgence-seeking could easily invite less than spiritual dispositions, as when indulgences were bought and sold. Luther rightly objected to this aberration. See [5, pp. 487-488].

CONTEMPORARY CATHOLIC VIEWS
ON DEATH AND DYING

To a non-Catholic observer the most striking feature of a Catholic funeral today is probably its emphasis on *risen life*. The music is joyous and hopeful, the vestments are white (no longer black), the scriptural readings are about resurrection and promise, the Easter Candle burns, the preaching is anything but morbid, and all of this occurs in the presence of honest and healthy tears. 1 Corinthians 15:54 seems pervasive: "Death is swallowed up; victory is won."

What had happened to cause this transformation? The causes are surely too many and too complicated to enumerate, but a few may be signaled: 1) The centrality of Jesus' resurrection had been reclaimed in Catholic theology, overcoming the one-sided emphasis on the Cross which was inherited from medieval Christianity;[16] even Luther and much classical Protestant thought shared the somewhat exclusive medieval emphasis on crucifixion-theology. 2) The Second Vatican Council, which ended in 1965, launched a reform of Catholic liturgical practices which affected all the sacraments (the Mass, Baptism, etc.) and, more germane to this essay, led to a revised *Rite of Funerals* in 1969.[17] 3) Various theologians had been writing on the "theology of death," such as Karl Rahner [15] and Edward Schillebeeckx [16], and such writings influenced catechetical materials and parish preaching. 4) The "mind" of the Catholic laity moved from a preoccupation with sin and death toward an orientation to the blessings of a Christian life, i.e., God's love for the individual, the Gospel promises, the hope for resurrection, etc. One might simply say that a healthy biblicism and pastoral practice, rooted in a sounder psychology, took hold.[18]

The Catholic funeral rite is an instructive source for the "Catholic view" of death. Not only is the rite an official document from the Vatican; the rite also gives expression to and further shapes the Catholic *mentality*. The introductory notes to the liturgical document capture the spirit animating the prescribed rituals so evident in a Catholic "death setting" today, i.e., the prayers for the dying person, the wake service which may or may not be in a funeral parlor, the funeral mass in the Church, and the final cemetery rituals.

---

[16]One notes the seminal study [13] by F. X. Durrwell, with the important introduction to the English translation by C. Davis.

[17]See [14] for the best study in English of the funeral rite.

[18]For literature on death from psychological and other scientific perspectives, see [17]; for a treatment of death and the cultural aspects of "sin" from a gerontological perspective, see [18, pp. 320-324].

That underlying spirit rather that the rituals themselves merits description.[19]

The Introduction's very first words, *Paschale Christi mysterium*, [the paschal mystery of Christ] set the basic Catholic vision. Paschal, from the Aramaic word for Passover, simply means the death-resurrection of Jesus considered as a single interconnected event; in dying Jesus passed over into risen life. As the life of a Christian began with incorporation into Jesus' personal passover (baptized into his death that one might be born or raised up anew) and was nourished by paschal food (the sacred elements of the Mass are for Catholics the food of Jesus' risen body), the death of a Christian is his or her consummate contact with the paschal mystery. The Christian follows Jesus into the mystery of death in order to find life like his own. For this reason the tone of the funeral is thanksgiving and consolation rather than morbidity, and the bereaved receive Holy Communion since the Eucharist is the sacrament *par excellence* of Jesus' paschal mystery. It had been the "food of hope" of the deceased during his or her active life as a Catholic. Celebrating Eucharist within a funeral rite is a specifically Catholic practice.[20]

Richard Rutherford detects in this Introduction to the 1969 *Rite of Funerals* two attitudes toward the funeral Mass which shape the pieties of ordinary Catholics. In one attitude the Mass is a prayer proclaiming that Jesus' death-resurrection has reconciled the Christian with God. The other attitude, which was the prevailing one in the recent past, underscores the funeral Mass "being *offered* on behalf of the deceased." The benefits of the Mass[21] are felt to apply to the deceased, even to the point of aiding him or her on the other side of death in a propitiatory way. Rutherford rightly argues that the former attitude is primary in the document, and that the latter attitude can too easily slip into quantitative calculations and a quasi-magical view of prayer in popular pieties. Nevertheless, the ancient practice of prayer on behalf of the dead, prayer that is beneficial to the deceased and not mere trappings or just therapy for the bereaved, is clearly affirmed in the Catholic rite.

The bereaved, however, do benefit directly from the funeral rite. Their personal faith expressed during the prayerful services for the

---

[19]My descriptions are indebted to Rutherford [14].

[20]Within "high church" parishes of the Protestant Episcopal Church one also meets this practice.

[21]An older theology spoke of the "fruits of the Mass." See [14, pp. 122-123]. As the reader will note, the reality of post-death purgation is not denied in contemporary Catholicism but it no longer is an emotional focus.

deceased gives them "the consolation of hope" in the words of the document. Their hope is in Jesus' promise of victory over death, at once a hope for the deceased and a hope for *themselves* when they die. The funeral rites put them into an environment where the priorities of Catholic faith are expressed. "I believe in the resurrection of the dead and the life of the world to come" [14, p. 126].

The official funeral ritual, furthermore, recognizes the local customs and family traditions which might prevail. It cautions against any customs, especially those from the funeral industry, which might obscure the paschal mystery by an attempt to cosmetically mask death. As Rutherford notes, "the Christian funeral proclaims life through death and not through the appearance of life" [14, p. 131]. Contrariwise, it affirms those customs which enhance the paschal mystery. The priest who conducts the rites can better accentuate an Easter faith if he had been with the deceased and the bereaved during the dying process; in this case genuine grief is part of the shared experience that also prays in hope of God's promises. The custom, also, of friends and parish community coming to the wake and to the funeral Mass provides the social supports to the bereaved to begin the process of coping, of adapting to the loss of the deceased. "The *Rite* is founded on the principle of Christian community" [14, p. 132]. While the Risen Christ is the support of any Christian in a death, both of the deceased and the bereaved, the assembled community of believers provides the "social vehicle" through which Christ especially supports the bereaved.

From the liturgical practice of Catholics a further observation may be made about the Sacrament of the Anointing of the Sick and Dying. This ritual anointing, popularly called in the past "the Last Rites," has been restored by the Vatican to its ancient and fuller usage. It is meant for the seriously ill, who may or may not be in danger of death. From medieval times until recently it had been restricted to the death bed situation, and the arrival of the priest at the home or hospital presaged final leave-taking. In its healthier present context of being a sacramental support during serious illness, the rite is administered at the onset of a serious illness, whether that illness leads or does not lead to death.

Priest, family and friends, and most often with the ill person consciously participating, gather in special prayer at the bedside. The prayer is for healing to occur, but if in God's providence it should not, the deeper purpose of the prayer and the anointing is that this illness will not cause the faith of the ill person to waiver. When a dying process does ensue, such emboldened faith casts an entirely salutary aura over "dying and grief." Christ is already accompanying the dying person on the final steps of a "gospel life" toward the rewards of the kingdom. The effects of this sacramental anointing as well as the renewed funeral rites cannot be overestimated on the salutary attitudes of Catholics to dying, death, and grief.

Contemporary Catholic theology has also contributed to salutary attitudes toward death, and with one such vision from Edward Schillebeeckx [16] this essay concludes.[22] Considered from a purely natural perspective, death is unintelligible and even absurd. Whatever one has formed of relationships and however much one has accumulated in this life, all these things pass from grasp. Death snatches everything away. The Judeo-Christian community perceives in this absurdity the power of sin (Genesis, Romans 5:12). Because sin is absurd, destroying piece by piece the humanity of the sinner who freely chooses to sin, death is the visibly absurd appearance within human existence of a corporate sinfulness afflicting all who are born.[23] This religious insight, which is not meant to compete with biological or medical explanations of death that view the same reality from a different vantage, affirms that death (in its absurdity) is something that we humans have invented; for "God did not make death, neither has he pleasure in the destruction of the living" (Wisdom 1:13).

This absurdity within human existence touched the being of God when God "dared to become man. Nevertheless, when this happened, death itself entered in the kingdom of God. The last absurd scandal of the tyranny of death, the death of the man Jesus who is God, in fact brought life back to humanity, because whatever the living God touches becomes itself alive, even though it be very death" [16, pp. 69-70]. Humanity can offer God many things, which are God's already. Death alone, humanity's doing, was the only thing God did not possess. Death itself having been experienced by God (in Jesus), death can now offer "possibilities" of a way of reaching toward life with God, and these become for the dying Christian an alternative to death's hitherto absurdity. The solitary confinements of death when viewed naturally, i.e., the loss of all contact with what lives and had surrounded the dead person, can give way to contact with the One who truly and forever lives, God.

With the above religious view of death, Prof. Schillebeeckx proposes that "dying is not an act; but the attitude of mind in which we accept death can give it the value of an act [of faith in God]" [16, pp. 74-75].

---

[22]In addition to Schillebeeckx, see also the work of Rahner [15, 19].

[23]The Judeo-Christian understanding of the "Fall," as related in *Genesis*, must not be equated with its mythological description of Adam/Eve/fruit of the tree. The deeper truth is the rebellious spirit of humanity before the all-holy God, and of the consequences which ensue.

Dying is not an action a person does; it is something that happens or overcomes one. In its absurdity, death *alienates* a person from the only existence he or she has ever known, one's own life and the lives of loved ones. "Death can therefore only have a positive, Christian and salutary significance when we freely accept this alienation from self" out of love for God [16, pp. 74-75]. Only one who loves God above all things, with one's whole heart and soul, who loves in the face of the absurd, can inherit the Kingdom of God, as the Gospels teach.

Such an act of "accepting" death has certain features, all Gospel grounded. It is an attitude of *obedient* love, an acceptance of God's intervention in our life, as and when God wills. It is an act of *contrite* sorrow for the sins of our life, for it is the experience of a sinner who feels the near approach of the holy God who can only be approached by the "pure of heart." It is an attitude that *affirms* the one true priority of a religious life, God. "Death is our most lonely moment: a dying man is cut off, uprooted, the great solitary who knows time and earth, loved ones and friends, fame, prestige and success, all things and everybody to be slipping away, and who comes at last before the one thing necessary, the One who judges all. 'My God and my all': this is the frame of mind in which a Christian ought to die" [16, p. 76]. Accepting death in this fashion can be so complete and intense that it expels every last vestige of self-love. Self-love is used here in its religious sense to mean selfish love, the detrimental love of self that is sin, the very self-centering love that *caused* death to be.

Such an attitude toward death cannot be constructed at a life's last moments. It is an attitude resulting from one's life as a whole. "Whatever during his life a man has made of the whole of his life, that he is at the moment of death. . . . The attitude finally achieved is decisive, but this itself depends to a large extent on earlier attitudes which prepare the way for the final one" [16, pp. 80-81]. One could have pretended and "acted a part" during a life of actually chosen priorities, but in the moment of death all pretense is stilled. The convictions of obedience, contrition and the felt sovereignty of God, were they not one' true self in life, can unlikely be constructed in one's dying moments. If Jesus is the model for the dying Christian, then it must be recollected that his statement on the Cross, "not my will but Yours be done," was an attitude Jesus had possessed and lived out long before.

COUNSELING POSTSCRIPTS

For the counselor working with Catholic people who either have experienced the death of a loved one or who are dealing with an impending death, some suggestions are offered. Catholics, like members of other faiths, may or may not be active congregants. For active and committed members of Roman Catholicism, the counselor Catholics seek is likely to be a priest, either a friend of the family or someone staffing the local parish. Since Vatican Council II, the parish staff member might also be a deacon, a brother or nun from a religious order, and in some cases a Catholic layperson suitably trained for this "ministry," as this assistance is now termed.

In the above situation the Catholic person or party looks to the parish for counseling support. It is also true that Catholics utilize other professional counselors for support in "dying and death" situations. Whatever the counseling supports, the following observations are offered as helpful and suggestive. Catholics with an active and strong faith should be urged to call upon the central sensitivities suggested above in the essay. These sensitivities involve recollection that Jesus himself experienced grief, suffering, and death itself. Thus, the God to whom Catholics pray for support is poignantly aware of the pain that is being endured. Furthermore, their Church through its sacraments and funeral rites intends and is meant to be a "community of support" for Catholics in times of grief. For the benefit of counselors I have attempted to elaborate what these community supports are and how Catholics understand them.

Even when a counselor is dealing with a so-called "lapsed" or inactive Catholic, it must be remembered that such a person likely bears "Catholic instincts" at a deeply subconscious level. While the Catholic viewpoints about dying and death, which I have described earlier, primarily had in mind those views of active and participating Roman Catholics, I was attempting a description of the social *ethos* of Catholicism at a more fundamental level. Inactive Catholics were socialized at an earlier time into such an ethos, and it is never fully eradicated, even by those who have ceased participating in the Catholic community. When such Catholics unburden themselves to the counselor, it is unlikely that the language will be exclusively "secular."

The professional counselor whose own background is not Catholic may encounter issues in a Catholic client that are rooted in misconceptions or exaggerations of Catholic teaching or rituals. For example, the bereaved may be experiencing anxiety about the deceased person "suffering in purgatory." The above essay was not intended as a theological primer to handle such delicate issues then and there but only to give the reader an orientation to Catholic viewpoints and to give the further sense that developments have occurred within the Catholic community. When confronted with such issues, the non-Catholic counselor could profitably refer the client to someone conversant with those aspects of Catholic teaching and practice.

Death and dying pose a fundamental question to human existence, perhaps the most poignant and fundamental question that can be posed. Such a question does not tolerate an "answer" since the question deals with an unfathomable mystery, and mysteries are never answered. They are lived through and endured. To the mystery of death, Catholics juxtapose another mystery: Jesus Christ and their faith in him. Catholic sacraments are also mysteries, not in the English denotation of mysterious, but in the Greek biblical sense of *mysterion*,[24] which connotes that the reality of God has expressed itself in and through visible things like bread and wine, the anointing oils, the words and gestures of the priest, etc. These, too, are brought to bear on the mystery of death, not as answers, not as placebos, but as prayerful experiences of the mystery of the Risen Jesus, who endured death and unmasked it as the entry to where He is.

REFERENCES

1. E. Schillebeeckx, *Jezus: Het Verhaal van een Levende,* Nelissen, Bloemendaal, Netherlands, 1974; ET *Jesus: An Experiment in Christology,* Seabury, New York, 1979.
2. J. Gonzales, *A History of Christian Thought,* Vol. 3, Abingdon, Nashville, Tennessee, 1975.
3. R. E. Brown, *The Gospel According to John,* Doubleday Publishing Co., Garden City, New York, 1966.
4. R. E. Brown, *The Virginal Conception and Bodily Resurrection of Jesus,* Paulist Press, New York, 1973.
5. *The Teaching of Christ,* R. Lawler, D. Wuerl, T. Comerford (eds.), Our Sunday Visitor, Huntington, Indiana, 1976.
6. R. P. McBrien, *Catholicism,* Winston Press, Minneapolis, Minnesota, 1980.
7. *A New Catechism,* Cathechetical Institute of Nijmegen (ed.), Herder and Herder, New York, 1967.
8. D. Senior, *Jesus: A Gospel Portrait,* Pflaum Press, Dayton, Ohio, 1975.
9. B. Vawter, *This Man Jesus,* Doubleday Publishing Co., Garden City, New York, 1973.
10. L. Bouyer, *History of Christian Spirituality,* Desclee, New York and Paris, 1963.
11. J. Ryan, Purgatory, *The New Catholic Encyclopedia, 11*:cols., 1034-1039, 1967.

[24]The Latin translation of the biblical Greek *mysterion* is *sacramentum,* from which source the word "sacrament" is derived.

12. A. Michel, Purgatoire, *Dictionnaire de Théologie Catholique, 13*:cols., 1164-1326, 1936.
13. F. X. Durrwell, *The Resurrection: A Biblical Study,* Sheed and Ward Publishing Co., New York, 1960.
14. Richard Rutherford, *The Death of a Christian: The Rite of Funerals,* Pueblo, New York, 1980.
15. K. Rahner, *On the Theology of Death,* Seabury, New York, 1961.
16. E. Schillebeeckx, The Death of a Christian, *The Layman in the Church,* Alba House, Staten Island, New York, 1963.
17. A. J. Miller and M. J. Acri, *Death: A Bibliographical Guide,* Scarecrow Press, Metuchen, New Jersey, 1977.
18. *Life Change, Live Events, and Illness,* T. H. Holmes and E. David (eds.), Praeger, New York, 1989.
19. K. Rahner, Tod, *Lexikon Für Theologie und Kirche, 10*: cols., 22-26 and *Eschatologie, 3*:cols. 1094-1098, 1965.

CHAPTER 5

Spirituality, Protestantism, and Death

Dennis Klass

This volume is about *spirituality* and death. This chapter is about a *religion,* Protestantism. As a beginning, we ought to spend a moment thinking about the relationship between *spirituality* and *religion.*

SPIRITUALITY AND RELIGION

The *spiritual* is a dimension of our humanness. Most dimensions of our humanness are not uniquely human. We share with all matter the quality of physical existence, for we have weight, chemical composition, and spatial relationship to all other hunks of matter. We share with all living beings the processes of reproduction and adaptation to our environment. We share with vertebrates a sense of bonding with others of our species as well as a need to guard ourselves from some other members of our own species and from some other species. We share with many animals consciousness of our environment, of our selves within that environment, of our own pain, and, sometimes, of the pain of others. Spirituality, however, probably is limited to our earlier ancestors, *homo habilis* and *homo erectus,* who had tools and fire, and to ourselves, *homo sapiens.*

Like *life, spirituality* is not a thing or a state of being, but is a process of interaction. Like *consciousness, spirituality* is an awareness of relationship. As consciousness is an awareness of ourselves in relation to objects of our senses, spirituality is an awareness of a relationship to that which is beyond our senses. We know our spirituality in the awe we feel, as Kant told us, when we stare into the vastness of the starry sky above and in the righteousness we feel when we act against our own immediate advantage and follow, instead, the moral law within. We know our spirituality when we feel the boundaries of our individual ego soften and we know the truth that is in us is also out there: or in Christian terms, when we know that the reality in our hearts is also the reality of the creator of heaven and earth; or in Buddhist terms, when we know that the separateness of the reality I call my "I" is an illusion.

Spirituality is experienced at the meeting point, or as some would say, the merging point, between our self and that which we usually feel is not our self. D. W. Winnicott told of a realm of experience which is both inner experience and outer experience [1]. It is like music which is a series of notes mathematically related, but which, when we are open to it, feels like flight in our soul. Ken Wilber tells us that we know the spiritual when we break through the boundaries of our ordinary self and come into contact with that which used to feel only outside ourselves [2].

And *death* seems the end of that spirituality, for it would be the end of life, of consciousness, of contact with the eternal. To be sure spiritual teachers have often talked of death in a metaphoric sense as necessary to the spiritual life: "Unless you die and are born again you are not fit for the Kingdom of Heaven." But death as a metaphor is quite different from death as a physical, bloody, painful reality. Yet the spiritual is our aid and comfort in the face of death, for it is our sense of connection with that which is beyond the limitations of this physical and conscious self. To understand the lived relationship of the spiritual to death we must turn to *religion,* for there is no spiritual to be lived in the abstract. The spiritual, like the soul, must wear a body if we are to see it; the body is *religion.*

Religion is a cultural institution. It exists in a particular form in a particular place and changes over time. In many ways, the religion to which we belong is an accident of birth. A Presbyterian elder in suburban St. Louis would have been of a quite different religion if he had been born in Boston in 1670, and of a very different religion had he lived in South America during the time of the Inca civilization. Religions bind communities together in shared symbols, ritual, myth, and ethical norms.

At best, the symbols, myth, ritual, and ethics of a religion provide the means by which the spiritual may be channeled and nurtured. And at their beginnings, all religions seem to have been the effect of a burst of spirituality. But there is another side as well. Religion is also a way to kill the spirit and turn it into letter. Religious symbols, myths, rituals, and ethics often become ends in themselves, preserved and passed on for the habitual comfort or social advantage they afford the pious. Still, no matter now hypocritical it seems to the outsider, religion always seems genuine to those who order their lives by its map, so in this chapter we shall treat religion with the respect due to spirituality.

We turn now to one religion, *Protestantism*. At its best, it provides its members a map by which their spiritual encounter with death can be navigated. At its worst it has offered dead-end channels or rocky shoals for those who have tried to follow its charts. We will try to give a brief overview of its map. The metaphor of religion as a navigational chart is appropriate for Protestantism, for the image of the individual making his or her way through a difficult passage is at the heart of the Protestant view of life. One well-known Protestant hymn reads:

> Jesus, Savior, pilot me
> Over life's tempestuous sea;
> Unknown waves before me roll,
> Hiding rock and treacherous shaol.
> Chart and compass come from thee.
> Jesus, Savior, pilot me.

In some ways, it is difficult to distinguish the spirituality of Protestantism from the general spirituality in North American civil religion, for U.S. and English Canadian culture was born out of Protestantism. European settlement came from the Protestant sections of Europe. When Catholics and Jews came in sufficient numbers to do so, they started their own schools for their children, for it seemed to them that the "public" schools were Protestant. For some of the Protestant settlers, North America was to be the proving ground of their ideas. They would found a "city on a hill" for all the world to see the perfect society of men which could be built on Protestant principles. Most scholarship on contemporary North America culture finds that the "protestant hegemony" is over. Often the election of Catholic John Kennedy as president is cited as a date to mark the end of the dominance of Protestantism. But still, for the first three and a half centuries, North American politics, art, economics, and home life grew out of the Protestant heritage. The intellectual questions grew from Protestant soil.

In this chapter, we will try to stick to Protestantism as it has provided forms for the spiritual dimension of humanness. But we will bear in mind that the themes we will see in Protestantism, such as the importance of the individual and the individual's immediate access to God, are often the unexamined assumptions of a wide range of spiritual alternatives which have moved out of the church but remain essentially Protestant in their worldview.

AN OVERVIEW OF PROTESTANTISM

In its very soul, Protestantism is a diverse and fragmented religious tradition, for in its beginning it was a protest against the standing order; and throughout its history, renewed protests ended in the creation of new schools, denominations, and movements. Historically we think of Protestantism as beginning when Martin Luther protested against the corruption of the Catholic indulgence system or when John Calvin set up his theocratic government in Geneva, or perhaps when the anabaptist communities vowed to live the simple communal life they found in the New Testament. We can also think of Protestantism beginning with a change in historical consciousness, *individualism,* and with a change in technology, the invention of the *printing press.* As a way of outlining the diversity of origin and historical development, we will look at a series of interrelating themes in Protestantism: its individualism, its view of authority, its understanding of God, its understanding of the God/person relationship, and its organization of the community of believers.

Individualism

For whatever reasons, beginning about 1300, Europeans began, for the first time since antiquity, to feel themselves to have an individual soul whose destiny was their individual responsibility. By 1200, Western Christianity had recovered from the fall of Roman Civilization, and from its split from the Eastern Church. Western Christianity had made accommodation to the triumph of Islam in most of Christianity's old territory. The papacy had asserted spiritual and temporal powers, worked out methods of dominating kings and emperors, and tamed the monastic piety into orders obedient to Rome. Northern Europe began to feel a new autonomy. Rome seemed a long way away. Latin did not seem to fit the world as did the native tongues. The kings and nobles did not like the heavy hand of the church restricting their powers. At the same time, trade was increasing and serfs were being freed. A new class of merchants emerged whose wealth depended on commerce, not on the land as did the wealth of the nobility. In some places, this new class gained control of their own political lives. In Geneva, after a series of other arrangements, the Town Council, an elected body, was free from any interference from the nobility and from the church.

Individuals began to have more of a sense of themselves apart from their collective identifications. They began to feel that there was a "me" who is important in my own right, and that "my life" counts in the eyes of God and in my eyes. Phillipe Ariés notes that the period saw a change in the way death was understood. Earlier, he argues, death had been tamed, for it was a part of the natural processes and could be made acceptable by the rituals provided by the church. With the sense that "I am an individual," death became a crisis which Ariés names, "My Death" [3].

People became concerned with the destiny of their own soul. Among the earliest indications of this development was a flood of visions akin to the present near death experiences [4]. Individuals who thought themselves as just back from the edge of death reported that their soul journeyed to another world where they were judged by the quality of the life they had led on earth. From those visions, an idea of the after-life developed rather fully. It included a Heaven where the souls of good people went and a Hell where the souls of sinners went. We can see another indication of this rise of concern with the individual's death in the woodcuts of the dance of death. Everyone, regardless of their station in this life, must dance their individual dance with the smiling skeleton.

The new autonomous individuals began to trust their own reason and conscience to test religious truths. With the rediscovery of the ancient philosophers, the new knowledge of the world gained by expanded trade, and the establishment of independent universities, learning moved out of the narrow, deductive limitations imposed by scholasticism. With intellectual autonomy, science as we know it now began to develop, first as practical experiment with new tools for competitive advantage in the rapidly developing commercial world, and later as the human mind seeking to comprehend nature. Astrology gave way to astronomy and later alchemy to chemistry. We already feel ourselves in modernity when in 1408 the early reformer, John Huss, in an address at the University of Prague said [5, p. 39]:

> From the beginning of my studies, I have made it a rule, whenever I found a better opinion on any matter, gladly and without a struggle to give up the old one, being well aware that what we know is vastly less than what we do not know.

Religious Authority

The introduction of the printing press in the late medieval world made as much difference in the way humans processed information as the introductions of the computer and satellite television are making in ours. Hand copied manuscripts were usually read aloud. Their use could be controlled. With the rise of mass reading, the eye replaced the ear as the primary sense that gathered abstract information. The linear thinking described by McLuhan replaced the more uncritical, holistic thinking of the oral world. A text could be discussed, read again, and compared to other texts in the privacy of the home. The Bible, translated into the languages of the people, could be an authority against which to judge all other authority. It could be the authority for the new autonomous individual and it could be the authority on which to base the political struggles against the Pope. The Word was not the Body of Christ which was the church. The Word was on the page. The people could read it and search for their own truth; and they would then be responsible for that truth as they stood alone and autonomous before the Judgment Seat.

While the Bible is in theory available to each believer to interpret according to his/her own faith and reason, the history of Protestantism can largely be read as a history of conflict, often bitter, about the correct interpretation of the Bible. The major conflict today is over the nature of the revelation in the Bible. Conservatives hold that the Bible was given word for word by God and is therefore without error and should be interpreted literally. Liberals tend to hold that the Bible is a product of a historical process, and that it should be interpreted in light of its time and in light of human scientific reason.

God

Just as the Protestant could not feel the spiritual outside of his/her sense of unique individuality, neither could the Protestant experience the spiritual outside of a sense that there is one God who is the Father in Heaven. God is understood to be a single being who existed at the beginning of time, created the world, spoke to his people through the law and prophets of the Old Testament, and, especially, who came to earth as Jesus, who was God in human form. God remains for Protestantism a God who is transcendent, creator, judge, and redeemer. Although Protestantism came into being almost at the same time as astronomy proclaimed a heliocentric solar system rather than an earth surrounded by crystal spheres, the new science did not affect the basic cosmology which Protestantism brought from its Catholic roots. The God of the Protestants remained the Heavenly Father and the reformers firmly remained His children. This God had a history. He created the world. He made Adam and Eve and drove them out of the Garden when they tried to usurp His place by knowing Good and Evil.

He had chosen the people of Israel to be His own and given them the Law through Moses when He had led them to their promised land. He had reproved His people by the prophets when they did evil. And finally, though modern revisionists often wish otherwise, the reformers believed that God had withdrawn his choice from the Israelites (now called Jews) and had sent his son in the form of a man, Jesus. Jesus was sinless, but died to take away the sins of all humans. After Jesus died, he rose from the dead and is now in heaven. All who believed in him were now the chosen people and at death, they would also rise and join him.

The experience of God has been described in many ways in the history of Protestantism, but for the most part it remains within the experience of a child with a parent. Jesus used the word "Abba" when addressing God. It literally means "daddy." Like a parent God is felt to be all powerful and all knowing. Protestant founder Martin Luther wrote a hymn, "A mighty fortress is our God, a bulwark never failing." God is a being who the believer can trust as a child trusts a parent, and in return God cares for the believer. Jesus once asked what parent whose child asked for bread would give a stone. So God the father should be experienced as caring for the believer. Fredrick Schliermacher distilled the experience of the Protestant with God as "the feeling of absolute dependence." Another Protestant, Rudolph Otto, said the experience of God is the *Mysterium Tremendum* made up of awe, fascination, fear, and a sense of belonging.

Because the presence of God is offered by Protestantism as so immediate, the absence of God can be felt just as strongly. The individual can feel a lack of autonomy if God is not there for support. The plaintive gospel hymn "I need thee every hour" and the joyful claim of "Leaning, leaning, leaning on the everlasting arms" point to the potential terror that could be felt were the everlasting arms to fail or one's hour of need be unmet.

Priesthood of All Believers

In a radical sense, the understanding of access to God changed for the autonomous individuals of Protestantism. Each Protestant has a direct and personal relationship with God unmediated by priest or sacrament. The reformers believed that salvation was to be had only by faith and the only authority was scripture. They removed the church as the mediating institution between humans and God. The idea of sainthood changed in Protestantism. In some places, statues of saints were smashed. No longer could the believer find a saint who could grant special favors or insure that petitions would get through to God. In some later Protestantism, the "saints" became a word that referred to believers (as when they "go marching in").

The ritual aspect of worship was simplified by the early reformers as native languages were substituted for Latin, so the action no longer seemed far off and removed from the life of the worshipper. The medieval church had developed a doctrine that the bread and wine of the mass were turned into actual body and blood of Christ on the altar. In language which seems strange to us today, Luther argued for "consubstantiation" rather than the Catholic "transubstantiation." But for most Protestants such fine distinctions were not enough and the bread and wine which Jesus had shared with his disciples on the night before he was executed became a meal which the community of believers shared with each other in memory of Jesus. For many Protestants, the alter became a table. We can see the simplification of worship in the clean and unadorned lines of the New England "meeting house." The central focus is a pulpit. From there the Word was preached to members of the community who sit in pews. In front of the pulpit is a small table which may be pulled out so the minister and deacons can sit behind it as the sacrament is shared. The human-scale table replaced the awe-inspiring altar.

Nothing stands between the believer and God. Indeed, the direct access to God became the center of much Protestantism. Luther's exposition of the commandment "You shall have no other gods," begins with [6, p. 9]:

> A god is that to which we look for all good and in which we find refuge in every time of need. To have a god is nothing else than to trust and believe in him with our whole heart. As I have often said, the trust and faith of the heart alone make both God and an idol. If your faith and trust are right, then your God is the true God. On the other hand, if your trust is false and wrong, then you have not the true God. For these two belong together, faith and God. That to which your heart clings and entrusts itself is, I say, really your God.

Later evangelical Americans would not admit anyone as saved until they could individually testify that they had a "personal relationship" with God. There is no sense in the Protestant soul that any other person or office has special access to God. God can be experienced in the life and in the heart of the individual. Prayers are not directed toward saints who have closer access to God. Confession may be made directly to God and forgiveness may be received directly from God. A priest is not needed to mediate the confession-forgiveness process. It is the individual and the individual's relationship with the divine which is important. As the spiritual says, "It's a me; it's a me; it's a me, Oh Lord, standing in the need of prayer."

But if God be a judgmental parent, then the individual stands in terror with no protection before the wrath. Jonathan Edwards' sermon "Sinners in the Hands of an Angry God" has a flavor of the more frightening side of the idea of priesthood of all believers [7, p. 159]:

> The God that holds you over the pit of hell, much as one holds a spider, or some loathsome insect over the fire, abhors you, and is dreadfully provoked; his wrath towards you burns like fire; he looks upon you as worthy of nothing else, but to be cast into the fire; he is of purer eyes than to bear to have you in his sight; you are ten thousand times more abominable in his eyes, than the most hateful venomous serpent is in ours. You have offended him infinitely more than ever a stubborn rebel did his prince; and yet it is nothing but his hand that holds you from falling into the fire every moment.

Since all were equal before God, all were responsible for God's work. The clergy became preachers and teachers of the Word. But preaching and teaching are not accepted automatically. Criticizing the minister's sermon is often a favorite activity among Protestants. The goal of preaching and teaching is to enable an individual believer to live out his or her life in the faith, for the important action in Protestantism is not the sacrament in church, but the individual life in the world. Thus, the Protestant soul is often called to higher than average living. As the hymn says:

> Rise up, oh men of God.
> Have done with lesser things.
> Give heart and soul and mind and strength
> To serve the King of Kings.

The priesthood of believers means that each individual has direct access to God, so it would seem that the gap between man and God is closed, and so it seemed to the early reformers. But it is difficult to relate directly to God, for He is maker of heaven and earth, who was before all things and will be after all things. This God not only protects, but also judges. Soren Kierkegaard, the Protestant existentialist, described worship as a theatre [8]. The preacher is the prompter in the wings; the individual worshipper in on stage; and God is the audience. Such lonely self consciousness has often been the hallmark of the Protestant inner life, especially among the intellectuals (see for example, Dag Hammarskjold [9]).

Most Protestants in the pew, however, would be uncomfortable with Kierkegaard's stage or on Edward's spider thread. They find it easier to focus on Jesus, God in human form with whom one may have personal attachment.

> I've found a friend, O such a friend!
> He loved me ere I knew him.
> He drew me with the chords of love
> And thus he bound me to him.

Thus Protestantism maintains a tension between a sense of aloneness and unworthiness in the face of God the father and a sense of immediate presence of the God who came as Jesus. In the high moments of Protestant experience, the tension is resolved in *justification* or *atonement* as the individual feels him or herself to be known, to be called, and to respond. A well-known account of one of those very Protestant moments was written by John Newton:

> Amazing Grace, how sweet the sound
> That saved a wretch like me!
> I once was lost, but now I'm found;
> Was blind, but now I see.

The individual alone encounters the infinity of the universe and the depth of his/her own soul. Such a disparity produces the feelings of fear, guilt, and smallness. When those feelings are overcome, the individual knows him/herself to be safe, forgiven, and important in God's eyes.

The Community of Believers

If the individual is radically alone in the presence of God, the individual need not be alone in human society. In Protestantism, the church became a voluntary association of believers. Humans needed an institution in which they can study the Word, and gather to worship. This varies a good deal from place to place, but in many groups which are important to the development of North American Protestantism, church membership was a voluntary act, made in a public confession of belief and public testimony of an inner experience.

Thus the membership the Protestant feels is a particular membership. While a few clergy or very active laypeople might feel themselves affiliated with other believers around the world, the Protestant community of reference is, for the most part, a local *congregation* or a particular *denomination*. The church is a series of interpersonal relationships. The traditions of moral correctness and upright behavior are vested in senior matriarchs of the congregation whose approval or disapproval is communicated though a network of family and organizational relationships. If the Protestant stands alone before God in his inner faith, the Protestant stands before the congregation in the moral and behavioral life. For this reason, Protestant congregations tend to be split along racial, ethnic, and social class lines. While the ideal held by the official theology is of the inclusiveness of humanity and while the Sunday School children are taught to sing, "Red and yellow, black and white, all are precious in His sight," Black folk tend to congregate with Black folk and White folk with Whites, while rich and poor each have their own church. The feeling, then, is being with one's own. The congregation is often referred to as a family. The community gathering for a hot-dish supper may be as important as the community gathering to study the Word. The communal singing in worship blends into communal singing of "spirituals" for the joy of "fellowship." Larger congregations are divided into smaller groups of young people, young married, singles, middle-aged couples, men's fellowships, and women's guilds.

DEATH, SALVATION, AND SUFFERING

Death is a challenge to Protestant spirituality, first because it opens the possibility that the individual might not survive death. That challenge is answered in Protestantism in the theme of salvation. Second, death is a challenge because it often raises the problem of evil and the problem of the meaningfulness of suffering. We will deal first with the salvation, then with the issue of suffering.

Salvation

In the individualistic spirituality of Protestantism, death raises the possibility that the individual ends with the demise of the physical. For Protestants, the answer to death is salvation. Indeed, the goal of Protestant religion is salvation. At its simplest, the idea is that the human is born into a condition of damnable sinfulness because Adam and Eve disobeyed God and lost their original goodness. Protestants of most theological stripes have preached that God made salvation possible because He became human in Jesus, who was sinless. Jesus' dying and rising from the dead means that those who participate in Jesus' death and resurrection no longer participate in the sinful human nature and thus are fit for the Kingdom of God.

Christianity was founded in a world which had competing ideas of the new world. In the exile (598-521, BCE) the hope of the Jewish

people shifted from a this-worldly nationalism to a vision of a perfect
world beyond history. We see this primarily in the latter sections of
Ezekiel in the Old Testament. But some also looked to a perfect world
in a New Jerusalem on an Earth transformed by the intervention of
God. There was also the idea that each individual has two bodies, one
physical and one spiritual. Within this tradition, St. Paul explained,
"So it is with the resurrection of the dead. . . . It is sown a physical
body, it is raised a spiritual body. If there is a physical body, there is
also a spiritual body." (I Corinthians 15:42-44). Both Jesus and Paul
speak at different times as if the resurrection of the dead will come on
earth after a final act of God and also as if there is a Heaven and Hell
which occurs immediately after the death of the individual. Most of the
possibilities which might arise from this mixture of competing ideas
have been emphasized at one time or another in various Protestant
groups.

Over the history of Protestantism, the actual possibility and nature
of salvation has varied considerably. Indeed, one of the conflicts of the
English reformation was whether the burial service in the prayer book
should omit the words "sure and certain" in the line "we therefore
commit his body to the ground in the sure and certain hope of resurrection to eternal life" [10, p. 73]. The Calvinists, best known in America
as the Puritans, thought that God rightly damned everyone, for no one
deserved to be saved. But from his love, God elected a few and pre-
destined them for a heavenly life after death. One could never be sure,
however, that one was a member of this select few, so one had constantly to be monitoring one's thoughts and actions for vestiges of the
lower man. On the other hand, among the Pentecostals, salvation is
self-evident, for God's primary activity in the present world is as the
Holy Spirit who will come to anyone who opens the self to the Spirit.
One needs to "Give your heart to Jesus," and the Holy Spirit will enter
the person. Pentecostals know when the Spirit has possessed a
believer, for the Spirit speaks through them in the phenomenon of
glossolalia, "speaking in tongues." Thus, so long as one still believes
and so long as the spiritual gift of tongues lasts, one can be sure of a
place in heaven.

Contemporary conservative or evangelical Protestants make salvation the center of their organizational life. The prime reason for the
church is to spread the Word and provide opportunities for people's
salvation. Most religious programs on television are put on by conservatives in the service of saving souls. For liberals, on the other hand,
salvation seems more elusive. Since liberals accept a greater role for
human reason, the experience of salvation is less likely to be highly
emotional. Rather a liberal is more likely to gain conviction over a

longer period of time. Further, liberals are less likely to believe that God would damn anyone to Hell, so the question of what is one "saved from" and "saved to" is somewhat more difficult to articulate. In the face of death, both the liberal and conservative come against the test of their faith. For the liberal, the test may be whether anything is known surely enough to overcome the pain, doubt, and fear of death. For the conservative, the test is whether the certainty, which was supported by the church community and which often brought higher social status in the church community, can now hold in the very solitary experience of dying.

Salvation has both the *eschatological* and an *ethical* dimension. The eschatological idea is that there is another world or age after this one. Jesus' teaching that the Kingdom is at hand, that it is like a mustard seed or the yeast in the dough, has led liberal scholars to the idea of "realized" eschatology"—that the Kingdom of God is actually a present reality. But for most Protestants in the pew, salvation has a future orientation. Throughout Protestant history, there have been groups which have read the Bible as a guide to present history and have predicted that the Kingdom of God will be an event on earth, that it is coming soon, and that the dead will be raised and judged as the sinners are damned forever. But too many predictions about the end of time dull the nerves. Individually, people bet on the future by marrying and having children. They grow old, get sick, and know that they will probably die before history ends. Several Protestant denominations had begun with the claim that the end of history was coming soon, but as the first generation passed on, the churches became more comfortable in the present.

The basic teaching in the New Testament is an eschatological understanding of history, with a new age—a new relationship of humans to God; but for most Protestants in the pew, the teachings about the Kingdom of God and a "new world a happening" come down to the question, "What happens to me after I die?" It is about what will happen to the individual after death.

The ethical dimension of salvation determines the answer, because the autonomous individual of Protestantism is responsible for the moral quality of life lived on earth. If one is saved, it is salvation to a more moral and ethical life than that of the sinner. That moral life in this world is an indication that the individual is qualified for Heaven in the afterlife. The sins which have been of most concern to Protestants are those which are immediately applicable to the autonomous individual's decision. In general, Protestants have been more concerned with sins which are private and personal than with sins which are public and corporate. Thus, Protestants are more likely to fear

God's judgment for extra-marital sex or thoughts about extra-marital sex, than they fear God's judgment because they work for a corporation which pollutes the environment.

The question of how strict a judge God will be has been a matter of disagreement among Protestants throughout their history. All Protestants would probably agree that there is a Heaven. Protestant funeral sermons offer a better world after this one. At times Protestant literature has been rather detailed in its description of the world after death. For example, in the consolidation literature of the middle 19th century United States, the writers seemed to know the streets and houses of heaven as well as they knew their own neighborhood. Usually, however, Protestants have been content to offer Heaven, but leave the details to the individual imagination and later experience.

Hell, the other possibility for a life after death, brings considerably more disagreement among Protestants. For some, there cannot be a just God without Hell, for there is no purpose in leading a moral life if there is no punishment for the immoral. For others, however, the idea of a loving God seems to exclude the idea that God would leave anyone out of heaven. At present, those for whom Hell is a live possibility seem outnumbered by those for whom Heaven is the only possible destination they can imagine for themselves and for those they love. Still, in counseling we see people for whom the fear of death is linked to fear of punishment for real or imagined shortcomings.

It would seem that the more sure a person is that there is life after death and that the soul is bound for heaven, the more the shock of death would be softened. If the soul will be in heaven, death is not final; it is just a temporary separation. And for some people, heaven seems a sure thing. But for most Protestants, heaven is known in hope, not in guarantee, so the anxiety at one's own death can only be partly assuaged by belief.

If we ask what kind of experiences do Protestants bring to their hope of an afterlife, we find phenomena which sometimes seem surer than the data-free speculation about God's judgment and the existence of Hell. There is a difference between the life-after-death people experience when others die and the life-after-death we hope for in our own death. Almost everyone in my study of parents whose children have died experiences their child in heaven [11]. We found no parents with a sense of their child in Hell. I know of no research in which contemporary people experience significant others who have died as in Hell. For those in the study with active prayer lives, when they experience the presence of God, they also experience the presence of the child who had died. When others feel the wonder of the natural world, they also feel the presence of their child. In the study, we also found several parents who said that intellectually they did not believe in an afterlife, but still they felt in touch with a dead child who seemed to be in heaven. For many people, the inner representations of everyone they had grieved were joined. It is not unusual for people to think of someone dying and going to heaven to join another significant person who has died. Thus, the belief in an afterlife holds together experiences of memory, of a sense of presence, a sense of the enduring quality of a person who has died and a sense of the human community which we have shared. These experiences are strongly supported in Protestantism, though the theology is apt to be softer than the sentiment. The experiences which support the belief in the afterlife have little place in the prevailing theology of most Protestants, but still, they remain a strong part of the resolution of grief and are supported within the practical life of a Protestant congregation.

For the people facing their own death, afterlife may be somewhat harder to verify. The specific theological issue that began the Protestant reformation was the sale of indulgences, a kind of sacramental coupon redeemable at death. The Catholic church had provided prayers and masses for the dead which would insure heaven. The sacrament of last rites could absolve dying persons of their sins and give a guarantee of heaven. The sacrament of confession and penance could give immediate assurance of the soul's worthiness for a good afterlife. But the Protestant faces death with none of those aids. The individual faces the cosmos alone.

For those whom William James called the "sick soul"—who feel that the world and themselves are not right and that evil may have the final innings—death may hold the terror that there is nothing after life [12]. Or they may feel the judgment they face in the same way Kierkegaard described the individual on the stage with God as an audience. This individual Protestant alone with death and with God may well have experiences upon which to draw which provide what Wordsworth called "intimations of immortality." A saving experience where God seemed personal and close may very well be enough to last a lifetime so that on the deathbed, the believer may still know the certainty of the "hour I first believed." For others, however, an untimely death and great suffering may very well make such certainty seem dim indeed.

For those whom James called the "healthy minded," life seems basically good and their life in conformity to prevailing ethical standards seems blessed by God. The healthy minded have lived with a sense of blessedness all their lives, so the blessing of heaven, if death be acceptable, seems a natural extension of their habitual way of living.

All religious belief is held as part of the individual's affiliation with the community, that is, we verify our mental world by holding much the same world as the community in which we are members. If the individual is in synch with the community—that there is a heaven and that the individual's life merits entry—and if the individual feels the community bonds as he or she dies, then the bond with God can be maintained easier. But if the individual is out of synch with the community, the bond with God may be less sure. Except for the faith in the center of the soul and the bonds with the community of faith, Protestantism provides few certainties with which to face the terror of one's own death.

The Problem of Evil and the Meaningfulness of Suffering

Salvation answers the challenge death presents that the individual may end with the end of the physical body. The second challenge death presents is the problem of evil and the potential meaninglessness of suffering. The problem of evil may be defined simply as: Does the spiritual force work for good, especially my good, or is there a force working against the good, especially against my good? The problem of the meaningfulness of suffering is an important subset of the problem of evil. It may be simply defined as: Does the physical, social, and psychological pain I experience have any positive value?

Because the question of evil and the meaningfulness of suffering are so central a challenge to the spiritual, religions make the issues central to their teachings. The first noble truth in Buddhism is that "All life is suffering." Suffering is in the core of Protestant teaching. Jesus died a painful death on a cross. The broken body and shed blood are central themes in Protestant preaching. Yet it is not easy for any believer to bring the teaching of religion to bear as the pain of bone cancer does not respond to the medication. Overcoming evil is at the core of Protestant teaching. Jesus rose from the dead, so death, sin, and the devil have been overcome. Yet the resurrection of the Son of God may be scant solace to parents who stand at the bedside of their teen-age son lying brain-dead from a self-inflicted gunshot wound. We will look at the means Protestantism has to meet this challenge.

Evil

Protestantism has rather mixed answers to the problem of evil. For most of the first two centuries of Protestantism, there was little question in anyone's mind that the Devil did exist, that evil spirits could be loose in the world, and that the Protestant needed to be wary. Luther thought he was personally beset by devils. He wrote the hymn words:

For still our ancient foe
Doth seek to work us woe.
His craft and power are great
And armed with cruel hate.
On earth is not his equal.

There are still a good many Protestants for whom evil is an active and personal force in their world. They believe that there is a large cult of devil worshippers who speak in the lyrics of heavy metal rock songs. Symbols like the '60s peace symbol and the ancient Egyptian life symbol are displayed and solemnly pronounced the marks of Satanic cults. Obviously, there is a cultural need for such Protestant theology, for these ideas get rather full airing in the mass media.

Another Protestant answer to the presence of death and suffering is that these came into the world as a result and as a punishment for humanity's disobedience and sin. "The wages of sin is death," said St. Paul. One of the possibilities of faith is that the faithful no longer need fear God's extracting those wages. Protestantism's God is a powerful protective father who is said to count the hairs of the believer's head and know when the sparrow falls. There is a kind of contract in the belief of many people that if they are good, then God will protect them personally from harm. The reverse of that contract is that harm comes to those who have not been good. There are few people who, when they are diagnosed with a serious illness do not spend at least moments considering whether they are being punished for some real or imagined shortcoming.

For most moderate and liberal Protestants, however much their necks tingle at reports of satanic rites and however much they might wonder about their sins being punished, the problem of evil is more likely to be cast as a problem of the limitation of the power of God; that is, moderate and liberal Protestantism has tended to move to an old tradition which sees evil as the absence of good, just as cold is the absence of heat. In matters of suffering and death, good tends to be defined as "good for me." When we are in pain, we tend not to care that as a severe infection is harming one human, it is also the flowering of bacterial civilization. Though written by a Jewish Rabbi, Harold Kushner's book *When Bad Things Happen to Good People* has been widely read by Protestants trying to understand why bad things are happening to them [13]. He argues that there is a God, but that God's omnipotence is limited. That is, God does not interfere with natural laws; so that if two cars are headed toward each other at 60 miles per hour, the natural laws by which the universe is sustained cannot be abridged for the sake of the people in those cars. Obviously, those who find comfort in the limitation of God's omnipotence are also likely to believe in a more active and responsible role for humans. If God is not all powerful, many other questions of faith and salvation must be reworked if the theology of the belief system is to be kept consistent. Most people, however, seem not to need a great deal of consistency in their working theology.

Suffering

Suffering is physical as we experience our body's pain or incapacity. It is social as we experience the loneliness of being isolated from family and community. It is psychological as we feel the accusations of shortcomings from our conscience and memory. Obviously, there are many kinds of suffering from the economic devastation of homelessness to the social outcast status of the homosexual to the uncontrolled inner conflict of schizophrenia. But this volume is about death and dying, so we will limit ourselves. Each year I survey my class about what frightens them about death. The answer for most is that death itself is less frightening than dying. When I ask what is worse than death, the majority speak of long, unrelenting suffering or of losing bodily function without a full loss of consciousness. Most people in the modern world would like a quick death, or at least a painless one.

Quick and painless deaths are a rarity. For example, the trajectory of a terminal cancer is several months to several years with a cycle of hope and dashed hope, with a gradual loss of bodily functions, and with treatment which may bring as much pain as the disease. Suffering is difficult for the person dying and is difficult for family and friends.

Some of the answer to the problem of suffering is found in the answer to the general problem of evil: Why does it happen? But the more immediate problem of suffering is: How shall I live through it? How shall I play the role? How do I do this? We do not live life as if no one had ever lived before. We use models on which to pattern parts of our lives: a good father is a model for our own parenting; a sports hero is our model for gracious winning and losing. Protestantism has basically two models for suffering. Those models are personified by *Job* and *Jesus*.

Job is the central character of a story in the Old Testament which deals with whether faith in God is dependent on God providing the believer with the good life. Satan, in this story is God's debating opponent rather than the personification of evil. Satan says the only reason Job is faithful is that Job and his family are healthy and he is rich. Satan challenges God, "Put forth thy hand now and touch all that he has, he will curse thee to thy face" (Job 2:11). God takes the challenge and with the proviso that Job not die, allows the destruction of Job's crops, livestock, and finally his children. Then Job gets sores all over his body and he sits in the ashes scraping the sores with a broken piece of pottery. Then begins a long series of dialogues first between Job and his wife, then between Job and three friends, then between Job and one younger friend, and finally between God and Job. All the dialogues center on the question: Should Job accuse God for what has happened to him? Or should Job accept responsibility for his suffering? Job refuses to admit that he did anything to deserve his condition (Job 23:11-12):

> My foot has held fast to his steps;
> I have kept his way and have not turned aside.
> I have not departed from the commandment of his lips.

But it is not enough for Job to find himself righteous, the later arguments of the story insist that the sufferer must also find God is without fault even though He created a world that included Job's suffering. Near the end of the story, God, himself, speaks out of a whirlwind, "Where were you when I laid the foundations of the earth?" (Job 38:1). God then goes on at some length showing that He has power and knowledge, neither of which Job has. Job's right to question God is denied, for it is only for God to question Job. God says to Job (Job 40:7-8):

> I will question you, and you will declare to me.
> Will you even put me in the wrong?
> Will you condemn me that you may be justified?

At the end, Job gives up any claim to his own goodness and he gives up any claim to understanding why this is happening. As he understands that only God knows the truth and only God has the power to understand, Job sees the truth about Man's relationship to God (Job 42:2-6):

> I know that thou canst do all things,
>   and that no purpose of thine can be thwarted . . .
> Therefore I have uttered what I did not understand,
>   things too wonderful for me, which I did not know . . .
> I had heard of thee by the hearing of the ear,
>   but now my eye sees thee;
> Therefore I despire myself
>   and repent in dust and ashes.

With that confession, the argument is won, for God has proved to Satan that Job's faith does not depend on Job's being rich and healthy. To give the story a happy ending, Job's family and possessions are restored.

In Job's model, the Protestant endures suffering without the loss of faith because the Protestant has no claim of righteousness or goodness on his or her own account, and because any answers about why and to whom suffering comes are human answers which do not count. Though Job seems not to know it in the story, his sufferings happened merely to settle an argument between Satan and God. Yet even this is discounted, because it is not for Job to understand; it is for Job to be faithful. When Job stops asking questions, stops thinking that humans can know the answers, then Job moves to a new level of faith, for before he had "heard of thee by the hearing of the ear, but now my eye sees thee."

The high theology and philosophy of Job is encapsulated for Protestants in the pew by the phrase "the patience of Job," for it is not the arguments which need to be understood in the face of suffering. The patient is to endure as Job did. Job is an oft-used model for Protestants. The mere fact of endurance without complaint against God and without self righteousness is proof of faith and therefore proof of the suffering Protestant's fitness for Heaven.

Jesus provides a quite different model of suffering, for Jesus was the sacrificial lamb who in death took the sins of all of humanity upon himself. It is his death which redeems humankind. The first idea of this model of suffering is in Isaiah in the Old Testament (Isaiah 53:3-6):

> He was despised and rejected by men;
>   a man of sorrows, and acquainted with grief . . .
> Surely he has borne our griefs and carried our sorrows;
>   yet we esteemed him stricken, smitten by God, and afflicted.
> But he was wounded for our transgressions,
>   he was bruised for our iniquities;
>   upon him was the chastisement that made us whole.

Suffering is here not to be endured as if it were a test of faith. Rather, suffering is self-chosen because by Jesus Christ's suffering the effects of sin and evil are removed.

Although Christ's suffering is a central part of the Protestant theology, too much talk of humans sharing the suffering of Jesus sounds too Catholic for Protestant sensibility. Protestants read the Word and wrestle with God within their own soul like Job did. There is no place in Protestantism for the stigmata such as St. Francis had when the wounds of Jesus' crucifixion appeared on the saint's body. There is no place in Protestantism for pilgrims to whip themselves bloody in order to share Jesus' pain. Protestants of all sorts tend to think of Jesus' suffering as something Jesus did "for my sake." Therefore the issue for Protestants is whether the individual can accept the gift of God's grace in Jesus' death, not how the individual can participate in Jesus's suffering. Indeed, this difference between Protestant and Catholic Christians is exemplified in the representations of the cross. Catholics tend to display the cross with the limp, dying body of Jesus on it, while Protestants tend to display the bare cross, that is, the cross after the crucifixion, which represents the resurrection rather than the suffering.

Because Protestantism has so often been a protest against what it considered a degenerate standing order, Protestants have often spoken of suffering on behalf of Jesus when they were persecuted or opposed by those they believed to be in league with the devil. This kind of suffering is real, but somewhat beyond the scope of the theme of this book: death and spirituality.

There have been significant movements of non-violence in Protestantism in which the powerless suffering of Jesus has been understood as a way to redeem those who rule in society as well as to change the power relationships. For example, George Fox, the founder of the Quakers, would not return hate for hate or blow for blow because the kindness of love could be stronger than the cruelty of the world. In the mid-twentieth century, American Protestant minister Martin Luther King, Jr., developed the idea of suffering for others in a political direction. Hundreds of Protestant clergy from around the country traveled the South to march, facing death while pledging neither to run away nor fight back. They would, they believed, redeem the souls of the racists who opposed them. But while King is honored as a person, his ideas about redemptive suffering have not been incorporated into the common fund of Protestant theology.

Still sometimes we do find that the suffering of Jesus is a model for Protestants as they face their own death. Often cited are the deaths of heroes or the deaths of those who have sacrificed their lives or have suffered for others. Suffering of the innocent children has often evoked a sense of the suffering of Jesus who was innocent, without sin. The theme of innocent suffering, as the suffering of Jesus, was strong in Victorian American Protestantism. The dying child in *Uncle Tom's Cabin* had insight beyond the learned men and could be the incarnation of the dying Christ [14].

Rather than the theme of the believer participating in Jesus' sufferings, contemporary Protestant pastors seem more likely to turn the focus around. Unlike Job whose suffering seemed to put him beyond the scope of God's care, and who only saw God when he confessed he could not understand, Protestants find comfort in the fact that God can empathize with humans. "God understands our pain because he experienced pain himself," is a theme which finds resonance in the present day when understanding is defined as the feeling of empathy rather than intellectual rational comprehension. Thus, because God suffered in Jesus' dying, suffering does not put the believer out of harmony with God, but is an occasion in which God can empathize and understand the experience of the believer. In my study of parents whose children have died, some identified their suffering with God's. They say, "God is a bereaved parent." So long as God understands and cares, suffering does not separate them from God.

CONCLUSION

The core of Protestant Christianity is the relationship of the individual to his or her God. Death challenges this relationship in that it may end with the disappearance of the individual. Protestantism answers that challenge with the claim of salvation: that there is life after death and that faith will deliver the believer into the better world. Death also challenges the relationship between the individual and God in so far as death often brings with it the problems of the meaningfulness of suffering and the existence of evil. Protestant answers to the problem of evil range from the existence of a Devil who has been overcome by Jesus' death to defining God as limited in power. Two models are available to the Protestant to find meaning in suffering: Job, whose suffering teaches the limits of human understanding, and Jesus, whose suffering redeems humankind.

REFERENCES

1. D. W. Winnicott, *Playing and Reality,* Basic Books, New York, 1971.
2. K. Wilbur, *Up From Eden,* Shambhala Press, Boulder, Colorado, 1981.
3. P. Ariés, *Western Attitudes Toward Death,* P. M. Ranum (trans.), Johns Hopkins University Press, Baltimore, 1974.
4. C. Zaleski, *Otherworld Journeys: Accounts of Near-Death Experiences in Medieval and Modern Times,* Oxford University Press, New York, 1987.
5. H. B. Workman, *The Dawn of the Reformation,* Vol. 1, Epworth Press, London, 1933.
6. M. Luther, *The Large Catechism,* R. H. Fischer (trans.), Fortress Press, Philadelphia, 1959.
7. J. Edwards, *Basic Writings,* O. E. Winslow (ed.), New American Library, New York, 1966.

8. S. Kierkegaard, *Purity of Heart is to Will One Thing*, D. V. Steere (trans.), Harper & Row, New York, 1938.
9. D. Hammarskjold, *Markings*, Leif Sjoberg and W. H. Auden (trans.), Alfred A. Knopf, New York, 1964.
10. D. E. Stannard, *The Puritan Way of Death*, Oxford University Press, New York, 1988.
11. D. Klass, *Parental Grief: Solace and Restoration*, Springer, New York, 1988.
12. W. James, *Varieties of Religious Experience*, New American Library, New York, 1958.
13. H. Kishner, *When Bad Things Happen to Good People*, Schocken, New York, 1981.
14. A. Douglas, *Feminization of American Culture*, Alfred E. Knopf, New York, 1977.

FURTHER READING

In this chapter I have passed over a great deal of the history and denominational differences within Protestantism. The following books are good general introductions to Protestant history, thought, and practice. Some are quite old, but they were widely distributed and should be found in many libraries.

R. M. Brown, *The Spirit of Protestantism*, Oxford University Press, New York, 1964.
J. B. Cobb, *Varieties of Protestantism*, Westminster Press, Philadelphia, 1980.
J. L. Dunstan (ed.), *Protestantism*, George Braziller, New York, 1962.
M. E. Marty, *Protestantism*, Holt, Rinehart and Winston, New York, 1972.
D. A. Rausch and C. H. Voss, *Protestant—Its Modern Meaning*, Fortress Press, Philadelphia, 1987.

CHAPTER 6

Death: Eastern Perspectives

Dennis Ryan

INTRODUCTION

"Please burn incense to Lord Buddha for me."

The words startled the chaplain. She had visited the old Chinese male patient every day for almost two weeks. Each day he had hardly uttered a word in response to her inquiries. He just lay there under the starched hospital sheets stoically bearing the pain of his dying.

She felt sad for him. He was so poor that he was ending his life in a dingy ward for indigents in one of New York City's large, over-crowded hospitals. No one came to visit him and he had given neither an address nor the name of his next of kin. He was dying alone.

"Is there anything I can do for you?" the chaplain would ask each afternoon on her rounds through his ward. Usually he shook his head ever so slightly, but this time was different. He looked at her, right in the eyes, scrutinizing her, and then he softly said, "Please burn incense for me to Lord Buddha."

The request startled her. No one had ever asked her such a favor. She recovered rapidly, and asked, "Where would you like me to do this for you?"

"At the Grace Gratitude Buddhist Temple on the Bowery," he answered.

Fortunately she knew her way around Chinatown and felt sure that she would be able to find the place. "Fine," she said, "I'll do it for you tonight." She saw him visibly relax and give a very slight sigh; he closed his eyes and nodded. She imagined a smile, but it really didn't appear. "Anything else," she asked. He just shook his head.

Knowing the dying's sense of urgency and true to her word, she went to Chinatown and found the temple. She bought a pack of the most expensive incense and with the help of a friendly Buddhist monk, she burned it all before a large golden image of Buddha.

She had never really studied the image of Buddha before, but as the incense burned, she stared at the calm serene face of Buddha. She found it comforting and imagined the old man holding the memory of this image in his mind as he lay dying.

When she returned to work the next morning, she went directly to his ward to tell him that it was done. Someone else was already in his bed. He had died during the night. She was disappointed, but the memory of the image of the Buddha with the incense burning before it made her smile; his death was easier to accept.

Every culture has images that communicate something about death. Such cultures as those in Europe and the Americas are referred to collectively as Western Culture. Greek philosophy, Judaism and Christianity are fundamental to this perspective on death. Most cultures of the East, however, have their roots in India and China. India produced two major spiritual traditions, Hinduism and Buddhism. China also produced two, Confucianism and Taoism. Each of these presents its ideas and images of dying and death. In both East and West, spiritual traditions are important supports for the dying and those caring for them. Common features exist in both eastern and western perspectives. One idea is that a part of one's self or one's life transcends the limits of birth and death. Dying is a transition of some sort, like the caterpillar turning into a butterfly; what seems to be the end is not; it is a passage to a new beginning. This is similar to ideas in the West. The methods by which this viewpoint is presented are familiar too. All peoples express their beliefs and attitudes about death by means of stories, images, and teachings. What then are some of the stories, teachings, and images of these eastern perspectives?

HINDUISM

In Hinduism, one finds expressions of successive creations and dissolutions of the universe. Unlike the western view of one creation and one apocalyptic ending, there are endless series of creations, dissolutions and recreations. Even the gods are part of this process.

There is a story of one of the gods, Indra, who was very demanding in the construction of his heavenly palace. Even though his architect was a genius, Indra kept increasing his demands even as the work was in progress. After years of this, the architect finally begged for relief from the highest deity in the universe, Vishnu. Vishnu heard his plea.

On the next morning, a young boy appeared at Indra's residence. When Indra came out to see the guest, he was startled by some mysterious power about the child. He invited him in, offered him refreshment and asked the child why he had come.

The child answered, saying that he had heard about the wonderful palace Indra was building and he was curious about how many more demands he would make on his architect. And then he concluded, "No Indra before you has ever succeeded in completing such a palace as yours is to be" [1, p. 93].

Indra was both startled and amused by the boy's pretension to knowledge of previous Indras and questioned the child about his source. The boy replied [1, p. 93]:

> I have known the dreadful dissolution of the universe. I have seen all perish, again and again, at the end of every cycle. . . . Who will count the universes that have passed away, or the creations that have risen afresh, again and again, from the formless abyss . . . the endless series cannot be told.

At the end of the story, the boy disappears leaving the god quite shaken and humbled.

About twenty-five hundred years ago, wise men in India wrote the *Upanishads,* considered very sacred by the Hindus. These scriptures teach the belief in karma; that is, that every act of a human being, even an internal act such as a desire, has an effect on what that person becomes [2, p. 62-63].

> According as one acts, according as one conducts himself, so does he become. The doer of good becomes good. The doer of evil becomes evil. One becomes virtuous by virtuous action, bad by bad action.

> Accordingly, those who are of pleasant conduct here—the prospect is indeed that they will enter a pleasant womb. . . . But those who are of stinking conduct here—the prospect is indeed that they will enter a stinking womb, either the womb of a dog, or the womb of a swine or the womb of an outcast.

Besides this fundamental belief in karma and rebirth, the *Upanishads* also teach that beyond these transient worlds and creations, beyond the cycles of lives in which humans are caught up, there exists a Supreme Being [3, p. 32].

> He is the unseen Seer, the unheard Hearer,
> the unthought Thinker

the not understood Understander.
there is no Seer other than He,
no Hearer other than He,
no Thinker other than He,
no understander other than He.
He is your soul,
the Inner Controller, Immortal.

And the *Upanishads* teach that there is an important relationship between the Supreme Being and the individual self with its consciousness [4, p. 156].

This is my Soul within the heart,
greater than the earth . . . greater than the sky,
greater than these worlds . . .
encompassing all this universe . . .
This is my Soul within the heart,
this is Brahman;
When I depart from hence,
I shall merge into it.

Later Hindu teachers all based their ideas on these texts, but interpretations differed. Shankara, who lived around the beginning of the ninth century, taught an absolute identity of Brahman and the individual. He taught there was really only the one reality and that multiplicity was only apparent, not real. Ramanuja, two centuries later, taught that the right interpretation was that a real difference existed between Brahman and the soul. After death the liberated soul could be united with Brahman, not fused into it. Shankara used the image of separate puddles of water being collected and returned into the one great ocean. Ramanuja taught the union was like the different parts of the body being united together in one body. The very ambiguities of the primary texts, the *Upanishads*, left open the possibilities for these differences in Hindu teachings.

The *Bhagavad Gita* is another sacred writing for Hindus. It is about seventeen hundred years old and contains the teachings of the Supreme Being who appeared on earth as the counselor, Krishna. He taught this about death [5. p. 36]:

The wise do not grieve for the dead or for the living. Never was there a time when I was not, nor when you were not, nor these other human lords. Never will there be a time hereafter when we shall not be. As in this body, there are for the soul childhood, youth, and old age, even so there is the taking on another body after death. The wise are not confused by this.

The image of Krishna teaching his warrior disciple, Arjuna is a popular Hindu image that reminds Hindus of their beliefs. Hinduism is well known for the many images it has of its gods. Another of these images, the Lord of the Dance, is another source from which Hindus may learn the meaning of death. It is an image of the god Shiva who is pictured as in a frame of movie film. He is in the midst of a dance; one foot is raised and his arms are outstretched; he is balanced and graceful. In one hand he plays a small drum that gives rhythm and regularity to life; he determines the time and the pulse of life. In another hand he holds a small brazier which has a fire in it; it represents both the forces that consume the universe at the end of a cycle as well as the fire and warmth that is essential to the preservation of life. A third hand points down to the demon dwarf being crushed under foot in the dance; the demon is ignorance. Finally, a fourth hand is held in a classic hand gesture found in hundreds of images. The open palm is held facing the viewer expressing the message, do not be afraid. All this is encompassed in a circle that represents everything. Therefore a believer beholds that not only at the center of the universe but also in the center of each individual there is only Shiva, dancing (see Figure 1) [6].

In sum, the Hindu perspective on death includes these elements: 1) cycles of being born and dying in an infinite series of lives, in a universe that itself goes through countless cycles of creation, destruction and recreation; 2) karma, the cosmic principle of ethical consequences; an unceasing moral evaluation process, causing the subsequent becomings of individuals; 3) a supreme being who exists in the universe in the individual souls and is the ultimate end of all. One consequence of these basic Hindu beliefs is that fear of death is considered based on a false identification of our true Soul with the temporary self of this life. Another consequence is the belief that our moral effort will not only affect our state after death but also our ability to attain release from the cycle of births and deaths. And finally, that one should accept one's present situation as just retribution for past karma and strive to respond as one ought to the moral challenges of the present, in the hope of making spiritual progress.

BUDDHISM

The second tradition from India is Buddhism. Perhaps no image from the East is so well known in the West as that of Buddha. When a Buddhist contemplates the image of Buddha sitting crossed-legged and meditating, he or she is reminded of the teachings of the Buddha and the spiritual path he left his followers (see Figure 2).

Figure 1. The Lord of the Dance.

Figure 2. Buddha.

Many of the beliefs of Hinduism are present in Buddhism, such as the belief in karma and rebirth. The Jataka Tales are stories of the five hundred and fifty states of existence both animal and human which preceded Buddha's birth as Buddha. One of the spiritual signs of Buddha's achievement is his detailed knowledge of his previous lives. For example, one time he was a rabbit who was willing to give up his own life to provide food for a hungry human. These good deeds caused him to eventually become the Buddha [7].

In a later work, a Buddhist monk, Nagasena, is asked by King Milinda why some people live long lives and others short lives, some sickly and some healthy lives. Nagasena replies [8, p. 25]:

> They are not alike because of different karmas. As the Lord (Buddha) said . . . Beings each have their own karma. They are . . . born through karma, they become members of tribes and families through karma, each is ruled by karma; it is karma that divides them into high and low.

Buddhists believe that it was the sight of a dead man in part that led Buddha on his six year intensive search for the truth. The truth he discovered and passed on is that life is filled with the pain of grief because humans constantly desire that life should not change, that death never occur. This is a fundamental flaw, a radical ignorance of reality. The first step is to realize this truth about life.

One early and popular Buddhist story is of Kisa Gotami. She is the daughter of a dirt poor peasant whose family is constantly struggling with starvation. Her life is miserable until fate enables her father to marry her into a family that is financially secure. She is full of hope that her life will now be happy, but when she arrives in the household of her new husband, she is not accepted by the women of the family because of her background. When she becomes pregnant their attitudes change. Should she give birth to a son, her status would improve greatly. She does, and she is accepted by all the family now. She has never been happier. This happiness lasts only two short years when, suddenly, her son dies. She is out of her mind with grief and wanders around carrying the body of her son, asking whomever she meets for medicine to cure him. She chances to meet the Buddha who understands her state. He tells her that she has come to the right person for medicine. He tells her to bring a handful of mustard seeds, but they must be from a household where no one has ever died. She sets out immediately and begins to seek the seeds. After spending hours trying to find such a household, she realizes what medicine Buddha was talking about. She takes the body of her dead son to the cremation grounds, lays him down and says [9, p. 45]:

> Dear little son, I thought that you alone had been overtaken by this thing which men call death. But you are not the only one death has overtaken. This is a law common to all mankind.

Buddha taught a way to overcome this ignorance and attain truth, a path to enlightenment. He taught that if we could come to a right understanding of life, we could correct our desires accordingly. The subsequent experience of life is very different from that of someone still in the state of ignorance. This changed state of awareness is called Nirvana. One does not need to die in order to attain Nirvana. It is a transformed inner state of consciousness, difficult to describe to those still in ignorance.

It is significant that when followers asked Buddha about his experience, he compared it to waking up after a very vivid dream. While dreaming, one thinks he/she is in the real world, but after waking up, it is clear that it was not real. Buddha did not use any of the Hindu terms for his spiritual attainment; rather he said, "I am awake." That is the meaning of his title, the Buddha.

The Buddhist monk, Nagasena, explained that if anyone truly sought to follow Buddha's teachings and attain Nirvana he or she should meditate on the subjects of meditation such as the dissatisfaction with things in the world, the impermanence of things manifested in sickness and death [8, p. 32]:

> Whoever wishes to be free from age and death takes one of these as a subject for meditation and thus he is set free from passion, hatred, and dullness, from pride and from false views; he crosses the ocean of rebirth, dams the torrent of his cravings . . . and destroys all evil within him. So he enters the glorious city of Nirvana, stainless and undefiled, pure and white, unaging, deathless, secure, and calm and happy, and his mind is emancipated as a perfect being.

Most Buddhists think that this state is very difficult to attain. The image of the Buddha sitting in meditation reminds them that the truth is found within each person. Theravada monks in Sri Lanka and Zen nuns in Japan strive with great effort and concentration to achieve this goal. Most Buddhists believe that it takes many lifetimes to accomplish this spiritual task.

Other Buddhists believe there is another way, a way of faith. This form of Buddhism is known as Pure Land Buddhism. The Pure Land, sometimes also called the Western Paradise, is a heavenly realm which is ruled by the Buddha Amitabha. It is believed that when Amitabha, the human, attained Nirvana, he was overcome with compassion for his fellow humans who were unable to attain Nirvana. So he made a solemn vow that by his merits he would set himself up in heavenly realm which would be free from the temptations and distractions found on earth, hence the name, the Pure Land. Pure Land Buddhists believe that if they call to Amitabha, full of faith in his vow, that he will bring them to his realm when they die where they can pursue Nirvana more easily than on earth. These Buddhists invoke the name of Amitabha Buddha. Sometimes they call to one of his companions, Guan-yin, the goddess of mercy. This is a more popular form of Buddhism found in China, Korea, and Japan.

CONFUCIANISM

Confucius is probably the most well-known ancient Chinese. A widely known saying of his speaks of the treatment of parents [10, p. 89]:

> While they are alive, serve them according to ritual. When they die, bury them according to ritual and sacrifice to them according to ritual.

Confucius was primarily interested in improving human relationships. He said that if all agreed on the right way to speak and behave toward each other, there would be peace and harmony and happiness among humans. He believed that these right ways of interacting could be taught. Social rituals, such as greetings, asking favors, serving food, could all be learned. These rituals were ways of expressing the respect that was appropriate in different relationships. For example, there is a right way to address one's parents which is different from how we address anyone else. Through ritual, Confucius was trying to correct serious errors in society [10, p. 155]:

> Filial sons nowadays are people who see to it that their parents get enough to eat. But even dogs and horses are cared for to that extent. If there is no feeling of respect, wherein lies the difference.

The way one does things is very important; it is as important as what one does. One should learn the right ways of relating to others.

A later Confucian teacher, Chang Tsai, explained the proper relationship one should have for the dead [11, p. 497]:

> Death does not sever the relationship of the departed with the living; but merely changes it to a different level. Far from being characterized by fear, the attitude of the living toward the departed members of the family or clan is one of continuous remembrance and affection.

By the time of Confucius, the custom of family-centered worship of ancestors was already well established, as were many aspects of popular beliefs. "Confucius accepted these and left it to each individual to make of them what he could or would" [12]. When Confucius was asked about the spirits of the dead, his answer was, "Until you are able to serve men, how can you be able to serve spirits. . . . Until you know about the living, how are you to know about the dead?" [10]. This ambiguous answer develops into scepticism in later Confucian teachers, but the emphasis on observing the proper rituals is maintained [13]:

> The sacrificial rites originate in the emotions of remembrance and longing for the dead. Everyone is at times visited by sudden feelings of depression and melancholy longing. A loyal minister who has lost his lord or a filial son who has lost a parent, even when he is enjoying himself among congenial company, will be overcome by such feelings. If they come to him and he is greatly moved, but does nothing to give them expression, then his emotions of remembrance and longing will be frustrated and unfulfilled and he will feel a sense of deficiency in his ritual behavior. . . . Hence the sacrificial rites originate in the emotions of remembrance and longing. . . To the gentleman they are part of the way of man; to the common people they are something pertaining to the spirits.

These words of the Confucian, Hsun Tzu, express great scepticism but acknowledge the continued belief in spirits on the part of most Chinese. What they highlight is the value that Confucians saw in rituals. As Herbert Fingarette writes, the central theme of Confucius was the "flowering of humanity in the ceremonial acts of men" [14, p. 16].

To summarize, Confucianism teaches that one should carefully attend to the rituals that relate the living with the dead. One ought to keep alive the memory of one's parents and ancestors through regular rituals of remembrance. By these one expresses gratitude for the gift of life which ancestors and parents passed on as well as the sacrifices they made and all the other benefits the living received from them. Another reason to perform these rituals is that they provide a vehicle for the expression of the human emotions of grief and affection. One learns and is provided specific ways of expressing grief, ways that follow the middle way, always avoiding extremes. These rituals bring grace, beauty, and harmony to human behavior, and continuity with the past and tradition. Ritual reveals the ultimate dignity of human relationships, the moral perfection implicit in achieving one's ends by freely choosing to deal with others as having equal dignity [14, p. 76].

Others see the importance of social immortality in this Confucian tradition. The core of life is social responsibility starting with our own families. One lives in such a way that after death, one will be well remembered [15, p. 111].

> Chinese are convinced that what counts in an individual life is its contribution to family and society, through education, hard work, and ethical integrity. Society keeps going on after we die, so by strengthening it our own influence continues; we have not lived for nothing.

TAOISM (DAOISM)

Taoism is the second spiritual tradition begun in China. At first glance it does not seem especially profound. Taoist writers seem to be saying "not to worry, but to take life as it comes, not to become entrapped by soaring ambition, and to savor and enjoy life as one can, day by day" [16]. But there is much more. Taoism focuses on nature, not man as Confucians do. The Taoist focus on nature developed as a sceptical response to the Confucian optimism about remedying society's disorder and lack of harmony. Instead of the value of social involvement and social conventions, Taoism offers a way of transcending the limits of one's world [12].

Of all the Taoist writers, Chuang Tzu is probably the best exponent. He wrote about finding happiness in life. He thinks the greatest obstacle to this goal is taking conventions seriously [12]. Chuang Tzu invites the reader to free himself from the world. Specifically, one is challenged to let go of the "baggage of conventional wisdom." He writes that these ideas and attitudes contribute to a great extent to the grief, oppression, and the anxieties that torture human beings. Education, highly recommended by the Confucians, creates a "web of values" which imprisons us [17]. Chuang Tzu writes to help the reader be free from such traps. He does so sometimes by poking fun at social do-gooders [18, p. 66]:

> The South Sea King was named Act-on-Your-Hunch. The North Sea King was named Act-in-a-Flash. The King of the place between them was named No-Form. Now Act-on-Your-Hunch and Act-in-a-Flash used to meet often in the Land of No-Form. He always treated them well. So they consulted together and thought to do him a good turn. In token of their appreciation they would think up a pleasant surprise. They said, "Humans have seven openings for seeing, hearing, eating, breathing, and so on, but poor No-Form has none. let's make him a few holes." So after that, they put holes in

No-Form, one a day for seven days. And when they finished the seventh opening, their friend lay dead.

Taoists, like Chuang Tzu, looked to nature to discover the principles of life. They became keen observers of nature, using their imaginations to express what they found [17, p. 4]:

The life of things is a gallop, a headlong dash—with every movement things alter, with every moment they shift. What should you do and what should you not do? Everything will change of itself, that is certain.

Once you have realized that everything is in a natural state of continuous change, one should adjust one's self [19, p. 138]:

Bring your mind into a state of quiet, and your energy into a state of indifference. Follow the spontaneity of things and hold within you no element of ego.

Being tranquil, one can see life from this elevated perspective. Being free of conventional wisdom, one can be open to whatever changes life brings. And one can accept it [19, p. 229]:

Those who at night dream of a banquet, may the next morning wail and weep. Those who dream of wailing and weeping, may in the morning go out and hunt. When they dream, they do not know that they are dreaming. In their dream, they may even interpret dreams. Only when they are awake, do they begin to know that they dreamed. By and by comes the Great Awakening, and then we shall find out that life itself is a great dream.

Death is part of this natural change and Chuang Tzu explains his point of view on death this way [17, p. 80]:

. . . things have their life and death—you cannot rely upon their fulfillment. One moment empty, the next moment full—you cannot depend on their form. The years cannot be held off; time cannot be stopped. Decay, growth, fullness and emptiness end and then begin again. . . . Everything will change of itself, that is certain! . . . Life is the companion of death, death is the beginning of life. Who understands their workings? Man's life is a coming together of breath. If it comes together, there is life; if it scatters, there is death. And if life and death are companions to each other, then what is there for us to be anxious about?

This view of unending change, of ceaseless transformations, of infinite variations in the forms of life and death, this is the idea of Chuang Tzu. This is the "Way" things are and continue to be, or better, become. It does no good to wish it were different. Nor need one be anxious about it. There is a beauty and a wonder about this process which one might not only respect but even admire. The tone of acceptance in Chuang Tzu is a tone of positive admiration. The process of death is part of the life-death process and should be embraced with equanimity and even joy.

The Chinese symbol of the Supreme Reality is the circle of yin and yang (see Figure 3); these are the bases of all natural change. The light half represents yang and the dark half yin [20]. Yang originally meant sunshine, while yin meant darkness. Later they became the cosmic

Figure 3. The Chinese symbol of the Supreme Reality (yin and yang).

symbols of forces: yang being the masculine, active, hot, bright, dry, and hard; yin being the feminine, passive, cold, dark, wet, and soft. Through the eternal interaction of these two complementary forces, all the many things of the universe arise, develop, decline, and are transformed [21].

Each force constantly transforms into its opposite. There is no feminine without the masculine, no day without night, no evil without good, no life without death.

One story that well exemplifies this idea is the story of what happened when the wife of Chuang Tzu died. His friends came to express their condolences and were expecting to find Chuang Tzu grief stricken and, perhaps, inconsolable. Instead, they found him sitting on the ground, merrily tapping out a beat on a turned over bucket and singing. This was shocking Confucian friends, so Chuang tried to explain [17, p. 182]:

> When she first died, do you think I didn't grieve like anyone else? But I looked back to her beginning and the time before she was born. Not only the time before she was born, but the time before she had a body. Not only the time before she had a body but the time before she had a spirit. In the midst of the jumble of wonder and mystery, a change took place and she had a spirit. Another change and she had a body. Another change and she was born. Now there's been another change and she's dead. It's just like the progression of the four seasons, spring, summer, fall, and winter. Now she is going to lie down in a vast room. If I were to follow after her bawling and sobbing, it would show that I don't understand anything about fate. So I stopped.

Chuang Tzu had come to accept the way things are, the process of change that includes disease and death but also birth, growth and life He had experienced grief but had found a strong support for getting through his grief in this view of life. Nor is he anxious that his ego or that of his wife is lost at death. It is not lost; it is transformed [16, p. 183].

> The universe is the unity of all things. If one recognizes his identity with this unity, then the parts of his body mean no more to him than so much dirt, and death and life, end and beginning, disturb his tranquility no more than the succession of day and night.

It seems clear that even with ambiguities and exceptions one can find, the dominant perspective on death in both the Confucian and the Taoist Traditions is one of acceptance. For the Confucians, humans are part of an infinite biological and social chain in which each individual has value because of his or her part in one's family and society. For the Taoists, beyond the limits of human biology and society, there is vast cosmos, "carrying all within its never-ending cycles of transformation" [22].

CONCLUSION

Trying to offer support to dying Asians can be frustrating to a Westerner. Many Asians are influenced by the Confucian Tradition. They value formal learned behavior while Americans especially value spontaneity and informality. Chinese, Japanese, Koreans and others have learned to value social ritual and public formalities. They learn that such behavior contributes to human dignity. To bear one's own troubles in silence expresses human dignity. Emotions such as grief and sorrow may be expressed but only in prescribed public rituals. Private sadness should be kept private.

And this behavior sets a good example for others and contributes to one's good reputation after death. Accepting one's fate and the conditions of one's dying is an expression of moral development; to do less would reveal a fault in one's character, and one would be remembered for this failure.

Such a lack of acceptance would reveal another weakness, a lack of wisdom. In the Eastern Traditions there are numerous expressions of death as a natural process; we have looked at some. To rebel against death and not to recognize when it is inevitable and appropriate is to lack a fundamental understanding of life.

Westerners who work with these people as they die, should understand this point of view. It may not be comfortable or easy, but it is essential for more than just a superficial relationship.

Some people with this perspective may seek comfort in images of saviors like one of the Buddhas or Krishna or the Divine Mother. More likely, they will silently hold these images in their minds or seek to achieve a tranquil view of things by quietly repeating holy mantras or formulas, sometimes with the help of prayer beads.

Many of those from these traditions believe in reincarnation. Teachers have taught them that their dying thoughts and desires are crucial in determining their next rebirth. For example, if a man's final thought is of his pet dog, he might very well be reborn as a dog. If on the other hand, a woman's last thoughts are of Amitabha Buddha who rules over the Western Paradise, she will be reborn there. A person with such beliefs might welcome an image of Amitabha to help her fix her attention on this goal.

Some Hindus might desire to return to India and die there, especially in the holy city of Banaras. Many Hindus believe that to die in Banaras insures a rebirth in Heaven or even release from continued rebirth. To a Westerner, the obstacles to such a trip may seem so large that the idea seems irrational; but one should try to understand the importance of the request to the one making it.

Chinese may express the desire to be buried in China or to have their ashes returned to China and placed with the remains of their ancestors in the town from which their family originally came. Again, to a Westerner, this might not seem like an important request, but if that person were to know that it would be done, his dying might be much easier.

This chapter is only a limited attempt to introduce the reader to some perspectives on death from eastern spiritual traditions and some possible applications. It is like the image of Buddha in one of the stone shrines in Borobodur, in Indonesia. The statue is a life size image of Buddha sitting in meditation. The stone shrine, called a stupa, is shaped like a bell, but it is just large enough to contain the statue. The stupa has no windows or doors but its walls are pierced at regular intervals with three inch diamond shaped holes. These openings are randomly placed all over the stupa and allow light to filter in and make the statue visible. However, the openings are so positioned that no matter which one is used, the viewer can only see a small part of the entire image. So this chapter has sought to provide a few openings by which the reader could see part of something that is much larger and impossible to fully comprehend so that one may begin to enter into and participate in the eastern perspective on death.

REFERENCES

1. J. Henderson and M. Oakes, *The Wisdom of the Serpent*, Macmillan, New York, 1963.
2. Ainslee Embree, *The Hindu Tradition*, Random House, New York, 1966.
3. Geoffrey Parrinder, *The Indestructible Soul*, George Allen and Unwin, London, 1973.
4. Sarvapelli Radhakrishnan (trans.), *The Principle Upanishads*, George Allen and Unwin, London, 1953.
5. Winthrop Sargent, *The Bhagavad Gita*, Doubleday, New York, p. 36, 1979.
6. H. Zimmer, *Myths and Symbols in Indian Art and Civilization*, Pantheon, New York, 1946.
7. Lucien Stryk, *The World of the Buddha*, Doubleday, New York, p. 9, 1968.
8. Wm. T. deBary, *The Buddhist Tradition*, Random House, New York, 1969.
9. E. A. Burtt, *Teachings of the Compassionate Buddha*, New American, New York, 1955.

10. A. Waley (trans.), *The Analects of Confucius*, Random House, New York, 1938.
11. Chan Wing Tsit, *Sourcebook of Chinese Philosophy*, Princeton University Press, New Jersey, 1963.
12. Frederick Mote, *Intellectual Foundations of China*, Alfred Knopf, New York, 1989.
13. Burton Watsons (trans.), *Hsun Tzu, Basic Writings*, Columbia University, New York, 1963.
14. Herbert Fingarette, *Confucius—The Secular As Sacred*, Harper and Row, New York, 1972.
15. Daniel Overmyer, *Religions of China*, Harper and Row, New York, 1987.
16. H. G. Creel, *Chinese Thought: From Confucius to Mao Tse-Tung*, University of Chicago Press, Chicago, 1953.
17. Burton Watson (trans.), *Chuang Tzu: The Complete Works*, Columbia University Press, New York, 1968.
18. Thomas Merton, *The Way of Chuang Tzu*, New Directions Press, New York, 1965.
19. Fung Yu-lan, *History of Chinese Philosophy*, Vol. I, Derk Bodde (trans.), Princeton University Press, New Jersey, 1952.
20. C. Joachim, *Chinese Religions*, Prentice-Hall, Englewood Cliffs, New Jersey, 1986.
21. K. Kramer, *The Sacred Art of Dying*, Paulist Press, New York, 1988.
22. Frederick Holck, *Death and Eastern Thought*, Abingdon Press, New York, 1974.

CHAPTER 7

Spiritual Issues in Death and Dying for Those Who Do Not Have Conventional Religious Belief

Paul E. Irion

Because the comforts of religious faith in the face of death have been described for so many centuries, it has often been assumed that people who are not committed to a traditional religious belief system face death without comfort. It is on such persons that this chapter is focused in an effort to demonstrate that the portion of our population without commitment to a traditional belief system can and does develop understandings of death which may or may not serve them well in time of crisis.

What kind of people are we talking about here? We are not thinking simply of people who are unaffiliated with any religious community although they may hold personally to a very traditional belief system (Christian, Jewish, Buddhist, Islamic, etc.). This chapter is focused on people who might be described as secularists, humanists, or naturalists (as distinguished from supernaturalists). To simplify matters in this chapter we shall call these persons secularists.

SECULARISTS

These secularists have to be considered in two groups. First, there are people who thoughtfully develop and articulate their own position. They understand their lives on the basis of a twentieth century scientific worldview. They consider the world of the here and now to be the real world. They take full responsibility for making the decisions life requires of them and accept the consequences of those decisions,

without metaphysically positing either benevolent or evil powers outside of human beings.

The second group merely functions in today's world on the terms
that world sets without giving it serious thought. There is sometimes a
kind of intellectual nihilism that characterizes such folk. They are
apathetic, perhaps even disdainful, about philosophical searching and
are unaware of the thinking that influences their lives. They
have never heard of existentialism or scientific naturalism, but they
unknowingly live by tenets such as these.

Our focus in this chapter will be largely on the first group, the
thoughtful secularists, because they are struggling to make some sense
of life and death. It will apply only obliquely to the second group
because they do not really participate intentionally in the search for
meaning.

In spite of the games of denial humans play, death is inevitable for
everyone. The vast majority of persons want, consciously or unconsciously, to transcend death in some way, to find some way to mitigate
its radical consequences for themselves and their loved ones. They try
to come to terms with the possibility of nothingness, the ending of time,
the injustice of untimely death.

SECULARISTS AND DEATH

If we assume that the need to cope with death is universal,
secularists have the same need as religious people. They suffer the
pain of loss and separation, they look to find some meaning in their
suffering, they search for answers to the questions death has always
raised for human rationality.

This can be thought of as a spiritual quest. The spiritual is defined
in this volume as that which reaches beyond material limits. This does
not have to be defined in terms of platonic dualism with distinct realms
of matter and spirit but as a kind of ultimate abstraction. Spirituality
is seen as a stepping back from our experience of the world and
reflecting upon it. John Morgan suggests that in doing this, one
suspends time and space as the context for reflection. Or we may think
of these interpretations of facts being expressed as artistic abstractions; that is, they lift one imaginatively beyond the factual. Morgan
also proposes that spirituality makes persons aware of their participation in a larger whole, transcending the bounds of singular existence [1].

This volume narrows the focus to consider spirituality and death.
In other words: How can one reflect on the experience of death and
articulate interpretations, probably artistic, of that phenomenon? How

can one interpret the facts of death and its consequences in ways that enable her or him to cope with death and loss?

This is usually seen as the role of religion. Through the centuries the various world religions have provided "answers" to questions about death. They have offered a perspective for understanding death and have developed a vocabulary for talking about death. They have framed interpretive images and stories, which are seen factually by some and metaphorically by others. In short, they have enabled an abstraction from the experience of death and provided a context for interpreting that experience. Thus they have provided comfort for many of their devotees. However, various empirical studies have failed to demonstrate conclusively that religion *invariably* helps people to cope with death [2]. We all have observed some people who have been helped greatly by their religious faith and other sincerely religious persons who struggled unsuccessfully to cope with death.

The question raised in this essay is: Is the secular world silent in the face of death or does it simply speak with a different language? It can be argued that the secular world includes the spiritual as it is defined for this volume. The secularist can step back from the experience of the death of another and reflect on it (although totally suspending time and space is the context may be difficult because of commitment to the here and now as the world of reality), making artistic interpretations of that phenomenon, affirming himself or herself as part of the larger whole. The secularist will certainly rest on somewhat different assumptions than the person with conventional religious faith, but these assumptions also enable an effective coping with death.

THE SECULAR MYTH

It is doubtful that a person can approach death, seeking its meaning, in any way but through myth. Myth is many things. Myth is not simply a primitive or prescientific attempt to understand existence. Rather myth is a para-rational, para-logical mode for interpreting existence from the inside out. It fits well into the understanding of spirituality upon which this volume is based, for myth is a pattern of interpretation of facts. Myth is not a way in which one gains knowledge; knowledge which is somehow beyond the reach of scientific investigation. Creation myths, for instance, provide no knowledge whatsoever about the origins of the universe. Rather they are expressions of values, of the sense of wonder and participation which wells up in humans when they reflect on their environment. Myths regarding death do not fill gaps in our scientific understanding of the cessation of life but are mitigating human responses to what is often seen as the brevity of existence. Myths make contact with the deep satisfactions and fears of the human spirit.

For the secularist the need of our day is for a mythological interpretation which has greater congruence with the contemporary scientific worldview and the best knowledge of the present age. Science and myth are not necessarily opponents, because in a way science itself is a myth, an interpretation of observed and experienced facts.

Humans know that they will die, but have a need somehow to transcend death, not simply to deny death. This they have done by proposing some sort of way to get beyond the limits set by death in our experience. Humans make abstractions from this experience which portray some sort of existence beyond death. The most familiar of these are abstractions which are made by devotees of many religions, expressing their faith and hope in a life after death in a realm beyond time and space. Others might frame their abstractions in terms of biological immortality, living on in the genetic pool—one's descendants. This is living on as a part of ongoing nature, the ongoing life process. Or some will make abstract interpretations which can be described as social immortality, living on in the memories of others or in the contributions which have been made by one's life. All of these interpretations are spiritual, mythic.

It has been suggested that one of the causes of the pervasive pattern of death denial has been the collapse of old meanings. As the traditional interpretations became less satisfactory for many persons, lacking anything to put in their place, many people turned away from any real search for meaning. In so doing they impoverished their grasp on life because they sought to blot out its tragic dimensions. Rather than coming of age by accepting tragedy maturely, they simply closed their minds to the tragic, blotting out a significant dimension of living.

The vocabulary of the Judeo-Christian faith tradition and its mythology has supplied the words and symbols by which most western thought traditionally has dealt with the questions about death. The very way in which questions are raised tends to presuppose this vocabulary.

"Why did God let him die?"
"In the divine plan of creation why does death come to everyone?"
"If a person dies, shall he or she live again?"
"Is there justice in a world in which the good die and evil-doers survive?"

SECULARIST "ANSWERS" TO QUESTIONS ABOUT DEATH

Secularist views of the world may well provide "answers" to the same questions as do religious views but they employ the vocabulary of the secular scientific mythology of our time. This vocabulary is used in daily discourse and now needs to be applied to those crisis occasions in which an attempt is made to speak about meaning.

Religious meanings have the support of a religious community and the institutions it involves. For the most part secularists lack an institutional component to support meanings. Often their meanings may seem idiosyncratic rather than growing out of the consensus of an organized group.

The institutions of a secular age lack the metaphysical basis for absolutizing their meanings. So meanings are expressed tentatively and relatively. Even the presuppositions of secularism are such that they do not produce a critical synthesis upon which common meanings are built. Only a relatively few secularists would understand themselves as formally part of the scientific community or as members of a humanist association. Because the consensus is unavoidably vague, the institutional basis indistinct, there is little foundation for rituals to support the secularist interpretations of death.

Many persons are devoid of common rituals and patterns which help them deal meaningfully with the crisis of death. Their struggle against the painful experiences of separation and loss find them with only very limited resources of language, symbol, and ritual to bring the event of death into some kind of helpful perspective. But this does not have to be.

Brian and Esther are well-educated, retired professionals. Brian experienced Protestant Sunday School in childhood and Esther grew up in a non-observant Jewish family. Neither has ever had a sustained or meaningful connection with organized religion. They are not hostile to nor disdainful of the religious beliefs of others, but it is not a felt need on their part. Both of them are reflective, thoughtful people, who have worked out for themselves a satisfactory understanding of death as the end of personal existence. Neither finds thought of an afterlife important or meaningful.

Both of them have experienced deaths, Brian's father and Esther's brother, in the past year. Their views are well portrayed in a brief ritual which they prepared and shared with a few of their close friends when Brian's father died. Esther described some of their reflections on what death means to them: the ending of A LIFE and the ongoingness of LIFE. They talked of the life of Brian's father, culminating with his final debilitating illness. Brian shared some of his memories of earlier experiences from childhood and young adulthood. He spoke touchingly of what would be missing from his life now that his father was no longer alive.

There was none of the hopelessness, the emptiness, the meaninglessness which would be the conventional religious expectation for those confronting this death of loved ones without any traditional belief system. They had developed an understanding of death and its consequences which was meaningful and helpful for them. They were not without comfort.

A good deal has been written about the plight of contemporary humans in a world of collapsed mythology. The lack of an affirming religious mythology produces a loss of emotional reassurance. The question then is: Is it possible to understand the secularist's world view as resting on the mythology of twentieth-century science? In that mythology the basis for perceived reality is this-worldly rather than other-wordly; a dynamic existence is regarded as the ideal rather than an endless, static existence; the future is characterized by on-goingness rather than a final *denouement* in which a static equilibrium of perfection arrives. So one finds people saying that afterlife is not part of the mythology of our age; that they see death as the end of existence for them; that moral judgments, rewards and punishments occur in the here and now in the consequences of our actions. Still, life goes on.

DEMYTHOLOGIZING AND REMYTHOLOGIZING

In a time when old myths are no longer satisfying to everyone, two processes usually emerge: demythologizing and remythologizing. Demythologizing can be an effort to divest life of all mythic meaning and to seek to live without myth, thus reducing life to a prosaic, limited, one-dimensional focus. But it also can clear the way for new myth. Remythologizing recognizes the necessity for some sort of mythic dimensions to life but seeks myths that are more firmly in touch with contemporary worldviews and life patterns.

Death defies knowledge through empirical investigation and must be understood poetically and mythologically. No one really knows what it is to die, because one can only experience the death of another person and reflect on it as one who is still living. When a person actually dies, to the best of our knowledge and experience, the capacity for such reflection ends, and certainly the ability to communicate the experience to the living no longer exists. So the work of remythologizing is the task of creative imagination, of poetry, of art, of mythology, to interpret richly our very limited knowledge and understanding of death, increasing our appreciation of its function and necessity.

Remythologizing is a work of art, broadly understood, done in community. Art is centrally involved in the human effort to give death meaning. The creative artist works in her or his medium to communicate her or his experience of what and how life is. As John Dewey says,

"Science states meanings; art expresses them" [3, p. 84]. Because meanings grow out of experience, it is understandable that the creative artist, as one who experiences deeply, is among the first to attempt articulation. We are well familiar with the way in which great art in past centuries has expressed the meanings which were also articulated by the major religions. In our time most of the great art articulates meanings for the secularist.

Art is hardly divorced from the intellect, but it is also closely related to the emotive, the feeling, the inner psychical level. Art is very much part of what has been defined for this volume as spiritual. Art is not the prelude to an experience nor simply a description of an experience. It is an experience itself. The artist, then, does not merely describe death and delineate its meanings. The artist participates in the awareness of mortality, and those who observe the work, participate in it with the artist. This is true regardless of the art form: whether it be Picasso's *Guernica,* Hemingway's *Death in the Afternoon,* Eberhart's *The Groundhog,* Bernstein's *Mass,* or deCoppola's *Apocalypse Now.*

The artist's fundamental contribution is the application of the creative imagination to death and dying. The artist can no more directly experience death before her or his own dying than any other person; but she or he does bring creative imagination to bear on death as a part of life. The merging of experience of life (and death in life) with the artist's imagination produces his or her picture or story or poem or movie.

The artist does not say, "I tell you for a fact, this is what death is!" Rather the artist says, "Here is my picture (in words, or paint, or music) of the way I experience death in life. How do you respond to it?" If the beholder feels, "Yes, I hadn't really seen it just that way; but, yes, that is the way I experience death in life," meaning has been communicated. The imaginative way in which the artist has reflected upon and portrayed her or his experience of death in life finds resonance in the imagination of the beholder, reflecting and augmenting at a deeper level that person's own experience. That is a form of secularist spirituality.

Usually, when dealing with facts, one immediately becomes caught up in the categories of true or false, correct or incorrect, and rightly so. Anything that is purported to be fact must be subject to such judgments. The product of the creative imagination of the artist is not seen as fact. Its adequacy is tested by its communicability: does it produce a resonance in the beholder? Is the resonance widely shared? This establishes not its truthfulness but its value as a carrier of meaning. A poetic story, when it is widely and resonantly shared within a culture or community, assumes the stature of myth.

SECULARISTS AND LIFE BEYOND DEATH

Having thus examined the process by which death can be interpreted, let us now examine the content of that interpretation which the
secularist gives to death. One of the marks found in a good deal of
twentieth-century thought is the measurement of human existence on
a this-worldly scale. A university professor of anthropology said, "I
can't remember ever in my whole life having believed in eternal life;
that my life would be eternal. I went to Sunday School as a child. They
talked about it, but I never believed it. I've always thought of this life
as all that I know about or all that I can count on." Earlier notions of
humankind transcending nature have been largely eclipsed for many.
Each person participates in the natural order and is simply a portion of
nature, a complex part to be sure. While a human being is a distinct
species within nature, there is no part of him or her that is not totally
natural. Teilhard de Chardin put it this way [4, pp. 12-13]:

> The prevailing view has been that the body . . . is a *fragment* of the
> Universe, a piece completely detached from the rest and handed
> over to a spirit that informs it. In the future we shall have to say
> that the Body is the very Universality of things. . . . My own body is
> not these cells that belong *exclusively* to me; it is *what,* in these cells
> *and* in the rest of the world feels my influence and reacts against
> me. *My* matter is not a *part* of the Universe that I possess *totaliter*:
> it is the *totality* of the Universe possessed by me *partialiter*.

This in a sense is the opposite of dualism. The scientific naturalism
which informs our age, as distinct from romantic naturalism, is monis-
tic, seeing the physical, material world as the only real order of existence. That which has been called spiritual or mental is understood as a
function of the physical, just as thinking is a function of the brain. A
human being is subject to natural law in his or her whole being. This
means that a person's death is seen as thoroughly natural, that is, it is
like the death of any other living thing. Like trees or beasts, persons
die, and when they die, their life is over and the atoms of which they
were composed and which made possible their functioning are dis-
persed and reconstituted in the natural process. The older affirmations
of immortality of the soul or literal resurrection of the body from the
dead, or of essential distinctions between body and spirit, are not made
by the secularist. Rather affirmations are made of the sustaining continuity of the life process in the face of individual death.

The facts of death described in this naturalistic view are the same
facts that are verifiable in any other view of death. When a person dies,
we know from empirical observation that: 1) death brings an end to

consciousness and all bodily functions; 2) there is a severing of all interactive human interpersonal relationships; 3) the cells of the body begin to dissolve almost immediately; and 4) their matter is reconstituted. The processes of demythologizing and remythologizing neither add to nor subtract from these demonstrable facts.

The mythic dimension of the human struggle for meaning grows out of the person's inner response to these factual realities. It deals with the individual's awareness of his or her mortality and the desire somehow to transcend it.

It does make a difference that we live in a scientific age. The older myth of survival after death by immortality or resurrection, particularly when understood literally, is out of step with the scientific assumptions, insights, and discoveries which inform contemporary thinking. For some people the meaning has been lost from older mythological interpretations of death's inevitability in terms of punishment for sin, of death's acceptability as the working out of a benign providential purpose, and of the transcendence of death through receiving an endless, timeless, static existence beyond the grave. They have demythologized ancient patterns of heaven and hell, mortal body and immortal soul, reward and punishment, eternity. So, for the secularist, a new myth must evolve which does not contradict that scientific naturalistic context, even though the myth itself is not scientific, but which still ministers to the needs of those who confront their mortality.

Some have remythologized in naturalistic terms. For them death is understood as inevitable because all living things die. One middle-aged man put it, "I see death as a part of a natural process. The world couldn't go on if everyone kept living. Some are born, some die. It's entirely a natural thing. Personal continuation is through what we hand on to our children and the people around us . . . a kind of rebirth, not literally, but a handing down of self." A person's full participation in nature makes him or her subject to death. Unavoidably one is part of a process of dissolution and reconstitution. In a sense this process passes through the person, in a sense the individual's life is an episode in the extended process. The needs to acknowledge death as the end of life and somehow to transcend death require that both discontinuity and continuity be involved in the patterns by which death is interpreted.

Although the "story" by which the naturalistic myth is told may take many forms, the basic structural components are constant. If one is to be fully human, one must confront one's own death in the midst of living. This death is the end of his or her personal existence. Any residue of the person's living will be found in the resorption of his or her body cells, the continuing genetic chain in which the individual was a link, and the effective influence of her or his social contributions to other individuals and institutions. An individual life has a discernible beginning and ending, but the life process is ongoing and for practical purposes appears to be continuing indefinitely. These are not facts but interpretations by which a person who holds the presuppositions of scientific naturalism confronts his or her own death and the desire to transcend it.

SECULARISTS AND
THE AWARENESS OF MORTALITY

The naturalistic secular understanding of death regards death realistically as the final limit on a human being. The alternative to this confrontation is the neurotic evasive pattern one detects all too readily in western culture in which people exert great energy to keep from facing up to the reality of death. The naturalistic view holds that death is real and final, inescapable and inevitable. It is a mark of humanity's solidarity with nature and with the evolutionary process. A journalist stated his point of view, "The death of every living thing is essentially the same. The physical happening is part of the ecological process. Death is seen as a natural necessity, when once it was understood in terms of moral necessity."

Still, even in death a person can recognize that he or she is part of an ongoing evolutionary pattern which does not end at the individual's death but reconstitutes to include the residue of that person's existence. The contemporary interest in ecology reminds us of the interdependence of all parts of nature, making clear the assumption of humankind's unity with all the rest of nature.

But so often human beings have not accepted readily their place within nature. They have assumed that somehow they are above nature, participating only partially in the mortality they observe in nature. The ecological theme, for the secularist, asserts that nature is one interdependent whole and thus undercuts the notion that there is an immunity to death in any special part of nature.

Death is always present as the outer limit of human possibility. It is a terrible threat to a human, meaningless destruction, unless the person accepts and uses the thought of it as a springboard to move him or her to live to a fuller extent of potentiality.

A woman in early middle age shared a personal experience. "A couple years ago I had a very nasty shock health-wise. I felt I wouldn't live to a ripe old age. I thought I've got to get more out of life, to value every day for itself. This was a very enriching experience, although it was terrifying at first. Once I had accepted it, I could make the most of it."

The value of life is asserted by naturalism through the inclusiveness of its view of existence. The twentieth-century mind, influenced by evolutionary models, sees nature in terms of process, described as ongoing life. Death does not stop the process but alters the direction of its living elements in an apparently endless sequence of recombinations. A particular life is short and seemingly inconsequential when viewed by itself, but assumes value and importance as a significant element in the entire ongoing process. Whether this process is defined in physical or in social terms, continuity of the molecules of the body after death or of the social group after the death of a member, the brevity of the individual's participation does not suggest insignificance or negativity. Life, even brief life, is a contribution to the process. The secularist is not left without a sense of purpose in life just because he or she does not anticipate personal existence after death.

THE ART OF SECULAR DYING

Humans have long said, "As one lives, so one dies." Sometimes this has been said with appreciation, sometimes with dreadful foreboding. Ultimately, one's views of death have to come into focus in terms of one's own dying. So it is important to ask: How can the secularist look at dying?

"Death is for the general good," one man reflected. "If people didn't die, earth would have problems. There are always people around you with whom it is necessary to relate in order to be human. That is what is primary, but the old scheme of life being preparation for death is in a way replaced with a scheme of death being a preparation for life in this world."

New interests have developed in medicine which have urged stronger consideration for enabling the terminally ill to die with meaning and dignity. The question is "Is a person dying?" has been extended to include, "How is the person dying?" which is another way of asking, "How is the person living?"

In a sense, what was called in the past "the art of holy dying" has been translated into psychotherapy for the dying and hospice care. Psychotherapy has been taking a more active part than religion in urging the confrontation of life and death and providing support for that task.

Where in traditional religious views life was understood as a probationary period in which one prepared for death and the final judgment it occasioned, the naturalistic understanding sees the quality of life one lives making a contribution to the ongoing life process.

This change in perspective is part of the humanizing tendency which is so much a facet of contemporary secular thinking. The realization of human potentialities, even imperfect realization, is regarded as a legitimate goal. Tempering the notion of inevitably escalating human progress, which was part of the old, overly-optimistic liberalism, it has become possible to accept the tragic limitations of human nature and still work toward the goal of realizing potentiality. Weakness, suffering, and death are accepted as parts of life with which one must come to terms.

Human beings are active rather than passive in this process. Individuals accept the responsibility not only for their own living, but also for their own being human. Their goal is to be more human rather than less human, so some of the older ways of "denaturalizing" a person's life and death are unsatisfying to this point of view because they result in a reduction of human persons to a fraction of their being.

Human beings as part of the natural order are dying all the time they are living. Only as one becomes aware of this fact and accepts it, does personal existence assume a new quality. Death is still very real, a tragic threat which hangs over life, but life reaches its fullness though acceptance of the fact of this death.

Naturalism talks about death in language which describes a natural process. Of course, humans do not have complete knowledge of this process. They can only make interpretations based on what they experience and observe of the process. Naturalism leads an effort to place the death of an individual into the framework of the process of living and dying, emergence and extinction which is seen everywhere in the natural realm. All death, therefore, is from natural causes. There is nothing arbitrary about it; it occurs everywhere in nature when certain conditions prevail.

In a way this describes death as no less inexorable than the old view of God calling individuals from this life. But there is an important difference. Nature is not regarded as conscious and intelligent; cause and effect processes are not regarded in any moral light. Death is a natural event that happens. It is determined only by the total process, not by any deliberate exercise of will or purposeful intelligence. Call death the work of "Mother Nature" and the whole interpretation becomes unacceptable.

This issue of inexorability offers a paradigm for examining the use of language and its significance. The traditional language is no longer satisfying to many modern minds for a number of reasons. To speak of God calling persons from this life does not coincide with the contemporary scientific understanding of natural law but speaks in terms of an arbitrary divine will operating out of moral judgment. Its basic imagery portrays supernatural intervention into natural process or contravention of natural laws, a theme inimical to the twentieth century scientific mind. It implies that humans are subject to a power outside nature, an inference unsupported by the contemporary scientific worldview. The naturalistic interpretation, talking about death as totally natural, affirms its inevitability, describes the human condition as mortal, construes death as morally neutral. Such language is in agreement with the best knowledge of our day. It is interpretive and tentative because it is talking about death as a mystery, but it is an interpretation which can bear more weight because it is in tune with a contemporary, rather than a prescientific, world view.

DEATH AND IDENTITY

Or, let us look at another example in the way continuity and discontinuity are involved in traditional and naturalistic language about death. Traditional religious language talks of the end of this life and the giving of a new life in which there is continuity of personal identity. We know that when a person is confronted with the death of another, when a person becomes aware of his or her own mortality, his or her participation in the process of dying, the individual faces the inevitable possibility of not remaining as he or she is. Death has an impact on identity.

There are two dimensions of identity that become involved here. For one, body sense and identity are closely related. We live only as embodied persons. We know one another as embodied persons. It is through our bodies that we are in contact with the world and establish a measure of control over our world. The obvious effect of death on the body (dissolution) indicates a similar impact on selfhood.

Much the same thing can be said of the effect of death described as the cessation of consciousness. The current understandings of brain death are based on an irreversible cessation of consciousness. For the vast majority of people consciousness is so highly prized that its termination is not desired. Still the behavioral sciences see that loss as inevitable and confront humans with the task of accepting it.

Both body sense and consciousness are essential ingredients of personal identity. Death clearly brings an end to both. It follows logically in this point of view that death then also brings an end to personal identity. But those who offer the resources of psychotherapy to the dying would affirm that it is the facing of this very fact that gives impetus to a positive and constructive coping with approaching death by enhancing and sustaining identity now. Traditional language and naturalistic language affirm personal identity: the former affirms it as continuing into some other world and the latter in the here and now.

It would be quite possible to make naturalistic translations of much of traditional language about death which gave meaning in a prescientific context. Without going into the detail of the illustrations of body loss and identity loss offered above, one could find significant meanings in time-honored phrases by putting them in the language of scientific naturalism. Death seen traditionally as the will of God is interpreted by the secularist as the working out of natural law by which all living things die. Death seen as going home is interpreted as the absorption of the differentiated person in the natural process. Death as sacrifice is spoken of in terms of the contribution one makes to the evolutionary process by dying. Death as the occasion for final judgment is understood as the cessation of life's potentiality for both positive or negative contributions. Death as fulfillment is understood in terms of the contribution one's life has made, physically and socially, to the evolutionary process in which all living things participate. Death as entering into oneness with God is interpreted as the human's resorption in new ways into nature which he or she has never left, even during the brief time the individual was a differentiated part.

This approach can be criticized as mere reductionism. One can only counter that these naturalistic interpretations form, in the light of the twentieth-century worldview, a more significantly credible and useful basis for human feelings and for poetic expression that the traditional pre-scientific meanings of death and its consequences.

ISN'T THERE MORE TO LIFE?

Humans have long reflected: Life is so partial and incomplete when it culminates in death that there must be something more. It is frustrating to see that dreams will not be realized, goals will not be achieved, potentialities will not be realized. In many instances, from our perspective, life ends too soon.

The need to cope with such frustrations brought by death also can be met by naturalism. The fulfillment death can bring is understood not as the achievement of personal perfection or the completion of the partial. Rather it is a matter of moving beyond seeing death only as dissolution or the end of individual consciousness to recognize it as *natural* transition, in the literal sense. That which has been the person is redistributed or reconstituted in the existence that continues. The molecules of the body are combined with the molecules in earth and air to form new substances; the social and psychological consequences of a person having lived have their effect on those who continue to live. The understanding of an afterlife with personal identity intact is replaced with the idea of a person entering into a new kind of relationship with all that is, the personal as well as the natural world.

These meanings are expressed in terms of relating the individual instance to the dimly perceived "totality," the individual to the "community," the single life to the "whole of existence." The "entities" denoted in the preceding sentence are not regarded as states of perfection or completeness. They may well be little more than constructs through which we define ourselves. Meanings of this kind are not extensions of time into eternity or of finitude into infinity. They are simply extensions *beyond* the person. They can be conceived in terms of the reconstitution of the molecules of the body of the deceased, the carrying of genes into offspring, the effect of one's contribution to and influence on others. Such extensions are understood in terms of demonstrable rather than hypothetical features. They are related to the world of the here and now.

This unity with the natural world cannot be warmly personalized nor hypostasized because the data of the natural world do not sustain the attribution to the natural process of love or justice or communication. The consequences of death are mitigated in the acceptance of being a part of nature rather than in sentimentalizing or personalizing nature. This is a here and now existence in which life and death are taken seriously, in which a person finds new courage for decisive living, because the fact of one's own dying is admitted. Hospice care is a good illustration because it demonstrates in so many instances the possibility of adding a quality of richness, even to the final days of life, because of the intentionality with which death in life is confronted. Fulfillment comes now in an improved quality of present existence, even in the face of approaching death.

However, we must recognize that some die after a more negative than positive experience. There are those who have been truly victimized, those whose days and nights have been filled with unrelieved pain, those who have rarely known happiness or satisfaction, the really miserable. We must be aware of the possibility that the mythic patterns growing out of scientific naturalism or existentialism may not benefit everyone, any more than the older myths brought certain comfort to every person.

SECULARISTS AND THE FEAR OF DEATH

Death is mysterious and awesome. Its experienced consequences are drastic, often very painful. Quite naturally it is feared because it appears to end everything. Many of the comforts of religious faith are believed to reduce this fear, and for many this is true. But the secularist can also confront the fearfulness of death in his or her understanding.

Even though death necessarily involves separation, it does not have to be estrangement from existence. Everything dies but existence goes on, thriving precisely because of death. Scientific naturalism is prepared to accept the possibility that matter and energy are in an endless dynamic flow, constantly interchanging form. The person does come to an end in death, just as a species may become extinct, but the process of which he or she has been a part continues and rearranges. It is quite natural since this is a *vital* process, that there is a struggle to live and a reluctance to die, but that does not mean that death cannot be faced and accepted. Individuals can be supported in this acceptance by knowing that they are parts not only of the human community, but also of the entire natural process.

Life can be understood as a process that has a purposeful quality. To ask whether this purpose is actually operative in a meta-physical sense or formally operative in a strictly physical sense, rooted in the regularities of natural law, or part of a construct by which a person's mind organizes life in a patterned way to gain understanding is not critical at this point, because in any instance the function is the same. If life is regarded as purposeful, and if death is a part of life, then it is possible to assume that somehow death fits into the purposeful nature of things. But we need to be reminded that it is also possible to understand nature operating randomly, thus resisting the temptation to develop elaborate teleologies or serious hypostasization of nature. The human need for the security of order may well be the prime basis for perceiving order in nature. It would thus appear that there is a relationship between the capacity to tolerate death and the extent to which one can see it as part of the natural order.

When death is seen as part of the natural "order," or as part of the universal human condition, it can be tolerated more easily. On the whole this process is regarded as helpful and beneficial since life is enabled by it. Life and death are continuous parts of the whole. Like the century-old rhythm of seedtime and harvest, death is understood as enabling life, which life, in turn, leads again to death.

Existentialism, somewhat like naturalism, seeks to make death less fearful by showing its universality and inevitability without minimiz-ing its totally destructive consequences for the person. The fear of death is faced in the midst of life rather than just at the moment of dying. Emphasis is laid on the courage needed to decide to face death honestly. Attention is devoted to the quality of life within that limit. Once death is accepted, the quality of authentic existence improves and the fear of death is diminished.

SUMMARY

All of this involves creative imagination. A woman said when she was describing her views of death, "But this is probably purely and simply my imagination. It's something I've wondered about for a long time." While this may sound like oversimplification, it is honest recognition that the imagination is employed in seeking some understanding of death.

We must dissociate imagination from delusion and recognize that it is a legitimate way of grappling with that which is beyond empirical investigation. It is extremely important that the imaginative process be recognized for what it is—and is not. It begins with what a person knows and on the basis of that limited knowledge proceeds to make an imaginative *interpretation*, speculatively pressing that knowledge for meaning.

We have to learn to deal imaginatively, poetically, with existence as we perceive it, to find our place in it. Unfortunately, perceptions get absolutized and developed into unquestionable prosaic systems of "truth." If one sees the process frankly as one's imagination dealing with reality as it is perceived, a more honest and believable myth emerges.

The application of creative imagination to death has several major facets: It deals with the inevitability of death, with the ambivalent need to accept and deny it, and with the effort to transcend it.

Some very literal believers in the ancient myths thought of life after death as continuation and augmentation of the good elements of the present life. Such myths described death as entrance into an existence which was pictured as perfection and bliss, with the person continuing while the setting changed. The naturalistic remythologizing tends to reverse this—the person changes radically while the setting (i.e., the natural process) continues. As a result of the person's participation in the ongoing process, the process itself evolves. In various ways the naturalistic myth involves the residue of the individual life whether it be in terms of reconstitution of the molecules of the body, of genetic legacy, or social contribution. The individual can accept death more readily by imagining some element of participation in the continuity of the process, even though one's life may be discontinuous.

Mythologies have sought to portray the possibility of transcending death in a sense of winning a victory even in the act of dying. This is true whether or not the myth involves personal survival. Those who have remythologized the victory, described earlier in terms of inheriting endless heavenly life, often find new meaning in the victory described in existentialism. One finds the victory in facing and accepting death. Even though in the end one dies, he or she has won the victory of the courage to be, to exist. Life has been lived in the light of death's darkness.

IMPLICATIONS FOR CAREGIVERS

Those who work to provide care for the dying and the grieving are dealing with people who are grappling with what mortality means to them. These caregivers are faced with the task of bringing together two perspectives: their own understandings of death and its consequences and the perspective of the person receiving care. In some instances these perspectives are fairly congruent, at other times there may be wide divergences. For the caregiver who is personally committed to the meanings usually associated with traditional Judeo-Christian belief systems, working with a secularist requires thoughtful and sensitive responses.

A first step in such caregiving involves laying aside the assumption that the only real comfort for mourners is through a religious belief system. Once one has found in one's own belief system meanings which enable coping with thoughts of mortality, it is easy to assume that coping is impossible without similar meanings. We commonly observe extreme defensiveness when confronted with alternatives to our own understandings of death and its consequences, as if the very articulation of those alternate views threatens the "truthfulness" of our personal views.

Alfred North Whitehead defined faith as the willing suspension of disbelief. Perhaps we can slightly skew this definition to suggest that the best expression of the caregiver's own faith may be the willing suspension of disbelief in the position of the mourner. If a particular perspective has meaning for the dying person or the mourner, it works for them, whether or not it is a belief shared by the caregiver. The prime criterion for judging a perspective on the meaning of death is not the effectiveness of a belief system for the caregiver, but for the mourner.

Providing supportive care for those who are dying or who are trying to cope with the death of a loved one involves enabling them to strengthen the meanings by which they struggle with their crisis. This may raise the question for some caregivers: How does one nurture in mourners their own belief system, beliefs which the caregiver may not share? For example, can a clergy person to a lay caregiver seriously committed to a traditional religious faith minister to bereaved individuals who are secularists, who do not share belief in resurrection and life eternal? This is a question of conscience for the caregiver. It may be helpful to reflect on the paradigm of the world-wide relief efforts carried out by religious groups when confronted by famine, earthquake, war. Religious communities respond to such need without insisting that recipients share their belief system. Food and clothing are provided for Muslims, Hindus, animists who have need. No effort is made to proselytize; it is enough that they are hungry. In the same way mourners have profound needs, whether they are Christian, Jewish, or secularist.

There is a natural desire to share one's own belief because it has become so central in one's own living. This is particularly true when that belief system has met one's own needs, e.g., confronting the loss of a loved one through death. It is so easy to assume that a person who has a belief system quite different from our own naturally is going to miss completely all the benefits which we feel we derive from our own beliefs. Sometimes, if we do not hear words or symbolic images familiar to us, we assume that there is a spiritual vacuum, a *tabula rasa*. But as this essay has tried to indicate, absence of a traditional belief system does not necessarily mean that the secularist has no workable system of meaning. The caregiver's function is to hear those meanings with sensitivity.

We recognize that, even for those with traditional religious beliefs, there may be times when those beliefs are not fully effective in meeting their needs. Many pastors or hospital chaplains have seen persons who sincerely held the Christian belief in resurrection, who suffered almost inconsolably their sense of loss. Often only after a long struggle did their belief system begin to provide perspective for relating to their loss in new ways.

So it is no less unusual for the secularist to struggle with grief. It is easy to jump to the conclusion that the pain of the mourner occurs because the mourner does not espouse a traditional belief system. It should not be assumed automatically that their secularist beliefs have failed them.

Evidence of such struggle can easily be perceived as a license for the caregiver to impose his or her personal belief system on the mourner. The effective caregiver offers his or her own beliefs only on request. Even when a caregiver is invited to share personal belief, it should be in terms of what has been found personally to be helpful, rather than staking a claim to eternal truth.

This is not to say that the caregiver needs to be without personal beliefs, without values. But one of the prime values of the effective caregiver is to honor the right of the one being cared for to hold to that which he or she has found meaningful and helpful.

The important function for the caregiver is to provide an opportunity for people to articulate their belief systems and to indicate the ways in which they are finding it helpful (or not helpful) in meeting their crisis. As we have said, this is not a license for the caregiver to try to convert the mourner to the caregiver's point of view. Nor is it effective caregiving to become a critic of the person's own belief system.

The role of the caregiver is that of mid-wife, helping a meaning system to emerge from the mourner: clarifying, empathizing with the struggle. This requires the full attention of the caregiver because the non-traditional meanings may not be expressed in familiar or easily understood terms. It may be helpful for the caregiver from time to time to try to paraphrase what the person has been expressing both to test the accuracy of the communication and to reinforce the personal statement of the other person.

Rather than talking only in abstract terms it is helpful for the caregiver to try to reflect objectively how the person is finding his or her particular perspective helpful in dealing with the present crisis. This has to be done with sensitive appreciation, whether or not the caregiver would find such insight personally helpful.

The basic issue for the caregiver is this: Is my confidence that the grieving person will be helped based on the affirmation of the meanings of a traditional religious belief system or on the working through of a process which could involve any one of many alternative beliefs? Caregivers in the past would have answered that question very much in favor of the former resource: espousal of a traditional faith. In recent decades, as we have understood much better the functioning of the mourning process, we are in a position to affirm that for many help comes by working through the process, even with unconventional or non-traditional beliefs and meanings. The approach of the caregiver will be profoundly influenced by the way in which this issue is understood. Serious grappling with this important question is a crucial prerequisite for working with the bereaved.

REFERENCES

1. J. Morgan, Death and Bereavement: Spiritual, Ethical, and Pastoral Issues, *Death Studies, 13*, pp. 85-89, 1988.
2. H. Feifel, The Problem of Death, in *Death Interpretations*, H. M. Ruitenbeck (ed.), Delta Books, New York, 1969.
3. J. Dewey, *Art as Experience*, G. P. Putnam and Sons, New York, 1958.
4. P. Teilhard de Chardin, *Science and Christ*, Harper and Row, New York, 1968.

CHAPTER 8

Perspectives on Death in
the Africa-American Community

David K. Meagher and Craig P. Bell

INTRODUCTION

In attempting to analyze or discuss the meaning of death in the African-American community, one is struck by the paucity of research on the topic. This lack of research raises interesting yet disturbing questions regarding:

1. the existing professional assumptions being made about the death-related needs of the African-American community; and
2. the justification for this apparent lack of interest in this community's need for assistance in death-related matters.

Is this situation simply the result of professional oversight, disinterest or, to quote Dubois, is it "The result of age-long complexes sunk into unconscious habit and irrational urge?" [1]. Is the profession of thanatology merely accepting traditional assumptions regarding death and bereavement and extrapolating that data on the African-American community?

Kalish and Reynolds wrote that one must examine African-American perspectives of death by means of one or more of four conceptual frameworks [2]:

1. as a form of African survival;
2. as an imprint of the dominant culture within which Blacks have, involuntarily from a historical perspective, spent the last three centuries;

3. as a representation of the value system of the socioeconomic group within which they are disproportionately found; and
4. as an idiosyncratic consequence of being black in America.

A more realistic approach would be to consider all four as integral and related variables influencing the perspective. Anything less is tantamount to researcher bias. The historical and contemporary realities of being black in America impact very significantly on the attitude about life and death. In essence, to analyze the African-American attitude toward death would ultimately involve analyzing the relationship, if any, between being black in America and dying. Is there an unusual or pathological relationship in this country between culture and morbidity or is the relationship more a reflection of socio-economic status?

The thrust of this chapter is to pose questions regarding the issues of death and bereavement within the African-American community. The inherent assumption throughout the chapter will be that *there are differences* in attitudes, feelings, and behaviors associated with death between the white community (those of European descent) and the black community (those of African descent). [In the context of this chapter, *black* is used interchangeably with *African-American* to connote a common cultural tradition among a specific population and not a condition of color.] These differences are the result of the dissimilarity of the life experiences between the two groups—specifically life experiences with death. We recognize the difficulties involved in attempting to make statements and raise questions regarding an entire ethnic/cultural group. We clearly comprehend that African-Americans come from all dispositions, capabilities and aspirations—there are many conditions of blackness. Contrary to popular impressions, this community is not a homogenous group and we do them a disservice by lumping them together and reacting to them in terms of socially constructed stereotypes. As with all other cultural groups, African-Americans are a very diverse population who do not have a singular set of needs and no singular set of services will accommodate their needs. West, however, cautions that any inquiry into African-American belief systems must include the experiences of the past and the present: the doings and the sufferings of African people in the United States [3]. These doings and sufferings are the manifestation and outcomes to prejudice and racism that have impacted on the socio-economic, spiritual life of the black American. One must recognize that the life experiences of this community reflect a continuous historical reality-racial discrimination. No matter the socio-economic classification, racist norms and standards lead to the detrimental, preconceived judgment of the individual. These racist norms and standards become the criteria for meaningful participation in the on-going process of institutional life. Racial discrimination is the mutual commonality in the life experiences of African-Americans. It is an ideology of racial domination and exploitation which becomes the shared environmental condition of the African-American.

The Meaning of Death

News Report: The United States National Center for Health Statistics reported that the life-expectancy gap between blacks and whites is growing. According to the researchers, a black infant born in 1988 could expect to live 69.2 years while his/her white counterpart has an expected life span of 75.6 years. This greater death rate in the black population is described as "unconscionable" as most of these deaths are unnecessary; they could be affected by changes in the health care policy of the country. The greatest increases in death were from AIDS and drug and alcohol abuse. A second study released to the press reported that while blacks make up approximately 13 percent of the population, they account for nearly 80 percent of premature deaths due to curable diseases. The reason given for this disparity was the lack of access to the health care system. A co-author of this study was quoted as saying that some of these premature deaths were a "function of hopelessness, a disenfranchisement from the community."

(New York Times, December 2, 1990)

The attitudes an individual holds toward death and dying are embedded in his/her social, cultural and religious values. Values affect the way in which one conceptualizes death. Values also affect one's behavior in relation to death because values underlie the guidelines on which the individual bases his/her behavior [4]. Conversely, experience and behavior influence the strength of the values and attitudes. Americans, it is argued, respond to death in a manner consistent with their general orientation to life. This orientation to life may be summarized as "instrumental activism" [5]. An important component of instrumental activism is the scientific method and since scientists are committed to realism, one should not expect to find "an attitude so drastically discrepant with the realism of science in an area [death] so close to biology and medicine" [5].

The attitudes and behaviors of African-Americans in regard to death cannot be understood without reference to the accompanying persistent presence of death in their history [2] and to the experience with dying and death and the expectations for life within a modern technological society.

The Myth/Reality of Black Religion

Within the religious conceptual model, the origins of the philosophical and spiritual meanings of death are universally similar. Many religions of the world have defined the purpose of life and the reason for death, have taught that there is a supreme being, that death is not the complete end of the human spirit, and that there is some type of ongoing existence after death, the form of which is determined by how one lived. This promised postmortem existence ranges from the belief in reincarnation to a heavenly experience to Nirvana [6]. God, Allah, Buddha or a deity by some other name has always promised that "He who believes in me shall not die a complete, permanent and absolute death." Clearly, there are religious similarities between cultural groups which ultimately have a similar impact on their attitude towards death. With the religious conceptual model, death offers the glorious reward of everlasting life for a life governed by the belief in the redeemer (e.g., sanctified peace). May wrote that the belief in the absolute rightness of promise is essential. He stated it in the following way: "There is nothing to be done toward the sacred except to let it be what it is, permit it to run its course, and let one's own life be caught up in its force" [5, p. 100)]. Lifton described this as the spiritual power that is at the heart of all religions [6]. This spiritual force is the power of death. Traditionally, for many in the African-American community, this promise of everlasting peace was the reward for enduring an oppressive existence under the black codes of slavery or the Jim Crow laws on segregation or for the benign neglect of isolation. The anticipated security and peace of death was an alternative to a life of oppression and brutality. Within this context one can clearly comprehend the significance of the ritualization of death and bereavement within the black community (the shouting, crying, singing at a Baptist funeral or the laughing, eating, drinking revelry of the wake, etc.). Yet one must not make the mistake of assuming that there is a "Black Church" or a "Black Religion." While the idea of a "Black Church" may have a certain heuristic value [7, p. 12], the reality is that there are many churches and beliefs to which large groups of American Blacks affiliate: Muslim, Islam, Judaism, and Christianity. No matter the sect or the belief system, the total may be grouped into a single concept of Black Religion. This concept has been defined as the many forms of belief in which Black people, in Africa and later in America, attempt to explain the universe and humans' relationship to the universe [8]. The ultimate end of this attempt is to create a set of norms and standards that would govern man's relationship to man.

While there is no one black church, there is one shared theme of all Black Churches; namely, the element of a protest against the racist and socially-stratified structure of American society [7]. The major consequences of the slave experience were a loss of culture and the resultant loss of self-image and self-determination. Black Americans labored under the burden of a triple crisis of self-recognition and cultural predicament: African appearance and unconscious cultural mores, involuntary displacement to America without American status, and American alienation from European ethos complicated through domination by European Americans [3].

A black spirituality is very connected to the issue of forced transportation of Africans from their own culture to the dehumanizing servitude of slavery in culture and self-determination that is almost without precedent in the history of the world. The Black Church is the only institution in existence that was capable of reversing a trend of thinking that brought Black people to the very banks of annihilation [8].

Initially the traditional Black Church offered the newly freed blacks a spiritual means of surviving in bondage and it offered the promise of a better post-mortem life in Heaven. West proffers the reasons why a large number of American Blacks became Christians [3]. Christianity, West suggests, is a religion especially fitted to the oppressed. It looks at the world from the perspective of those who are on the bottom of the socio-economic ladder. It is a theodicy, a triumphant account of good over evil.

The spirituals and sermons, as Smith described, grew out of a consistent belief that the better life, which has yet to come, was what gave one the ability to endure and in doing so, made the unendurable bearable [9]. The promised reward of a life of joy and happiness after death which the person earned for all his/her suffering in life was a major source of life-sustenance. The black family managed to survive largely because it has drawn upon the church for inspiration and for resources. But this was not a one-way transaction. The black family and the church have had to draw on each other for support and nurture. In order to do this, each party had to understand the several shared realities which constituted the problems both had to confront. The first was that the black community is a suffering yet hopeful community. More than a community in the usual sense, the concepts of family and community became almost synonymous. Blacks perceived each other as "Brother" and "Sister." These were not some abstract terms or code words of a secret society. They were, and still are, concrete ways of expressing, through the church, the familial inter-relatedness and the structure of the nuclear or extended family unit which blacks, through the slave system, were often denied [9].

The implications for this family/community identification on the ways in which the family unit perceives responsibility of its members are interesting. The black family has developed as an adoptive/absorptive entity-practiced in the care of the elderly and the practice of informal adoptions. This absorption mechanism is an important facet of the mutual aid system within the black extended family. The process of adoption/absorption is clearly explained in the following passage [9, p. 29]:

> The strength of the black family must ultimately be measured by its extraordinary contribution to black Ecclesiology. As the nuclear family in all its brokenness comes to the church, it finds a place where surrogate mothers and fathers, brothers, sisters, uncles and aunts are willing to receive them and adopt into their fold.

Over the last 150 years, four types of black religious sects that have relevancy to the strategies of social action and attitudinal orientation have evolved. These sects have been categorized in the following way [7, p. 8]:

1. mainstream religious groups (Baptist, Methodist, and Presbyterian) generally made up of middle-class blacks who believe that change comes from within the social system;
2. nationalistic religious groups (Muslim, Islamic, and Jewish sects along with the African Orthodox Church and the Shrines of the Black Madonna) desirous of a counterculture that rejects many of the values and goals of the larger society;
3. conversionist sects (Pentecostal, Holiness and smaller Baptist congregations) emphasizing a puritanical life-style and ecstatic behavior;
4. thaumaturgical groups (the Black Spiritual movement) employing the use of magico-religious rituals to acquire esoteric knowledge of self as a means of obtaining the "good life."

Each of these groups share the common themes of justice and respect that will lead to self-determination. Out of the extended family concept of a suffering community came the pastor who became responsible for the radical political action necessary to achieve for the church-family the material necessities to deal with a racist world [9]. Thus, one sees that the black preacher did not remain behind the pulpit within the physical confines of the church. He truly became the shepherd of his flock. The black preachers are the historical leaders of most black

Americans and their words are heard by more blacks, whether they regularly attend church or not, than those words communicated by any other organization [8]. The title of reverend is often seen before the names of those individuals identified as the black leaders of this nation. The roster includes such luminaries as the Reverends Martin Luther King, Jr., Jesse Jackson, Benjamin Hooks, Calvin O. Butts, Louis Farakaan and Al Sharpton. These leaders are leading their people to a promised land in which all are free and in control of their own destiny. "For freedom Christ has set us free; stand fast therefore, and do not submit again to the yoke of slavery" (Galatians 4:5).

While the throngs who marched with Rev. Martin Luther King, Jr. sang "We shall overcome-someday" and King preached his now famous "I Have a Dream" sermon, it is no longer accepted that the promised land is a goal of the future or the next world. The group now chants:

> What do we want?
> Freedom-Justice-Equality!
> When do we want it?
> Now!

THE SECULARISM OF DEATH

Present theory sees modern Western society as experiencing a movement away from this religious, spiritual meaning of death toward one in which secular (scientific and medical) meanings define life and death (brain life and brain death definitions). Within this secular conceptualization, death is no longer seen as a necessary experience which results in the transformation of the human soul or essence from the confines of the physical body to a spiritual existence in an other than earthly place. More frequently death is being seen merely as an experience of this world, albeit the final experience, and nothing more. This perception includes the belief that there is no altered or continued postmortem existence. Life and death are antithetical potentials. Death is the absence of life; dying is defined medically as the final stage of life, the stage of ultimate exhaustion ending in the complete and permanent cessation and termination of all life processes. Consistent with instrumental activism, this society distinguishes between death as the natural and inevitable term of human life, which it strives in it ceremonies to accept, and adventitious, premature death which it has increasingly subjected to prevention and/or control [5].

It is in this sense that death has lost its sacred meaning. How one lives as the means to achieve an everlasting reward in heaven has become less important. The achievement of a heaven on earth where one will be able to live a very long life of happiness, well-being, personal satisfaction and accomplishment, has become the important goal of life [10]. Death is the enemy. Religion, for the believers in and recipients of modern medicine, is no longer the essential institution called upon to answer the question of life and death. This continuing process of divestment results in the progressive annexation of religious values and beliefs into medical values and beliefs [11].

The result of this secularism is that death, having undergone this significant attitudinal/belief change, is no longer seen as a necessary event in nature. The reason for death as the will of God is no longer an acceptable explanation. It is now an event that is explained by using the medical model: a disease that medicine, science and technology will and should be able to control and eliminate. This manner of avoiding death is known as emortality (the elimination of disease-related deaths) [12]; and its accomplishment is financially related.

Without a sacred meaning to neutralize its evil nature, death becomes almost "dirty"—not fit for polite society. This shift toward a secular conception of death and the resulting confrontation with the finality of death have given rise to the coping attitudes of death avoidance and denial. The evidence of the presence in society of the attitudes of denial and avoidance are given as [4]:

1. the institutionalization of the dying with death being removed to special sites;
2. the removal of the elderly, the carriers of dying, to old age homes and retirement villages; and
3. the eschewing of death-related discussions and conversations.

The Inequality of Death

Clearly, the secular model represents some drastic changes in societal attitudes and behaviors toward death. Yet, the inherent assumption of the secular model is that changes will impact equally on all groups within the American society. However, in terms of the African-American community, one can question whether the secular model has had the predicted impact on death attitudes and behavior. It would appear that the secular conceptualization of death carries with it a vastly different set of expectations and values for blacks in this country. Indeed, the clear implication of secular technology is to remove death as much as possible from the human continuum. Even though it is an experience of this world and, as such, natural and inevitable, it must also be viewed as a preventable and unacceptable experience. For the individual it must become a rarity within the societal context. Death must be distanced from the experience of everyday living: removing death from the house, institutionalizing those most apt to die (the aged and the terminally ill) and placing a censor's R or X rating on death-related presentations. But what of those communities in which death is a more common experience? Death in the African-American community is not a rarity. On the contrary, death, especially for inner city blacks, is an everyday occurrence. One study examining the influence of race on the attitudes toward death reported that blacks had more contact with those who died during the previous two years of the study than any other racial group [2]. Yet institutions like trauma centers, intensive care centers, hospices, and grief support programs do not locate in predominately black communities. Old age homes and retirement villages permitting the removal of the death prone require financial resources that are generally beyond the means of many black families along with the possibility of these services not being perceived as acceptable alternatives to the usual way of caring for the elderly [2]. As a result, death-related conversations cannot be avoided and become necessary as families attempt to survive and cope with the greater frequency of losses due to death. Blacks, as a consequence of race and economics, are more likely to be death accepting, believing there is a high probability that I or someone I know will die very soon and prematurely.

Recent statistical data on the morbidity and mortality rates within the African-American community clearly indicate that this group has not benefitted from medical technology as well as the rest of society. An inexcusably large gap in expected longevity exists between white and non-white. So the secular reality of death being a medically-controlled entity in which all may live a long, happy, and satisfying life is not a complete or all encompassing reality within the African-American population. Blacks do not share completely in the secular materialism; therefore they do not reap the benefit of technology that is available to the rest of society. The promises of a long life, of a caring medical care system, and of a dignified, peaceful death after a life of accomplishment, are not fulfilled. Racial/socioeconomic factors have produced a population that is not afforded the opportunity to participate in this life- extending medical system in the same way as the rest of the society. As was described in the news summary from the *New York Times* and presented earlier in the chapter, blacks constitute a major group of this population.

According to the National Center for Health Statistics, African-Americans do not have the luxury to demand, as a right, a long happy life of personal or family security. Blacks, according to these statistics, have a great deal of difficulty in surviving each day. Many in this group, experience severe problems in keeping their children alive from infancy to childhood (inadequate prenatal care, higher infant mortality rates); face almost insurmountable opposition from the physical and social environment in successfully getting their children from childhood to adolescence (nutritional deprivation, lead poisoning, etc.), through adolescence (drug abuse and violent deaths) to early adulthood (AIDS, violent deaths, suicide) and on to middle age and old age that, according to the statistics, seems to be medically guaranteed to the rest of society.

What are the potential pathologies in the type of child loss mentioned above? One of the most difficult tasks for parents [13], but one that is most important in grief resolution [14] is the search for some meaning in a child's death. What is the impact on parental grief when the meaning arrived at is incomprehensible and serves only to strengthen senses of helplessness and hopelessness? In this situation are parents expected to engage in anticipatory bereavement from the moment of the birth of their children? These questions beg for the answers that are necessary to understand the spiritual/philosophical meaning of death held by the African-American parent. The answers may be reflected in the Kalish and Reynolds report that death was not only a central theme of black literature, as it is in white literature, but the depiction of death seemed to reflect the reality of death in the black community [2]. Neither romantic death (the idyllic scene of death in "A Love Story") nor death as the culmination of a long life (the "On Golden Pond" promise of death in old age and reconciliation) permeated the writings. In contrast, death as a sudden violent experience was what was consistently described. Homicide and suicide were the major causes of death depicted in the literature surveyed. These themes seem not only to reflect the reality but they may be accurate indicators of the African-American perception of death.

The failure of African-Americans to participate fully in and enjoy the rewards of a modern medical society is, in addition to the earlier statistics, evidenced by the fact that:

1. black males have the highest death rates from accidents and violence of any statistical group;
2. the suicide rates have risen at a faster rate for blacks than for whites;
3. infant mortality rates in the black community are double that of whites;
4. one third of all American casualties in Viet Nam were African-Americans;

5. the odds of an African-American male being murdered are six times greater than for his white counterpart (eight times greater between the ages of 24 and 34);
6. a black female is three times more likely to be a homicide victim than her white counterpart; and
7. the survival rates (5-year survival rates) for most forms of cancer are significantly less for the black patient than for the population of patients as a whole.

In addition to these statistical differences between the races, it is known that most suicides and homicides black men experience are committed between the ages of 20 to 35. This fact may be an indication that after 35, the black individual ceases to struggle against his environment and accepts a fate in it for himself; thus returning to the philosophical attitudes of the Lord's will taught him in black churches when he was very young [8].

These statistics described common causes of death in the black community. It has long been recognized that the cause of death affects the grief response and ultimately bereavement outcome. While there is a lack of reliable information on race and ethnic differences in bereavement outcome, the few studies that have been reported suggest black survivors are at greater risk of increased morbidity and mortality than whites [15].

In view of the limited data, discussions of the impact of race on the grieving process and bereavement outcome need to be examined prior to the development of support programs. It may well be that the grief counselor/therapist, a person trained to offer support to the bereft, needs to become more involved in the political-social-economic arenas that are part of the problem as well as part of the solution. Grief support, in these instances, may be more involved with prevention of like loss in the future than in postvention designed to cope with loss already experienced.

It would appear that the secularization of death and the creation of dying as a medical construct facilitate a political and economic reality to the process and for many in the African-American community the parameters of their existence exclude them from this political-economic reality. There are those members of the society who have the economic resources and expect, even demand, that scientific technological medicine produce increased longevity and prevent death. The demand, more frequently in recent times, assumes the quality of a right. If death occurs, one's rights have been violated and the violator must be held accountable. Money is seen as the answer to all medical problems and threats for it provides the power and accessibility to technological health care. There is an imperative that states medicine can and must do something about every condition. An infallibility of science presupposes that there is always one more thing medicine can do. We are asked to have faith and trust in the system and it will take very good care of us all providing we are compliant and have the means to pay. There is some justification for this belief. Medicine, as a scientific technological endeavor, has been instrumental in improving both the quantity and quality of life for many, if not for all of us.

Yet, there are those who do not have the means to pay and/or, even with the means, are considered undesired consumers of the system. Again, analyses indicate that the African-American community receives a disproportionately low share of the economic resources and opportunities available to the citizens of the country. Without the available economic resources to purchase scientific technological medical solutions, death within this community is uniquely different. It occurs at younger ages, from sudden (perceived as unanticipated and unexpected in the non-black community) causes, and often for unnecessary (senseless) reasons. Within this context, increased longevity and preventable death is not a right but a nonexistent illusion. In the community, secularization of death, death as an unnecessary or preventable state, is not a logical or resultant conclusion. Death represents the ultimate victimization of the individual for it is a daily, uncontrollable, unpredictable, culturally predetermined event. There is no possibility for intervention or prevention. In essence, all forms of death become acceptable and expected. Even money loses its potency for often accessibility of the more advanced forms of medical intervention will be futile because of the advanced stage of illness or the weakened condition of the body due to malnutrition, repeated infection, etc.

Another consequence of death as a medical construct is that a greater attention is focused on how one dies. Not only has death become an object worthy of contempt in the greater society but so have certain forms of dying. Categories of desired and appropriate deaths, implying the diametrically opposite categories of undesired and inappropriate deaths, begin to appear in the attitude literature. Desired deaths include the absence of pain, little or no change in one's physical appearance and going gently into the night of death. Among the many undesirable forms of dying that people would rather avoid are:

1. metastasized cancer after severe, aggressive, invasive treatments;

2. diseases and conditions associated with old age and loss of control;
3. AIDS and AIDS-related diseases;
4. suicide; and
5. acts of violence that cause extreme bodily mutilation.

These most undesired deaths, with the exception of those associated with old age, tend to be the more frequent death experiences in African-American communities. So, whether death is classified as natural, accidental, suicidal, or homicidal, the reality is that the rates are higher in black communities than in the society in general. This difference is not a recent phenomenon and it cannot be explained away simply as a statistical anomaly. Most of the deaths listed were preventable. This includes those deaths from conditions such as cancer and AIDS. The investment in long-term programs of prevention and intervention is negligible necessitating a greater need for postventive support that addresses the results of the deprivations and inequalities.

It is not only the death of self that is at issue. The dying and death of others, as opposed to the death of self, carry with them a different set of concerns. The death of one's infant/child or the death of one's spouse raises fears and anxieties that are distinct from the concerns of death of self. In addition, a death that was preventable, one that is the result of a lack of money or a lack of available resources, has a very distinct effect on the bereavement process and on the attitudes and beliefs about life and death. Sanders wrote that certain situational moderator variables can have a debilitating effect on bereavement outcome [14]. These variables, she continued, contribute significantly to complicated bereavement and, in many cases, if experienced strongly enough, may be the sole reason for the complication. The variables about which she wrote are those described above as frequent experiences in the African-American community. Among the important variables mentioned are social variables (socio-economic status), situational variables surrounding the death (frequency of sudden deaths, suicide, AIDS, drug overdose), and variables surrounding the bereavement (lack of social supports and concurrent crises). Each of the preceding variables alone can affect the adaptability to loss. When present in combinations, as is the case in many African-American families, they may reach overwhelming proportions and increase the possibility of complications that make a pathological bereavement outcome more likely [14]. Research is desperately needed to examine how race, as a constant, combines with each of these variables in creating an idiosyncratic death attitude and a unique susceptibility to complicated grief and pathological outcomes.

The Ethical Dilemmas of Death

The disparity in the access to health care and the availability of modern interventive technologies are not more evident than in the medical-ethical arena of dilemmas this society seems to confront daily. To the best knowledge of the authors, there have not been any reported landmark, legally precedent setting, cases of the right to remove life-sustaining technologies from a patient who was black. The Karen Ann Quinlans and Nancy Cruzans were white. It has been hypothesized that this disparity may be the result of one or more of the following: the lack of technologies in the hospitals utilized by blacks; the lack of financial resources to pay for those intensive forms of intervention necessary to create the dilemma; the nature and/or stage of the life-threatening conditions when presented to the medical care system rendering the interventions useless; or an attitude of disinterest or disdain on the part of the medical caregiver. A recent report from The Center for Health Policy Studies at the Georgetown University School of Medicine supports the economic hypothesis. It was reported (*New York Times*, January 16, 1991) that hospital patients who lack medical insurance die up to three times the rate of similar patients with insurance. The authors of the report suggest that physicians are less likely to order expensive procedures for patients who could not pay and were more likely to forego procedures that could be judged as optional. Support for the other theories is also easily found in the professional literature [16].

Neubauer and Hamilton, in an examination of racial differences in attitudes toward hospice, report that blacks were more likely to differ significantly from whites on two issues [17]. Blacks surveyed wanted to live as long as possible under any circumstances and they stated that death should be avoided at all costs. Hospice, in these subjects, may have been perceived as a place where people go to die. The difference in attitudes addressing the right to die issue may reflect the absence of the potential for the dilemma to be confronted. In addition, it may reflect the fact that the researchers did not pose the question of choosing between a life completely dependent on mechanical support systems and a "living will" death. If, as the data suggest, blacks are not the recipients of life extending technologies because of racial and economic factors, then the ethical dilemma about their utilization may be moot.

Implications for the Caregiver

The authors, in attempting to determine the implications for the caregiver of the impact of the black experience make two assumptions with which the reader may or may not agree. These assumptions are:

1. we live in a racist society, and
2. the social/medical programs and services offered to African-American communities are generally a replication of services based on a need evaluation of white, middle-class populations.

As was stated earlier, the concerned caregiver in order to provide greater support to the black community may need to become more involved in grass roots social, economic, political movements aimed at the prevention of a problem than to be focused only on those services designed to allow the problem to manifest itself in the first place, as in the case of programs of intervention and postvention.

It had also been noted earlier that race as a single variable influencing death-related behavior or in combination with socioeconomic status has not received a great deal of attention in the thanatology research community. Data, empirically arrived at, describing the importance, if any, of race in American society as a variable impacting on the patient's response to terminal illness and/or the chances for increased risk of adverse bereavement consequences in the survivors do not exist. Therefore, the caregiver/counselor is left with models, the bases of which are built on situational factors such as: the expectation of the death (sudden and unexpected, sudden and expected, or chronic and expected), socioeconomic status, degree of religiosity of the patient and family, past death experiences within the family, and the degree of social recognition of the grief (recognized and sanctioned or disenfranchised and unsupported). The utility of the existing models tend to be most efficient when applied to white, middle-class populations. Terminally-ill black patients, especially poor blacks, seem not to be a desired or targeted population for hospice care. The caregiver may be surprised to learn that this exclusion may, in fact, be a mutually arrived at reality. Not only is there a lack of hospice programs within the black communities, it is likely these services would have been rejected had they been instituted. The distrust of the medical system in the black community is very pervasive and would likely influence significantly the acceptance of ancillary programs like hospice. In addition, there is a value of life that seems to be present in the African-American community that may be considered unique given the current debates of patients' rights and living wills. This value, described by Neubauer and Hamilton, may be stated as [17]:

Life must not be surrendered, death is not a phenomenon to which one meekly acquiesces. Intervention, in the form of aggressive care, should be continued. Death will occur in its own time. It does not need any help.

In the absence of models based on the African-American experience, the caregiver/counselor who seeks to understand the dynamics of death-related behaviors in this population may have to spend some time and energy constructing his/her own models of intervention and support. The accomplishment of this model development is made easier by addressing a variety of hypotheses derived from social and historical observations about the black experience. The following are three such hypotheses.

1. The adoptive-absorptive nature of the inclusive community of the traditional black family/religion [9], described earlier, results in a lessening of the desirability of non-community-based support programs as an option for care. A black, terminally-ill patient and the family in search of support may not respond favorably or positively to a suggestion or offer of assistance from institutionalized palliative care units or from well-intentioned hospice caregivers. In addition to a locus of control attitude described above, giving care to the aged, the abandoned young and the dying are family/religion spiritual matters.
2. The definition of and the spiritual value given to life result in the belief that the death of any one member of the inclusive community/family increases the vulnerability of all family members. Systems of care designed to accept or permit death may not be acceptable options.
3. The impact of slavery and the racism that followed the black American after the Emancipation Proclamation resulted in significant differences in the way pain and suffering are perceived when compared to the white majority. What a community evolved question might ask for is the rationale for palliation at the end of life when in the greater society there is little or no concern about the life-long deprivation and pain experienced by this group?

Assuming a difference in the racial make-up between the counselor and client the caregiver/counselor needs to:

1. begin to address his/her own racial needs and how they impact on the delivery of care;
2. be sensitive to the history of being black in white America, understanding the perception of distrust and that the reality of medical abuses allow for one to conclude that the goal of all assistance programs offered have not been for the betterment of the recipient;

3. understand the spiritual make-up of the family (understanding who is family) and that the responsibility of family is to be there for all its members (adoptive/absorptive behavior);
4. be prepared to support or provide care to this family structure with the same verve she/he brings to her/his other caregiving experiences;
5. be more sensitive to the impact of death on the immediate survivors as well as the community, extending the parameters of who might normally be considered primary grievers in the development of support services and the acceptance of persons for grief counseling; and
6. be prepared to support a grief whose signs and symptoms might be best described as a mix of expected and sudden, and unanticipated death experiences.

Death, as in the case of life, is defined in part as an outcome to the racial biases that seems to permeate the very fiber of society. An attempt at offering sympathy and understanding by telling the survivors that "the doctors did all they could" or "we are here to help you in this time of need" generally is not consistent with the experience of the community.

Providing care to a person without taking into account the social factors that may have contributed to the death and the familial circumstances that may now be presenting major obstacles to a successful grief resolution will result in inadequate support. Inadequate support may become a factor in the perpetuation of an attitude which questions and/or doubts the purpose of the offer of care and the design of the structure of the care offered. Systems of social support designed to facilitate recovery from bereavement should result in at least the enhancement of self-esteem and the provision of resources that will assist the person in grief with his/her coping tasks.

SUMMARY

In summary, three sources of black culture in American society that are significant in the value and meaning African-Americans give to death may be offered [18]. These sources are slavery, the sub-culture of the American south, and the Emancipation Proclamation with the promises and betrayals that followed upon release from slavery. Blacks could not assimilate like other ethnic groups because they exist in a racist society that strongly resisted assimilation [18]. Their historical roots in slavery and its policies brought about the disintegration of culture, family and possibly even a sense of self. This entire arrangement has been described as the most implacable example of race-consciousness, observed in any society [6]. This reality raises a series of questions that come through the statistical data presented in this chapter. How is this secular, medical disenfranchisement of blacks manifested in the system of death beliefs? How is the spirituality of the person affected by the realization that what others describe as unexpected deaths are the expected ways I and my loved ones will probably die? These questions are difficult, at best, to answer. The difficulty is rooted, in part, in the absence of good research examining these issues.

REFERENCES

1. W. E. B. Dubois, *Dusk of Dawn*, Schocken Books, New York, 1969.
2. R. Kalish and D. Reynolds, *Death and Ethnicity*, Baywood Publishing, Amityville, New York, 1981.
3. C. West, *Prophesy Deliverance! An Afro-American Revolutionary*, Christianity, The Westminster Press, Philadelphia, 1982.
4. J. B. Kamerman, *Death in the Midst of Life*, Prentice Hall, Englewood Cliffs, New Jersey, 1988.
5. W. May, The Sacral Power of Death in Contemporary Experience, in *Death in American Experience*, A. Mack (ed.), Schocken Books, New York, pp. 97-122, 1973.
6. R. J. Lifton, *The Broken Connection*, Simon and Schuster, New York, 1979.
7. H. A. Baer, *The Black Spiritual Movement*, University of Tennessee Press, Knoxville, 1984.
8. S. D. Plumpp, *Black Rituals*, Third World Press, Chicago, 1972.
9. W. A. Smith, *The Church in the Life of the Black Family*, Judson Smith, Valley Forge, 1985.
10. T. A. Rando, *Parental Loss of a Child*, Research Press, Champaign, Illinois, 1986.
11. R. C. Fox, The Medicalization and Demedicalization of American Society, in *Doing Better and Feeling Worse: Health in the United States*, J. H. Knowles (ed.), W. W. Norton Publishing, New York, pp. 9-22, 1977.
12. A. Silverstein, *Conquest of Death*, Macmillan Publishing, New York, 1979.
13. T. A. Rando, *Grief, Dying and Death*, Research Press, Champaign, Illinois, 1984.
14. C. M. Sanders, *Grief: The Mourning After*, John Wiley and Sons, New York, 1989.
15. W. Stroebe and M. S. Stroebe, *Bereavement and Health*, Cambridge University Press, New York, 1978.
16. S. M. Miller, Race in the Health of America, in *The Nation's Health*, P. R. Lee and C. L. Estes (eds.), Jones and Bartlett, Boston, pp. 54-71, 1990.
17. B. Neubauer and C. Hamilton, Racial Differences in Attitudes Toward Hospice, Hospice Journal, 6:1, pp. 37-38, 1990.
18. R. Blauner, Black Culture: Myth or Reality, in *Afro-American Anthropology*, N. Whitten and J. Szwed (eds.), The Free Press, New York, 1970.

PART III

Spiritual Concerns in Counseling the Dying

However one defines faith, whatever one's beliefs, that faith may be called into question as one faces life-threatening illness. Life-threatening illness is a crisis on many levels—medical, physical, logical, familial, and social. It is also a spiritual crisis. As such, it may raise significant spiritual issues.

In addressing these spiritual issues and concerns, it is critical to emphasize one point—the individuality of each person. People vary psychologically, socially, culturally. Because of the different backgrounds, experiences, spiritual needs and concerns of persons with life-threatening illness, one cannot assume common language, definitions beliefs, experiences, or needs. Caregivers then should explore each individual's spiritual perspective separately.

O'Connor's contribution to this work may provide a valued guide for that exploration. Ever sensitive to the individual spiritual journeys of different persons, she offers clinicians a paradigm for exploring spiritual concerns. To O'Connor, effective and caring spiritual care is an integral part of holistic care and involves understanding spiritual orientations and assisting individuals in exploring spiritual issues, spiritual needs and spiritual pain.

Not only should the individuality of each person be emphasized, the nature of life-threatening illness needs to be understood. Generally there is a considerable period of time between the diagnosis and subsequent death. Thus, it may be helpful to recognize varied phases of life-threatening illness. The acute phase is that period where the individual confronts the crisis of diagnosis. The chronic phase is often a long transitional one. People begin in attempting to accommodate their life to the new reality of life-threatening illness. But as that phase goes on they may face continued deterioration and decline. In short then, in

131

this phase, individuals begin by attempting to live with disease. They may end it recognizing that they will die from the disease. In the terminal phase, one must deal with the inescapable reality of death.

Doka's chapter recognizes that spiritual issues and concerns may develop at any point in life-threatening illness. His emphasis, however is on the terminal phase. Here, as individuals experience the nearness of death they are likely to struggle with three inherently spiritual issues: to find meaning in life, to die appropriately, and to find hope that extends beyond the grave.

Both O'Connor and Doka emphasize that one significant issue that is likely to be faced in life-threatening illness is the issue of suffering. In many ways, this is largely an issue of a secular age. Ariés points out that in the Middle Ages, suffering was often welcomed [1]. It was the quick death that was feared. Suffering provided opportunity for preparation and repentance. And suffering was, in itself, cleansing, for it allowed for the atonement or payment of sins. Ariés' analysis may perhaps be too glib. Thousands of years ago, the Old Testament book of Job portrayed the same concerns and issues, the "why me's?" that are still echoed today. But Ariés does make a valued point: there is little role or point in suffering in secular, scientific thought. We lack, as Pope John Paul once said, a theology of philosophical framework for interpreting suffering.

Since suffering is such a central issue in spiritual care of the dying patient, both Kollar and Kauffman consider it. Kollar provides both an overview of the ways that suffering may be interpreted as well as a valued series of guidelines for caregivers interested in assisting clients, both dying persons and bereaved, in exploring the issue of suffering. Kauffman's chapter complements Kollar. To Kauffman the essence of caregiving to those who are experiencing suffering is to provide a safe opportunity to suffer, to provide a "context" where clients can fully explore rather than deny that part of life. Finally, Ley's chapter on "Spiritual Care in Hospice" indicates how hospice, at least partially, seeks to provide a context for all these spiritual concerns to be addressed.

REFERENCE

1. P. Ariés, *The Hour of Our Death*, Alfred Knopf, New York, 1981.

CHAPTER 9

A Clinical Paradigm for Exploring Spiritual Concerns

Patrice O'Connor

INTRODUCTION

Although it is a fact that we are each dying daily, the idea of interacting with dying persons and their families may be very terrifying for some caregivers. This fear may inhibit the caregiver in his or her role thus it needs to be explored. One of the areas that need to be addressed in this process is the spirituality of the person which also reflects or mirrors the spirituality of the family, friends and caregivers.

There is a wide agreement that holistic care of persons nearing the end of their life span should include a dimension of spiritual care. Unfortunately, viewpoints differ on the commonalities of spiritual care in spite of the contribution of Dame Cicily Saunders, founder of the modern hospice movement, that spiritual care is not an "optional extra" [1].

An effort to resolve some of these issues began with the Conferences on Secular and Non-secular Issues on Death and Dying at Yale University in 1985 and 1986. Proceedings from these colloquia contributed to the agenda of both the International Work Group on Death, Dying, and Bereavement, and the Sixth World Congress on the Care of the Terminally Ill. In accordance with this concept the International Work Group on Death, Dying, and Bereavement has produced a statement of the Assumptions and Principles of Spiritual Care (see Chapter 2). These 31 Assumptions and Principles cover a wide range of issues from a) general principles, b) individuals and families, c) patients and families, d) caregivers, e) community coordination, and f) education and research [2]. The hope is that by putting emphasis on spiritual care in such broad terms, it will be addressed on an international level and seen as an essential element of care. This will not be a simple task, as each person, team, program and then health care system, in general, struggles to define and implement its understanding of the concept. This was forcefully manifested during the committee process of developing these assumptions and principles within the international group, when the problem of linguistics occurred after a Japanese minister remarked that "each person should be in control of his own destiny." A Norwegian minister replied that this idea would be interpreted in his country as an approval of euthanasia and/or suicide.

Any interpretation of the work "spiritual" presents confusion when discussed outside of the framework of religion or beyond one's personal beliefs. Likewise, the concepts of spiritual care becomes even more elusive when a non-dogmatic approach to spirituality attempts to explain a dimension of health care that is provided by a variety of professional disciplines. Does spiritual care refer to religious endeavors that have been stripped of doctrine? Or is spiritual care an element of secular that is clothed in religious undertones? The terms "religious care" and "spiritual care" are frequently used synonymously. Perhaps religious care is spiritual care, but I submit that spiritual is not necessarily religious care.

How does this spiritual care translate to daily practice for caregivers (the term caregiver will be used in this chapter in order to emphasize a nurturing relationship)? Using a conceptual framework for spiritual care, some aspects of this care will be discussed in the areas of patient's spiritual orientation, spiritual issues, spiritual needs, spiritual pain, spiritual care yielding to homeostasis (Figure 1) [3].

SPIRITUAL ORIENTATION

Patients and families do not come to a situation having had a spiritual vacuum in their own lives. An awareness and appreciation of a patient's spiritual orientation is essential to holistic care. Therefore, the role and function of the caregiver is to create an environment where the patient's spiritual orientation can flourish.

When, for example, one considers Saunders' five types of pain—physical, psychological, social, emotional, and spiritual—it is obvious that religious suffering comes under the last category. Yet in selecting the word "spiritual," she was able to encompass all pain that was not physical, psychological, etc. [1].

Just as in physical pain, spiritual pain requires assessment on a continuous basis, not just checking the box on the form as to patient's religious affiliation. As a lack of homeostasis may manifest itself as

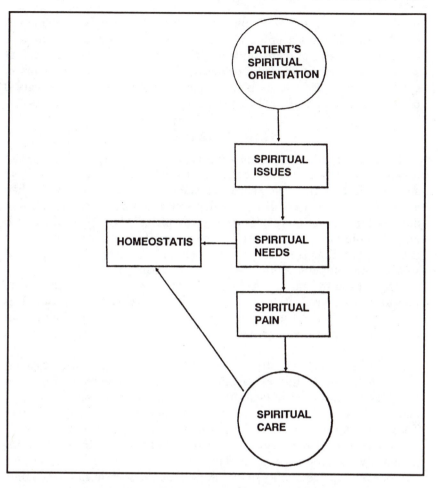

Figure 1. Conceptual framework for spiritual care.
Courtesy of Marjorie Pawling Kaplan, MPH, St. Luke's/Roosevelt
Hospital Center, New York City.

physical pain, spiritual pain also represents a lack of balance or adjustment to one's immediate self. Consequently, an evaluation of a patient's spiritual orientation seems appropriate in order to diagnose spiritual pain. With spiritual pain, one cannot simply point a finger to exactly where it hurts. Cassell has written that transcendence is probably the most powerful way that one is restored to wholeness after an injury to personhood. The sufferer is not isolated by pain, but is brought closer to the transpersonal source of meaning and to the human community that share these meanings. Such an experience need not involve religion in any formal sense, however, in its transpersonal dimension it is deeply spiritual. For example, patriotism can be a secular expression of transcendence [4]. Therefore, one needs to look at some dimensions of spiritual orientation. Some of the components of spiritual orientation are: spiritual issues, spiritual needs, spiritual pain—which are nurtured by spiritual care.

SPIRITUAL ISSUES

Perhaps, in the area of spiritual issues, caregivers are hesitant to invade privacy or feel this area should be left to clergy. However, if we are to give holistic care, there are times we need to be bold when assessing the spiritual. It can be done in a non-threatening manner. Some sample questions of "How are your spirits?," "Can you share with me your spiritual journey?," "How do you define your spirit?" may open the dialogue. Spiritual issues may include nurturing of the soul, the solace from religious traditions, or external stimuli.

These need to be addressed when reviewing a patient's total plan of care and always reflective of the individual's spiritual orientation. It is not the caregiver's responsibility to solve all spiritual problems, but rather to create an environment to nurture the patient's exploration whenever possible.

Patients may have strong affiliation with religious institutions. Effort to continue and bridge this connection is important. However, religious affiliation may facilitate or hinder spiritual issues. Patients and families are in a vulnerable state at the time of a terminal illness. They may be reluctant to reject the role of a clergyperson perceiving it as a rejection of God. Clergy need to remember that it is the needs of the patient that dictate their role and not the other way around. In addition, in order to enhance quality of life for patients, it is essential to evaluate the strengths and the resources of the patient to enable him to participate in meeting his own issues based on his life patterns of behavior.

Dealing with dying patients frequently raises spiritual issues for caregivers, such as coping under stress or watching suffering, which raise theological and philosophical questions that challenge basic beliefs of concepts. Caregivers should be aware that this can happen and address their own issues in order to assist patients and families. This can be a very enriching opportunity for growth for the caregiver.

SPIRITUAL NEEDS

One does not change a lifetime of examining spiritual needs just because one is dying. It is important when assessing these needs to be able to recognize the resources that patient has identified as having helped to meet these needs in the past. We may learn more about the patient by asking "What nourishes your spirit?" instead of the usual "What church do you belong to?" Patient needs may range from religious ritual (such as prayers, holy communion, blessing of the sick) to secular observances (sunsets, music, poetry, etc.). The process continually needs to be assessed frequently in order to identify spiritual needs. Even the most sensitive staff members can be frustrated by miscommunication.

Separating our needs from the needs of the patient, how do we react to the spiritual needs of the atheist or the metaphysician? First, we listen carefully for verbal and non-verbal messages that may indicate the patient's feeling. A statement such as "I do not believe in God" may reveal a strong sense of belief in a Universal Source, while for another patient it may convey a special plea for help in facing adversity. "We do not want patients to think the way we are thinking, we want them to think more deeply in their own way" [5].

Likewise, one does not change a lifetime of examining spiritual needs just because one is caring for the dying. This need intensifies spiritual awareness since caregivers need to give of their extra and replenish the essence of their own spirit.

SPIRITUAL PAIN

When comparing the assessment of spiritual pain to physical pain, there are a few guidelines that can be utilized. It is mainly the lack of objective symptoms of spiritual pain that hinders the diagnostic process. Friends and families may be a resource for eliciting information about the suffering of a patient. Caregivers must be realistic in their expectations—there is just so much we can do—and not always assume that care will produce a positive effect. As with physical pain, there are some patients who feel the need to suffer from spiritual pain for important specific reasons. We must appreciate that for them pain is not a "problem" in our sense of the word. When assessing a patient's spiritual pain the questions, "How have you addressed your spiritual pain before?" and "What helped to relieve this pain?," can be addressed to the patient, family, and friends. Some responses to this question have been, "If only I could smell true fresh air again," or "When I was truly low, listening to the Mormon Tabernacle Choir relieved my suffering," or "Sometimes just sitting in a quiet church raised my spirits." The responses are often simple, but full of meaning. And, as with physical pain that changes over the course of time, so spiritual pain may change and the need to be assessed continuously, e.g., "How are your spirits today?" Spiritual pain represents the agony of unmet need.

Still, it is crucial to realize that the time of dying may raise spiritual issues, but not necessarily spiritual pain.

SPIRITUAL CARE

Feifel stresses that it is not necessary to understand fully a patient's spiritual orientation when creating an environment to offer nurturing [6]. We may be holding back this nurturing ability in order to be perceived as credible caregivers. Yet, spiritual care need not trigger inferences of faith healing or hocus pocus. An understanding of clergy within a person's cultural background can influence spiritual care. Perhaps in leaving the function of spiritual care to the clergy, caregivers have not addressed the patient's total needs for spiritual care, since clergy represent institutional religion or religious affiliation.

The caregiver must not assume that since a patient expresses religious affiliation that spiritual care is being given. In a survey of several interdisciplinary teams from one program with a twelve-year history of delivery of hospice care, the respondents reported a relatively low rating on the importance of religion to an individual patient's coping ability during the dying process [7].

Healing is a daily process that can change from moment to moment, especially as a terminal patient perceives time. Healing, inner healing, is more sensed than seen. For some patients it is a continuing of a life pattern with religious beliefs and practices. For others, it is a total "renewal-rebirth" of a relationship to a "Higher Being" and for some, a deep awareness of self.

Reed has commented that he believes that any human being can minister in a situation where the ultimate meaning must be pursued [8]. Munley further states that the essence of spiritual caregiving is not doctrine or dogma, but the capacity to enter into the world of others and respond with feeling. This fundamental human capacity involves touching another at a level that is deeper than ideological or doctrinal differences [9].

Spiritual care is promoted though presence, compassion, hopefulness and the recognition that, although life may no longer be productive, it remains nonetheless fruitful [3]. These elements of spiritual care form the understanding partnership that helps to protect the patient from dying alone and the family from feeling alone [10]. The willingness to allow a patient or family to be themselves by supporting them with our presence is essential. In the spiritual realm, presence implies an "unconditional acceptance" of people. To be present with the terminally ill and their families is to listen in the broadest sense of the word in order to hear clearly what is being communicated. Presence does not require many words. Sometimes it requires none. The French philosopher, Gabriel Marcel, describes the journey: Every human is to wrestle his being and owning up to responsibilities. Presence is such a situation: always risky, potentially painful, but allowing those who enter is to be more richly human [11]. The spiritual aspects of presence imply the reciprocation of giving and receiving: a process of nourishment. To extend presence to patient and family requires us to examine the manner in which this presence is reflected. For presence to be of benefit, its intervention must be done with compassion. Nouwen defines compassion as "entering into solidarity with our suffering fellow human beings. Compassion broadens your view, compassion makes you see and feel around you, compassion makes you aware of all possibilities" [12].

Caregivers do not aim to restore the patient's biological integrity, but to assist the patient and family to live as fully as possible. Both patient and caregiver reach out beyond themselves. Caregivers try to generate hope in what appears to be a hopeless situation. Hope becomes an essential ingredient in the religious and spiritual aspects of care; a major component of our contribution to the healing process; and for some patients, a major determinant between life and death [13]. Vaillot comments that it is the relationship between the caregiver and the patient which sustains the presence of hope [14]. A spiritual person inspires hope more by who he or she is, than by what he or she does. To be effective, hope—no matter now transient—must be realistic.

In the Denial of Death, Becker comments that "Man must reach out for support to a dream, a metaphysic hope that sustains him and makes his life worthwhile. To talk about hope is to give fruitful focus to the problems at hand [15]. The spiritual aspects of hope for a terminally ill patient afford him or her the continued experience of being fruitful. It is not unusual to observe patients who have been alienated from friends and family return to their loved ones and share a fruitful existence, no matter how brief. Caregivers will often say they receive more than they give. Patients enrich our lives with their fruitfulness by exhibiting courage, peace, and joy. How gracious our patients and families are to allow us to walk with them during this stressful, most intimate time of their lives. Frequently caregivers need to understand that they can have a gently acceptance of the incongruities of life and the ability not to take themselves too seriously through humor. We cannot change the course of the dying, but we can help ourselves and others humanize the situation and this can be done with humor. Humor, incidentally, is not the same as laughter or telling jokes. Humor doesn't deny the hurt, it is vehicle through which anger and defiance and pain be handled [16].

CONCLUSION

While biomedical technology in American health care is rapidly changing, psychosocial aspects—although not as rapidly—are similarly changing. A more humanistic approach is apparent at the beginning of life, evidenced in the increased numbers of birthing rooms around the nation, and at the end of life, with the continued development of new hospice programs. It is becoming clear that individuals are gradually seeking control over more of the processes of their own health care. Perhaps the desire for more control over our own lives is in response to a universal threat of death.

Norman Cousins restates a common theme, "Death is not the ultimate tragedy of life. The ultimate tragedy is depersonalization—dying in an alien and sterile area, separated from the spiritual nourishment that comes from being able to reach out to a loving hand, separated from a desire to experience the things that make life worth living, separated from hope" [17]. Perhaps our greatest task as caregivers is to protect our patients from this ultimate tragedy of depersonalization and to sustain them in a "personalized" environment that recognizes individual needs and attempts to reduce individual fears. Without denying death, the caregiver accepts the limitation of a brief prognosis to promote maximum physical and psychological comfort. Patients come with no hope of recovery from physical disease, yet full of hope for relief from suffering. The caregiver can generate hope in what often appears to be a hopeless situation; and the caring for these patients, in turn, will make us aware of our own mortality.

Fortunately, caregivers are becoming increasingly aware of the fact that spiritual care is not a pro rae nata intervention. Therefore, the ability to address spiritual issues is no longer a matter of choice, but rather a fundamental principle of total patient care.

REFERENCES

1. C. Saunders, *The Management of Terminal Malignant Disease,* Edward Arnold, London, 1984.
2. I. Corless, Assumptions and Principles of Spiritual Care, *Death Studies, 14,* pp. 75-81d, 1990.
3. P. O'Connor, The Role of Spiritual Care in Hospice, *The American Journal of Hospice Care, 5,* pp. 31-37, 1988.
4. E. Cassell, Nature of Suffering and the Goals of Medicine, *New England Journal of Medicine,* pp. 639-645, 1982.
5. C. Saunders, Living with the Dying, *Radiography, 49,* pp. 79-83, 1983.

6. H. Feifel, The Overlap Between Humanism, Spirituality, Religion and Philosophy, Sixth World Congress on the Care of the Terminally Ill, Montreal, 1986.
7. F. Wald, *In Quest of the Spiritual Component of Care for the Terminally Ill,* Yale University Press, New Haven, 1986.
8. A. Reed, Image of the Hospice Chaplain, *The Hospice Journal,* pp. 111-117, 1985.
9. A. Munley, *The Hospice Alternative,* Basic Books, New York, 1983.
10. P. O'Connor, Spiritual Element of Hospice Care, *The Hospice Journal,* 2:2, pp. 99-108, 1986.
11. G. Marcel, *Presence and Immortality,* University Press, Pittsburgh, 1967.
12. H. Nouwen, Reflection on Compassion, Address presented at the Annual Convention of the Catholic Health Association of Canada, Ottawa, 1978.
13. J. Bruhn, Therapeutic Value of Hope, *Southern Medical Journal,* 77, pp. 215-219, 1984.
14. M. Vaillot, Hope: An Invitation to Live, *American Journal of Nursing,* 7, pp. 268-275, 1970.
15. E. Becker, *The Denial of Death,* Macmillan, New York, 1974.
16. D. Donnelly, The Blessing Called Humor, *Origins,* 17:4, pp. 806-812, 1988.
17. N. Cousins, *Anatomy of an Illness,* Norton, New York, 1979.

CHAPTER 10

The Spiritual Needs of the Dying*

Kenneth J. Doka

It has become a truism to describe contemporary American culture as secular. To Becker it is that very secularization that has led to the denial of death [1]. Yet the term "secularization" often has very ambiguous, different, and even conflicting meanings [2]. To many, secularization is essentially a social process whereby religious symbols and doctrines lack social significance and societal decisions are made on a rational and pragmatic rather than on a theological or spiritual basis. Such definition does not deny the potency of both religion and spirituality on an individual level. Gallop polls affirm that vast majorities of Americans both believe in God and consider religion and spirituality important in their lives. This is clearly evident when one faces the crisis of dying, a crisis when scientific explanations are largely silent.

Individuals, of course, differ in the extent that religion plays a part in their lives. These differences continue even throughout the dying process. As Pattison noted, dying persons will use belief systems as they have used throughout life—constructively, destructively, or not at all [3]. To some individuals, belief systems can be a source of comfort and support; to others, it will be a cause for anxiety. Pattison even notes that individuals who seem to find religion in terminal illness often show a basic continuity, for these "foxhole" religionists are likely to be individuals who seek out and grasp each new treatment, diet, or drug.

*A section of this chapter has been previously published by the author in the *Newsletter of the Forum for Death Education and Counseling, 6,* pp. 2-3.

Counselors are increasingly recognizing the value in exploring religious and spiritual themes with the dying; for dying is not only a medical and personal crisis, it is a spiritual one as well. Though individuals may adhere to different religious beliefs and explanations, or even then lack them, dying focuses one on questions such as the meaning of life, the purpose of one's own existence, and the reason for death, that have an inherently spiritual quality. Thus as individuals struggle with dying, spiritual and religious themes are likely to emerge. In fact, often these spiritual interpretations are, to paraphrase Freud "a royal road into the unconscious."

While this chapter will emphasize religious and spiritual themes in the terminal phase of disease, it is important to recognize the presence of these themes throughout the illness. Even at the point of diagnosis, persons may interpret the disease in a spiritual or religious sense. For example, one person may define AIDS as a punishment from God. That interpretation is likely to have very different reverberations throughout the illness than those from someone who sees the disease as a result from an unfortunate exposure to a virus.

It is not unusual for a person's interpretation of the disease to have religious and spiritual dimensions. Every disease has a component of mystery. Why does one smoker get lung cancer and another not? Why does a disease manifest itself at any given time? Why, in fact, do we die? None of these questions yield to totally satisfactory scientific and rational explanations.

Hence in exploring someone's interpretation of disease, it is essential to be sensitive to these religious or spiritual dimensions. Often because religious or spiritual explanations are not socially validated, individuals may be reluctant to share them or even be fully aware of them. There is a need then for counselors to probe for such issues in a permissive and nonjudgmental atmosphere.

Religions of spiritual themes may also be intertwined with affective responses evident in the living-dying interval. Numerous observers have noted that persons with a life-threatening or terminal disease often exhibit emotions such as anger, guilt, bargaining, resignation, hope and anxiety [4, 5]. All of these responses may be tied to spiritual concerns. Anger may not only be directed against significant others but also cosmically—against nature, the universe, fate, or God. And such anger can be combined with both guilt and fear that anger toward the deity or other transcendental power is both wrong and dangerous. One person, for example, as both angry at God for her disease, but also was fearful that God would continue to punish her for that anger. In counseling, the woman has been able to reinterpret her anger as a form of prayer, and with that a reaffirmation of both her relationship to God (e.g., she had the freedom to communicate such anger) and his power. A comment by Easson helped [6]. In describing the anger of a thirteen-year-old boy with leukemia, he noted the child's comment that "if God is God, He will understand my anger, if He does not understand my anger, He is not God" [6, p. 91]. This allowed the woman to see her anger as an aspect of faith.

Similarly bargaining may be directed toward God leading to a sense of hope or resignation if the bargain is perceived as accepted and a sense of anger, guilt and fear is perceived as denied. One man with leukemia gave up hope at the time of his first relapse. In his mind he had made a "bargain" with God at the time of his first hospitalization. At that time he had hoped for the health to participate in a family event. When a relapse soon followed, he now believed that God had fulfilled his part of the deal—the man was now resigned to dying. Such bargains do not have to be theistic in nature. One woman once had made a deal with "the universe" to give something back if she achieved a desired success. In her own intensely spiritual frame of reference, her illness was a manifestation of her selfishness and unwillingness to part with her time or possessions. She had not fulfilled her promise, her illness was the result.

It is important then for counselors to recognize that *any* response to life-threatening illness can be intertwined with religious themes. Throughout the illness, these religious or spiritual interpretations should be explored as they can facilitate or complicate a person's response to illness.

Religious and spiritual values may also influence treatment decisions. Extreme examples of this may be found when adherence to particular beliefs precludes certain medical procedures such as blood transfusions or even causes patients to reject any conventional medical therapies. But even in other cases, religious and philosophical perspectives may certainly be part of treatment decisions. For example, persons may decline treatments because of personal perspectives on quality of life or because they perceive a value to life or an obligation to God or fellow humans. Perspectives in euthanasia may be profoundly influenced by religious and spiritual values.

While religious and spiritual themes are often found throughout the struggle with life-threatening illness, they are often especially critical in the terminal phase. For beyond the medical, social, and psychological needs of dying individuals, there are spiritual needs as well. The terminally ill patient recognizes Becker's paradox that humans are aware of finitude yet have a sense of transcendence [1]. It is this paradox that underlies the three spiritual needs of dying persons:

1) the search for meaning of life, 2) to die appropriately, and 3) to find hope that extends beyond the grave.

1. THE SEARCH FOR MEANING OF LIFE

One major crisis precipitated by dying is a search for the meaning of one's life. Theoreticians of various disciplines have long recognized that we are creatures who create and share meaning. This purposiveness extends to self as well. In the prologue of the play *Ross,* a biography of Lawrence of Arabia, various characters posthumously assess Lawrence's life. As the spotlight descends on one Arab chieftain, he defiantly exclaims "that history will sigh and say 'this was a man!' " It is a statement that in one way or another we wish to make that our life had purpose, significance, and meaning. Developmental psychologists and sociologists, such as Erickson, Butler, and Marshall, assert that the knowledge of impending death creates a crisis in which one reviews life in order to integrate one's goals, values and experience [7-9]. This awareness of finitude can be a consequence of either old age or serious illness. Even very young children, and their families, will review the child's life to find that sense of purpose.

The failure to find meaning can create a deep sense of spiritual pain. Individuals may feel that their lives changed or meant nothing. This has implications for caregivers. One of the most important things that caregivers can do for dying persons is to provide time for that personal reflection. While the caregiver can help dying persons find significance in their lives, things they have done, events they have witnessed, history that they have experienced all provide fruitful areas for exploration. Counselors may use varied techniques to facilitate this process. Reviewing life and family histories, viewing family or period photographs and mementos or sharing family humor and stories can facilitate this process. Films, music, books, or art that evoke earlier periods or phases of life can encourage reminiscence and life review.

Religious beliefs or philosophical and spiritual systems can be very important here. They can give one's life a sense of cosmic significance. And, they can provide a sense of forgiveness—to oneself and to others— for acts of commission and omission and for dreams not accomplished.

2. TO DIE APPROPRIATELY

People not only need assurance that they have lived meaningfully, they must die meaningfully as well. First, people want to die in ways consistent with their own self-identity. For example, a group of elderly women have established a call system to each other. Each woman has a set of multiple keys to each other's apartment. "This," one woman assured, "was so we don't die stinking up the apartment and nobody has to break down any doors." To these old-world women, cleanliness and orderliness are key virtues. The thought of leaving dirt and disorder even at the moment of demise is painful. They wish to die congruent with the ways in which they lived.

Dying appropriately also means dying comprehendingly. It means being able to understand and interpret one's death. If one suffers, it means having a framework to explain suffering. Pope John Paul noted that our secular and comfort-oriented society lacks a theology of pain. This suggests that caregivers need to explore with patients their beliefs about pain and death.

To die appropriately is difficult in a technological world. The fantasy of a quick death surrounded by loving relatives contrasts starkly with the reality of dying by chronic disease, alone, and institutionalized. It is little wonder that people fear not so much the fact of death as the process of dying. Caregivers can be helpful here in a number of ways. First, by empathetic listening, they allow the dying space to interpret their deaths. Second, whatever control can be left to the dying aids in their construction of their deaths. The opportunity to discuss one's death with relatives, either near the time of death or earlier, permits occasion to prepare to die as one lived. This allows specifying modes of treatment, ritual requests, special bequests, or simply educating families in the details that accompany death.

3. TO FIND HOPE THAT EXTENDS BEYOND THE GRAVE

Another spiritual need is transcendental. We seek assurance in some way that our life, or what we left, will continue. Perhaps the popularity of Moody's *Life After Life* [10] is that it recasts traditional images of the afterlife in a quasiscientific framework.

But there are many ways that we can look toward continued existence. Lifton and Olson spoke of five modes of symbolic immortality in our progeny [11]. A second mode is the creative mode in which we see continuance in our creations. This can include the singular accomplishments of the great or the more mundane contributions of the average. The last three modes, theological, eternal nature, and transcendental, relate to conceptualizations of immortality proferred in various belief systems. We might add a sixth—a communal mode where we see our life as part of a larger group. The continued survival of the group gives each life significance and each person lives in the community's memory. Such a theme is often evidence in Jewish thought.

Religion and other belief systems are one way to provide critical reassurance of immortality. Religious rituals may affirm a sense of continuity even beyond death. Yet Lifton and Olson's typology remind that there are other things that help as well. Actions of caregivers are important too. The presence of personal artifacts and dignified treatment of the terminally ill reaffirm personhood and suggest significance. Institutional policies that encourage intergenerational visiting provide subtle reminders of one's biological legacy.

SUMMARY

Yet while there seems some recognition of these spiritual needs, it remains unclear as to how well these needs are being met. Observers have recognized a variety of obstacles to religious or spiritual wholeness [12]. Some of these obstacles may be structural. Lack of access to clergy, a lack of privacy, or a reluctance of caregivers to explore religious and spiritual issues can inhibit any attempt to address there spiritual concerns.

The lack of structure may also be an inhibitor. Within the Christian tradition, there is an absence of recognized ritual that mandates the presence of clergy and focuses on spiritual issues such as reconciliation and closure. Such a ritual has never been particularly significant in Protestant liturgy or theology. In the Roman Catholic tradition, the sacrament of extreme unction, or popularly "last rites," has changed its meaning significantly since 1974. Retitled (or restored to the title of) "anointing of the sick," it now emphasizes a holistic notion of healing that is rooted in a context of prayer and counseling. While much is gained by this change, it ends the notion of a sacramental rite of passage into death. Death becomes simply a medical event where clergy have no defined role. There then is an absence of any structure of ritual that focuses on addressing these spiritual needs.

Other failures may be failures of personnel. Clergy or clinicians may be unable to facilitate this process. There may be a number of reasons for this. Clergy may be intolerant of other beliefs or seek to proselytize. They may fail to be understanding. They may hide behind prayer or ritual. Intellectually or emotionally they may have little to offer dying persons. Other caregivers ma not be religious, may not have explored their own spiritual beliefs, or are hesitant to explore beliefs of others.

Finally, dying persons may be unable to meet their own spiritual needs. They may lack conviction in their own beliefs, fail to appreciate or explore their own spiritual needs, or be consumed by dysfunctional elements of their own belief system [12].

Clergy and clinicians can facilitate spiritual wholeness in a number of ways. First, in their own conversations with dying persons, they can provide individuals with opportunities to explore these concerns in a nonthreatening and nonjudgmental atmosphere. These are times to listen and explore the individual's perspective. Should some of these beliefs have dysfunctional elements, counselors can explore the ways that these issues can be addressed within the belief structure. For example, in one case, a man was consumed with religious guilt. Exploration of his own beliefs allowed him to address how that guilt could be expiated.

Varied rituals may facilitate this process. Rituals such as confession or communion can provide a visible sign of forgiveness. As DeArment notes, prayer can be a powerful way to express emotion or approach intimate reflection without the patient feeling exposed or vulnerable [13]. It can also be useful to explore faith stories or "paricopes" with individuals. By asking persons to relate faith stories that they believe speak to their situations. One can assess significant issues and themes in their own spiritual journeys. Sometimes one can help individuals reframe these faith stories to derive additional support. For example, many individuals in the Judaic-Christian tradition interpret Job as fatalistically responding to loss. "The Lord givith and taketh." Another way to view that story, though, is as a long intense struggle of Job as he experiences loss. The latter is often more helpful to people in struggle and is quite faithful to text. In those cases in which the counselor cannot utilize such rituals or beliefs, they are still able to assist in locating empathic clergy or layperson of the person's own faith. This also reminds one that faith communities—the churches, congregations, and temples—that individuals may belong to can be helpful resources.

In recent years, there has been increasing recognition that dying persons not only have medical needs but psychological and social needs as well. Recognition of spiritual needs, too, will allow individuals to approach death as they have approached life—wholly.

REFERENCES

1. E. Becker, *The Denial of Death,* Free Press, New York, 1973.
2. J. A. Winter, *Continuities in the Sociology of Religion.* Harper and Row, New York, 1977.
3. G. M. Pattison, *Religion, Faith, and Healing, The Experience of Dying,* Prentice Hall, New Jersey, 1977.
4. E. Kubler-Ross, *On Death and Dying,* Macmillan, New York, 1969.
5. T. Rando, Grief, *Dying and Death: Clinical Interventions for Caregivers,* Research Press, Champaign, Illinois, 1984.

6. W. Easson, *The Dying Child: The Management of the Child or Adolescent Who is Dying,* Charles C. Thomas, Springfield, Illinois, 1970.
7. E. Erickson, *Childhood and Society,* Macmillan, New York, 1963.
8. R. Butler, The Life Review: An Interpretation of Reminiscence in the Aged, *Psychiatry, 26,* p. 1, 1963.
9. V. Marshall, *Last Chapters: A Sociology of Aging and Dying,* Brooks/Cole, Monteray, California, 1980.
10. R. Moody, *Life After Life,* Bantam Books, New York, 1975.
11. R. Lifton and E. Olson, *Living and Dying,* Bantam Books, New York, 1974.
12. T. Attig, Respecting the Dying and Bereaved as Believers, *Newsletter of the Forum for Death Education and Counseling, 6,* pp. 10-11, 1983.
13. D. DeArment, Prayer and the Dying Patient: Intimacy Without Exposure, in *Death and Ministry,* J. Bane, Kutcher, Neale and Reeves, Jr. (eds.), Seabury Press, New York, 1975.

CHAPTER 11

Spiritualities of
Suffering and Grief

Nathan R. Kollar

The death of another person is a painful reminder that we are interdependent. Grief many times brings back the joyful memories of interdependence: loving touches, harmonious laughter, quiet presence in shared danger or prideful success—the symbols of the person's presence surround us. In their grief-filled and haunting presence we remember that all we have are the symbols—he or she will never again freely touch, laugh, or spontaneously share our life. Our joys as well as our sorrows are multiplied by a number equal to those with whom we are interdependent.

Our interdependence, however, is not something which grew up serendipitously—without consciousness, without pain, without joy. There is a style of interdependence which characterizes the way those who share life deeply differ one group from the other—a style which gives *this* group of people a certain direction that is different from *that* group of people. In the context of this chapter, perhaps the word "spirit" is better than "style." One group of people is distinguished from another group of people by their spirit, their style. A "spirituality" is the conscious recognition and acceptance of a certain spirit or style of life as normative for present and future living. A religious spirituality is the conscious recognition and acceptance of a spirit of living that manifests and causes an ultimately, healthy, responsible, belonging, and meaningful life.

We have all witnessed these various group-spirits as well as shared them. Our team has a different spirit than your team. Our school has a different spirit than your school. Every group's spirit and spirituality is linked together by symbols of memory and a certain spirit that enlivens both these symbols and the memories associated with them.

Grief finds us remembering. Grief finds us at times dispirited. Grief finds us at times dispirited and alone in our memories of those who are important to us. The spirit, the memories, the symbols of interdependence pour forth when we are asked: "What happened?" The response to a simple question such as this begins the story of the death and the life of the person for whom we grieve. This story also reflects his or her spirituality and the spirituality of those who remember.

This chapter will review the spiritualities which enliven the answer to that question "What happened?" It will review the role of questions in the counseling process as well as some basic ways of responding to those questions which attempt to tell the suffering person's story from the perspective of our religious traditions. It will review, too, how the counselor must respect and enhance the stories of the individual and the individual's universe. At the same time we must look at those situations where one's story may be dysfunctional to his, her, or our life.

STORIES, PLOTS, AND VALUES

Every life's story has a plot. In the telling of our story, we tie our life together. As we apply for a job, make small talk, recall our early adventures to our children, we do so by tying our life together in some sort of plot and showing that our life does make sense. The way we tell our story speaks volumes about our style of life: why we do the things we do, what we think is important and unimportant, how we prioritize our values and valuables. But telling a story is more than an expression of what has happened, it is also an indicator of our future direction. To be able to enter into the story of the storyteller: to affirm by a nod of the head; to question by the raise of an eyebrow, to somehow enter into the story is important for the storyteller as well as the listener.

QUESTIONS IN LIFE AND ABOUT LIFE

Every life story has its exclamation points, periods, and question marks. Here we are interested in the question marks. We ask questions about life as it happens as well as when it is over. Noticing a cut on my daughter's arm I ask, "How did it happen?" Facing a dentist's drill I inquire, "Will it hurt?" and losing a position in a factory I demand, "Why me? What did I do?"

Questions have a way of probing the world around us. They stretch to the past and probe the present in order to allow us to live better in the future. To know that my daughter's cut was caused by a piece of metal on her bike, that the dentist will give me something for the pain, and that everyone fifty-nine and older was let go makes a difference for future living by allowing me to plan for that future.

Some questions and answers are larger than themselves. They point to larger questions and answers than are presently available. Why do we suffer? Why do we die? Do we have a future?—are types of questions which are never fully answered. Our attempts to answer them make a difference in the way we live our lives. These are what might be described as making-sense-questions. Questions which both when asked and when answered bring our story together differently than when they were not asked or answered. They express the plot of our life's story. To even ask these questions about suffering, death, and future is to proclaim that we know these experiences and to suggest that the world should have some purpose—otherwise why ask? To receive an answer to these questions, no matter how tentative, suggests a plot for our life's story and that of everyone we know. To live one's life with an awareness of that plot is to test both question and answer. It is not unusual that in living the answer, we discover a new question. Making-sense-questions are like that—once we think we know the "sense," we are anxious to know if they are really non-sense.

Questions and answers are never individual questions and answers. Because we are interdependent, because our stories are part of a mutual history, questions and answers are shared. Questions and answers about suffering, death, and future are also shared. The questions you have as a professional, the questions your clients have, are all part of larger communities of shared questions and answers. These may be national, religious, philosophical, or cultural groups which over time have developed ways of asking and answering these making-sense-questions.

When we suggest large categories of thought and action we always risk leaving someone out and/or not allowing room for mixtures of categories. Such are risks worthwhile, however, when we are able to present paradigms which are easily understandable and useful for dealing with those who grieve. There are four famous answers to our three questions: Why do we suffer? Why do we die? Do we have a future?

FOUR ANSWERS

It's Absurd

Life is absurd. Death is absurd. It's absurd to even ask the question about the future since all we know and experience is the here and now.

After all life is just one damn thing after another, so what is the use of even thinking about it?

It is no use thinking about it, but there is a benefit to doing something about it. You prove you can beat life's absurdity. Get up in the morning and face the boredom of life knowing that in facing it you prove you will not let its absurdity do you in. To be human and alive is to thumb your nose at the boredom, absurdity, and stupidity of life itself.

The ancient myth of Sisyphus is a good example of this response to our questions. The story is told that Sisyphus was condemned to push a huge boulder up an enormous mountain. Through rain, snow, sleet, cold and hot he strained to get the boulder to the top of the mountain. Day after day, night after night, his only goal was to push the boulder to the top. Strained muscles, scraped knees and arms, bruised shoulders and face did not stop him. Every day he pushed. Every day he inched his way to the top. Then one day he reached the top. In exultation he paused in triumph. While he paused the boulder rolled down the mountain. His eternity was to push the boulder to the top. His humanity was to look from the top of the mountain at the boulder below and with shoulders square, turn to begin again. Death? Suffering? Future? Absurd! But damn it, I'll keep pushing.

That's Life

"That's life," is another response. Some see life as a set of immutable laws, patterns, relationships, or recognized expectations which, if broken, result in suffering or death. The immutable laws may be titled natural, physical, social; they may be seen as the deep and expected relationships between all beings. Whereas the "it's absurd" perspective looks at life in a negative way, this present perspective may have a positive or negative outlook on life. But it is accepting of what causes the suffering or the death because it sees all of life in a give-and-take perspective where everything must be balanced. It is enough to say that the person died of cancer or that the war was caused by people's dislike of their dictator. The future, from this perspective, is determined by the present. There are no surprises. If one does everything that is proper physically, socially, and emotionally then one will live forever. Life is an interlocking network of relationships which, when broken, cause suffering and death.

Down Deep We Don't Suffer

"Down deep we don't suffer," is a third perspective. Some believe that all that is tangible and passing is not real. Suffering is derived from being too attached to what is passing. All that is real is what is permanent. This "permanent" reality may be called "soul" by some; self, by others; God, by still others.

There are many names used to describe this permanency but behind the names there is either a claim that there is some personal individuality which never changes or there is a common shared oneness that we all are. In either case when we get caught up in this changing world, suffering occurs. When we get caught up in our changing individual desires, suffering occurs. Death is the deliverance from this suffering. But an awareness that all of this is not real is also a way to move beyond the suffering. To realize that down deep, where the real me is, there is no suffering, is to go beyond death to be a reality which stands still and there is no difference between past, present, and future.

It All Fits In Somehow

"It all fits in somehow," is a perspective many of us have since it is dependent upon our western culture. It sees time and reality not as some permanent circle, as "down deep we don't suffer," but as a vector, a line going somewhere because it has reasons to go somewhere. Our personal history takes a personal direction which results from the interplay of our freedom, loving, and working with the world we are part of. We are very much our body, our changing emotions, and our relationships. We would be nothing without these dynamic and enfleshed realities. The "why" question is very important to those who approach life from this perspective because its answer indicates to them the direction of their future and the reasonableness of their death. Suffering and death must fit into something more than one's self. This something may be titled history, God, God's will, the Kingdom of God. Again there are many images for the plan but behind the plan is always a suggestion that it is a personal plan. The universe and all of life is the consequence of a relationship between the individual, all living and non-living beings, and that which supports the life and direction of this universe and life. When one asks, "Why do we suffer?" from this perspective, an expected answer is along the lines of the answer to the question "why did your parent or friend hang up the phone?" The expected answer is a personal answer involving love, responsibility, value or something similar.

The "why" question in the other three perspectives is an impersonal question and looks for an impersonal answer. "Why did he die?" in "it's absurd" expects a response of "There is no reason; it doesn't make sense." Why did he die?" in "that's life" will understand an answer framed in impersonal logic such as, "It's a terrible disease. Almost everyone dies because of it." "Why did he die?" in "down deep we don't suffer," is a question seldom asked. If asked, the expected reply would indicate that the person has not changed by death, that we really never knew him, that suffering is part of the life we live until we dig deeper into life and get to where it is really lived. The "why?" question may be asked in the "it all fits in somehow" not expecting an answer.

The way one phrases the unknowns of the cause is significant. We just don't know what it is all about. We think that what happened is bad, but we know that even from bad good may come. Or, in a sort of ultimate personal relationship, we describe how God suffered and died and that this seems stupid yet it is believed. Notice that the general, "it all fits in somehow," is accepted but how it fits becomes lost in the mystery of the stories that are part of this approach.

QUESTIONS AND ANSWERS WITHIN TRADITIONAL SPIRITUALITIES

These four answers are really spiritualities: a spirituality of the absurd, a spirituality of consequence, of illusion, and of providence. We live as well as speak questions and answers. When recognized and affirmed as the plot of life, each is spirituality which directs our life. These four answers are also institutionalized in specific historical religious tradition.

Humans have faced suffering and death since the beginning of time. The manner in which they have responded to these two basic realities has become enfleshed in a number of traditions. Traditions, after all, are our patterned response to the foundational realities of life. We have traditions of eating, of sleeping, of speaking, and suffering. This patterned response to suffering and death may be found expressed in each of the foundational human realities. Thus, we have traditions of bodily care, social ritual, emotional linking, and seeking for meaning associated with death and suffering. Because suffering and death are so all encompassing, so involved with the foundational realities of life, those traditions which are deeply involved with these questions are those we generally describe as religions. Religious communities have always responded to the whole person in their dealing with death and suffering. Some commentators in the last century, because of their philosophical orientation, suggested that religions always were concerned with the future, especially the future after this life. But if one looks at the major world religions, one sees a wholistic commitment to the alleviation of suffering and care for the dead.

There is care from the perspective of physical well-being. Care and concern for the sick and infirm have been so much a part of religion, especially in the West, that we have the tradition of hospitals and the vocation of doctor as evidence of a long tradition of care for one's physical well-being. Every religion will have a way of dealing with those who suffer. The one suffering should be aware of this; those who aid the sufferer should be aware of where religious help may be obtained. The yellow pages will direct one to the proper religious agency for housing, food, grief, and/or other physical needs.

Every religion demands right living from its members. Right living looks toward the diminution of suffering by erasing its immediate cause. It sets the stage for a world free of the suffering caused by humans. Judaism, for instance, has given us many principles of justice and concern. The statement of God in Hosea 6:6 ". . . what I want is love, not sacrifice," sets the prophetic theme of justice and love for all. And Nathan's statement to David, "You are the man" (2 Samuel 12:7), i.e., you are responsible and accountable to God for the suffering you cause—places the burden upon the individual to relieve suffering. The Christian's obligation vis-à-vis suffering is found both in Jesus' words on the Sermon on the Mount (Matthew 5:1-12 and Luke 6:20-26) and in his example in healing the blind, the lame, and the deaf. Islam's *Five Pillars* includes a direct attack on poverty and demands the giving of alms. As the Koran says, "Did he not find you wandering and give you guidance? As for the orphans, then, do him no harm; as for the beggar, turn him not away" (Smriti xciii). For the Hindu, right living consists of specifying duties for each state of life. If lived, they decrease the suffering in the world. In essence, one should cause harm to no one. Buddhism and Hinduism find a common bond in a compassion that seeks unity with the suffering of others in order to destroy all suffering. These are some of the ways the classical forms of religion deal with the suffering that surrounds them.

Religions also offer many means of engaging the emotions surrounding suffering and death. This engagement of the emotions is found especially in the tradition of "devotion," and the tradition of "mystical union." Not everyone within the various religions engages in these two traditions but they are present in most religions.

"Devotion" is prayer and life-style committed to a significant religious figure—for example, Krishna or Jesus. Prayer is a communication with this most significant religious figure. Our suffering takes on a meaning because of our relationship to this significant religious figure. At the same time our consecration to him or her opens up patterns of endurance, compassion, and forgiveness, because we want to base our life upon the object of our devotion who has also suffered.

"Mystical union" is consecration brought to completion by accomplishing oneness with the ultimate in our life. We see this in the Eastern religions, where the ultimate identity of each of us is found in the permanent (Brahman); or in the far East, in Tao, where we can reach an inner perception of self only with Tao. The union is with that which is beyond the here and now. In the union there is no suffering.

The social dimensions of religion are many—most of which have become ingrained in ritual. The ritual surrounding the preparation and the disposal of the body, the rituals associated with the days and/or weeks following the death, and the prayer rituals within the gathering of the community petitioning for health or comfort. Ritual action copes with suffering in many ways: for example, by enlisting the support of the religious community as in Jewish mourning practice of Shiva or the Catholic mass; or by placing sufferings in a positive frame of mind by putting them in contact with their ultimate concern and consequently relativizing the suffering. Some ritual actions are believed to reduce suffering itself, as in forms of faith healing.

Every wholistic approach must also include the human drive to understand the surrounding world. The religious traditions in response to the "why" question have developed over the centuries. Especially in those religious traditions which acknowledge a personal God (Judaism, Christianity, and Islam) there have been various attempts to understand why we suffer, why we die, and what influences our future. There are three basic responses: the instrumental, the punitive, and the redemptive.

The *instrumental* model of suffering is found, for instance, in the Islamic belief that suffering is an instrument of God's purposes; in Christianity, that God made Jesus perfect through suffering (Hebrews 12:3-10). In any discussion of suffering, this way of understanding the "why" of suffering comes to the fore as we tell one another that few good things are produced without pain or as we ask how we can develop into mature persons without suffering. The belief is that suffering is an instrument, sometimes sharp, sometimes blunt, of individual and communal development. A personal God uses it to bring about his goal for humanity.

Suffering considered as *punishment* changes the emphasis slightly yet significantly. Punishment highlights the judgmental character of a personal God. We suffer because we or others have sinned. Suffering is a way of righting the imbalance of evil over good. As Rabbi Ruba (1500 c.e.) said, "If a man sees that painful suffering visits him, let him examine his conduct." This approach is found in many prayer books of classic religions. But classic religion is not alone in such an approach: the blood of many people flows in reparation for the sins of their colonial forefathers; a woman in public office is hounded from it for an offense committed in her teens; those who commit crimes against society are punished for past deeds. The model of suffering as a punishment for wrong doing is evident to anyone who makes a child suffer because of some misdeed. It is a short step to complete the circle and ask of the sufferer what he or she has done wrong because suffering is supposedly always linked to wrong doing. As a Sufi saying has it, "When you suffer pain, your conscience is awakened, you are stricken with remorse and pray God to forgive your trespasses."

The belief in suffering as *redemptive* is found in many stories and songs: someone takes upon himself or herself the sins and burdens of others so that all will be free of the consequences of sin. In this view, whenever anyone suffers so that others may live, redemption occurs. The prophets of Israel make this clear in describing the role of the Babylonian captivity in the nation's life. Isaiah summarized it when he said, "By his suffering shall my servant justify many, taking their faults on himself." John's Gospel applies this same principle of Christianity when John the Baptist claims that Jesus is the one who takes away the sins of the world (John 1:29).

ENHANCING THE SPIRITUALITY
OF THE SUFFERER

A spirituality is made up of all the devotions, demands for proper living, rituals, ways of understanding suffering and the stories which tie them all together. The religious traditions, when consciously accepted, become a spirituality. The world religions originated long before our modern world. They presuppose a closeness of community and a continuity of religious membership which their contemporary adherents may not recognize. There is no conscious acceptance of the entire religious system of symbols and values. As a consequence, individuals may profess adherence to a specific religion but not know what they profess nor do they expect social obligations as a consequence of their profession. They may also not understand the rituals, devotions, literature, and stories of their professed religious membership. While not understanding these expressions of their religion they may wish the comfort of it and the rituals associated with it.

A funeral ritual, for instance, may be found in most of the world religions. Let us use the Episcopal church as an example. Individuals may have been born, baptized, and confirmed in this faith, may also not have gone to church for twenty years, and their close relatives may not have gone to church. The person's spouse dies at seventy-two years of age. She expects the church to provide a funeral ritual for her deceased, the priest to preach a homily, and the parish to support her in her husband's death. The probability is, however, that she will not understand the ritual because these symbols and stories are foreign to her; the homily will not be personal because no one knows her spouse; and, the service will be attended by few because of their limited connections with the religious community. This person's professed religious membership did not reflect their true spirituality which easily may have been a style or spirit quite foreign to their religion.

The non-religious professional must be aware that a person's declared religious membership may easily not reflect the true spirituality of her or his life. At the same time a knowledge of what we have mentioned so far does give the professional an ability to recognize some patterns and an opportunity to re-enforce them where possible. The patterns are important, not the labels we given them.

In our pluralistic society we have been exposed to most of what I have already mentioned. When we ask, "What happened?" the response engages us in the other person's spirituality. The present death or deep suffering may be an overwhelming challenge to that spirituality or it may not be. Our ability to understand the story and its underlying spirituality will determine the level of our involvement with that person's spirituality. The following are practical markers for enhancing the spirituality of those we serve.

Respecting the Questions and Answers of the Sufferer

Get to Know Their Values within Their Story

The only way to know something about a person is to enter into conversation with him or her. The professional comes to the interaction with certain categories of diagnosis, prognosis and remedy. The client comes to the professional to take advantage of this skill and knowledge. The skill, the knowledge, and the expectations are generalized. In dying and death situations we face the universal realities of death as they occur in this human being. No one is totally the same as everyone else. A professional should be able to discern the communality and uniqueness of his/her client. The principal way to exercise this discernment is to listen to the client's story. "What happened?" is always a more important first question than "How do you feel about it?" Listening to the story, asking, in sincere conversation, for elaboration or repetition helps you know more of the story and what the person values. How do they make sense of the world? Not in the abstract "why" question that we began with, but in the specific questions of "Do you love her?," "What are you going to do now?," "Can I help?" These are just a few of those questions which bring out one's spirituality of the absurd, of consequence, of illusion, of providence. But each professional also has his or her own answers to life's questions of suffering, death, and future. We must be careful not to give our answers to their questions.

Respect the Importance of Their Values; Their Story

We meet people for a short time each day, each week, each month. No matter how much time we spend with the client it is still a relationship which does not span their entire life. These making-sense answers are foundational to a person's life. One does not change the foundation of life easily. Anyone who has attempted to change a small habit of eating, smoking, or speaking knows a fraction of what is involved when one tries to change a foundational habit of life that is expressed by these answers. It is better to enter into the client's story and, within their setting, urge them to be authentic to their spirituality. That means that you must avoid intolerance and proselytizing: respect their view; be humble about yours.

Provide Opportunities for Seeing and Establishing Connections

A story makes sense as the connections become evident. An enjoyable mystery story is one that leads us down one path only to realize that it is a dead end or going outside the story's plot. To know how the story is connected is an amazing experience. The story of life is no different. When we can see and live the connections, life itself becomes more whole and more enjoyable. Making-sense questions or answers enable the person to put it all together or realize how together life really is. Thus it is important that we help our clients, inasmuch as possible, see and live the connections inherent in their spirituality. We do this by encouraging them to make connections with their religious community. This is best done by attending to the following.

1. Encourage them to make connections with their story in public and private religious rituals. If they have an active religious spirituality the first hearing of their story should be sufficient to give you an idea of which rituals are of significance to them. Rituals encourage any of the items mentioned under classical spiritualities. We do not have to know the rituals. It is enough to ask our clients. If they are actively involved with their religion they will know their own inclinations. What they need is encouragement to initiate the ritual action and support as they engage in it. Take, for instance, night prayer. A Christian with an established spirituality will have a place for regular prayer in his or her life. This easily may surround preparations for sleep. The intense suffering surrounding dying and death many times throws the person off their religious rituals—the rituals of suffering challenge the rituals of spirituality. If the client is not actively involved, but claims adherence to, a classic religious tradition you will need another hearing of their story. What was important to them in

their childhood? Are their patterns of latter life suggestive of another religious pattern? It would certainly be appropriate to encourage a devotional approach to someone who easily establishes personal relationships with others.

2. While encouraging the development of their spirituality, be willing to become involved with their story when it becomes highly emotional—emotions are constitutive of every spirituality.

3. Provide opportunities for the sufferer to see the connections between their experience and their belief system.

Every religion has many beliefs which are helpful for encouraging a person to stretch beyond their current hurt to another way of life. Each classical religion gives reasons, founded within its belief system, for dealing with suffering, death, and the future. These systems have proven quite effective for thousands of years. The client whose spirituality is founded in one of these systems should be encouraged to talk about what their co-religionists believe about suffering, death, the future. More than likely the person, in speaking about the others, will suggest the lines of thought which he or she is more comfortable with.

When Questions and Answers Do Not Match

Our spirituality of suffering is a story written by our answers to the foundational questions of life: Do I have a future? What can I hope for? What should I do to bring about my future and establish a hope in it? Sometimes the answers suggested by our client's religion are dysfunctional to their spiritual life. Instead of the religion affirming the person's responses to his or her suffering, it intensifies that suffering. Certainly various religions have grown out of the blood of martyrs. Certainly, too, all religious stories include ways of living through suffering. There are times, however, when the practitioner is faced with clear evidence that a person is being destroyed physically and psychologically by their religion. The religion as lived by the client is destructive of that client.

If we understand personality as a human pattern of response both to the internal world of consciousness and subconscious and the external world of interdependence, a dysfunctional religion is one which destroys or inhibits the growth of this patterning. Certainly the manifestation of certain psychosis together with prolonged aimlessness suggests destruction of the personality. If we also find that the religion causes the person to destroy their relationship with others, as well as with their physical environment, there is no doubt something must be done.

Many of us would be hesitant to withdraw our support for a person's religion. After seeing its importance for one's spirituality, we might hesitate to acknowledge its destructive capacities. But we must. If we answer "no" to the following questions we must suppose that this person's religion is destructive of his or her spirituality.

1. Does the person's religion destroy his or her relationship to others? Suffering can disrupt, or at least fail to build, community when it isolates persons from one another, destroys individuality, and neglects the demand of sufferers for recognition. If the person's religion intensifies this disruption, it may be destructive of their spirituality.
2. Does the client's religion contribute to his or her personality development? If so, it is a source of life. Self-actualization is a process of becoming more and more what we are, everything that we are capable of becoming. It implies progression through a sequential series of stages toward increasingly higher levels of motivation and self-organization. We grow in confidence and per- sonality development by making good choices and being respon- sible for them. If we find, therefore, that our religious way of life narrows our view of the world, that we are becoming self- centered, sarcastic in our humor, and rigid in action, then it is obvious that our religion is destroying us and reducing our ability to cope with life.
3. Does the religion lead to the person's engagement with the foun- dational questions and the hope associated with them? Religion must provide a person with hope. A hopeful attitude may not be easily articulated in the midst of deep suffering but it certainly is expressive in the person's conviction of transcending this imme- diate suffering. A hopeful attitude enables a person to hold on when life's purposes seem to be at an end.

If all these questions are answered "no," it becomes evident that the person's religion may be more destructive of his or her spirituality rather than enlivening it. We cannot become embittered toward all religions because of the way this person's religion is affecting him or her. Religion is a powerful force for good and for evil. The way each of us lives it varies, and, thus, its personal embodiment will differ. Our spirituality depends on the spirituality of others. When we encounter certain masochistic forms of religion, it is easy to be overwhelmed by the evil present in what we presupposed was consumate goodness. Sometimes we may forget the mysterious nature of both religion and suffering. To forget such mystery is to unnecessarily test the limits of our own spirituality. If we remember that we are not alone, that we cannot do everything, and that sharing suffering is shaping it, we will enhance rather than weaken our spirituality.

We Are Not Alone

Peer professionals, our family, the person's family all are present in some way facing the suffering with us. Peer professionals are present with their knowledge and skills to assist us both in encountering the suffering of others as well as in dealing with our own reaction to that suffering. Our family and those who are closely tied to our life are present to sustain our spirituality in difficult times. The person's family, too, is an essential component of this network. They are a way of connecting to our client and a means of becoming aware of the client's spirituality.

We Cannot Do Everything

When we engage in enhancing the spirituality of others there is always the danger of losing ourself in their story. If we listen to enough significantly different stories, we sometimes forget our own. What are our significant values? Stories? Celebrations of these stories? We must attend to our spirituality in the midst of engaging the spirituality of others. Sometimes the most prudent thing to do is refer the person to someone else when we sense that our own spirituality is disappearing.

Sharing is Shaping

Ultimately, we all face the fact that suffering is an encounter with the mysteries of life. An engagement with mysteries of this sort is an engagement not with a simple question and answer, but with a question and an answer which affects us and is part of the complexity of being human.

Spirit always goes beyond simple answers and simple solutions. Spirit always hovers within chaos bringing it together in some mysterious way. Our spirituality brings together the personal unknowns of past, present, and future and enables us to live. Dealing with the chaos of our client's suffering we many times must imitate the spirit within which silently hovers over all chaos. We must reach out in non-verbal ways to share the suffering of our clients. A held hand, a silent waiting, a back rub, a phone call of concern—these many times are significant answers to suffering's questions. And sometimes, just sometimes, our answers enhance the spirituality of those we deal with. Our spirit speaking to theirs at this moment of life. At this moment we share their suffering, their deaths, their grieving, their future because we have helped life make sense at its most profound level. For them and for you and in these truly spiritual moments—life, broken by suffering, opens to a deeper sense to all concerned. In our sharing we shape the spiritualities of others and ourself.

CHAPTER 12

Spiritual Perspectives on Suffering the Pain of Death

Jeffrey Kauffman

COMPASSION AND THE PAIN OF DEATH

In order for us as caregivers to get our bearings on, and be in touch with the spiritual needs of the dying and the bereaved, we need, in our own spiritual experience, within ourselves, to be opened to the pain of death. The starting place in working with another's pain in the face of death is to open ourselves to this pain. This is the one basic psychospiritual insight. To maintain openness to another's pain is a process of ongoing spiritual growth for the caregiver. Openness to the pain of another is the difficult spiritual pathway of *compassion*. Caring for the dying and the bereaved, being there in the force of their pain, is a practice both based on and nurtured in great spiritual discipline. The dual risks of: 1) being overwhelmed and too deeply touched by the psychospiritual power of the pain of death and loss, or else 2) becoming closed, untouched, spiritually numbed and beyond vulnerability are always present.

As compassion deepens and matures, and the spirit of the caregiver begins to ripen in its capacity to contain the pain of death, the psychospiritual caregiver may experience the flow of *gratitude* towards those cared for.

Being open within ourselves to the pain of another requires that we have cleared a space where our own death anxiety and our own pain have once been—a space that shall be *hospitable* to the pain of others. The caregiver for the dying and bereaved must carefully cultivate an awareness of yet undiscovered closures to the psychospiritual reality of death within him/herself that may be touched by the pain of others. The spiritual healing work that takes place in our relationship to the dying and bereaved is a give-and-take and a mutual healing. Our yearning for closure, our subtle denials, our whispers of self-assurance, our urges to fly from the agonizing emptiness, our dread and numbness, our aching for release of tensions, and our "passion to cure" the helplessness of those we care for must be recognized as *signals*. These signals tell us we must process some aspect of our relationship to death and dying. *Courage* and *humility,* required for this processing, ensure the safe passage and spiritual growth of compassion in the caregiver.

SUFFERING THE PAIN OF DEATH

We do not choose to suffer the pain of death. When the reality of death is present, human nature will do all it can do to block it out of consciousness. Psychoanalytic psychology has taught us to call this *denial*. Denial is the ego's earliest defense against dangers. The ego expels the danger from its intrapsychic space, but then is prone to re-experience the danger as a threat from outside. The most primitive belief about death is that it is an act of violence inflicted from outside. Psychologically, the origin of the ego's defensive nature is to create a boundary which excludes the existence of death. As the ego matures, it gradually reintegrates the originally excluded reality of death. The psychoanalytic description of this process speaks of an increased tolerance for frustration, an increased capacity to tolerate reality, and higher levels of psychic organization. Developmental process in depth psychology is a process of suffering a loss and gradually integrating this into "psychic structure."

Wilfred Bion suggested that pain that is not suffered may cause mental illness [1]. He writes, ". . . people exist who are so intolerant of pain or frustration (in whom pain or frustration are so intolerable) that they feel the pain but will not suffer it." In the face of death it is the normal human reaction to regress to such a state. The mourning process, which begins in this regression to the primitive defense of denial as a reaction to the presence of death, is a gradual process of suffering the pain of death and loss (healing) and integrating the whole process into self (growth).

In the initial shock and numbness into which we are thrown, *we are overwhelmed by the extraordinary eruption of the presence of death and loss in our consciousness.* The presence of death changes an otherwise secular consciousness into a sacred space, and defines the nature of the pain and mourning that follow as not simply psychological, but also spiritual. The normal course of mourning involves a struggle or dialogue between denial and realization. Realization of the loss occurs again and again over an extended period of time as aspects of helplessness, guilt, shame, anger, fear, disbelief, etc. are processed. *This process of healing through repeated suffering the pain of death is a spiritual process.*

The task of the caregiver for persons living with the pain of death is to be compassionately present, open to the pain that is there, even to the pain that is there which the dying or bereaved person may have not yet discovered—to facilitate the suffering of the pain that is there and to be a touchstone through which this pain may be realized, suffered and affirmed.

TRANSFORMATIONS IN SUFFERING

The Crisis of Meaninglessness

In the face of one's own imminent death or the loss of a loved one, the meaningfulness of reality may be shattered. There may occur the sense that nothing means anything anymore, that there is no purpose in life. The meaningfulness which orders the sense of value and of action may be ripped away. The very sense of reality that before was simply taken for granted as given—that life itself has meaning—may be threatened.

The opening upon the *mystery of life* in the crisis of meaninglessness, the opening forged by the presence of death and the injury it inflicts, is not an opening upon oceanic bliss or joyfulness of the freedom of the spirit. It is an opening in which meaning is threatened with annihilation and the cohesion of reality is undermined. The urge to find meaning as an escape from the painfulness of the unknown may seek to prematurely seal off this tremendous upsurge of psychological and spiritual disturbance. To abide by the compelling and sacred force of grief and the unknown that opens in us requires strength of soul and faith. Gentleness, comfort and solace within oneself and from others are needed. *Openness to the unknown and the deep mystery of life that may be awakened in the face of death is incubated in suffering the pain of death.* Let us focus on a common way in which this spiritual pain of death and the presence of the unknown is expressed in the mourning process.

The crisis of meaninglessness is sometimes expressed through the word "why." When this question comes up, it often serves the dying and bereaved well to force us out of our "knowing" and "helping" position and brings us closer to them. It reaches out and invites us into the unbearable agony and disordering of spiritual reality in the pain of the dying and the bereaved. In handling this question with a person who is grieving, it is necessary first to *assess what is really being asked*. Sometimes the question "Why?" expresses guilt. Often the question "Why?" expresses disbelief. The question "Why?" may express a variety of affects and cognition or a combination of feelings and thoughts condensed into one word. The question "Why?" may be a form of cursing in which, for example, rage and anguish are attempting to blast away a sense of helplessness. It is out of this helplessness that the "Giver of Meaning" is questioned: "What is the meaning of this violence and destruction!?," "What is the meaning of this pain!?," "What is the meaning of life?!," "Does goodness really exist?!," "Does God exist?!," "Why was I born?!," "Why," here, is the language of profound *injury*. It is the language of psychological or spiritual injury. It is not a question to be answered. The task of the caregiver is in trying to find a way of being opened to and validating of the profound depth of injury. The question may appear to ask for a justification. It does not. There is no justification.

The question "Why?" may be the pain of helplessness peering into loneliness and disbelief, yearning to be held. The question "Why?" may come to be reflective, seeking a deeper sense in the senselessness of death. The question "Why?" is born in the chaos and meaninglessness wrought by death—which cannot be accepted but which must be sustained. The opening upon spiritual reality in the mourning process harnesses the possibility of spiritual growth in being able to stay with the pain that is most difficult to suffer. Death may force us out of the ordinariness and everydayness of sleepwalking consciousness in which we are unaware of being alive, being sentient, and being conscious. There is also the risk that meaninglessness may erode the capacity to love, and the annihilating significance of death may root deeply in the self. Depression and spiritual emptiness may settle in. The crisis of meaninglessness puts one in the position where there is risk and possibility. The question "Why?" is poised on this spiritual pivot point.

Spiritual rebirth into meaning, the reintegration and regeneration of the self, may also heal long-lasting alienation from spiritual meaning in one's life. In the spiritual healing process, the present situation is focal, but in more intensive spiritual working through, the whole of life is recognized to be present. Loss and grief that may have affected one's entire life may be activated in the crisis and in the psychospiritual treatment of dying and bereavement.

Guilt, the Psychology of Internalization and the Transformation of the Self

When dying or when grieving the death of a loved one, a part of the mourning process is "settling accounts." In the psychological literature on mourning, this need is seen to come from *ambivalence in the relationship,* so that the mourner needs to resolve his guilt. It should be noted that guilt occurs in the mourning process due to other sources in addition to ambivalence in a relationship. A sense of guilt tends to occur normally in the face of death out of feelings of love; i.e., guilt is present out of being responsible rather than being ambivalent. The deep spiritual connection to our fellowman, our common bond and destiny, heightened in a love relationship, is a source of guilt. Even irrational guilt should, then, be respected and affirmed, at the same time the irrationality and self-blamefulness is caringly acknowledged.

The spiritual meaning of healing guilt in the mourning process is in the act of *gratitude*—returning thanks for what is given. In Plato's *Republic,* before Socrates and his interlocutors begin the dialogue which founds the "perfect city," the aged Cephalus, head of the household where they are gathered, excuses himself. He says he will soon die, and that he must go to make an offering to the gods, to *return to them their due* [2]. This is the justice our mortality compels in us. "Settling accounts" or resolving guilt in the mourning process is an act of paying a sacred debt. Giving to the other, to oneself, and to God what is due—*returning* what is due—is an act of gratitude. The psychospiritual healing of ambivalence and guilt in the mourning process is an act of gratitude. Nietzsche wrote that "one should part from this life as Ulysses parted by Nausicaa—blessing it rather than loving it" [3].

The deep psychological dynamic of gratitude in the mourning process is a process of "internalization." While the outward action is "letting go"—the psychodynamic process is a "process whereby intersubjective relations are transformed into intrasubjective ones" [4]. Another way of talking about internalization that occurs in mourning is that the other is taken into oneself in such a way that the other is transformed into a part of the self. One also gathers back in parts of the self that have been invested in the other, restoring the self to a renewed sense of wholeness and at-one-ment. The whole psychospiritual mourning experience becomes a part of oneself.

Imbued with the profound pain of death and its psychospiritual impact on the self, the process of internalization is also a process of *sanctification.* As guilt and anger that cling to the other as an intersubjective relationship are transformed by gratitude, and the other is released into the self, the self is spiritually nurtured, the spiritual meaning of life is deepened, and the capacity for compassion strengthened.

Loss of Self and Psychospiritual Healing

The pain of death in the mourning process precipitates a *regression* in psychological functioning in which the self may open upon its deepest vulnerabilities and may experience itself to be disintegrating. In normal grief one is thrown into helplessness, and tends to be overwhelmed also by feelings of abandonment, exposure, worthlessness and being out of control. These are *loss of self* anxieties. In being helpless to reverse the power of death, the very ground of the self is threatened: one is powerless to do what is most urgently wished for and needed. The self, experiencing itself falling into utter helplessness, and terrified by abandonment anxiety, is in dire spiritual danger. The deep, vulnerable core of the self is injured. Sometimes this is glaringly and disturbingly evident; sometimes it is covered over by shame and unseen.

The caregiver's *being there*, securing a sense of safety, recognition and understanding of the *unbearable aloneness* and injury inflicted in loss of self anxiety in the face of death—is his/her primary task. Care is provided in sanctioning and validating, in providing safe space for recognizing and acknowledging this vulnerability. Where this pain is not hidden away beyond the healing power of the mourning process, or stuck—as pain that is felt but not suffered (chronic grief), or fled from into pseudo-wellness where there has been no psychological or spiritual healing process—but, where it is suffered, its flowing through us may cut a deep passageway. Like a cave, with unexpected, hidden vaults, the psychospiritual dimension of the self opens. God's presence is not in removing the pain, but in securing safe passage through it.

REFERENCES

1. W. Bion, *Attention and Interpretation in Seven Servants*, Jason Aronson, New York, 1977.
2. Plato, *The Republic*, P. Shorey (trans.), Harvard University Press, Cambridge, Massachusetts, 1930.
3. F. Nietzsche, *Beyond Good and Evil*, W. Kaufmann (trans.), Vintage Books, New York, 1966.
4. J. La Planche and J. B. Pontalis, *The Language of Psychoanalysis*, W. W. Norton and Co., New York, 1973.

CHAPTER 13

Spiritual Care in Hospice

Dorothy C. H. Ley

> Questions of value-belief lie at the heart of the human experience
> and existence, of life and death. . . . Our contemporary Utopian
> movements are truculently secular and scientific. There was a time
> when angels walked the earth; now we doubt that they are even in
> heaven.
>
> Herman Feifel

Spiritual care lies at the heart of hospice. Yet, in a world of
"truculently secular and scientific movements" [1] the hospice movement is questioning its ability to give such care and is searching for
ways to provide spiritual support in a multicultural, pluralistic society.
Spiritual care is one of the philosophical pillars of the modern concept
of hospice care. However, it is dangerous to assume that after the
narcotics and the nursing, the counselling and psychosocial support,
the family counselling, spiritual care falls neatly into place—particularly if the chaplain is involved. Over 90 percent of American
hospice programs surveyed by the Joint Commission on Hospital
Accreditation failed to demonstrate adequate spiritual care. Only 2
percent of Canadian community programs provided formal spiritual
counselling or had a chaplain designated as a member of the team [2].

Modern society tends to compartmentalize care, to identify care
with the profession of the caregiver, and to allocate responsibility for
different kinds of care to a series of interconnected circles each with its
own label. Spiritual care thus becomes the responsibility of the
chaplain. This attitude spills over into the hospice setting in subtle
ways. Cicely Saunders has said that the measure of a hospice program
is the quality of the spiritual care that it provides. If indeed hospice is
struggling to provide effective spiritual care, what characteristic of

spirituality is not being recognized? What is it that is not being done or that is being done? Each member of the hospice team has the capacity to provide spiritual care, although each person's perception of such care will be different. One's concept of spirituality is both intimate and personal—and so it should be. We are spiritual beings deep within ourselves. It is from that well that each must draw when caring for dying people.

To understand the nature of spiritual care and the place of spirituality in hospice care, we have to go back a long way—to the meaning of spirituality and the roots of hospice. What is spirituality? The word "spiritual" is commonly used to describe the differences that exist between mankind and other animals. The dictionary defines spiritual as "that which concerns the spirit or higher or moral qualities, especially as regarded in a religious aspect." The concept of a spiritual soul is not found in the same way in Judaism or non-Western religions as it is in Christianity. To quote John Morgan, "We who live in a Western culture shaped by both the language of the Greek intellectual experience and the Christian religious experience identify the idea of spirituality with religion" [3].

A distinction should be made between religion and spirituality. Religion can be defined as an organized set of practices that surround a traditionally-defined belief in the existence of a God or divine, super-human, ruling power. Such practices are set down in sacred writings or declared by authoritative teachers. There are other definitions. Religion is, in some respects, a set of tools used to express or practice one's beliefs. Spirituality may be (and hopefully is) a part of religious belief or practice, but religion may or may not be part of one's spirituality. Those with strong religious ties may have difficulty recognizing that fact.

Spirituality is our relationship with the infinite and, it should be added, with our fellows. It has been said that it integrates our identities. It is the essence of self. It is the I. It is the God within each of us, the part that can commune with the transcendent. It underlies our capacity to forgive, to create, to love and to accept love. It frequently is intensified by approaching death. Our spirituality is what we seek when we search for meaning in our lives.

Both Christian religion and spiritual care have been at the heart of hospice from its beginnings in the fourth century A.D. when Fabiola established a hospice in pagan Rome for Christian pilgrims from Africa. The tradition of the medieval Knights Hospitaller was based on the injunction of Christ in the 25th Chapter of the Gospel according to St. Matthew, "Inasmuch as you have done it unto one of the least of these, my brethren, you have done it unto Me." The medieval hospices, whether the great fortress-hospital of St. John at Rhodes, the elegant hospice of Beaune, or the myriad of small hospices associated with monasteries throughout Europe—were dedicated to the physical and spiritual care of the sick and the dying—and the Christian burial of the dead. Whether the traveller was a knight on the journey to Jerusalem, or a poor beggar on the journey of life, the ancient hospice was a way station, a resting place, a place of care and concern for both the body and the spirit.

But the world changed. Society changed. With the waning of monastic influence and changing social patterns, the number of hospices in the old sense decreased. A different pattern of care developed—the hospital. Gradually, a society developed that increasingly valued order, efficiency and social discipline and came to regard a human being as an economic unit. The modern hospital became the repository of those who were unable to contribute to an industrialized society or a place to repair its damaged tools.

At the same time, a change in attitude to death was taking place. No discussion of spirituality is complete without examining society's attitudes to death. The moral and ethical issues of our time (abortion, euthanasia) are those related to death. From an event in medieval times accepted as the completion of life, to be shared with family and friends, it came to be seen as a violent disruption of living, calling forth grief, a pervasive sense of loss and intense fear.

In the seventeenth century, in the midst of profound social change, Descartes put forward the concept of the dualism of mind and body. The Church assumed responsibility for the mind (and soul) and science (or medicine) for the body. This philosophy has had a profound and lasting effect on the practice of medicine and ultimately on both society's and medicine's attitude toward death and dying. Today we are still caught in the dichotomy that Descartes enunciated so long ago, the separation of mind and body. Scientific medicine became increasingly intrusive in the process of dying, so much so that Ivan Illich coined the phrase "the medicalization of death" to describe a society in which death had become faceless, secularized, institutionalized and robbed of its humanity. Ariés subsequently wrote that the modern hospital was the only place where death could hide [4].

The scientific explosion of the twentieth century combined with rapid urbanization to isolate people from normal birth and death. The locus of care shifted from the community to "high tech" institutions. The role of the physician changed from a family friend and confidante to that of a distant, authoritative, scientific figure. The new technology and the increased availability of medical care as a result of universal or private health care insurance plans justified the public's belief that health was a right and fostered the illusion of medical infallibility and the indefinite deferment of death.

We became a death-denying society cared for by health professionals who saw the maintenance of life and not the quality of that life as a measure of competence and turned away from death as an expression of failure. The stage was set for the modern hospice movement. Hospice, in the twentieth century, began as a revolt against medical attitudes and practice and the rigid institutional bureaucracy that reduced dying people to the state of a disease in a bed.

The social revolution of the sixties rejected establishment power, including medical power, and in part led to the questioning of the validity of the Cartesian philosophy of separation of mind and body. Cicely Saunders, in Great Britain, developed the hospice as an alternative form of holistic care for people dying difficult deaths with cancer. Kubler-Ross, in America, conceptualized a series of stages in coming to terms with one's dying and promoted the concept of dying at home, surrounded by family and friends. It was a return, philosophically at least, to the medieval perspective of dying. There is a strong spiritual component to the philosophy of hospice as developed by both these women. Spirituality was and is an essential part of modern hospice care.

No discussion of spiritual care in hospice would be complete without a consideration of the concept of total pain and the meaning of suffering. Total pain is made up of different components: physical, psychological, social, emotional, and spiritual. Pain embraces the whole person. There is growing expertise in the relief of physical pain and the management of symptoms to maintain activity and to provide a degree of independence and self-esteem. Nevertheless, significantly more people than should suffer from unrelieved pain and poorly managed symptoms because of lack of education and faulty attitudes on the part of health care professionals.

If hospice is to care for the whole person, the family and community must be included. A fundamental principle of hospice is that the unit of care must be the person who is dying and that person's family. "No man is an island" wrote John Donne. We cannot live apart from our relationships with others. In modern society the "family" unit frequently differs from the so-called "nuclear family." To relieve social pain, to provide spiritual support, the hospice caregiver must be able to recognize the needs of the family and community and help them to come to terms with those needs and their own fears. It may be necessary to re-establish communication within the unit of care, to assist in the process of reconciliation. In many families there is much reconciliation to be done; there is some in every family. The goal of hospice care is to facilitate that reconciliation and help people to tie up loose ends, to take their farewells. However, as Saunders has so wisely pointed out, this is "not just a salvage operation, but an original opportunity, a moment for creation" [5].

When we care for persons who are dying we must find out who they are. Who is that person? What is their essential being? There is a tendency in modern society to think of ourselves in terms of what we do. We consider a person to be manifested in their work, their interests, their accomplishments, but a person is more than that. Who are we deep inside ourselves? What are our inner concerns, our values? How can we make sense of it all at the end? How can we find meaning in our living and in our dying? That surely is the spiritual dimension of a person. For some, their religious values and practices provide deep support and allow them to come to terms with their lives. For them the chaplain in a program is an essential member of the team. Others may have no relationship to a religion, or may have a sense of guilt, or unease, or a feeling that they were never able to measure up to the expectations of their family, their church or their God. The sermons, the sacraments, and the services do not reach them. As hospice caregivers, we must reach them, whether we wear our collar back-wards, wear a white coat or a nurses' cap, or a volunteer's smock or push a broom as a housekeeper. Death is a spiritual event. It generates a desire to identify what is valuable and true in one's life. We want to tidy up the ends, to put first things first. The inability to do so in a person's life may generate a desolate feeling of meaningless.

This is the essence of spiritual pain, to feel that one is meaningless or that one's life has been meaningless. In Viktor Frankl's book *Man's Search for Meaning*, he writes that if there is no way out of suffering then we have a responsibility for our attitude toward that suffering [6]. In *When Bad Things Happen to Good People* Kushner makes much the same point, that the pain is the reason and out of the pain and suffering comes understanding, comes the answer [7]. Kushner also reiterates (as Job learned) that God does not ask us to do things that he does not give us the strength to do.

Frankl reminds us that no one can tell another person what the meaning of their life should be. Sometimes we in hospice care tend to sermonize. It is tempting to preach but we do not have the right to tell dying people the meaning of their lives, only to help them find it. The key to spiritual care is to give them the opportunity and the time to work through and solve their problems—to find their own meaning. We may need to be no more than a presence—to be there. As Saunders has remarked there is a striking analogy between hospice care and Gethsemane. Christ was asking for meaning in what He had to do. He was asking that it not happen, but that if it did, He would be able to endure the pain and the suffering that He knew lay ahead. How often our patients say to us, "I know I'm dying, I don't want to die and I don't want to be in pain, but if you help me I can do it. Just be here and help me." As Christ said to the disciples, "Could you not watch with me one hour?," so often we are asked, "Watch with me." One cannot die for another or grant them a good death. One can never walk in a dying person's shoes. It is their death. All we can do is walk beside them. Spiritual care is helping them to find the way to acceptance and peace.

Nouwen's concept of the wounded healer is important in hospice care [8]. We understand because we too are wounded, because we too have pain. We understand because we are and because we have come to accept our own mortality. We must dig down deep inside and integrate the scattered parts of ourselves in order to be able to respond, even imperfectly, to a dying person's needs.

How do we help others? We caregivers are so diverse. We come from different backgrounds, from different beliefs, from different religions or no religion at all, and we are not dying. It is said that no one can imagine their own death. This means that when we care for dying people we cannot imagine what they are experiencing. However, we too can feel suffering, we can feel pain, we can feel loss. What can we do? We can give them freedom and space by controlling their pain. We can listen. We may not have the answers, but we can listen. We can listen in such a way that we help them to find their own answers, and the gift of listening belongs to everyone on the team.

What is suffering? There are many definitions. Cassel has written eloquently about it and has focused new attention on the interrelationship between pain and suffering [9]. We suffer when we perceive an impending threat to our personality, to our personhood. Suffering is unique. Only humans can suffer. Furthermore, we can suffer for others. We suffer until the threat to our personhood is removed or until we can come to terms with it. Recognizing suffering and helping people to deal with their suffering is part of spiritual care. Part of the ability to recognize suffering as distinct from pain lies in overcoming the concept of the dichotomy between mind and body.

As Delton Glebe has so accurately observed spirituality is implicit in the grieving process. If we, as hospice caregivers, accept the premise that our responsibility for care encompasses both patient and family, then our spiritual care must extend into the period of bereavement and include all those who grieve. The pain of grief is as real as the pain of cancer and, as in the management of physical pain, hospice care holds out the promise of relief. The bereaved, too, search for meaning in their loss and in the face of death. Like the dying, they need our skills, our compassion and the sense that we are there. Spiritual care should lead to the opportunity for both personal and community growth. To quote Glebe, "The spirituality of pain is the healing that is hidden in the hurting" [10].

There are a number of issues that affect spiritual care in modern society. There are global reasons, for example, for the current awareness of the need for spiritual care. Lifton makes some interesting and challenging comments in his book, *The Broken Connection* [11]. He reminds us that our sense of immortality depends on the link between life and death. In modern society our concept of that link has often been destroyed, for example, by nuclear war. We think of our immortality in terms of the world we leave behind. If there will be no world how, then, do we conceptualize immortality?

The world has been struck recently with a series of natural disasters, in which thousands of people have perished. Chernobyl faced the world with sudden, insidious death over which there was no control. It could not be anticipated, could not be seen and struck silently thousands of miles from its source. It reinforced the world's sense of vulnerability. The death of seven astronauts was witnessed on television by millions of viewers. It, too, threatened our sense of control and shook our faith in science. There is a growing tendency at this time to question science and technology, and an increased impetus to examine the meaning of our lives.

AIDS is a world-wide pandemic that has generated a sense of fear and hopelessness and an increasing perception of man's helplessness and human frailty. Organized religion in the Western world has not been at the forefront of care for people with AIDS or their family and friends. In part this has been because AIDS first appeared in two marginalized groups in society—homosexuals and drug abusers—that the modern church, both theologically and spiritually, has difficulty accepting. The Third World on the other hand—particularly Africa—has been and continues to be devastated by a pandemic of HIV infection that has the potential for destroying the fragile economy of many countries and wiping out the first generation of people with modern education. The face of AIDS is clearly visible in Africa. It is the face of ignorance, of disease, of poverty and promiscuity, of social dislocation and changing lifestyle. The Western world, faced with escalating infection of women and children and rapid spread of HIV in the community, only now is beginning to recognize the true nature of this pandemic. Only now are we beginning to look at the broader problems underlying the spread of this virus—problems that are directly related to the spiritual values of modern society.

We still must care for those people in our society who are infected with HIV and who have AIDS. Hospice caregivers not only require special medical and nursing skills to care for terminally ill AIDS patients, but they must learn new counselling skills for people and communities that they may not understand. Traditionally, caregivers have been white and middle class. AIDS should be a stimulus to an increase in the numbers of homosexuals and lesbians and visible minorities who are active in hospice care. The ability to provide spiritual care depends on the recognition of the nature of the spirituality of others, although it may differ from ours. Those of us who profess to be Christian must examine the ways in which we treat both our fellow Christians and others. AIDS is calling on the church to examine its role in providing pastoral care for people who are infected with HIV, their families and friends, and pastoral care for caregivers who become infected. AIDS is calling the church to look at itself in a way it has not done for centuries.

Another issue facing hospice and spiritual care in hospice is the rapid increase in the number of elderly in North American society. By the year 2000 there will have been a 130 percent increase in the number of people over 85 since 1980. Over 70 percent of the people in hospice care are over 65 years of age. We live in a competitive and materialistic society that puts a premium on dominance and power. Our perception of aging is one of decline in productivity and potential and increasing dependency and powerlessness. As caregivers we must resist the temptation to practice benign paternalism. There may be a gap of two or three generations between the dying elderly person and their caregivers. To provide spiritual care for the terminally ill elderly we must recognize the real nature of the person who is dying, the poignancy of their losses, the uniqueness of their perception of spirituality and their relationship to their religions. The elderly are more concerned about the quality of their lives than the length. They are frequently afraid of being abandoned physically and emotionally. Hospice must find a way to reinforce their personhood and give them back the control that we so easily take away from them.

There are problems facing spiritual care in hospice that are associated with ethnic differences. Modern hospice care began in a white, Anglo-Saxon, Christian community in Great Britain. We now live and practice hospice care in a multi-cultural, pluralistic society. We try to care for people from different ethnic and religious backgrounds and we, the people who provide care, come from differing beliefs and have different spiritual concepts. There is compassion and concern in the Buddhist teaching. There is compassion and concern in the Jewish faith. Humanists are concerned with social justice and ethics, compassion and abiding commitment. All can and do provide spiritual care in hospice—and not only to their own. Indeed, Florence Wald has suggested that we could and should develop ecumenical spiritual care in hospice.

Spiritual care has been described as the "unfinished revolution in palliative care" [12]. Spirituality is difficult to describe and even more difficult to define. Norman Cousins stated the problem facing hospice care most eloquently in his book *The Anatomy of An Illness*: "Death is not the ultimate tragedy of life. The ultimate tragedy is de-personalization—dying in an alien and sterile area, separated from the spiritual nourishment that comes from being able to reach out to a loving hand, separated from a desire to experience the things that make life worth living. Separated from hope" [13].

In answer to the cry of the spirit, hospice says: "We are here. We will be with you in your living and your dying. We will free you from pain and give you the freedom to find your own meaning in your own life—your way. We will comfort you and those you love—not always with words, often with a touch or a glance. We will bring you hope—not for tomorrow but for this day. We will not leave you. We will watch with you. We will be there."

REFERENCES

1. H. Feifel, Foreword, in *In Quest of the Spiritual Component of Care for the Terminally Ill*, F. Wald (ed.), Yale University Press, New Haven, 1986.
2. E. G. Heidemann, Palliative Care in Canada: 1986, *Journal of Palliative Care, 5*:3, pp. 37-42, 1989.
3. J. D. Morgan (ed.), Death and Bereavement: Spiritual, Ethical and Pastoral Issues, *Death Studies, 12*, pp. 85-89, 1988.
4. P. Ariés, *The Hour of Our Death*, Knopf, New York, 1951.
5. C. Saunders, Spiritual Pain, *Journal of Palliative Care, 4*:3, pp. 29-32, 1988.
6. V. E. Frankl, *Man's Search for Meaning* (Revised Edition), Hodder and Stoughton, London, 1987.
7. H. S. Kushner, *When Bad Things Happen to Good People*, Schocken Books, New York, 1981.
8. H. J. M. Nouwen, *The Wounded Healer: Ministry in Contemporary Society*, Doubleday, New York, 1972.
9. E. J. Cassel, The Nature of Suffering and the Goals of Medicine, *New England Journal of Medicine, 306*, pp. 639-645, 1982.
10. D. Glebe, Spirituality in the Grief Process, in *Saying Goodbye: Essays*, TVOntario Publications, Toronto, 1990.
11. R. J. Lifton, *The Broken Connection*, Simon and Schuster, New York, 1979.
12. I. B. Corless, Talk Given in New Paltz, New York, September 5, 1986.
13. N. Cousins, *Anatomy of an Illness*, Norton, New York, 1979.

PART IV

Spiritual Issues in Bereavement

While the previous section focuses on the spiritual needs of the dying, this section considers the spiritual needs of the survivors. However, this is not so neatly sequential as language and placement may seem to imply. Fulton and Fulton describe a process of "anticipatory grief," indication that grief is not only a response to loss that has occurred but also to anticipated or threatened losses [1]. Thus grieving may begin at the point that life-threatening illness is suspected or diagnosed. And griever, in this anticipatory period, may include not only the survivors but the patients as well.

This section begins with three introductory chapters. Doka begins by providing an overview of the spiritual crisis of bereavement. Doka emphasizes two major points. The first is that ritual can become a powerful therapeutic tool in resolving grief. This role can be enhanced when the bereaved have the opportunity to personalize and participate in rituals, and when they can mark with rituals, varied points in the grieving process. Doka also believes that current conceptualizations of the grieving process may not fully recognize the spiritual needs of the bereaved. He suggests that such models both incorporate remembrance and reintegrate belied systems. In Chapter 15, "Bereavement and the Sacred Art of Spiritual Care," Cullinan addresses similar issues. She emphasizes the great diversity of spiritual perspectives and beliefs as well as significant issues and needs that clients may have. And she provides some interventive strategies counselors can employ in facilitating these spiritual needs. While Cullinan explores spiritual counselling, Raether further examines the role of ritual, emphasizing through a brief review its psychological and social benefits.

Four additional chapters explore the particular issues raised in different types of losses. While selective, these chapters together reemphasize the fact that every situation and circumstance of loss raises its own unique spiritual issues. Echelbarger's chapter on suicide describes particular problems resulting from self-inflicted deaths. To Echelbarger the process of providing means to life, telling a story of a person's life and death, is the heart of the spiritual struggle in bereavement. In suicide this process can become thwarted by guilt and confusion, and the spiritual struggle complicated by the church's historical condemnation of the suicide act. While Echelbarger writes from a Christian perspective, many of his themes such as suffering, God's will, guilt and forgiveness can be applied to other traditions.

Cullinan, too, in her chapter "The Spiritual Care of the Traumatized: A Critical Need," explores the unique spiritual issues raised in sudden tragedy and disaster. These, too, raise profound questions about the fairness and will that affect any spiritual belief system. Cullinan's chapter has value for both its overview of literature on critical incident stress and its sensitivity to these spiritual concerns.

Doka and Nichol's chapter describes the spiritual needs and reactions of survivors of perinatal loss. Central to this essay is utilizing the funeral service as a therapeutic vehicle. Doka and Nichol's discussion of the context of the sermon, again written from a Christian perspective, may be easily applied to other traditions and to other circumstances of loss.

Wolfe's chapter provides an overview of the special bereavement problems caused by AIDS. Wolfe's review notes the special concerns of different groups of survivors. Underlying is the theme that AIDS provides a case where definitions of mortality and the fear of death often create a strong sense of stigma that exacerbates grief and raises distinct spiritual issues for survivors.

Perhaps there is a connecting thread in these last chapters. In earlier work, Doka defined "disenfranchised grief" as grief resulting from losses that cannot be publicly shared, openly acknowledged, or socially sanctioned [2]. The griever has experienced a loss, but lacks any socially perceived "right" to grieve. Grief may be disenfranchised for a number of reasons. In some cases, the griever's capacity to grieve may not be recognized as, for example, with the developmentally disabled. In other cases, such as perinatal loss, the loss may not be recognized. Sometimes relationships, like that of a lover or ex-spouse may not be recognized. Finally, some deaths can be disenfranchising; that is, the deaths are considered so shameful or horrible that survivors are reluctant to seek support. AIDS, suicide, and even some homicides or disasters may fall into that category. Such disenfranchised losses may place survivors in a disturbing double bind. On one hand, the loss may raise strong spiritual issues related to mortality and/or meaning. But sources of support such as religious beliefs and community or ritual may be neither forthcoming nor helpful.

REFERENCES

1. A. Fulton, A Psychological Aspect of Terminal Care: Anticipatory Grief, *Omega, 2,* pp. 91-100, 1971.
2. K. J. Doka, *Disenfranchised Grief,* Lexington Press, Lexington, Massachusetts, 1989.

CHAPTER 14

The Spiritual Crisis of Bereavement

Kenneth J. Doka

INTRODUCTION

Loss can be exceedingly painful. Both clinicians and novelists have explored the extraordinary pain that bereavement can bring. They have described in vivid detail the psychological trauma, the social loss, and the existential ache that can accompany significant loss.

Faith, with its rituals and beliefs, can be a powerful elixir at times of loss. Its ritual can provide structure and succor. Its beliefs may offer comfort and conciliation.

Yet like many powerful tools, faith can have both constructive and destructive aspects. It may promise reunion and resurrection, yet also haunt the bereaved with fears of retribution and damnation. To some it may offer forgiveness, while in others it exacerbates guilt. Its rituals may comfort some and trouble others.

But faith, whether in a theistic religious system or a philosophical system is likely to be part of the bereavement process. Just as dying has a spiritual dimension, so does death and bereavement. Questions about the value of the deceased's life, the meaningfulness of the survivor's existence in the face of loss, and the reason for death are common concerns in times of loss and have an inherently spiritual character.

This chapter seeks to explore the ways that beliefs and the rituals that accompany them can both facilitate and complicate bereavement. And it offers suggestions to clinicians on ways that they may assist clients in effectively utilizing their belief systems in resolving grief.

RITUAL AND LOSS

Rituals may be defined as "prescribed symbolic acts that must be performed in a certain way and in a certain order, and may or may not be accompanied by verbal formulas" [1, p. 8]. Often rituals are rooted in a belief system. This is particularly true of rituals that mark significant life events such as birth, puberty, marriage and death. Here historically religious rituals are the commonly accepted "rite of passage" even to those who only nominally adhere to the underlying religious beliefs. Even when those religious beliefs are decisively rejected, persons may still adhere to the rituals or seek alternate rituals more compatible to their own belief system. For example, the British Humanist Society conducts funerals for members who have rejected any religious tradition. For, in any case, there seems a need to mark the transition from life.

Rituals, then, can be a powerful tool for facilitating bereavement. Clinicians and theorists such as Irion, Rando, and Hart have all emphasized the psychological, social, and spiritual benefits of the funeral ritual [1-4]. The funeral can provide an opportunity to reintegrate and reaffirm the group, allow the expression and expiation of emotion, affirm the value of the deceased's life, stimulate remembrance, provide support and structure, offer hope and comfort, and perhaps even teleologically justify loss. This value has also been supported by research that has emphasized the role of the funeral in facilitating grief adjustment [5-14].

Yet there is also evidence that funeral rituals may have dysfunctional elements as well. Anecdotal and newspaper accounts have described funeral rituals that would seem highly troubling to survivors. For example, a priest in a New York City funeral for a young boy mauled by a caged bear suggested in his funeral homily that this early and awful death might be God's way of preserving this child's soul from the peril of future deviance. Similarly it has been reported that some clergy have used funerals of persons who have died from AIDS as a forum to condemn homosexuality or drug abuse. And research has indicated that those who experience complicated bereavement often report troubling funerals [15].

While such dysfunctional funerals may be rare, it does seem that the power of funeral rituals often lies untapped. The increasing bureaucratization of death has resulted in families delegating the planning of rituals to professionals. Secularism and pluralism have narrowed the collective utility of religious language and rituals. It is little wonder, then, that only the mourners closest to the bereaved benefit from the ritual [12].

Funeral rituals remain, then, a powerful tool for resolving grief, yet one that is sometimes destructively used and more often untapped. But there are ways that the power of ritual can be enhanced.

The first is to personalize and individualize such rituals. Rituals that are individualized are both preferred by bereaved and much more likely to facilitate grief adjustment. There are many ways that this can be accomplished. Funeral eulogies or homilies can review the life of the deceased. Prayers, readings, or music can be selected for their special relevance to the deceased. Opportunities can be developed that will allow mourners acts that will express remembrance or affection. For example, in a child's funeral, mourners were invited to place items in the child's casket that represented aspects of that child's life. Montages of photographs, displays of awards, 'creations,' or trophies can all be ways that a funeral ritual is personalized.

Along with personalization, participation has also been identified as a factor in rituals that facilitate grief adjustment [7]. Participation allows symbolic mastery, often so important in the chaos that loss brings. Participation in planning is encouraged when rituals are personalized. But other types of participation can also be encouraged. Participants in rituals may select to read, speak, play music or even sing. They may serve as casket bearers or in other roles. Even children can participate. One widow shared that the most significant part of the funeral to her was when she saw her great-grandson handing out flowers at graveside. This act gave her a comforting sense of continuity.

Participation and personalization not only can enhance funeral rituals but other death rituals as well. Post-funeral rituals have largely disappeared from many religious traditions. This is problematic for three reasons. First, they can be critical in educating both the bereaved and others that grief is a long, time consuming process. For example, in the Orthodox Jewish tradition there are a series of rituals, occurring over a year, that symbolically mark phases in mourning (see Chapter 3). Underlying such rituals, is an expectation that healing is a slow process and that communal support is essential. In other traditions though, the absence of ritual beyond the funeral may suggest to the bereaved and their community that they should quietly resume their lives and resolve loss.

Secondly, post death rituals allow the bereaved continued public opportunity to express grief. The problem with funeral rituals is that they offer no opportunity beyond the initial time after the death to publicly express emotion, receive support, and act out therapeutically. Post-death rituals provide such opportunity.

Finally, the little research available suggests that post-death rituals can have a significant role in facilitating grief adjustments.

Yoder, for example, emphasized the significance of the funeral meal [14]. Bolton and Camp [16] found that post-funeral rituals such as sending acknowledgments, disposing of personal effects, and visits to the grave site, had even more effect on grief adjustment than funeral rites.

Most religious traditions have opportunities to structure such rituals. Masses of remembrance, services on Memorial Day or All Saints Day can provide bereaved with special times to commemorate the deceased.

Clinicians should also utilize the religious traditions and rituals in designing therapeutic rituals. Therapeutic rituals are individually-designed interventions that seek to assist the bereaved in resolving grief. Often religious ceremonies and acts can be well utilized in designing such interventions. For example, an eight-year-old boy had considerable guilt over the fact that he never told a deceased uncle how much he loved him. The counselor decided that the child needed some kind of formal, ritualized, public way to express that emotion. Both the counselor and the child designed a ritual where the child saved money and dedicated flowers in church in loving memory of his uncle. After the service he laid the flowers on his uncle's grave, expressing his love.

In summary then, ritual can be therapeutic interventions in resolving grief. But that role can be enhanced when they are participatory, personalized, and allow bereaved continued opportunity to mark phases in their own grief journeys.

BELIEFS AND BEREAVEMENT

Spiritual and religious beliefs may also have significant influence on the course of bereavement. To Worden the process of bereavement involves the completion of four basic tasks [16]:

1. To accept the reality of death;
2. To experience the pain of grief;
3. To adjust to an environment in which the deceased is missing;
4. To emotionally relocate the deceased and move on with life.

Rituals, of course, can facilitate the completion of these tasks. Rituals often provide opportunity both to encounter the reality of death and express and expiate emotion.

But spiritual belief systems may also influence the resolution of these tasks. This is particularly true of the second and fourth tasks. "Experiencing the pain of grief" means that survivors need to express and work through varied emotions that accompany grief. Often these may have spiritual overtones and/or perhaps spiritual solutions.

For example, one common emotion that survivors often experience is guilt. And guilt often may have a religious or spiritual component. Miles and Demi speak of moral guilt as one manifestation of guilt experience in bereavement [17]. In moral guilt, survivors often feel morally responsible for the death. Some bereaved parents, for instance, may believe that they are morally responsible for their child's death, that their child's death is a result of their own inadequacies or sins.

While such spiritual themes may be a factor in varied emotional responses to loss, spiritual beliefs may also provide effective ways to resolve such emotions. Survivors, for example, may often feel guilty over aspects of their relationship with the deceased. Every religious or philosophical tradition deals with themes of forgiveness. Clinicians then can draw upon these beliefs and acts in assisting clients in working through their guilt.

There may also be cases in which the bereaved's religious and spiritual views may impede emotional expression. Here bereaved persons may feel constrained by their beliefs in expressing certain emotions or in expressing emotion at all. In the former case, the bereaved may feel that certain emotions are unacceptable. For example, in one case, a bereaved mother felt considerable relief over the loss of her child after a long terminal illness. She had a difficult time acknowledging such emotion since she felt guilty over the feeling and fearful that its expression might result in further divine retribution. In the latter case, the experience of grief itself may be denied. In such cases the bereaved may feel that the very expression of grief denies the validity of their faith. The bereaved may believe that any expression of sadness belies belief in the promises of their beliefs, such as the belief in an afterlife. In both situations, counselors must be careful not to challenge that faith but to assist the bereaved in exploring ways that they can express feelings within the context of their own religious tradition.

Religious and spiritual themes may also intertwine with the fourth task, "emotionally relocating the deceased and moving on with life." This task really involves a series of complex acts, for it entails both that the bereaved determine how they wish to remember the deceased as well as how they will resume their own lives. Much as the dying person has needs to die an appropriate death, find meaning in life, and find hope beyond the grave, the bereaved survivors have to struggle with these issues as well. They may need to interpret the death, validate the deceased's life and their role in that life, and maintain a perspective that allows them a sense of the continuance of the deceased, perhaps in an afterlife, alternate mode of existence, memory, or in the life of the community.

Here, too, spiritual beliefs and rituals may have a role in resolving this task. Often rituals, particularly post-death rituals, can provide excellent vehicles for both saying goodbye and sustaining memories. Belief systems may also provide interpretations of the deceased's presence. For example, beliefs about an afterlife can offer reassurance to survivors that the deceased is cared for, allowing survivors a sense of freedom to continue their own lives. There may be another side to this too. Fears related to an afterlife may inhibit a survivor's ability to withdraw emotional energy from the deceased. Here concerns about the ultimate fate of the deceased may inhibit the resolution of grief. Other belief systems may provide different, perhaps equally reassuring and problematic interpretations. For example, beliefs that a person may live on in memory may be very reassuring to some. Others, however, may view this as very fragile. Thus, although one father started a scholarship fund for his late son, he often expressed the fear that in the future his son would simply be "a meaningless name on some award."

Relocating the deceased may mean that survivors find ways to *creatively retain a relationship with the deceased*. It is neither unusual nor problematic that one way of resolving loss can be a form of creative retention. In creative retention, the bereaved decides, in some way or another, to keep the memory of the deceased alive, and to organize at least part of his or her life in such a way to retain that memory and relationship. This need not be unhealthy, provided it recognizes the reality of the loss, allows for continued individual growth, and does not inhibit the development of new relationships. Examples of creative retention may be found in bereaved parents who spend significant time in organizations such as Compassionate Friends. In these cases, these parents often dedicate themselves in assisting other newly bereaved parents resolve loss. Coretta King, who dedicated her life to preserving both the memory and ideals of her late husband, would be another example of creative retention. Often in this response, religious and spiritual beliefs may play a large role. For the very act of creative retention has a transcendental and sacrificial quality that the bereaved need both to explore and understand.

One may also speak of a fifth task in bereavement. This would be *to rebuild faith and philosophical systems that are challenged by loss.* Often significant losses bring on a crisis of faith. All one's beliefs about the nature and fairness of the universe, the existence of a higher power, or even the very nature of God, may be challenged by that loss. C. S. Lewis, in *A Grief Observed* captures this spiritual crisis well [18, pp. 4-5]:

Meanwhile, where is God? . . . But go to Him when your help is desperate, when all other help is vain, and what do you find? A door slammed in your face. . . .

Not that I am (I think) in much danger of ceasing to believe in God. The real danger is of coming to believe such dreadful things about him.

Thus, bereaved persons may simultaneously struggle with two losses—the loss of the deceased and the loss of their own beliefs. In resolving grief then, both will have to be addressed.

These struggles of faith can be problematic on a number of levels. Not only can they remove a potentially significant source of comfort, these struggles can also displace energy from the resolution of grief. And they may separate the bereaved from both rituals and community of faith that can possibly provide solace and support.

Counselors, in taking a history of a bereaved person, may wish to ascertain any changes in religious beliefs and behaviors since the illness and death, and explore any faith struggles, Works such as C. S. Lewis *A Grief Observed* [18] or Kushner's *When Bad Things Happen to Good People* [19] can be valued resources, as are empathic clergy.

CONCLUSION

It is clear that persons counseling the bereaved will need to be well aware of both the spiritual issues that arise in the bereavement process as well as rituals and beliefs that may influence the process. In taking histories of the bereaved, counselors should ask about client's religious and spiritual affiliations, beliefs, practices, and rituals. In addition to providing counselors with useful information that may later be explored, such questions also communicate to the bereaved the counselor's openness to discuss such concerns. Naturally, in every action, the counselor needs to communicate respect for those values and traditions.

In exploring a client's religious and spiritual system, counselors need to be aware that there is often a discrepancy between the theologies and practices of denominations and their members [20]. Perhaps even more important than the actual beliefs, or even religiosity of a given individual, is the certainty of their belief and the faith themes around which people organize beliefs. While the latter is unresearched, it is well worthwhile to explore the underlying themes of a client's belief system. For example, one client may emphasize themes of human imperfection and forgiveness while others organize beliefs around themes such as righteous behavior or judgment.

Throughout this exploration, counselors can assess with clients both the importance of their belief system and its role in the bereavement process; that is, in what ways it facilitates and in what ways it impedes grief. This latter question has to be handled respectfully and sensitively. For example, dysfunctional beliefs should not be belittled or dismissed; rather, clients should be encouraged to find alternate interpretations within their tradition. Supportive clergy, religiously-oriented books or other resources may be very helpful here. In one illustrative case, a woman was troubled that her brother's suicide damned him—a basic belief in her fundamentalist faith. Yet a sympathetic clergyman helped her recognize that even within her tradition there were opportunities for continued hope.

The client's religious resources, then, can be utilized to support the bereavement process. Beliefs may be drawn upon to facilitate grief resolution. Rituals may offer powerful, symbolic therapeutic interventions. Clergy may provide additional counsel. Congregations can offer assistance and community. The goal of counseling is first to empower clients to utilize their strengths and resources. In the intensely spiritual crisis of bereavement, neither counselors nor clients can ignore the strength of those spiritual resources.

REFERENCES

1. O. Hart, *Rituals in Psychotherapy: Transitions and Continuity,* Irvington Press, New York, 1978.
2. P. Irion, The Funeral and the Bereaved in *Acute Grief and the Funeral,* V. Pine et al. (eds.), Charles C. Thomas, Springfield, Illinois, 1976.
3. T. Rando, *Dying and Death: Clinical Interventions for Caregivers,* Research Press, Champagne, Illinois, 1984.
4. O. Hart, *Coping with Loss: The Therapeutic Use of Leave-Taking Rituals,* Irvington Press, New York, 1988.
5. C. Bolton and D. Comp, Funeral Rituals and the Facilitation of Grief Work, *Omega, 17,* pp. 343-348, 1987.
6. J. Cook, Children's Funerals and Their Effect on Familial Grief Adjustment, *National Reporter, 4*:10, 11, 1981.
7. K. J. Doka, Expectation of Death, Participation in Funeral Arrangements, and Grief Adjustment, *Omega, 15,* pp. 119-130, 1984.
8. R. Duvall, The Effect of the Presence or the Absence of a Physical Memorial Site and Other Variables Upon the Intensity of a Widow's Grief, *National Reporter, 6*:5, 6, 1983.
9. D. Ferrell, Implications of Cremation for Grief Adjustment, *National Reporter, 6*:7, 1983.

10. D. Huan, Perceptions of the Bereaved, Clergy and Funeral Directors Concerning Bereavement, *National Reporter, 3*:7, 8, 1980.
11. M. Lieberman and L. Borman, Widows View the Helpfulness of the Funeral Service, *National Reporter, 5*:2, 1982.
12. E. Swanson and T. Bennett, Degree of Closeness: Does It Affect the Bereaved's Attitudes Toward Selected Funeral Practices?, *Omega, 13*, pp. 43-50, 1982.
13. R. Winn, Perceptions of the Funeral Service and Post Bereavement Adjustment in Widowed Individuals, *National Reporter, 5*:1, 1982.
14. L. Yoder, The Funeral Meal: A Significant Funerary Ritual, *Journal of Religion and Health, 25*, pp. 149-160, 1986.
15. M. S. Johnson-Arbor, The Effect of Bereavement on the Elderly, *National Reporter, 4*:1, 1981.
16. W. Worden, *Grief Counseling and Grief Therapy* 2nd Edition, Springer, New York, 1991.
17. M. Miles and A. Demi, Toward the Development of a Theory of Bereavement Guilt: Sources of Guilt in Bereaved Parents, *Omega, 14*, pp. 299-314, 1984.
18. C. S. Lewis, *A Grief Observed*, Seabury Press, New York, 1961.
19. H. Kushner, *When Bad Things Happen to Good People*, Avon, New York, 1981.
20. M. Strommen, M. Brekka, R. Underwager, and A. Johnson, *A Study of Generations*, Aubsberg, Minneapolis, Minnesota, 1972.
21. R. Fulton and G. Geis, Death and Social Values, in *Death and Identity*, R. Fulton (ed.), Wiley, New York, 1976.

CHAPTER 15

Bereavement and the
Sacred Art of Spiritual Care

Alice Cullinan

INTRODUCTION

Over two-thirds of Americans believe in a personal God who cares for, helps, and/or judges people [1]. The faith belief system of any of these believers can suffer considerable disruption when a significant loss occurs. Should persons with spiritual pain arising out of grief seek solace only from clergy or the churches, especially when they may not always be the best source of support? Many priests, ministers, and rabbis are not trained in bereavement counseling and are not able to cope therapeutically with grief and trauma. A common problem can be the conviction of some that faith keeps one immune from the pain of grieving and that strong faith alone is necessary and sufficient to handle loss. They do not realize that grieving is not a symptom of weakness or lack of faith, but a very human, normal—if painful—response. Consequently, men and women with existential questions, shattered faith belief systems, and heavy emotional burdens are reticent to raise their conflicted issues with clergy.

The grief-stricken ordinarily find it very difficult to speak their needs clearly. They have not only pain; they simply are an empty ache, and it can seem like nothing can help. As they cry out for security and look for comfort in a God who can bring life out of death, questions arise: "Why did God allow it?"; "What did I do to deserve this?"; "Is God punishing me?"; "How can a loving God allow such a senseless death?"; "How will I go on: I'm not sure any more there is a God or a heaven"; or "Why can't the Church help me?" An even more basic question can be: "Who is in control?" Many people have been taught that God is all-powerful, and so often the Deity is blamed for the death of a loved one. Clergy can find it hard to listen to and accept these human reactions when they are not aware of the dimensions of the grief process.

Bereavement is a universal life experience affecting one in his or her totality. The spiritual dimensions of one's being become affected as ultimate concerns and questions about life and death surface. Effective ministering to this spiritual suffering and the existential *angst* of the traumatized and broken-hearted does not have to be necessarily done only by pastorally-trained clergy persons. Mental health professionals can also be therapeutic bridges between despair and spiritual hope, providing safe environments, secure relationships, and compassionate spiritual care through which shattered spirituality and muddled meaning can be transformed into a more authentic, integrated, and renewed life.

WHAT IS SPIRITUAL CARE?

Is it the simple extension of a loving hand to prevent a grieving person from being separated from those things which make life worth living? [2]; or does it derive from the acknowledgment of the uniqueness of each individual (a condition frequently ignored by the medical profession)? [3]. Mount has cautioned that if spirituality is not defined, it will be understood as "watered-down humanistic psychodynamic pablum" [4]. Holland wrote that spiritual caregiving was an act transcending both personalities and professional turf [5], while Vaillot demonstrated the importance of the relationship between a caregiver and a grieving person in emotional pain in sustaining the presence of hope [6]. The answer can encompass an amalgam from each of the above: all of which assume the reaching out by a caregiver in a sacred act of ministering.

SPIRITUAL DIMENSIONS OF
COUNSELING THE BEREAVED

In defining spiritual *concerns,* the 1971 White House Council on Aging combined psychosocial considerations with those of the spiritual domain and defined them as "the human need to deal with socio-cultural deprivations, anxieties and fears, death and dying, personality integration, self-image, personal dignity, social alienation and philosophy of life" [7]. In contradistinction, spiritual *needs* were depicted as "factors necessary to establish and maintain a relationship with God, or some transcendental reality, however that reality is defined by the individual," whereas spiritual well-being was portrayed as "the affirmation of life in a relationship with God, self, community, and environment that nurtures and celebrates wholeness [7]. Highfield and Cason captured elements of both approaches when they showed that the spiritual dimension addressed the need to find satisfactory answers to ultimate questions about the meaning of life, illness, and death, and was concerned with deep relationships with self, others, and God [8].

Both the bereaved and mental health professionals have many ways of understanding spirituality within the counseling process. When seen largely in terms of pathology, a real danger exists of introducing a pathological skew into interpretations of the normal behavior of bereaved persons after a loss. Armed with psychosocial theories, *religiosity* can be viewed as a symptom calling for *enlightened* interpretation and resolution, rather than as a direct, cogent statement of a worldview or as a mature attitude toward suffering. While some bereaved people will use faith belief systems to block or deny their authentic feelings, most interweave spiritual, cognitive and emotional reactions. Spirituality can be treated as wholly sacred, not open to significant scrutiny. The spiritual and the emotional are thus (incorrectly) believed to be two separate, distinct areas within the person which do not impact on each other. A third strategy, which makes spirituality the centerpiece of the treatment process, sees God's holy will as causing all events, and faith demanding full acceptance and surrender to that will. This can lead to the belief that having faith means that one does not grieve, a way of thinking which can lead to a complicated grief process [8]. A fourth way and one which can be the most useful, sees spirituality affected by the course of individual development, available cultural modes of expression, shaded by one's personal and public prayer, and framed by the tenets of any denominational membership [9]. This adaptive type of psycho-spiritual approach can focus on a coming to new meanings of life under the influence of loss and draw upon philosophical and religious, as well as psychological resources. The counselor using this approach can respect the uniqueness of the formulation and expression of important life meanings by the bereaved [10]. Other approaches hold that there are spiritual dimensions to human experience, thinking, willing, freedom, and self determination, and in commitment of oneself to a goal. Spiritual meaning can also be found in music, art, and literature.

It is important for counselors to recognize these approaches within themselves and within the bereaved when they occur, and to respond appropriately to the pain and potential for growth in each.

SPIRITUAL CARE WORK GROUP OF THE INTERNATIONAL WORK GROUP ON DEATH, DYING, AND BEREAVEMENT

The International Work Group on Death, Dying, and Bereavement (see Chapter 2) issued a consensus statement with principles that can be helpful for counselors. The group wrote that spirituality was concerned with the transcendental, inspirational, and existential ways of being human and of living one's life. Caregivers working with the bereaved were urged to be sensitive to the interrelationship of mental, emotional and physical responses of the spiritually-oriented bereaved who will want to give spiritual questions time and attention. A person's spiritual nature was seen revealing itself in widely differing religious and philosophical beliefs and practices depending upon race, sex, class, spirituality, ethnic heritage and prior experience. No single approach to spiritual care, therefore, was deemed satisfactory for all, and many kinds of resources were considered appropriate. Spirituality was viewed as being expressed and enhanced in a broad range of opportunities for expressing and enhancing one's Relationship the Divine: formal and informal, in religious and secular symbols, rituals, practices, patterns and gestures, art forms, prayers and meditation.

Individuals and their families were recognized as having divergent spiritual insights and beliefs which they might not be aware of, so that caregivers were cautioned to be aware of spiritual differences within a family or close relationship and to be alert to any difficulties which might ensue. Caregivers were urged to be alert to the varying spiritual concerns that could be expressed directly or indirectly during different phases of grieving.

Because professionals can erroneously presume they understand the spiritual needs of the bereaved, they were cautioned to thoughtfully review the spiritual assumptions, beliefs, practices, experiences, goals and perceived individual needs of survivors and to be sensitive to unexpressed spiritual issues. Finally, the Work Group believed that much healing and spiritual growth could occur in a person without assistance and that many grieving people did not desire or need professional assistance in their spiritual development.

THE SACRED ART OF SPIRITUAL CARE

Personal Preparation of the Counselor

To appropriately address the spiritual concerns of grieving persons, the clinician (whether clergy or mental health professional) must be in touch with and address his or her own spiritual and existential issues. The counselor must be aware of the interface between one's personal conceptions of dying and death and experiences of death and loss. This time-consuming, ongoing process must be frequently attended to and is never completed. Research has demonstrated that when the care-taker's own grief is unresolved, he or she is not able to effectively minister to the bereaved [11]. Factors such as one's personal loss experience, constructs about death, family background, the institu-tional policies in the place of work, the people associated with, and most importantly, the personal value systems developed, must be examined and acknowledged. The caretaker must be comfortable with the concept of a spirituality before he or she attempts to meet spiritual needs of others. Some caregivers have, like the bereaved, various belief systems or religious backgrounds and insights, or may be uncom-fortable with spiritual matters. They may need to make appropriate referrals when the demand for spiritual care exceeds their abilities or resources.

Unresolved spiritual and psychological issues can emerge as one works with the bereaved, and they will need to be dealt with. Because ongoing involvement with grieving persons can cause a severe drain of energy, it is essential that the caregiver have a strong support system, lest burnout occur.

Professional Preparation

After coming to terms with his or her personal constructs and feelings about spirituality, death, and loss, the clergyperson or mental health professional should learn how religiousness and the meaning and value of religious faith functions within the cognitive and emo-tional makeup of the particular client [12]. This presupposes a willing-ness to learn about the nature of the various religious denominations likely to be found in this country. The clinician must be experienced in the technique of debriefing, which is now being more widely used in grief and trauma counseling [11]. Intimate knowledge of the grief process must be possessed. This knowledge is not commonly taught in schools of higher education and can be obtained through personal study and through participation in organizations such as the Association for Death Education and Counseling and the Foundation of Thanatology [13]. Even rarer than reference to the spiritual dimensions within higher education is mention within healthcare settings. However, the counselor must have this knowledge and training if the bereaved per-son is to feel comforted and supported in his or her spiritual pain and helped along the road to healing. Finally, counseling techniques of particular usefulness to bereaved persons must be learned, utilized and honed with careful and regular supervision.

Assessing Spiritual Needs of the Bereaved

Accurate assessment of spiritual needs prior to and during interventions can radically enrich the care of the whole person and thus facilitate healing. Spiritual concerns, which are often camouflaged beneath an array of behaviors and actions, can be discovered through a careful assessment that requires particular skills of observation, listening and intuitiveness on the part of the helper. Signs and symptoms of a spiritual need are seldom clear. However, listening to and observing what the bereaved person is really saying or not saying and attending to such variables as affect, attitude, behavior, and significant relationships will yield clues that can be followed up. An example is the young widowed woman who asked her counselor if there was any reason for her to go on living. Although on the surface, this might have seemed like suicidal ideation, closer inquiry found it to be a seeking for help in finding new meaning in life. Survivor's religious and cultural backgrounds should be discerned as well as where the prior meaning and purpose in life was centered. Spiritual distress related to a need for new meaning and purpose may be indicated by fears, feelings of uselessness, meaninglessness, or hopelessness expressed as loneliness and a sense of abandonment. This usually occurs after the initial crisis is over. The bereaved may seek advice or support for their decisions in a frantic way, look for spiritual assistance, or may rebel and be reluctant to participate in any spiritual rituals. They may display rage towards religious representatives and God, may verbalize inner conflict about prior beliefs, and question the credibility of any spirituality or relationship with God—whose compassion can be called into question. "If He really loved me, He would not have allowed this to happen to me"; "I feel God has abandoned me and I feel like my prayers don't reach past the ceiling"; "I feel no connectedness with God or any of the church people." The loss can be seen as punishment from God for deeds done or undone and clients may discontinue religious participation. This sense of disturbance in relationship to God and spirituality can be accompanied by an ambivalence over an expressed desire to feel close to and/or find comfort in spiritual rituals versus a felt alienation from everyone, even God. Self-pity, depression, insecurity, desperation, fear, apathy, withdrawal, depression, anxiety, a sense of exhaustion, and in extreme cases, engagement in self-destructive behavior are also indications that the client needs love and spiritual care from oneself, other people, and God. The expressions of this need go hand-in-hand with the necessity for new meaning and purpose in life—the search for which can become intense. Once new meaning begins to be established, the healing process has begun.

The need for forgiveness may be reflected by bitterness which is directed toward oneself, the lost loved one, family, friends, or God. The client may belittle him or herself or project blame for various events surrounding the bereavement onto others, often health professionals. Clients often express a wish to undo, redo, or relive the past—"If only I had the time back, I never would have . . . ," "I never should have let him ride his bicycle in the rain. . . ." Shame, regret, guilt, and sinfulness may be openly expressed or be accompanied by doubt that God could ever accept him or her. Survivor guilt can hinder the resolution of grief as it inhibits the bereaved person from meeting his or her needs. Self-punitive, haunting, and associated with a great deal of pain, guilt is extremely difficult to identify. With each of these feelings and thoughts, there can be sleep disturbances, psychosomatic complaints, anxiety, depression, and a temporary deterioration of short-term memory. These indicators can point to a spiritual need which can then be explored with the bereaved with skillful comfort and support.

Specific Techniques of Counseling

The counselor of the bereaved should reach out to the bereaved and not wait for the mourner to make the first contact. Home visits are very appropriate and effective. The caregiver should be actively supportive, reassuring that the often new and frightening emotions and thoughts experienced are typical. He or she should be consistently available for crisis intervention with the bereaved in the months following the loss. Catharsis should be encouraged, permission given to mourn, and skills to cope with the pain gradually taught. These skills include cognitive and behavioral strategies, including relaxation techniques, and learning how to seek out caring relationships. Support and guidance should be given as questions related to death and faith are explored. The bereaved can be invited to share whether they feel comforted or abandoned by their faith; what meaning or value they find in their religion or philosophy of life at any given time during the grief process; whether death for them means eternal life or the final end; whether the cause of death is perceived to be from divine or natural causes; what relationships are found between death, faith and meaning; and what messages they give themselves regarding the expression or repression of grief as related to their faith. Compassionately approaching mourners as fellow human beings and seeking to understand how their faith impacts on their experience with grief would seem to be much better than either one without the other. Early in the counseling process, the client should be encouraged to communicate how he or she first learned of the death and the circumstances surrounding it. The experience with the funeral and how it aided in the expression or repression of the grief should also be related. This *de-briefing* can help alleviate any traumatization and facilitate the grieving process immensely. Because there are no standing orders for spiritual care, no two helpers can be equally comfortable and prepared to meet spiritual needs. However, the counselor who is in touch with his or her own death constructs, who can be supportive, empathetic and a listener, who is knowledgeable in the theories and manifestations of normal and complicated grief, who is comfortable with spirituality in others, and who is able to cope with the emotional demands of bereavement counseling can be an effective therapist to the bereaved with spiritual concerns.

Long-Term Support

Although in our society and religious organizations much support is given at the time of a loss, too often the spiritual needs of the bereaved are neglected in the time following the bereavement. Long-term support is the most important critical element in ministry to the bereaved. The counselor must be able to maintain a long-term relationship if necessary, and recognize and affirm the on-going and ever-evolving spiritual journey of the grieving person. Grief is a long process and even though on the outside persons may seem to be adjusting well, inside the loss can be raw and new. It takes a long time to internalize death's reality and to integrate the changes that the loss brings.

The structure of the year itself prolongs grief because we are creatures who live in time. As the days, weeks, holidays, birthdays, and anniversaries pass, they become inexplicably associated with those we love. Death can crowd the family calendar with new and bleak anniversaries: the day of death, of diagnosis, of the accident, etc. Even weekdays can assume a new significance: if Tuesday was the day of death, every Tuesday can stand as a stark reminder. The nature of the grief process also prolongs mourning. A certain numbness or anesthesia initially cushions the blow. This wears off slowly over weeks and months. Thus the second Christmas may be the one that feels the most empty because the loss is starker and more concrete. Time alone has little power to heal the wounds left by death because grief is a process that must be worked through actively. Survivors face the task of internalizing the awful reality, of accepting the loss, and of developing a sense of self no longer defined by the interrupted relationship. The re-organization of self and of one's life that must occur for healing to transpire imperceptibly takes place along with the pain. Grief is experienced like waves that appear to come and go at will and with varying intensity. The grief process is often quite lengthy. When complicated by such factors as unsettled law suits, unresolved trauma, poor social support, little or no spiritual care, lack of time to grieve (as in the case of a widow with young children she believes she must constantly care for), this grieving can be blocked for years. At times, psychotropic medication may be needed for a short period so that severe depression can be ameliorated sufficiently for the grief process to proceed.

Role of Spirituality in the Bereavement Process

Having faith during the period of grief can add hope, comfort, strength, inner resources, and support to help through the pain of sudden or anticipated losses. Sorrow can have a refining influence on the soul, help an individual put priorities in their proper perspective, clarify values and be the occasion for growth and a finding of new meaning. The individual with a deep, abiding faith, however defined, may emerge from the experience stronger and is usually motivated to reach out to others going through similar tragedies.

Faith alone rarely gives full-enduring comfort in the face of the reality of the loss. For many, the solace they hoped to find in their religious tradition is not there. Doubts that might have been intellectual before became existential for some. For others, the simple faith they knew before matures when challenged by the tragedy of the death. Although former ways of relating to God often no longer *work*, new spiritualities, new meanings of who *God is for me*, can develop. These transformed belief systems and spirituality can give a rational and richer reason for living in a universe that can be irrational and full of pain. Openness to this possibility and reality of transformation can help strengthen the vitality of the response to catastrophe and loss.

However, having a prior spirituality can also find one suffering guilt and despair, or having feelings of being abandoned. Faith can be a constantly shifting source of strength or a cold comfort for the harsh reality of death [12]. A life-shattering loss can irrevocably shake one's beliefs about God, religion, one's sense of worth, and/or about the meaning of life. When this occurs and persists for years, it can be a sign of clinical depression and indicate the need for intensive psychotherapy.

One's Own Dying

Two major questions can face humans regarding dying: 1) "What happens to a person after death?" 2) "How can a person live without overwhelming anxiety in the face of the certainty of death?" [14]. Organized religion, while providing an answer to the first question, has responded with varying degrees of success to the second. The more that theological or sacred doctrines prevail within a family or society, the less death constitutes an important challenge to one's conceptions of self. The individual comes to regard his demise as natural and ordained, and the shock of death is assuaged through the promise of a renewed or continued existence. Spirituality provides just one approach to the questions of ultimate destination and existential anxiety and research has demonstrated that religious persons have no less anxiety about their death and dying than non-believing ones. However, persons without religious faith do appear to suffer more at the time of bereavement. As a rule they do not perceive that they are getting the support they need in times of grief, and they suffer from a high degree of pathological grief [15].

CONCLUSION

Most bereaved people can benefit from the assistance of caregivers who accept and understand a spiritual dimension and who can aid them in the journey toward recovery and growth that can be the legacy of resolved mourning. Although the process is long and arduous, it can be made measurably easier with the support of caregivers who not only value spirituality, but who have the counseling skills, openness to and knowledge about grief, fortitude to *be there for you* over the prolonged time of bereavement, and who have the inner attitudes that equip them to successfully *comfort the brokenhearted.*

A great need exists today for both clergy and secular clinicians to become more sensitive to the spiritual (as well as purely psychological) needs of the bereaved, to become aware of their own death attitudes, and to obtain adequate training to do effective grief counseling. The pain of grief is the greatest of all emotional pain. As members of the human family, we are obliged to help one another with it.

REFERENCES

1. J. Becker, We Believe We're Going to Heaven, *USA Weekend,* December 19-21, 1986.
2. N. Cousins, *The Anatomy of An Illness,* Norton, New York, 1979.
3. E. Cassell, The Nature of Suffering and the Goals of Medicine, *New England Journal of Medicine, 306,* pp. 639-645, 1982.
4. B. Mount, Reflections on Hospice, address presented at the Convention of the National Hospice Organization, Washington, D.C., 1982.

5. E. Holland, The Art of Hospice Spiritual Care, *Quality of Care for the Terminally Ill*, Joint Commission on Accreditation of Hospitals, Chicago, 1985.
6. M. D. Vaillot, Hope: An Invitation to Live, *American Journal of Nursing*, 70, pp. 268-275, 1986.
7. J. Ellerhorhost-Ryan, Selecting an Instrument to Measure Spiritual Distress, *Oncology Nursing Forum*, 12:2, pp. 93-99, 1985.
8. M. F. Highfield and C. Cason, Spiritual Needs of Patients: Are They Recognized?, *Cancer Nursing*, 6:(3), pp. 187-192, 1983.
9. A. D. Wolfett, *Death and Grief: A Guide for Clergy*, Accelerated Development, Inc., Muncie, Indiana.
10. D. Barnard, Illness as a Crisis of Meaning: Psychospiritual Agendas in Health Care, *Pastoral Psychology*, 33, pp. 74-82, 1984.
11. A. Cullinan, Teacher's Death Anxiety, Ability to Cope with Death, and Perceived Ability to Aid Bereaved Students, *Death Studies*, 14, pp. 147-160, 1990.
12. B. Raphael, *The Anatomy of Bereavement*, Basic Books, New York, 1985.
13. R. Dunlop, Training Bereavement Therapists, *Death Education*, 4, pp. 165-178, 1980.
14. R. J. Lifton and E. Olson, *Living and Dying*, Praeger, New York, 1974.
15. D. Kalekin-Fishman and A. Klingman, Bereavement and Mourning in Nonreligious Kibbutzim, *Death Studies*, 12, pp. 253-370, 1988.

CHAPTER 16

Rituals, Beliefs, and Grief

Howard C. Raether

For many years clergypersons and funeral directors believed that, for most, the funeral was primary theological-oriented religious ceremony. Paul E. Irion was one of the first clergymen to write and speak of the funeral as having more than simply theological value. In *The Funeral and the Mourner,* Irion suggested that the funeral could be an experience of value as it helped to meet other needs of those who mourn [1]. Increased interest in dying, death, and bereavement brought the psychological and sociological needs of the bereaved to the forefront. In his paper, "Changing Patterns of Ritual Response to Death," Irion recognizes the contributions of these disciplines [2]:

> The new funeral orders manifest an integrated, more comprehensive understanding of the function of ritual. This sounds obvious: isn't it natural that religious groups would have an appreciation for ritual—which is so much a part of their lives throughout centuries? Probably the most influential new development which is seen can be described as increased pastoral sensitivity based on psychology and sociology, as well as being theologically motivated.

Then too, as George LaMore, Jr. writes, "The word religion comes from the very instructive Latin root words meaning *perceiving how all of life is connected together.*" Such "life connection" can surface in the funeral ritual psychologically and sociologically, as well as theologically [3].

AN OVERVIEW OF POST-DEATH RITUAL
AND CEREMONY

The interweaving of psychology, sociology and theology in post-death rituals and ceremonies warrants a look at some basic definitions. Ritual is defined as "the symbolic affirmation of values by means of culturally standardized utterances and actions" and ceremony as "a given complex of rituals associated with a specific occasion" [4]. Although there is this distinction, popular usage of the words often has them as synonymous in some of the following definitions. But in each the value of ritual and ceremony is strongly affirmed.

He (man) is a being who buries his dead with ceremony [5].

I know of no people for whom the fact of death is not critical, and who have no ritual by which to deal with it [6].

Ritual is a means of communicating. We see funeral rituals as acting out—symbolic—behavior that carries certain meanings that might be more difficult to communicate in mere conversations [2].

It is our feeling that the Christian funeral can be the most significant group activity at the time of death, for it honestly faces reality, accepts deep feelings; affirms faith, and challenges life to seek its highest spiritual meaning. It is the time of ultimate relevance for seeking these purposes, and doing it, is clearly on sound psychological, social and spiritual ground [7].

Over the centuries rabbis have evolved distinctive patterns and rites which demonstrate both a respect for the dead and a deep concern for the living. Jewish laws of mourning revolve around a community structure enabling the bereaved to better confront those inevitable moments of darkness and despair [8].

Religious ritual, according to anthropologists, is one of six practices which death elicits the world over [9].

THE THERAPIES OF THE FUNERAL

As far back as the colonial period, the General Court of Massachusetts passed laws prohibiting "Extraordinary Expense at Funerals" [10]. Before and since then the alleged economic disutility of the funeral has been a recurring charge. Seldom was the *social/religious utility* of the funeral studied and evaluated publicly before Habenstein and Lamers spelled out some of the therapies of the funeral [5]. These topics included the following.

The Therapy of Direct Expression

The period of funeralization provides a setting and an occasion—sometimes a provocation—for the direct physical expression by the bereaved of the emotional surcharges generated by death.

The Therapy of Language

For the bereaved there are no silent funerals. The period of the funeral creates a climate for mourning which results in communication. Much of the language of the bereaved will be repetition often expressed in the simplest of words which helps them acknowledge what has happened. There is the exchange between those deeply affected and a stream of those less concerned. The bereaved vent their feelings and find relief in that outlet.

The Therapy of Sharing

Especially to be noted in all cultures is the manner in which the kinship group draws together to give emotional, physical, and frequently financial support to the bereaved when death occurs. . . . Equal recognition is given to the fact that visiting the bereaved is a meritorious phase of burying the dead. It is a truism that 'joy shared is joy increased, while grief shared is grief diminished.'

The Therapy of Activity

Funeralization for many persons provides routines by which they are aroused from immobility. You must be at the funeral home. You must speak to those who come to offer sympathy. You must put on your best clothes, polish your shoes, comb your hair. You cannot withdraw; you must keep busy.

While the first post-death responses may be listless, mechanical, the performance has therapeutic value because it prevents withdrawal from reality and activity, and provides an individually helpful and socially non-objectionable outlet for emotions.

The Therapy of Aesthetics

The type of funeral provided in Western culture improves aesthetic quality. It allows for ceremony with comfort, quiet, and beauty which can condition the mood of the bereaved and provide a therapy for grief and loss.

The Therapy of Viewing

To some death is so disturbing that they find it difficult to accept it as reality or to view it in its proper perspective against the whole of their lives. The healthy personality sees life wholly and steadily, accepts it for what it is and adjusts to it." Seeing is believing. The funeral reorientates the living to the dead and to death.

Viewing creates a final and corrected image of the dead, which image is likely to crowd out the images formed during the final illness and at the time of death.

The Therapy of Ceremony

Sociologists have long regarded ceremony as a powerful force in social control—in some cases a more powerful force than statutory law itself. For the bereaved the routines of ceremony in themselves represent the stability not only of the folkway but of the folk. New faces may come, old faces go, but the old order renews itself—a concept particularly important to those made insecure by death. Ceremony has the power of ennobling and glorifying. *Most funeral ceremonies represent an effort to bring death and burial within the framework of religious belief in the fact of a life hereafter, even though the nature of that life, and the relationship of the departed to it, may sometimes be vague or uncertain.* (The emphasis is that of the author.)

The Therapy of Self Denial, Suffering

The thread of guilt runs through funeral beliefs and practices of many cultures. "That which I should not have done, I did; that which I should have done, I failed to do. Therefore I am guilty of this death and must pay the penalty and make some kind of reparation to the dead. . . . Funeralization is a final summing up of accounts. It is an opportunity to say what has been left unsaid."

RITUALS AND COMPONENTS OF PRE- AND POST-DEATH ACTIVITIES INCLUDING THE FUNERAL

Up to this point this chapter has dealt with immediate post-death rites and ceremonies, including the therapies of the funeral for those who survive. Before becoming more specific as to the funeral as a *post-death* activity, it is important to point out that a growing number of persons arrange their own funeral or alternate to it *in advance of death*. This could be therapeutic to the prearranger as it provides him/her a "peace of mind." It also could be helpful to those who will be the immediate survivors, most times family members, if they are a part of or consulted as to the prearrangement. The funeral is *of* the person who has died. It is for those who survive who can benefit by the following components during the period of the funeral.

The Wake or Visitation

Wakes, funerals and burials are Cassem's first three steps beyond the grave [11]. Of these, Cassem says the wake is the most criticized if there is an open casket. Whether the casket is open or closed, the wake or visitation is one of the rituals which help to provide the previously referred to climate for mourning during which there are expressions of respect for the deceased and of condolence for the family. Family units are drawn together in an atmosphere which encourages such expression. The wake/visitation is one of the activities which re-emphasizes the social network of support [11]. Given mobile society, it is one of the first times, if not the only time, the family reassembles.

Where and when more people pay their respects during the wake/ visitation, then the funeral, participation of family or friends in an informal ceremony is becoming ritualistic. The new *Order of Christian Funerals* of the Catholic Church embraces prayer with the family before the visitation [12]. During the visitation there is either a prayer vigil or recitation of the rosary.

Despite or perhaps because of opposition of some to viewing the dead body, Cassem writes "Rituals reemphasize the reality that the deceased person is dead and gone, often by a view of the body (failure to see the dead body generally retards grieving)" [13].

> I was recently again reminded of how valuable and legitimate a funeral service can be. I accompanied a friend to the funeral of his mother. She had died of a chronic and wasting illness and I had been present at her death bed. My friend experienced a deep and profound consolation seeing his mother with the lines of suffering erased from her face and lying at peace. [C. Wahl, personal communication]

THE FUNERAL SERVICE

For a number of years the National Funeral Directors Association sponsored clergy-funeral director seminars. During these seminars, some clergypersons admitted concerns relating to the adequacy of their ministering to the survivors of a death. Some said questions would be asked during the visitation such as "Where is your God now? Here he lies dead while the reprobate down the street who never was inside any church is as healthy as the day he was born." Or, "Pastor, what happens now?"

For many of a religious faith, Habenstein and Lamers argue that ". . . When the doctrine that life persists after death is ceremoniously presented to the bereaved in moments of high suggestibility, and when it coincides with the hopes and wishes of the bereaved, then the acceptability of this belief is enhanced. The greater part of the human race finds consolation in this doctrine, and, to the extent to which ceremony increases its acceptance, another contribution to the therapy of the bereaved is indicated" [14].

Blauner adds [15]:

Its [religion's] rituals and beliefs impart to the funeral ceremonies those qualities of the sacred and the serious that help the stricken group reestablish and reintegrate itself through the collective reaffirmation of shared cultural assumptions. In all known societies it serves to reassure the individual against possible anxieties concerning destruction, nonbeing, and finitude by providing beliefs that make death meaningful, afterlife plausible, and the miseries and injustices of earthy existence endurable.

The ceremonial presentation most times consists of: Scripture reading, prayers, sermon, music, and committal service. Reference is made also to prose and poetry selections, often with laity participating. In the Catholic and some other churches, communion is celebrated as part of the funeral mass/ceremony [15].

THE COMMITTAL SERVICE

Irion in his *The Funeral and the Mourners* wrote: "The committal service provides, as nothing else . . . does so graphically, a symbolic demonstration that the kind of relationship which has existed between the mourner and the deceased is now at an end" [1].

The 1989 "Order of Christian Funerals" of the National Conference of Catholic Bishops confirmed by the Apostolic See sets forth the rite of committal as the concluding funeral rite. It is ". . . the final act of the community of faith in caring for the body of its deceased member (which) may be celebrated at the grave, tomb, or crematorium and may be used for burial at sea. Whenever possible, the rite of committal is to be celebrated at the site of committal; that is, beside the open grave or placement of interment, rather than at a cemetery chapel" [12].

There are denominations which do not agree with the positions given above. Their clergypersons "commit" the body at the church or funeral home following the funeral service or at an interment chapel at a cemetery or crematory. Many feel that this process is more symbolic than realistic and falls short of that which is best socially, psychologically and even theologically.

CHANGING RITUALS

Raether and Slater spelled out some changes in funeral rituals such as [16]:

- The humanistic funeral service as introduced by Irion almost ten years earlier for those who do not profess a specific religious belief.
- Placing of letters, pictures, shoulder patches and other items in the casket or grave.
- Music other than that taped or played on an organ.
- Witnessing the lowering of the casketed body into a receptacle or the ground and shoveling some earth thereon.
- The impact of youth and the adaptability of the funeral. There is not the same or similar service for a teenager killed on a trail bike as there is for an octogenarian.

Irion's previously referred to paper on "Changing Patterns of Ritual Response to Death" was based on a review of the new funeral rituals of the Roman Catholic Church, the United Methodist Church, The United Church of Christ, the Lutheran Church and Reform Judaism [2]. In addition to his findings that the above churches have a more integrated, comprehensive understanding of the function of ritual, he also learned of:

- The emergence of the funeral as a community function, not as a private exercise. The new funeral orders are devoid of any encouragement for strictly private services.
- The awareness of the importance of facing the reality of death with the casketed body present. Previously some faiths deemphasized attention to the body as "pagan." Also, there should be a committal of body in the presence of the mourners acknowledging that the lives of the mourners will never be the same again.

• The place of the funeral within the context of the mourning process. Focus on an extended grieving process rather than a single event, the funeral services.
• The responsiveness to the dynamics of pluralism. Rituals must be responsive to variations in religious beliefs, in communities, and within families.
• The recognition that there are ministries other than that of clergy. Mobilization of many resources in the community, religious and secular, demonstrates many ways to meet the needs of those who mourn.

CONCLUSION

Following most deaths, through rituals of the funeral, the clergy-person and the funeral director will perform a united service as they walk with the bereaved through the valley of the shadow. The need for that united service is enhanced as the new decade begins. For the recognition that the funeral ritual is an excellent way to address all needs of the bereaved—spiritual, psychological, and social.

REFERENCES

1. Paul E. Irion, *The Funeral and The Mourners*, Abingdon Press, New York, 1954.
2. Paul Irion, Changing Patterns of Ritual Response to Death, presentation before the Association for Death Education and Counselling, March 25, 1990.
3. George E. LaMore, Jr., Clergy and Funeral Directors: A Professional Partnership, in *The Funeral Directors' Practice Management Handbook*, Howard C. Raether (ed.), Prentice Hall, Englewood Cliffs, New Jersey, 1989.
4. George E. Dickenson, Cross Culture Patterns of Bereavement Behavior, in *Understanding Dying, Death, and Bereavement*, Michael R. Leming and George E. Dickenson (eds.), Holt, Rinehart, and Winston, New York, 1985.
5. Robert W. Habenstein and William M. Lamers, Sr., *Funeral Customs the World Over*, Second Revised Edition, Bulfin Printers, Inc., Milwaukee, 1974.
6. Margaret Mead, *Ritual in Social Crisis in Roots of Ritual*, James Shaughnessy (ed.), Eerdman's, Grand Rapids, Michigan, 1973.
7. Edgar N. Jackson, *The Christian Funeral—Its Meaning, Its Purpose and Its Practice*, Channel Press, New York, 1966.
8. Earl A. Grollman, Concerning Death: A Practical Guide for the Living, Beacon Press, Boston, 1974.

9. Vanderlyn R. Pine, Comparative Funeral Practice, *Practical Anthropology, 16*:2, March-April, 1969.
10. Robert W. Habenstein and William M. Lamers, Sr., *The History of American Funeral Directing,* Second Revised Edition, Bulfin Printers, Inc., Milwaukee, 1981.
11. Ned H. Cassem, The First Three Steps Beyond the Grave, in *Acute Grief and the Funeral,* Pine et al. (eds.), Charles C. Thomas, Springfield, Illinois, 1976.
12. Joint Commission of Bishops' Conference, *Order of Christian Funerals,* Catholic Book Publishing Co., New York, 1989.
13. Ned H. Cassem, Treating the Person Confronting Death, in *The Harvard Guide to Modern Psychiatry,* Armand M. Nicholi, Jr. (ed.), Belknop Press of Harvard University Press, Cambridge, Massachusetts, 1978.
14. Glenn Mosely, *Acceptance, Death and Bereavement,* Austin H. Kutscher (ed.), Springfield, Illinois, 1969.
15. Robert Blauner, Death and Social Structure, in *Psychiatry, 29*:4, November 1966.
16. Howard C. Raether and Robert C. Slater, United States: Document Profile, in *Funeral Customs the World Over,* Bulfin Printers, Inc., Milwaukee, 1974.

CHAPTER 17

Spirituality and Suicide

David Echelbarger

When death occurs, grieving friends and family exert considerable energy in trying to interpret the event in a meaningful way. Standing next to the casket, a story, attempting to comprehend a death, may be repeated dozens of times. Throughout the active grieving process this "life story" will be edited continually as additional insight is gained. Death is interruption and human beings do not like unfinished stories. It is left to the mourners to complete them.

We have heard this frequently: "Well Grandma lived to be 89 years old. She had a good long life. She loved her children. She always said she wanted to see all of her children married and when Jimmy and Sue walked down the aisle she felt her life was complete. It is time to let Grandma rest."

Even in more difficult situations where death is a severe interruption, such as the terminal illness of a young person, these stories seek to find a thread of meaning. "Bobby was only ten when he died, but he got to see Disney World, he had a loving family and he knew more love in those short years than many people will every know."

Many times we have taken this process for granted or interpreted it as the need for a person to express pain. In truth, life stories signify much more. The need to complete the unfinished portrait of a person's life is a spiritual process. This is the age-old attempt to ground the individual in the eternal. These intimate tellings are more than trying to "understand what happened to Uncle Fred." Rather they involve the griever in the question: What does this death mean in my life? This quest for meaning and comfort is spiritual even if it is not explicitly expressed in religious imagery.

When the death is a suicide this process becomes even more important, although often times it is thwarted because of swirling confusion,
guilt and self incrimination. Stories involving suicide are not easily
told. Many chose to avoid spiritual questions because they feel discon-
nected from their spiritual roots due to the widespread belief that God
condemns the suicide victim. This chapter seeks to draw the caregiver's
attention to the spiritual elements in the griever's presenting story. It
also will demonstrate how intense grief can be dealt with by addressing
the spiritual themes the mourners bring to their grief.

While it is not our primary purpose to discuss the theology of suicide
or its ethical implications; this cannot be wholly ignored since
the church and its ministers are often perceived as being judgmental
toward persons who commit suicide. More than once a family member
has responded with a surprised, "You will?," when I have agreed to
conduct a funeral for a person who has taken their life. Old attitudes
die hard.

The overt hostility of the church in previous times toward suicide
may still be perceived. The early church leaders harshly condemned it
because of the fear that scores of people willingly would seek death to
in order to enter heavenly bliss. It would seem that when idealized
portraits of heaven are presented, there is the fear that people
will storm the gates. It was thought suicide needed to be dis-
couraged through a repressive response, such as assigning the
person's soul to hell, refusing to conduct the funeral, or actually
maiming the corpse.

It can be said with confidence that most mainline denominations no
longer hold suicide as anathema. Presently the church's stand is essentially non-judgmental. Deep compassion is usually extended to the
family and most pastors will spend hours trying to assuage the fears
that a loved one is somehow outside of God's grace. Increasingly there
is the awareness that the biblical material is not specific in any consistent condemnation of suicide, whereas the predominate themes of love,
grace, and forgiveness imply care and understanding. Religious professionals are more aware of mental illness and how it can contribute to
many suicides.

Some church leaders are sensitive to the fact the church is not
adequately meeting the needs of the despairing. This also has
increased the church's sense of compassion. If suicide is understood
primarily as a means of escape from realities that are judged to be
worse than death, then perhaps the church has failed in providing
resources and spiritual strength. The fact that most mainline
denominations emphasize the importance of the present life, by seeking to live responsively and make a contribution to the world, means

that theology no longer focuses on an escape into bliss. This reduces the church's fear of actually offering an invitation to suicide.

Pastors, ministers, priests, and rabbis, therefore, can usually offer powerful support in dealing with those needing to come to terms with suicide. As always, however, before a caregiver makes a clergy referral, the minister's individual attitudes about suicide need to be determined in advance. In many cases the best way to overcome the feelings of guilt and hopelessness that are often perceived when a person has committed suicide, is through a representative of the church.

A grief practitioner working with families who have experienced loss through suicide needs to listen carefully to the family's story. This seems all too obvious, yet it is a corrective to a kind of overanalysis that completely misses where people are. The grief process is not an orderly calculus. It is complicated and each person is unique. Simply listening to the story will reveal much about the family and the path it needs to follow to healing. People suffering from shock, confusion and guilt are not interested in discussing the abstract issues relating to suicide. Neither are they able at times to reflect on their emotional response to events but they readily will share the most intimate thing they have, their story. This provides a highway into a person's spiritual dimension. Occasionally someone will ask stark questions: "Is Jim in hell because of what he did?" But oftentimes people are so fearful of the answers they cloak their fears, even from themselves, in their stories. When attended to, these very personal statements can serve as the basis for directing the grieving process. A caregiver may then work with the family at editing their story and blending it with their religious tradition. This makes for an intensely personal journey which is precisely what grief is—a creatively painful trip from one place to another.

Hearing the family story can embrace the present crisis and also address issues the family has never resolved stemming back to other painful events. Following are some major themes that flow from the stories of people struggling with suicide.

GRACE AND THE SUFFERING GOD

Once I was called by the neighbors of a woman whose husband had died of a self-inflicted gunshot wound. He had driven to an isolated place in the forest and ended his life. Ginger had just gotten word of his death. I only vaguely remembered her. She had introduced herself at a funeral I conducted by saying: "I belong to your church but you don't know me, I'm not there much." On my way to her house I recalled being told that something traumatic had happened in the past that distanced the family from church.

Ginger answered the door. She was alone in the house and very nervous. "Well I suppose you know what happened?," she said bluntly, carefully scrutinizing my response. "Mark killed himself this morning and they just found out."

When contact is made by the clergy it is important to state early on what the church is willing to do. "Ginger," I said, "I am terribly sorry about what has happened, I want you to know I want to be helpful to you in anyway you choose. If you need me to officiate at the funeral I would be glad to help in that way." I asked Ginger how she was feeling and she responded by saying she "didn't feel anything." I then asked her to tell me exactly what happened. Ginger did not know how she was feeling, but she talked for the better part of an hour. She could not grasp her emotions but she had something to say. Through her story I was able to grasp something of her emotional state and the issues that were beginning to surface.

Ginger said that several years ago her husband, Mark, had a stroke while undergoing surgery. It left him with some numbness on his left side and altered his mood. Whereas before he was kind and warm, after the stroke he was explosive. His outbursts caused him much emotional pain. He felt guilty and was deeply regretful. Just prior to taking his life, Mark learned he would have to undergo a surgical procedure to remove a tumor that was suspected to be malignant. "He was so worried about going to the hospital again," Ginger told me. "This morning he sat in that chair drinking his coffee just as always, he said he was going to the store, kissed me good-bye and drove away. I had no idea. I've had other heartaches you know, and now this."

Ginger then told in detail about a son who died at the age of eighteen from a brain aneurysm. Already she was linking the two deaths. "I don't know why this has happened. We've been good people and lived good lives." I followed up on this veiled statement and asked where she thought God was in all this. Her eyes flashed anger, "I have no idea!"

It became clear that Ginger and her husband had held God accountable for the death of their son. They saw God as a remote being who rewarded good and punished evil. They felt they had been shortchanged and therefore had resisted all efforts of the minister who attempted to do pastoral care with them after their son's death. Now she was perceiving the suicide of her husband in the same way—he was escaping his fear of hospitalization and the subsequent pain of his stroke that unfairly had been brought on by God. This spiritual attitude had left Ginger with repressed anger. She often vacillated from being hostile with others to being down and depressed.

Caregivers have the task of helping the grieving frame the death, understand its context and implications. For those families using the services of religious institutions this can take place in a public setting during a funeral sermon. Some pastors resist any personal references during a funeral. This is an opportunity missed. When a death is given a framework it opens avenues of discussion between the mourners. In a way it provides safe conversation. One can always quote the minister.

At Mark's service I made use of biblical themes that addressed the particular situation of Ginger's spiritual and emotional state. I spoke of the fact that the God many people picture as remote is not the God of the biblical materials. This God is involved in all of human life. He feels each moment of human experience which makes him the world's greatest sufferer. God goes with us in our pain and feels it just as intensely as we do. We have only to refer to the fact that God knows what it is like to lose a son and how he promised to send us the Holy Spirit, the comforter. In addition, I called upon Ginger's own story and transformed it slightly. "For many years now, Mark has been suffering. Life has declined, just the simple things that you and I take for granted have become a burden. There was the stroke, that made it difficult for him to control his moods. The very part of ourselves that we cherish the most, the ability to direct our actions and emotions, had faded for Mark. He had said that he couldn't cope with the prospects of facing still more surgery. Today we struggle to understand how illness contributed to his death."

After the service Ginger asked for a copy of the homily. During the service she heard some things about God that were new to her. She also found comfort in linking Mark's illness to his death. "It was very helpful," she told me, "the way you said his illness caused his death."

In the weeks that followed Ginger was able to address a number of spiritual issues that had been unresolved. She was grieving not only for her husband but also her son. When the spiritual dimension began to change, instead of being depressed and hostile she became openly warm and energetic. Instead of a victim of God, she was a survivor with His help. The spiritual strength that she gained was a great asset when six months later she herself was diagnosed as having cancer. Following her surgery and chemotherapy Ginger suffered a series of strokes. After an initial period of despondency she made such rapid progress through rehabilitation that she became part of the hospital's rehabilitation marketing program. Not only had Ginger become free of much inner resentment, now she was an inspiration to other patients.

This is an instance where spiritual issues formed the primary focus for a person's healing. Ginger was hostile to organized religion but that did not diminish the need for the spiritual, in fact the need increased.

By hearing her story and helping her at various points to "edit" it by linking illness to the suicide and focusing on a God who knows what it is like to suffer, she was able to improve the quality of her life. Elaborate theological reflections were not necessary, simple connections to her own inner struggle were sufficient.

GOD'S WILL

As in all deaths, questions arise regarding the will of God. The Smith family had been through much trauma. First, Barbara, the mother, had died six months earlier after a lingering illness that lasted seven years. Rick, the father, recently remarried and his six adult children seemed to approve. One week after the marriage, Rick's twenty-year-old son, George, committed suicide by purposely overdosing on drugs. While he never saw a therapist, George probably suffered from recurrent major depression. Rick's oldest sister also had similar difficulties and had herself attempted suicide several times. It became clear to the pastor working with the family, that Barbara also had long-standing psychological problems before she became ill.

This was a well-defended, codependent family which was organized around a depressed, needy mother while the father was weak and absent. When meeting with the family the pastor heard the following story: "Well, pastor we know it was God's will. God wanted to take George. He'll be better off now. He was never really happy during his life." Tears were shed but clearly the responsibility for the event was easily placed on God. Unlike Ginger, who also blamed God, the family was relaxed and comforted with its conclusion. The pastor decided to challenge the family's perception of George's death. He was worried that their easy acceptance of the death would give permission for the older sister to follow her brother's lead.

Due to some unusual circumstances, the funeral was delayed for a week. During this time the pastor worked intensely with the family. Coming from a Christian perspective, he told them that God did not cause George's death. George chose to do that himself. God was in the life business, that was why he sent Jesus that we might have life and have it abundantly. Death, in Christianity, was the enemy that Jesus came to conquer. When the family could no longer believe that George's death was God's will it was thrown into confusion. It had lost its primary denying principle: "What happens, happens." Together they began to realize the deep denial that had permeated their relationships for years. George did seem to have all of the patterns of being chronically mentally ill, so did Barbara, as a matter of fact the oldest sister might not just be depressed but also alcoholic.

This is an example of where the family's story abruptly changed in less than a week from a blithe acceptance to self-incrimination. "If only we would have done something. If we could have seen where this would have led we could have gotten some help for George. I guess he couldn't handle Mom's death or Dad's remarriage." An additional worry surfaced now that they understood God did not cause George's death, perhaps God would "damn George to hell." A day prior to the funeral the pastor spoke devotionally about God's grace and acceptance but nothing seemed to penetrate their despondency. A suicide watch was put on the oldest sister as the day for the funeral came. Once again the homily played a role in the family's recovery.

The pastor reviewed the history of the family's struggle from realizing that this was not God's will. He spoke plainly of the need to confront truths in families that we would like to ignore. The pastor also raised the issue of "what happens to George now?" He skillfully linked the biblical story to that of the family. He read a quotation from the Gospel of Luke chapter 9 verses 37-43. A boy had been throwing himself into the fire, in other words trying to kill himself. When the father learned Jesus was coming, he ran to Jesus and told of his suicidal son. Jesus said: "Bring the boy to me." This passage cut through the family's confusion like sun through fog. Jesus was saying the same words to their son, they decided—bring the boy to me. George would be cared for by God. He was not rejected, he was loved. The pastor concluded with a call for action. God aids in healing and helps families grow no matter what difficulty they encounter. Two days later the oldest sister checked herself into an alcohol treatment center. Her initial treatment was not successful, but this was a case in point where the spiritual dimension helped a family overcome pervasive denial. The family's story kept changing during the course of pastoral care and the minister took an active role in reshaping it. The result was successfully facing grief, with the bonus of restructuring a dysfunctional family system.

GUILT AND FORGIVENESS

Early in the afternoon Joyce committed suicide using carbon monoxide poisoning. Her death shocked the entire community. Her's seemed to be the ideal family. Joyce was in her early fifties, her husband Mike was respected and had a good job. Her children were settled with their families with the exception of her eighteen-year-old daughter, Mary. Joyce was extremely active in her church, a full-time volunteer. Her death was shrouded in mystery. Some people, including their minister, thought it must have been an accident, a suicide gesture that got carried away.

Joyce had driven to their cottage in the country, parked in the garage and went into the house for a pillow. She then climbed into the back seat and started the car. Curiously, she had also opened the garage window. Late that evening her body was discovered by Mike, her husband.

The autopsy revealed that she was legally intoxicated at the time of death. The conflicting message of opening the garage window was confusing, but the fact she was found in the back seat with a pillow convinced the authorities it was a suicide.

The family sought support at a local mental health agency. The counselor noted that despite the comfort they might have received, the family did not interpret the events as accidental. They were all very angry with the youngest daughter, Mary. There was much conflict in Mary and Joyce's relationship. The daughter told how on the morning her mother had committed suicide they had fought. Mary was pregnant and told her mother that she intended to keep the child. Her mother disagreed with this and a vehement argument ensued. The day following her mother's funeral, Mary had an abortion. Mary said that she did not want the abortion but felt she should go ahead with it because it was what her mother wanted. The family story was crystal clear. "If Mary hadn't gotten pregnant, this would never had happened, further Mary was supposed to meet her mother at the cottage in the afternoon and Mary never arrived. If she would have been there this would not have happened. Mom never intended to die, she was just trying to get Mary to listen."

In the weeks of therapy that followed, a different story of Mom began to emerge. "Mom always tried to run our lives. She often threatened to hurt herself if we wouldn't abide by her wishes. Once she left the gas stove on, but Dad got home just in time." The family was clearly angry at mom. They were angry that she had committed suicide, but there was more. Mom had a way of manipulating the family through guilt. Still, the family did not feel safe directing their anger at Joyce, in most respects she was a wonderful person they loved deeply. Mary served as the lightening rod which she was all too willing to do.

Spiritually, the issue of forgiveness arose on a number of fronts. The family soon realized that anger directed at Mary was unfair. Any of them could have been in her position but it was very uncomfortable to be angry at mom. The therapist helped the family define the issues that were long standing. Mom was a loving and warm person. She supported the family and was a cornerstone in the community, but on occasion she tried to force her will on the family. On such days mom withdraw into depression. Typically, the family would do what she wanted in order to rescue her. Sometimes her depression would rage out of control, especially when she drank. Suicide threats became gestures, some so serious they might have resulted in her death. It so happened that Mary's confrontation with her mother was such an occasion. Mary was supposed to discover her mother attempting to kill herself, but Mary did not arrive. The gesture became the reality.

The family worked through a process where it was okay to be angry at mom for what she had done. Only after their anger was expressed could they turn to the spiritual power of forgiveness for healing. Mary had a much more difficult time. She understood the ideas but could not believe that God could forgive her for her mother's death and her abortion. It was not safe for Mary to talk with mom's pastor, they had been too close. The counselor referred her to a priest who was skilled in twelve-step recovery programs.

The priest addressed Mary's inability to forgive herself. In effect they did a fifth step where Mary carefully detailed her "sins" to the priest while sitting in an empty church. They chose the very building where the funeral had been held months before. Mary's eyes never left the place where the casket had stood. She talked for over an hour about her failures as a daughter and the mistakes she had made. With her face tear-streaked the priest said this: "Do you believe that the word of forgiveness I speak to you comes from God himself?" "Yes," she answered weakly. "God is merciful and loving," the priest continued, "by the command of our Lord Jesus Christ, I, a called and ordained priest forgive you all your sins, in the name of the Father and the Son and the Holy Spirit. Amen."

Mary had been unable to forgive herself without a rigorous self examination. This process of personal confession brought God's healing into her life. She could then forgive herself only when she felt forgiven. In time she realized the anger she had at her mother and was able to forgive her too—completing the story and putting it to rest.

In most deaths spiritual realities are invoked as people struggle to come to terms with finality. These spiritual impulses are powerful though often camouflaged. By listening carefully to the family's story, the grieving process can be aided dramatically. The spiritual dimension comes from a person's self-understanding and the way that person feels linked with all of life. If this connection is severed, as it often is when a loved one has committed suicide, repercussions occur. The only successful way of restoring wholeness to the grievers of suicide is through addressing the ensuing spiritual crisis which often is not even fully articulated. Commonly, the crisis can only be observed between the lines of the grievers' life stories.

When a caregiver lacks confidence to engage in this process, involving clergy or counselors with backgrounds in pastoral care will be immensely helpful. Working with grief is multifaceted. A caregiver should always consider oneself as a member of a team and not responsible for the totality of a person's healing. Practitioners who readily turn to spiritual realities will find a healing presence which reaches beyond the caregiver and griever combined. It is nothing less than the touch of God mending a torn life.

CHAPTER 18

Spiritual Care of the Traumatized: A Necessary Component

Alice Cullinan

On November 26th, 1989, a school disaster in the Hudson Valley of New York State resulted in ten children dying and many others being injured. Shortly after the tragedy, while walking around the site, I heard comments such as, "They were so innocent: how could God allow this?"; "And there is supposed to be a God who cares for us?"; "God punish whoever was responsible for this!" A police lieutenant, returning from the disaster scene to his station house, said to a dispatcher: "God has seven new angels with Him today." He then fell into her arms, sobbed and cried out: "But they were so innocent—why them?" About a year after, a bereaved mother related that in the midst of all her shock and pain on learning that her 7-year-old son died in the same disaster, she was aware of having been "upheld by God" in a way she had never known before: "In the midst of my devastation, He was there all the way those first few days."

These are examples of two of the very many possible spiritual responses to trauma. Many centuries ago, there were recounted in the Hebrew Bible cries of suffering and lament addressed directly to God. These Psalms could well be prayers of the traumatized today. They include such lines as Psalm 6: "Have pity on me, Yahweh, for I am fading away. Heal me, Yahweh, my spirit is shaken to its very depths"; Psalm 9: "Have pity on me, Yahweh, see my affliction, pull me back from the gates of death. . . . Why Yahweh do you keep so distant, stay hidden in times of trouble . . . do not forget the cry of the afflicted"; Psalm 13: "How long, Yahweh will you forget me? Forever? How long will you turn away your face from me? How long must I nurse rebellion in my soul, sorrow in my heart day and night?" Psalm 22 (prayed by Jesus on the Cross as He endured the trauma which led to His death): "My God, my God, why have you forsaken me? . . . My God, I call by day, buy you do not answer, at night, but I find no respite . . . many bulls are encircling me . . . closing in on me. My strength is trickling away"; Psalm 38: "Yahweh . . . your arrows have pierced deep into me, your hand has pressed down upon me. Your indignation has left no part of me unscathed . . . I grown in distress of heart"; and Psalm 55: "My heart writhes within me, the terrors of death come upon me, fear and trembling overwhelm me, and shuddering grips me . . . I want to find a refuge from the storm of abuse, from the destructive tempest, Lord. . . . For I see violence and strife in the city" (New Jerusalem Bible).

Because trauma touches the survivor "Like an earthquake, shaking the soul to its very being" [1, p. 247], there is a critical need for caretakers of the traumatized to understand the effects of trauma on the soul and to know ways to help diminish those effects. This chapter will discuss spiritual aspects of trauma and how spiritually-oriented caretakers can help transform and heal the unique physical, psychological, cognitive, and spiritual symptoms of traumatized individuals and groups.

A DESCRIPTION OF TRAUMA

Incidents called *traumatic* or *critical* can include any crisis, disaster, or violent act producing immediate or delayed stress—altered physical, mental, emotional, psychological or social coping mechanisms for emergency personnel, survivors, family members, or bystanders [2]. Included can be aircrashes, fires, earthquakes or tornadoes, violent acts such as murders or suicides and other events involving sudden death or loss, injury, destruction and serious disruption, incest and other sexual abuse, childhood injury or the "psycho-social trauma of war" [3-6].

For one to be traumatized, it is not necessary to have been at the actual scene of the event. Learning of the vehicular homicide of a loved one and discovering the details can result in a visual imaging of the event which can parallel actually being at the scene.

Variables Affecting the Impact of Traumatic Events

Reactions to critical incidents involve the whole person: physical, emotional, cognitive, and spiritual—with response patterns being both predictable and individualistic. These responses can be influenced by the extent and severity of injuries and deaths, the number of people involved, demographic characteristics of the affected people, lack of predictability of the emergency, distress of the helpers, availability of psychological and spiritual counseling and debriefings, the quality of post-trauma environmental and social support, and the impact on the faith belief system of the victim. A higher anxiety level can occur when events threaten self-esteem because of a symbolic or actual loss of a significant other, and when there are components that can make horror personal. The more central and significant an experience or relationship affected, the more intense will be the reactions to trauma. Additional intervening factors can be the cumulative effect of the number and kind of past traumatic incidents, one's age, spiritual attitudes toward death, and strength of specific bodily, emotional and thought-coping processes.

EFFECTS OF TRAUMATIZATION

Individual and Collective

Survivors of disasters can have two related distinguishable trauma: individual and collective [6]. An traumatic blow to the individual psyche can break through one's defenses so suddenly and with such force that effective response is not possible. Deep shock suffered as a result of exposure to death and destruction can lead to a withdrawal into one's self with feelings of numbness, fear, vulnerability and aloneness; a terrifying awareness of being cut-off from others, from self and from God, or from the spiritual root of one's being.

By collective trauma is meant a "blow to the tissues of social life that damages the bonds linking people together and impairs the prevailing sense of communality" [7, p. 301]. Because collective trauma works its way slowly and even insidiously into the awareness of those who suffer from it, it does not have the quality of suddenness usually associated with the word *trauma*. It is, however, a form of shock with a developing realization that the community no longer exists as a source of nurturance and that a part of the self has disappeared. "I continue to exist, although damaged and maybe even permanently changed. 'You' continue to exist, although distant and hard to relate to. But 'we' no longer exist as a connected pair or as linked cells in a larger communal body" [7].

Physical Effects

Physical reactions to traumatization can include gastrointestinal disorders, respiratory difficulty, cardiovascular distress, and/or chronic fatigue. Sleep disorders are common and can include intrusive night-mares, recurrent dreams, disruptive or long sleep. The difficulties with memory and with concentrating which so often occur can be frightening to the victim who does not understand the normalcy of this reaction. One lacks the energy to pray, to work, to relate with others and sometimes can only just *survive.*

Psychological Effects

Victims often respond in the early phases of traumatization with psychological symptoms of disorientation, shock, confusion, apathy, and emotional lability and/or numbness. Survivors may harbor feelings of resentment toward those spared serious losses or toward caregivers or suffer self-blame with accompanying depression. Anger may be projected toward significant others, including clergy, or be introjected, becoming depression. Anxiety, irritability, depression and moodiness, numbing of affect, mental flashbacks, the developing of negative atti-tudes, chemical coping, markedly increased environmental and inter-personal vigilance, a flight into activity, increased personal cynicism or inter-personal hostility, and sexual hyperactivity or incapacity are among the symptoms that can emerge. Traditional psychological defense mechanisms such as denial, regression, reaction-formation, intellectualization, and rationalization may also be used to cope. People who prefer direct coping may act to alter the sources of stress, provide emergency interventions for others, participate in disaster debriefing, seek psychological counseling, and actively reconstruct their personal, family and social lives. However, those who tend to use indirect coping may try to alter the perceived significance of the stress or events through denial or burying oneself in activity. If adaptation or effective resistance to a trauma is not possible, unresolved distress reactions may reveal themselves physically and psychologically.

An enduring response to trauma's effects appears to be continued perception of threat in the environment. This can be accompanied by a corresponding need to remain vigilant as every new situation is seen as harboring a potential danger. The threat for the survivor is very specific and major: not only can it be a threat to competence, status, or happiness, but is also perceived as endangering the psychological sur-vival of self or loved ones. After the perceived threat is over, an exhaus-tion created by the great effort to survive often results.

Cognitive Impact of Trauma

Immediately after or even during a traumatic incident, cognitive processes become triggered so that a sense of mastery over what has occurred can be regained. The processes include: the beginning of a fear-driven search for as much information as possible about what happened; looking for a cause or reason; a repetitive, and intrusive replaying of the events surrounding the event and evaluation of one's behavior and competency in handling the situation, of any guilt experienced and a conscious decision to continue or to discontinue that role.

These processes can fuel on-going emotional over-involvement in the event's aftermath, interfere with a return to normal functioning or even lead to the development of Post-Traumatic Stress Disorder.

Spiritual Effects

Responses of traumatized victims often include spiritual dimensions. "The experience of trauma can transform the human spirit in a variety of ways, ranging from extreme diminution of the will to an existential transcendence which is spiritual in nature" [8, p. xiii]. The immediate and short-term spiritual effects of trauma can include anger at God, a disintegration of one's belief system, a frantic immersion into church activities and/or submission to what has happened as allowed by or even willed by God. Often solace is sought from clergy persons or other church workers and resentment generated if this is not forthcoming or is viewed as being inappropriate. More long-term effects can include the questioning of the overall meaning of one's life. This in turn can lead to a renewed commitment to life or to an often temporary giving up on God, self, and life itself. Occasionally, bitterness and resentment toward God becomes deeply rooted and can remain for the remainder of one's life. An example is that of an eighty-two-year-old man I recently counseled because of a deep depression. When I asked what the meaning of his life had been, he replied: "There ain't been no meaning since the crash. All that was any good in me got killed in it." He was referring to a train wreck he had witnessed fifty years previously in which several members of his closely knit town had died.

COPING WITH THE EFFECTS OF TRAUMA

To treat post-traumatic stress syndromes is to directly encounter the very harsh realities of what survivorship and victimization mean. Initial concern during and after a traumatic event should always be the preservation of life. Early emergency intervention can then embrace psychological, cognitive, and spiritual first aid. Active intervention on all four levels during a critical incident can often prevent the formation of posttraumatic stress disorder and therapeutically modulate the long-term effects of calamity for victims and emergency care providers

[2]. Sadly, the three latter components are most often deleted from emergency preparedness plains, leading to confusion, conflict between agencies and individuals, and lack of effective treatment of needs other than physical.

Effective provision of services to survivors must include pre-disaster preparedness such as the development of liaison teams comprised of emergency services personnel, mental health professionals, clergy, and volunteers who are familiar with one another, the promotion of awareness of potential stressors in relation to specific events, and provision of the opportunity for informal debriefing and counseling. Disaster intervention is very different from other pastoral or mental health work. Clergy and clinicians must aggressively establish their presence and seek out clients who may be in too much shock to seek help on their own. Victims may also believe they will be stigmatized as sick or abnormal if they admit how they feel. In providing spiritual and psychological first aid to victims and emergency responders, the clergy person and/or crisis worker should remain calm, provide information, honest reassurance and the comfort of presence.

During the actual critical incident, responders are encouraged to share factual information with one another and with survivors. This can facilitate psychological preparedness. A disaster intervention plan should address the needs of clinicians, rotating them in shifts to avoid burnout. Involved people must be informed of information within customary limits of tolerance, told the truth tempered with compassion, and given appropriate counseling, reassurance, advice and guidance. Family members should be told nothing that might promote psychopathology. An example is how details of dismemberment, decay, or other forms of extreme trauma are often omitted in the interest of mental health.

Clergy, mental health personnel and other crisis workers should not expect to take the pain away because there can be no magical amnesia. The encountering of volatile emotional reactions, such as intense bursts of ventilated grief, expressed feelings of helplessness, and possible hostility can be common. Response workers should accept the situation, tolerate the ventilation, and encourage physical and verbal support for those particularly affected. Those providing spiritual and psychological first aid should try to legitimize and normalize participants' reactions, and use coping strategies that promote resolution. Simultaneously, they should avoid endorsing destructive or dysfunctional strategies, such as emotional repression, chemical coping or denial of secondary losses. These can include loss of an element of self-concept, of the illusion of invulnerability for oneself or significant others, or loss of faith in a just world, where only good things happen to good people.

Crisis workers, including clergy, should operate on a buddy system and rotate care of difficult victims, while also monitoring one another for signs of fatigue, stress symptoms, or inappropriate conduct. Their own negative emotional responses should not compromise personal integrity, professional ethics, or humane delivery of psychological services. This presupposes a certain level of emotional maturity, an ability to tolerate inner psychic pain and awareness of the physical, psychic and spiritual pain of others, and a capacity to benefit from peer support.

The Critical Incident Stress Debriefing

"From all indications, it is clear that the initial phase of any disaster is characterized by a period of intense social disorganization. This state is somewhat generalized and pervasive, depending upon the extent of physical and social network disruption. It is during this time span that the scope of the disaster event is defined and the appropriate response mechanisms brought into play. A highly effective way of doing this is through use of the Critical Incident Stress Debriefing Process" [7].

The majority of participants in a critical incident want to talk about the event, their part in it, and the perceived spiritual and psychosocial meaning of the event. During debriefings, trained facilitators encourage participants, who should be grouped according to similar disciplines, to tell the story of what each experienced as fully as possible. After an occurrence is identified as a *critical incident,* plans to hold a debriefing should soon be made. Usually conducted within 24 to 72 hours of an incident, the debriefing should generally be done within one week for optimal effect. If large numbers of individuals are involved, debriefing begins with those most involved with the incident.

In planning debriefings, provision should be made for several factors: a) a location should be selected that is free of distractions and represents a neutral environment; i.e., school, church, or other meeting facility as opposed to crew quarters of an EMT station; b) all personnel involved in the incident should be invited and encouraged to attend. This includes, but is not limited to, fire, law enforcement, dispatch personnel, medical personnel, and clergy.

Debriefings typically have five phases in which all participants should try to share. There is first a fact phase which establishes the scene. There is self introduction of participants who then are encouraged to describe what they heard, saw, smelled and did during the incident. A feeling phase follows with a sharing of feelings at the scene, now and in past situations if applicable. The symptom phase is next, with attention paid to perceived unusual experiences at the time of and/or since the incident. Participants are encouraged to express their responses to stress. A teaching phase then follows in which the debriefing team discusses stress response syndrome and normal signs, symptoms and emotional reactions. Finally, in the re-entry phase loose ends are wrapped up, additional questions answered, final reassurances provided and subsequent plans of action are discussed. Effective coping is encouraged and regular physical activity, adequate nutrition and rest, and regular contact with one's social support network are highly encouraged. Assessment and referral may be made of those participants who may be at risk for PTSD.

When done within a safe and secure environment, a well-facilitated debriefing results in a *desensitization* of the effects of the event. Participants benefit from knowing that another human shares the story in a non-judgmental and accepting way. Though simple, the well-executed CISD has an enormous potential to alleviate overwhelming emotional feelings and potentially dangerous physical symptoms. When not done during the acute phase after a traumatic event, incident specific traumatic reminders are not as easily identifiable. With time's passage, two important psychological consequences: the contraction of ego functioning and the dulling of one's emotional life, can result in maladaptive traumatic trauma resolution and lead to PTSD [9]. The client can be left with the intrusive memories and neurological changes that can be mistaken over time as symptoms of pathological grief or evidence of an underlying personality disorder.

Post-disaster treatment can include modalities such as critical incident stress debriefing, grief counseling, brief multimodal therapy, referral to traditional therapies and follow up.

LONG-TERM EFFECTS OF TRAUMATIZATION

Many people are frightened by the intense emotional, cognitive, physical and spiritual reactions generated by trauma and grief and want to know if what they are experiencing is normal. Most times it is and persons suffering from trauma will recover without needing professional help especially if they receive timely assistance with debriefing and strong social support. At times, it will be necessary to treat the unaided survivor of traumatic loss with a psychotropic medication, along with psychotherapy.

The direction of personality change, toward pathology or toward health in persons exposed to trauma, depends not only on the nature and severity of the trauma, but also on the metaphorical significance of the event, the biological vulnerability to psychiatric illness, and the biopsychosocial context, before, during and after the trauma. As time passes, the psychological meaning of recalled trauma is subject to reorganization with changes in life circumstances and biopsychosocial and spiritual contexts. Environmental experiences have been shown to have a role in both anatomic and functional development and may lead to neurobiologic changes in the brain after psychological trauma [10]. Children and adults have been found to develop startle responses after critical incidents, suggesting that the traumatic experience can induce a long-lasting brainstem dysfunction [2, 11].

It is important to be aware of the effect that age, developmental stage and level of psychosocial development of participants in critical incidents has on symptomatology and response. For example, trauma victims of all ages report difficulty reestablishing trust after the event, but children appear to be especially vulnerable to a collapse of both basic trust and autonomy. There is a fairly consistent pattern of additional age differences in symptomatology following potentially traumatic events. An example is how adolescents have been found to become either very compliant and withdrawn, or aggressive, acting out sexually and in greater danger of abusing chemical substances [12].

Manifestations of anxiety, depression, anger, hysteria, and guilt are commonly observed in survivors of all ages [13]. Because sudden tragedy involving loved ones and especially children is so shattering, families undergo an acute psychic shock when confronted with the sudden death or threatened death of one of their family members. Initially within the family, the anxiety level heightens. This is followed by shock or denial, which seems to act as a psychological preparation for any further bad news the family may receive. Anger, which can next emerge, can take many forms, including rage, direct at first responders, medical staffs, clergy, etc., self blame or withdrawal. Ventilation of the anger must be encouraged. Guilt and/or self blame can be often followed by grief, the duration and intensity of which depend on such factors as the condition of survivors, length of hospitalizations, the family solidarity and degree of remorse suffered by the family. Over time, either a reconciliation with new growth or deterioration of the family system ensues [14]. Surviving family members can be helped with the offering of long-term support which can effectively be done by trained clergy, pastoral counselors and mental health workers. Through sharing the pain of their loss, by having someone to sorrow with them, and with encouragement to go forward with their lives, families can be helped to heal [3].

Spiritual Growth After Trauma

Selder has detailed a description of the reorganization of life's meaning that can occur after a traumatic event [15]. When the current meaning of life is disrupted by a traumatic event, a reorganization or reconstruction of the significance of one's life and spirituality occurs. A life transition is initiated. The disruption can originate in a trauma such as a sudden, crucial event or a determined decision such as a divorce. If a person does not acknowledge the change or disruption, engagement in active living may be greatly curtailed. Whenever a carefully constructed life meaning is disrupted, an ambiguity and a state of disconnectedness can ensue as the absence or order, logic, predictability, rootedness is experienced. If the unpredictable event can be dealt with in a predictable manner, control can be taken. However, if the sense of self or one's position is so compromised that the event or decision cannot be integrated or resolved within the formerly maintained system of meaning of the person, the event can intrude on and shatter every aspect of the person's life experience.

The old meaning no longer exists and a new one has not yet been constructed. For most people, this uncertainty is an intolerable state, so they attempt to reduce the stress of ambivalence and unsureness by actively engaging in a variety of activities. This reduces the uncertainty experienced following a disruption of one's life and former sense of purpose. One set of activities confronts the circumstances around the disrupted meaning. The permanency of what was lost is acknowledged and the dimensions of the changes recognized. Eventually one comes to understand that the prior reality is permanently and irreversibly altered and must be let go of.

Not knowing what to expect or what to do can lead to an experiencing of self as outside of ordinary life. Other people do not know or understand what is being endured and communication of the inner state of chaos and disorientation can be very difficult. Lacking a diagram of the recovery process can contribute to anxiety: the trauma survivor does not know what can be expected currently, or at any point in the future. Following the disruption of one's life, there is a preoccupation with what had gone on before, so a *connecting* up with what had been predictable and known can be attempted. For example, women who have had children die soon after birth report an incessant review of the nine months preceding the child's birth and a review of the infant's first few minutes/hours/days/months of life. This review of the past enables one to become aware both of the past and of changed circumstances. Indeed the preoccupation with the most recently held meanings is a requisite condition to the life transition which contributes to growth and acquisition of new meaning in life.

During the life transition, the perception of time and the marking of the passage of time changes. One is unable to acknowledge that the present experience will be completed or over in any foreseeable future and temporarily cannot see beyond the present pain and this can lead to a lack of hope.

Gradually, integration and healing occurs. Simple passage of time is one factor that helps people to acknowledge and participate in the changed circumstances and meaning of their life. There are also trigger events which precipitate awareness of the change of meaning in life, its consequences, and the permanency of the alteration and also function to structure a new reality. One such trigger event is reactivation: the remembering of thoughts, feelings and sensations that occurred earlier in the disrupted reality. As life transition progresses, this reactivation decreases in intensity and duration. A second trigger event includes the awareness of the finality of changes created within the new meaning—the new spirituality and identifying options no longer available. Important in reducing the uncertainty and in finding new meaning is normalization or engaging in behaviors that mirror the standard established by the core society, e.g., returning to work, returning to church. Following a disruption in reality, the person's sense of time collapses; there is no orientation to the future but only pre-occupation with the pre-disrupted reality and meaning of life. Gradually, the traumatic event is integrated with its consequences and new meaning is found as the old one is finally relinquished.

Successful Coping with Trauma

LaGrand has listed seven of the most frequently reported convictions of survivors of trauma which contributed to their psychological, cognitive, physical, and spiritual recovery [16].

1. Problems represented by life changes such as death are universal. Others in similar situations feel the way I do.
2. Reaching out to others in love transcends the inevitable changes which result after trauma.
3. Nurture and develop the strength within.
4. Inter-dependence with others is life affirming.
5. Communication and expression of feelings is essential.
6. There are common emotional and physical sensations after trauma and loss.

7. A faith in something or Someone outside the self integrates new meaning into life.

POST-TRAUMATIC STRESS DISORDER

Some investigators have denied that serious psychological harm can occur solely from the trauma of disaster [17, 18]. However, most have found that incidents resulting in human suffering beyond the normal range can produce immediate or delayed serious emotional reactions, resulting in individual, familial and other dysfunctions persisting through the life span [19-21].

The condition was described as early as 1818 in Goethe's play about Lila, a young woman traumatized by erroneous news of her husband's death in war [22]. Stephen Crane wrote of war-induced trauma in *The Red Badge of Courage* in the mid-18th century, and Da Costa noted anxiety disorders in Civil War soldiers [23].

Later, Freud recognized psychic trauma as a break in the protective shield against stimuli characterized by a sense of utter helplessness [24, 25]. In the late 1960s, the number of returning traumatized Viet Nam veterans resulted in the formal recognition of Post-Traumatic Stress Disorder (PTSD) as a psychiatric disorder through its inclusion in the Diagnostic and Statistical Manual III [26].

Those involved in a trauma can be at risk to develop Post-Traumatic Stress Disorders and pathological grief reactions. If a traumatized person's physical, psychosocial, and spiritual disequilibrium is prolonged and "directly associated with episodes of intrusive imagery and reliving, which often alternate with periods of depression, isolation, withdrawal, emotional constriction, and detachment," there can develop a disruption of the steady state of the autonomic nervous system [27]. This leads to a physiological hyperarousal associated with the condition called Post-Traumatic Stress Disorder. This condition should always be treated by therapists skilled in addressing the needs of traumatized survivors. Such treatment will often involve both medication and psychotherapy and can benefit also from a reevaluation and eventual restructuring of one's religious belief system. Healing from this condition involves the reestablishment of continuity and cohesion in the self and an integration of one's shattered core identity.

Groups at Risk for PTSD

At risk groups for Post-Traumatic Stress Disorder include survivors and bereaved families and friends of victims, especially when little or no social support is available. An example of this is the large number of veterans of the Vietnam War who developed PTSD after they returned to an environment which offered little recognition and poor social support to them.

Although anyone can be affected by a critical incident and need psychological care, emergency responders and crisis care workers, who intervene in situations of high stress to mitigate the suffering of others, especially need attention. They assume the risk of immediate or delayed, difficulties with the life-support patterns of body maintenance, psychological and emotional stability, occupational well-being, family and social relationships, and spiritual equanimity which they may adopt. Disaster workers who are exposed to gruesome sights, smells, and sounds which can leave lasting disturbing impressions can be at risk to PTSD especially when they see themselves or their loved ones as similar to the victims and form a personal identification with them. The risk for workers is increased when workers continue to work long beyond their normal endurance limits, a common phenomenon.

Coordinators and leaders, those in leadership positions, including clergy, sometimes suffer the most. They can be exposed to the same stressors as the workers and also have the burden of coordinating activities, making critical decisions, and monitoring the condition of their personnel. Although debriefing sessions and other primary prevention programs are becoming more common for disaster workers, their leaders frequently exclude themselves from these sessions to allow the workers more freedom to express their emotions.

Individuals providing spiritual and emotional assistance to victims and the bereaved are at high risk for spiritual and psychological distress. Increased role confusion and feelings of depression and helplessness have been reported in workers whose function was to provide spiritual and emotional support to bereaved families after accidents. An intense and intimate involvement between helpers and victims was related to increased muscle tension, fatigue, and sleep disturbances, especially for those workers providing spiritual and emotional support and counseling. Sources of stress for disaster helpers include: a) the close encounter with death, reminding helpers of their own vulnerability; b) the sharing of the anguish of victims and their families, which often results in a close empathic identification; and c) role ambiguity and role conflict [28].

In a study of rescue workers in a 1985 Dallas–Fort Worth plane crash, those who worked primarily with families of victims displayed more symptoms than any other group considered and both chaplains providing emotional support to the bereaved family members were reported to have fairly significant emotional reactions and symptoms [27].

Long-Term Effects of Unresolved Trauma

Individuals can triumph over what may at first seem to be insurmountable adversities, to live healthy and productive lives. However, if survivors do not learn to overcome the legacy of helplessness, victimization, fear of becoming hurt or destroyed which can result from unresolved trauma, they can develop increasing dependency and problems in adapting to retirement, bereavement, illness or disability [29]. Kinzie wrote of how depression, anxiety, denial and re-experiencing patterns, vulnerability to stress, nightmares (even years after), survivor guilt, can be ongoing symptoms of traumatic shock to the system [30]. Anderson discussed how after disasters, rescuers, including clergy, may suffer disturbing symptoms and mental disorders that could have been prevented with appropriate professional care [23].

CONCLUSION

Attention to the spiritual needs of the traumatized is intimately interconnected with attention to their emotional, cognitive, and even physiological needs. The ministering of love, concern for and attention to the pain caused by the shattering of life's meaning which can often occur after a traumatic event, the offering of the pastoral ministries of churches on a sustained and long-term basis after a traumatic event are several of the ways in which the traumatized can be spiritually ministered too.

Recently, an EMT was recounting to me how the meaning of his life was irrevocably changed over the twenty-month period following the school disaster alluded to at the beginning of this chapter. His comments can be a fitting close:

> Before the school disaster, I did my work as I had been trained to. . . . Do the rescue work, finish the paper work, see assisting the victim as a job . . . only that. After that November day, when I helped uncover and lift up all those bodies of dead children who were the ages of my children, I first felt rage at a God who could allow this slaughter of innocents. I stopped going to Church and stopped believing in my 'Sunday School God.' Gradually, I became aware that I could still love and in fact, loved my wife and children even more than before. I talked to a spiritually-oriented counselor who helped me make this power to love become my spirituality. . . . It took about eighteen months but I can choose now to continuously nurture it . . . and try never to overlook an opportunity to use it to give life to others.

REFERENCES

1. S. Kierkegaard, *The Concept of Dread*, W. Lowrie (trans.), Princeton University Press, Princeton, New Jersey, 1940.
2. G. Walker, Crisis-Care in Critical Incident Debriefing, *Death Studies, 12*, pp. 121-133, 1990.
3. M. Coolican, E. Vassar, and J. Grogan, Trauma's Other Victims: Helping Survivors Survive, *Nursing, 89*, pp. 53-57, 1989.
4. J. Middleton-Moz, *Children of Trauma, Shame and Guilt, in press.*
5. H. Martin, Parents and Children's Reactions to Burns and Scalds in Children, *British Journal of Medical Psychology, 43*, pp. 183-191, 1970.
6. I. Martin-Baro, War and the Psychosocial Trauma of Salvadoran Children, paper presented at the 198th annual meeting of the American Psychological Association, Boston, 1990.
7. J. T. Mitchell, When Disaster Strikes: The Critical Incident Stress Debriefing Process, *Journal of Emergency Medical Services*, pp. 36-39, January 1983.
8. J. P. Wilson, *Trauma, Transformation and Healing*, Brunner Mazel, New York, 1986.
9. J. Krystal, Trauma and Effects, *Psychoanalytic Study of the Child, 33*, pp. 81-116, 1978.
10. J. R. Rundell, ,R. J. Ursano, H. C. Holloway, and E. K. Silberman, Psychiatric Responses to Trauma, *Hospital and Community Psychiatry, 40*, pp. 68-74, 1989.
11. E. M. Ornitz and R. S. Pynoos, Startle Modulation in Children with Posttraumatic Stress Disorder, *American Journal of Psychiatry, 46*, pp. 866-869, 1989.
12. J. A. Lyons, Posttraumatic Stress Disorder in Children and Adolescents, *Developmental and Behavioral Pediatrics, 8*, pp. 349-356, 1987.
13. C. J. Frederick, Children Traumatized by Catastrophic Situations, in *Post Traumatic Stress Disorder in Children*, S. Eth and R. S. Pynoos (eds.), American Psychiatric Press, Washington, D.C., 1981.
14. M. M. Epperson, Families in Sudden Crisis, *Social Work in Health Care, 2*, pp. 265-273, 1977.
15. F. Selder, Life Transition Theory, *Nursing and Health Care, 10*, pp. 437-451, 1990.
16. L. E. LaGrand, *Changing Patterns of Human Existence*, Charles C. Thomas, Springfield, Illinois, 1988.
17. E. L. Quarentilli and R. R. Dynes, Response to Social Crisis and Disaster, *Annual Review of Sociology, 3*, pp. 23-49, 1977.
18. V. Taylor, Good News About Disaster, *Psychology Today*, October, 1977.
19. C. R. Figley, *Trauma and Its Wake: Vol. I & II*, Brunner Mazel, New York, 1986.
20. R. Pynoos, C. Frederick, and K. Nader, Life Threat and Posttraumatic Stress in School-age Children, *Archives of General Psychiatry, 44*, pp. 1057-1063, 1987.

21. M. Sugar, Children in a Disaster: An Overview, *Child Psychiatry and Human Development, 19*, pp. 163-179, 1989.
22. J. W. Goethe, *Lila*, C. Danielson (trans.), Highland, New York, 1973.
23. N. Anderson, Posttraumatic Stress Disorder, in *Comprehensive Textbook of Psychiatry/IV*, H. I. Kaplan and B. J. Sadock (eds.), Wilkins & Wilkins, Baltimore, pp. 918-924, 1988.
24. S. Freud, Beyond the Pleasure Principle, in *Standard Edition, Vol. 18*, J. Strachey (ed.), Hogarth Press, London, pp. 1-64, 1920.
25. S. Freud, Inhibitions, Symptoms, and Anxiety, in *Standard Edition, Vol. 20*, J. Strachey (ed.), Hogarth Press, London, pp. 75-175, 1926.
26. *Diagnostic and Statistical Manual of Mental Disorders* (Third Edition—Revised III). American Psychiatric Association, Washington, D.C., 1989.
27. A. Cullinan, A. Counseling Psychologist's Role in a School and Community Disaster, paper presented at the 198th annual meeting of the American Psychological Association, Boston, 1989.
28. B. Raphael, *When Disaster Strikes*, Basic Books, New York, 1986.
29. B. Kahana, Z. Harel, E. Kahana, and T. Rosner, Coping with Extreme Trauma, in *Human Adaptation of Extreme Stress: From the Holocaust to Vietnam*, J. P. Wilson, Z. Harel, and B. Kanahan (eds.), Plenum Press, New York, 1988.
30. D. Kinzie, The Psychiatric Effect of Massive Trauma on Cambodian Refugees, in *Human Adaptation to Extreme Stress: From the Holocaust to Vietnam*, J. P. Wilson, Z. Harel, and B. Kahana (eds.), Plenum Press, New York, 1988.

CHAPTER 19

No More Rosebuds:
A Perspective on Perinatal Death,
Funerals, and Pastoral Care*

Jane Nichols and Kenneth J. Doka

Several years ago, a young woman's second child was stillborn. The dead infant was buried privately in a distant city. The newly-delivered mother was still hospitalized and had never seen her child. Later as she searched to know whom or what she had lost, she asked the clergyman who performed the infant's graveside service to mail a copy of his remarks.

They were about rosebuds! "No blossom blooms in vain," he had said. Her reply: "I didn't lose a rosebud. I lost a son."

She folded the service copy and placed it in a drawer. It was a long time before she opened herself again to the efforts of clergy. Hence, she experienced a second loss: spiritual amputation . . . and the burden of her grief was multiplied. (true story)

The purpose of this chapter is: 1) to set forth a perspective on parental bereavement following perinatal death, especially as it interfaces with the role of pastoral care workers; 2) to suggest that the "rosebud" approach to newborn funerals estranges; rather than comforts, many (but not all) parents; and 3) to offer suggestions for personal design of newborn funerals.

*An earlier version of this chapter was presented to the 1987 Annual Meeting of the Association for Death Education and Counseling, London, Canada, May.

THE SCOPE

The term *perinatal* refers to the period of time between the twentieth week of gestation and the first twenty-eight days of life after birth. Each year in the United States, there are approximately 68,000 perinatal deaths affecting 136,000 mothers and fathers, an undetermined number of siblings, grandparents, aunts, uncles, and cousins who may be profoundly moved or who may be experiencing a close death for the first time.

Included in a broader definition of the term *perinatal* are the deaths of infants who die prior to the twentieth week of gestation. Data are not uniformly collected on these occurrences so it is impossible to report accurately how many there are; however, we do know they are high in number. The professional caregiving community frequently refers to these events as *spontaneous abortions, miscarriages, the passing of* fetal tissue, or *non-viable, non-deaths*. Most state health departments do not issue birth or death certificates for these infants. Social custom has largely negated the value of babies so young and burial or funeralization is not customary: hospitals simply cremate the *tissue*.

Perhaps because of raised awareness of *when life begins,* coming out of the abortion issue, or perhaps because of the common expectation that babies do not die nor pregnancies fail in these times, many (but not all) parents seem to attach to and hold great store in *the product of their conception* very early in pregnancy. They simply do not think of their infant as *non-viable fetal tissue,* but rather as *our baby.* This notable difference between professionals and parents in terms of the perception, meaning, and value of the child and the event can be the basis for the severing gap between what parents need and the care which is offered.

In addition to miscarriages, stillbirths, and newborn deaths, there are a growing number of infants who live for several months in Newborn Intensive Care Units (NICUs) before dying; these infants can also be included in the broad definition of perinatal death.

THE CONTEXT OF PERINATAL DEATH

Thanatologists have long noted a variety of factors which affect the way people grieve. Among them are the events which surround the death. It seems particularly helpful to bring to mind the context of perinatal deaths because it impacts greatly on parent response and need. Most perinatal deaths occur with little warning and little opportunity for anticipatory grieving. Suddenly and unexpectedly, a child dies in utero or is born prematurely and dies soon after, often separated from and never seen by his mother.

There are five other scenarios which occur less often, but which merit special note because of the nuances of individual responses and the difficulty caregivers, including clergy, might have in responding in helpful ways. One such small group includes those infants who die after many months in a Newborn Intensive Care Unit (NICU).

Another group includes parents of twin infants where one child and the other lives. Contrary to popular perception, many of these parents struggle with joy for the surviving twin which does not compensate for nor eradicate the sorrow for the twin who died. Grief and joy are cumbersome bedmates. Further, all too often, the surviving twin also dies at a later time and parents are burdened with dual grief.

Another delicate scene of perinatal death includes grandparents who not only mourn the death of a grandchild, but also suffer for the pain of their adult child. Many grandparents seek to help their 'children' by taking over decision-making, including decisions about funeralization.

Next, there are many parents for whom certain physiological or genetic conditions exist which place their offspring at a higher-than-average risk of death. Indeed, many *high-risk* parents have sustained the blow of several pregnancy-related deaths. Having such multiple *rehearsals,* these parents often have absolute clarity about the kinds of care and services which they find helpful; caregivers on the other hand, being accustomed to families who behave in more vulnerable ways, may find this assertive clarity *difficult.*

Finally, advancing medical knowledge and fairly accurate pre-natal diagnostic techniques, enable physicians to identify certain conditions in infants which will cause death after birth. Thus, growing numbers of parents are faced with the decision either to induce labor in mid-pregnancy, resulting in the death of the baby, or to carry the child to full-term and then see it die. Several of the issues in this scenario are obvious, including the ethical dilemmas and the potential for prolonged anticipatory grief. Less obvious is that many parents experience grief rather than relief, when they choose to terminate the pregnancy.

Each of these constellations represents the possibility of grief present, and, thus, the opportunity for caregivers to be helpful or harmful to the surviving family. Clergy carry a special role in the care they offer to these families.

REVIEW OF PARENTAL GRIEF

It is fair to say that when a perinatal death occurs, parental response is predictably unpredictable; that is, each parent's response is highly individual. Many (perhaps most), but not all, parents grieve. Others are deeply saddened, but do not grieve profoundly. In general, observation suggests that the longer the period of gestation, the more profound the grief. There are some parents, however, who grieve deeply for an infant of only a few weeks' gestation; others do not grieve the death of their full-term baby.

Overall, women tend to grieve longer and more intensely than men do when their baby has died. In addition to the many factors which account for personal differences in grieving noted in general grief literature, it has been theorized that the reasons mothers grieve infants more than fathers include a) mother's greater maternal-infant attachment because of constant physical contact throughout pregnancy; b) father's being comforted by their *mate's* survival of pregnancy and childbirth; c) the therapeutic effectiveness of father's being called upon to make funeral arrangements and deal with other death-related tasks, whereas mothers are often left out of these painful, but grief-relieving activities [1]; and d) the possibility that an infant, newly-conceived or full-term, may hold a very different meaning for a father than for a mother.

Parental grief following newborn death is characterized by most of the same physical, emotional, mental, and spiritual symptoms as other bereavements [2, 3]. In addition, it is marked by some unique circumstances which caregivers do well to recall so as to promote more precisely helpful caregiving responses.

First, when death occurs so soon after birth, it is difficult for parents to know whom or what they have lost . . . but they know they have lost something. It is an indefinable loss that makes grieving vague and shadowy, hard to *get a handle on.* Parents need concrete, tangible experiences and mementos related to the authenticity of their baby's life and death. Planning for, attending, and/or participating in the funeral service, although difficult, is one means of providing some of the needed definition. Viewed from this perspective, the funeral may create an important memory. One can see, too, how the *rosebud* metaphor can add to the vague reality of the child, rather than clarify it.

Next, even when a baby has died, parents often need to *be parents,* if only symbolically. For example, parents may wish to see, touch, or hold the child, name the child, give the baby gifts, take pictures, let family and friends see the child. Baptizing a dying or dead baby is often perceived by parents as the only parental *protection* they can offer their newborn, even though to many traditions it is theologically unnecessary. The baptismal cloth could be offered as a memento of their brief parenting.

Third, when a baby dies, there are two central grievers: mother and father. Because their needs may be very different, it is crucial that caregivers hear and honor the feelings, wishes, opinions, and styles of *both* parents, especially when making decisions about final disposition, funeral rituals, and so on.

Fourth, there is a tendency for caregivers, family, and friends to presume that parents do not or should not grieve when a newborn dies. Yet we know that grief is a normal response to a significant loss: it is nature's way. The two perceptions contradict each other.

Further, to discount grief precludes that caregivers *should* or *would* offer social, psychological, or spiritual support to parents, thus depriving them of significant assistance usually available to the grievers. For example, there is a tendency to minimize the funeral observance, restricting it to a few prayers at graveside. If funerals are helpful to survivors of other deaths, why not for parents or newborns? It is as though one were saying, *little person, little death, little grief, little fuss.* Negating grief isolates parents and smacks of avoidance and protectionism. It says "nothing *really* happened here."

Finally, when a baby dies so young, it is probable that few family members or friends had the opportunity to become acquainted with him. And not being acquainted, they do not share the grief. Parents, then, can be isolated in their bereavement.

COMFORT, RELIEF, AND FUNERALS

There are ways that clergy can be helpful. When a baby is dying or has died, the clergy's first role is to be present and to offer comfort and relief—to be quietly in the presence of parents, to put a hand on the shoulder, to embrace the weary, to evoke blessing for those in pain, to walk a while with them, to acknowledge with the heart the suffering which is present, to bear witness to the drama of the event without idle chatter.

Especially at this time, the clergy will need to be empathic listeners. Bereaved parents may challenge the fairness of God. They may bristle with anger at the apparent senselessness of this death. This is the point at which one simply listens and acknowledges diverse perspectives; this is not the time to argue theology. Some of the issues they raise may be touched upon in the funeral homily and certainly explored in greater depth at a later time in the counseling process.

It is also wise to avoid cliches. "You have your other children." "You're young, you can have other children." "We must accept God's will." Expressions like these bring comfort to some but arouse anger and a sense of alienation in others. Take your lead from the parents. If they say these things, clergy should go with them. If they do not they should not mention them.

The clergy's second role is to prepare and deliver the funeral service. There is abundant research supporting the position that funeral rituals can have great therapeutic value to survivors [4]. In the context of perinatal death, the funeral service can be an excellent vehicle by which parents, family friends, professional caregivers are reminded that these newly-born infants are children of God also, and that they are deserving of dignity, respect, and caring. The funeral, if individually designed, may also meet many of the post-death needs suggested above. Such a service may require composing a new, more relevant burial service; the creation of a *birth and death* announcement; ways of introducing the baby; a more fitting use of music. These approaches are not to be scaled-down versions of adult funerals, but examples of thoughtful response to the realities of a particular newborn death. Even within highly formalized church ritual, there is room for individualization.

Additionally, there is evidence that the therapeutic value of the funeral is enhanced when the bereaved take active roles in planning for and participating in funeral rituals [5, 6]. This suggests that after being present with a family to offer comfort and relief, one of the first things the pastor should do is meet with the family to discuss funeral options and plan the funeral service. On such occasions, there has been a tendency of fathers and grandparents to exclude the mother. While the goal of that behavior may be protective, it is potentially dangerous since *both* parents will have to live with the decisions that are made. Grievers are not incompetent, only vulnerable. If mothers wish to take part, they should not be excluded, even if the planning is painful. This further suggests that, if the mother is still hospitalized, part of the planning will be done at the hospital or delayed until the mother can participate. If her hospitalization is prolonged, the funeral itself could be conducted in the hospital. Similarly it might be well to incorporate siblings at some point in the planning process.

An important first step of the funeral planning sessions is to intentionally decide the purpose of the service. If clergy and parents decide together what the purpose of the funeral is; that is—what parents wish and need from the service, then parents are apt to benefit more from the service, thus heightening its therapeutic value. The very act of determining the purpose may itself by therapeutic.

Further, clergy will need to be patient. It may take a while before parents determine the "right" way to memorialize their child. The clergyperson may remind them of some options. For example, perhaps they would like to wait—not have a funeral service now, but a memorial service at a later time. Or they could have a committal service now and plan a special service of remembrance at a later time. Let families know they have options and be supportive of the decisions they make.

A second step for the planning is to ask parents to review their memories of and hopes for the child. Who was he or she? What did he or she bring? What were his/her gifts? What are the memories the parents have of this pregnancy? What were their dreams for this child? This review has dual value. First, it allows clergy to understand how the baby was perceived by the family. This awareness provides clergy with the opportunity to deepen the context of the funeral service as well as the pastoral care. Secondly, the review of memories is part of the healing process and gives parents permission to grieve legitimately. Public sharing of these thoughts can service to "introduce" the baby to family and friends; however, because they are personal, the pastor should ask permission to use them.

The incorporation of the family in the conduct of the service can be facilitated further by clergy's suggestions about possible opportunities for family involvement. Are there any readings that are particularly meaningful to them? Do they have any favorite music, hymns, or psalms? Are there people who should be recognized at the service? Could family members prerecord music to be used prior to or after the service? It is important to give attention to music, for it can be a valuable vehicle for expressing feelings that words cannot convey.

In reviewing the liturgy for the service, clergy might point out opportunities for involvement. Are there family members who would wish to do readings? Do family members wish to serve as ushers or pallbearers? Even children can be incorporated in the service as altar boys and girls, acolytes, crucifers, readers, or musicians. Young children can distribute materials or hold books for the clergy as they read. One option parents may select is not to personalize or to participate in the service. This, too, should be respected.

In summation, planning for meaningful funeral rituals involves considerable preparation. It means actively engaging the family. It means maintaining a sensitivity to ethnic or local customs. It means empowering parents to make choices within the liturgy so that they may fashion an individual service that has significance to them. This may result in the family choosing readings or hymns that the pastor considers inappropriate, mismatched, or even in questionable taste.

Unless there are sound, indisputable theological principles at stake, the family's wishes should prevail.

THE CONDUCT OF THE SERVICE

There are four themes which can be incorporated into the funeral: personal, spiritual, psychological, and social. While these aspects will be addressed in the hymns, readings, and in all contexts of the liturgy, it is the homily itself that will draw these themes together.

One preparatory note, this chapter is written from a Christian perspective. As such it draws upon the theology, rituals, and practices evident in that faith, particularly in its more liturgical branches. Denominations such as the Roman Catholic, Episcopal, and Lutheran church share a similar and more formal liturgical tradition than do many other Protestant denominations. The Orthodox churches would also be considered liturgical though their traditions and rituals are somewhat different. However, while illustrating these themes within the faith, the authors emphasize that the use of the personal, spiritual, psychological, and social themes can be incorporated in any tradition, for each faith tradition was its own spiritual answer to the problem of human death.

Personal Theme

One issue to be addressed is the personal. A child has died. Clergy should be prepared to consider and address the particular nature of this perinatal loss. Further, even if the baby never saw a moment of life outside the womb, the child still embodied hopes and dreams. In some degree, each family member has attached to the baby during the pregnancy. There are memories. The funeral sermon can recognize that a unique and special individual has died. Clergy can use the child's name and share the hopes and memories that parents are willing to have made public. These personal references can affirm the parents as well by noting their love and concern and assuaging their damaged self-esteem. Although personalizing the service in this way has been identified by the bereaved as one of the helpful and therapeutic aspects of the service, many clergy are reluctant to eulogize the funeral sermon [7, 8]. Often the concern is raised that personal reference will detract from the salvation message. Many parents do not agree; the challenge is to personalize the service while maintaining the gospel message.

Spiritual Theme

The sermon may also address the spiritual dimension of grief. This is the area which includes, "Why did this happen, why did it happen to me; what is the nature of life and the meaning of death?" Like the mother in our opening story, many parents, young and unprepared to grapple with the broadest questions of life, find themselves isolated and estranged by responses to the spiritual quest inherent in grief, which are either nonexistent, vague, hidden, too pat, inadequate, or just plain do not fit.

Clergy do not need to attempt to explain the senselessness of the baby's death. To do so is to defend God; God does not need defense. Clergy can express their own bewilderment (a child has died; we do not know why) and offer comfort and support.

Naturally, the sermon cannot fully explore and resolve spiritual issues, but it can set up a context that can be considered and reviewed in later counseling sessions. The death bed, the funeral home, the place of services, the time of crisis are not the settings for theological seminars. People who are in pain, who are so vulnerable, so fragile do not need religious education. They need comfort and relief. Education can come later.

The centerpiece of the sermon is the message of hope: even in the midst of grief and mystery, faith provides. The theological message within the Christian faith will express the paradox of faith; in grief, there is hope; in death, resurrection. This paradox is well expressed by Thielicke [9, p. 198]:

> I walk into the night of death, truly the darkest night; yet I know who awaits me in the glorious morn.

A sense of this paradox in the funeral sermon avoids the contrasting problem of a depressing service that offers no hope or a celebration of death that denies the legitimacy of grief.

Psychological Theme

Another theme to be addressed in the funeral service is the psychological. Here the goal is to help the bereaved recognize both the naturalness and the nature of their grief. As stated earlier, part of the particular context of perinatal loss is that many people may not recognize that true loss has occurred. Further, many people labor under the misunderstanding that if they were good Christians they would not grieve. They have forgotten that "Jesus wept." Parents and others need to be reassured that grief is a natural response to the loss they have experienced and that Christians do grieve. (This is an excellent, needed topic to pursue also in a sermon during a regular Sunday worship service.)

Further, the funeral sermon is an effective place to remind family and friends of the course of grief and that grief is a roller-coaster process that may take time to resolve [10, 11]. In this process grievers may experience emotions including anger, feelings of being cheated, a sense of guilt and myriad other emotions. One might briefly note the ambivalent feelings survivors may have toward the baby, themselves, each other, and caregivers. One might remind them that they may experience grief differently and that the intense needs of each family member may make it difficult for them to be there for each other. And plant the seeds of hope. Reassure them that, if they choose, these feelings will diminish even as the memories remain: the end of grief is not the end of memory but the end of pain.

This component of the sermon can interweave with the spiritual component of the service. It can reassure people that it is not sinful to be angry with God. Anger is natural. And anger toward God is a form of prayer. The pastor may affirm that the feelings of the bereaved are understood by God and respected by the church. Sorrow, anger, and grief are not inappropriate nor signs of a weak faith. Jesus was "a man of sorrows, acquainted with grief."

Clergy may further wish to develop theses of forgiveness and thankfulness. It is easy to blame—oneself, one's spouse, others. Yet blaming is counter-productive. Forgiveness (sooner or later) is essential both psychologically and spiritually. Thankfulness, too, may be appropriately mentioned since it is a part of the healing process. Express gratitude (if appropriate) for health care providers, for the lessons taught by the child, and for God receiving the baby into heaven.

Addressing the course and nature of grief within the funeral service can have therapeutic value by normalizing the feeling the bereaved may be experiencing and by educating others so that hopefully they will be more understanding and empathic. Again it is important to keep this treatment general enough so that the family does not feel that the confidentiality of the counseling process has been violated.

Social Context Theme

A fourth theme that could be useful is that of the social context of this death. This loss has taken place in the midst of a supportive community—the larger circle of family, friends, and congregational community. That community is witnessing its concern by its very presence. Yet the community may need to be empowered to act. Members of that community may want to help, but may be at a loss as to how to help. They may simply not know how they can be effective.

The pastor can suggest options. One might suggest the importance of listening and of neither minimizing nor romanticizing the loss. Further, one could outline tangible acts of support: babysitting, helping with errands, housework, food preparation in the months ahead. The pastor can encourage others to let the family decide the degree to which they will be incorporated into upcoming activities rather than unilaterally trying to spare them pain by omitting them, providing diversion, or by insisting upon participation. Finally the pastor may help parents to recognize and forgive insensitive and unknowing comments that might have been or still may be made by the social community.

THE SERVICE IN A CONTEXT OF CARE

The sermon and service can be excellent ways to begin the process of recovery, yet they are most effective when they involve action within the context of other aspects of congregational ministry. It is helpful for pastors to make themselves available to families after the funeral so as to provide additional opportunity for counseling, spiritual exploration, and referral to various self-help groups and other resources. Given the demographic characteristics of parents most at risk for perinatal loss, they may be reluctant to avail themselves of the church. This suggests that pastors will have to recognize the necessity of active outreach. One simple way for that outreach to begin is, some time after the funeral, to present parents with a taped or typed copy of the service. Such an act has many benefits. It provides an additional memento of the infant. It also provides parents with the opportunity to review and reconsider words which were only partially heard in the din of their early grief. Further, it continues a relationship with clergy and the church. Special outreach efforts should be directed toward fathers, regardless of whether they are married, cohabitating, or separated, since fathers can be doubly disenfranchised: not only may the loss of the child be unrecognized, but fathers' grief may also be unacknowledged.

In addition to the emotional support offered to all grievers, aftercare of parents of newborns who have died may need to focus particularly on spiritual and theological issues. As we have noted above, observation suggests that these issues are triggered early in parental grief. It is a challenge for all who presume to offer assistance to the bereaved to seek fulfilling ways for grievers to wrestle with, chew on, dwell on these questions as they do the spiritual work of grief. For just as there is physical and emotional work to grief, there is also spiritual work. Many caregivers have come to realize that we cannot do this work for them; it is for us to simply walk with them while they sort it out for themselves.

CONCLUSION

Which parents will grieve, which ones grieve profoundly, what particular issues they carry, whether they find solace in metaphors or prefer more clear language, what their needs are and what care seems to offer comfort and relief: these can only be determined by careful, thoughtful, listening, client-centered interviews with each individual, as caregiver and parent seek to determine who died and what meaning this child and this death had for him and her.

Ministry to the survivors of perinatal loss is a demanding task for the clergy. It is difficult to say both hello and goodbye simultaneously. Few families or churches have traditions where birth and death are acknowledged at the same time. To do so requires a special sensitivity and creativity on the part of the clergy. However, clergy may take comfort from the fact that in few other situations is their guidance, counseling, and leadership more necessary, for it is the reality of death that gives our faith its ultimate significance.

A mother was asked what was so wonderful about the clergyman of whom she had so often spoken. Face glowing, she responded:

> He loved my kid! He let down the barriers and was able to receive from her. He stayed with her, offering us respite. He left the social level and came to the hurting level, one-to-one. When she died, he stayed with us, let us talk, made suggestions about the funeral. He was full of love.
>
> At the funeral, he talked about her; he talked about her as a person, not a twisted body. There was no preaching . . . it was all love.

Amen. Amen. And Amen.

RESOURCES

The Compassionate Friends (Parental loss)
P.O. Box 3696
Oak Brook, IL 60522-3696
(708) 990-0010

National SHARE Office (for Perinatal loss)
c/o St. Joseph's Health Center
300 First Capitol Drive
St. Charles, MO 63301
(314) 947-6164

REFERENCES

1. J. Nichols, Issues of Perinatal Loss, paper presented to a Symposium of the Foundation of Thanatology, New York, 1987.
2. C. M. Parkes, *Bereavement*, Penguin, Baltimore, 1974.
3. W. J. Worden, *Grief Counseling and Grief Therapy*, Springer, New York, 1991.
4. T. A. Rando, *Grief, Dying and Death: Clinical Interventions for Caregivers*, Research Press, Champaign, Illinois, 1984.
5. K. J. Doka, Expectation of Death, Participation in Funeral Arrangements and Grief Adjustment, *Omega, 15*, pp. 119-130, 1984.
6. P. Estok and A. Lehman, Perinatal Death: Grief Support for Families, *Birth, 103*, pp. 17-25, 1983.
7. D. L. Huan, Perception of the Bereaved, Clergy, and Funeral Directors Concerning Bereavement, *National Reporters, 7*, pp. 7-8, 1980.
8. M. Okerson and S. Wheeler, Creating Memories, *Forum Newsletter, 10*, pp. 3-5, 1986.
9. H. Thelicke, *Death and Life*, Fortune Press, Philadelphia, 1970.
10. D. Klass, *Parental Grief: Solace and Resolution*, Springer, New York, 1988.
11. T. Rando, *Parental Loss of a Child*, Research Press, Champaign, Illinois, 1986.

CHAPTER 20

AIDS and Bereavement: Special Issues in Spiritual Counseling

Ben Wolfe

I was on the telephone when the call came in. The secretary took the message and told me, "The person said, if a man answers, just hang-up." The female caller did not leave her name, only her telephone number. This has happened a number of times before at the Grief Support Center.

When I called the number, a woman answered the phone. I asked if she had called the Center. Indicating she had, she started telling me her story. Her daughter's brother-in-law had AIDS. The concern was, she could not tell anyone and had to keep the "secret." Her own husband did not even know about their daughter's situation. I asked how the individual with AIDS was doing and she said he's had AIDS for two years and would die any day. I asked if she had seen or talked to him, sent him anything? Had she done anything at all? "No," was the reply. She, her daughter and son-in-law had not done anything, and they felt if they told anyone about their situation it would only cause problems. The story went on as so many others have, with each story sharing the same "secret." Grievers need not live with secrets, but unfortunately, many "hidden grievers" do.

Acquired Immune Deficiency Syndrome (AIDS) is a disease, but for many reasons, persons with AIDS (PWAs), their lovers/partners, parents, siblings, aunts, uncles, grandparents, spouses, ex-spouses, children and friends are shunned in many cases and struggle with finding unconditional support and love. In many cases, they keep the dying or the death a secret which can complicate their mourning.

257

What are some of the issues we as clinicians or clergy need to be aware of as we work with persons living with AIDS, their lovers, family, friends and the community-at-large? The focus of this chapter is on bereavement and AIDS, and its effect on the people we counsel and ourselves. Many health care providers, professionals and clergy are now just learning the many psychosocial problems associated with AIDS, while others have been on the front lines for years and are now exhausted or have already felt a need to move on to different areas. Additionally, our own anxiety over the fear of contacting the disease and the frustration of not having a "cure" need to be explored.

Spiritual concerns as they relate to bereavement and AIDS need to be considered. One of the primary considerations is, "Good spiritual caregiving for bereaved persons needs a fine balance between the human need to grieve adequately and the spiritual grounds for hope provided by formal religions or spiritual belief systems" [1]. Caregivers with religious convictions "must respect the powerful feelings of the bereaved during the transition period from grief to growth work" [1].

People live with AIDS and people die from AIDS. AIDS can be looked upon as a disease of compassion by support systems and a disease of courage by individuals living with AIDS. The struggle is not over. The disease is entering all segments of our society and statistically numbers are increasing. The statistics also appear in the 20- to 40-year-old age group, the "prime time of our lives" age, where death normally does not take place, leaving behind bereaved children, siblings, parents, spouses, lovers, relatives and friends. In Western culture, parents are supposed to be buried by their children, not the reverse. When a loved one has AIDS, the effect is like a pebble thrown in water with all the ripples created by the splash.

Stigma, anxiety, and fear have only added to the "AFRAIDS." Discrimination against persons living with AIDS has been documented in films such as the Ryan White story and his exclusion from school in Indiana as have other TV documentaries discussing the AIDS epidemic.

Bad things can and do happen to good people. In the early 1980s when the gay community was demonstrating symptoms of AIDS, some church leaders felt it was God's punishment as a result of the "sinful life-style." It is interesting to note from *The Biblical Perspectives On Death*, "The idea that human sinfulness causes premature death, found especially in Israel's Wisdom Literature, could lead to the conclusion that death itself (mortality) was a consequence of a sinful human condition. If that human condition (sinfulness) could be overcome, then death would be deprived of its reason for existence" [2, p. 77].

AIDS is not a gay disease, but a disease affecting individuals from all racial and ethnic groups, gay and straight, rich and poor, male and female, young and old, religious and those who are not. This disease, like other diseases and crises, can bring people together or divide them. Isolation and abandonment not only happen to PWAs, but also happen to their lovers, family, and friends. This disease asks us to redefine community and look at issues of hope. As a result of the disease, communities of compassion have been created, as well as communities rejecting the needs of human suffering.

How does one explore the spiritual dimension with the bereaved? Progoff states [3, p. 228]:

> In terms of the metaphor, we consider each human being to be a well which must be entered privately and separately, level after level. Progressively inward, we move through all the layers of psychic deposit, memory and habit and desire: All that comprises an individual existence. As we continue moving deeper into the well, we come to depths that are beyond the individuality of our personal life. Moving through the well, we ultimately go beyond the well itself, as we come to its source in the underground stream that unites all the wells. In this symbolic process, we reach beyond the personal to the source of individuality in what is greater than personal. It is both a personal and a self-transcending process.

He goes on to explain [3, p. 288]:

> The goal is to move from "depth unto depth" in our effort to make contact with the ultimate source from which our lives draw their substance. The underground stream carries in its flow the contents and the energies for life, and it supplies the well of our personal existence with waters of every kind. Operationally, it is the source to which we must go to find the contents that will bring spiritual creativity into our lives.

Spiritually, individuals living with AIDS and their lovers, relatives and friends, ride a psychological and emotional roller coaster. Many look at spirituality as the quest to discover there is more to their lives than material possessions, while for others the belief that if a God does exist, it is a God who stands with them and not in opposition to them. However, many people with AIDS, their lovers and caregivers have been shunned by the church before the person became sick. Seeking support from a community that is not supportive and, in some cases, shouts that AIDS is God's judgment, is difficult.

"The church has taught for centuries that good is rewarded and evil punished. Yet anyone old enough to read the headlines of their local newspaper knows that is untrue. What, then, is the value in being 'good?' What ought we to be teaching our children about the real nature of good and evil? How will we understand these ideas ourselves and how will we relate them to illness and death?" [4].

Meyer, in his book, *Surviving Death,* states that two major and opposing views of God appear to exist [4, p. 67]:

> The first posits an *active God in a responsive universe.* This belief system sees God as omniscient, omnipresent, all-powerful and in total control, while the rest of the universe (including illness and death) merely responds to God's command. The second view assumes a *responsive God in an active universe.* This system sees the universe actively, freely going about its natural business of building up and breaking down, living and dying, while God, supporting the free will of natural and human law, seeks to respond to that activity. This belief structure finds God not sending or controlling disease, but rather supporting and upholding those afflicted with illness—*suffering with them,* and grieving with them and their survivors.

Education about AIDS is needed in religious communities, as is the need to educate about "serving and ministering to the sick," regardless of a person's disease. Education is needed in every type of community and needs to be on-going. Utilizing persons living with AIDS as our teachers is imperative. AIDS also forces young people to think about mortality in ways Western culture has not asked of them before. The church and educational systems now talk about young people and death in the same breath, and also about homosexuality, gay rights, IV and drug use, and sexuality as it affects all ages of the community from the young to the aged. Being educated about AIDS and its prevention is the first step in overcoming biases and phobias before we can work with PWAs and their caregiving community. Feelings of discrimination and alienation take time to overcome, but can be accomplished. One does not have to approve of homosexuality or intravenous drug use to care for people who are ill or bereaved.

After a person dies from AIDS, what are some of the special issues in bereavement which need to be looked at? Each death brings old and new questions for those closely associated with the person who died, and can easily affect a wider group who may now start to look at self-evaluation. The stigma of AIDS has created a group of hidden grievers and has complicated the work of bereavement counseling.

Mourning the loss of a loved one is a painful experience. It involves dealing with psychological, emotional, physical, social, and spiritual experiences which may lead the individual into feeling disoriented, depressed, immobile, and suicidal. Structure and the world once known now changes, with confusion, disorganization, and anxiety the new form of temporary existence. Finding out that one is not "crazy," but rather grieving, is important. Mourning is not like a "still picture," instead it is like a video tape which is continually evolving and taking in all things at once. Special times like holidays, birthdays, anniversaries and other memorable occasions rekindle the griever in his or her "grief work." Like the roller coaster, there are ups and downs, but with time there are higher, longer ups, and downs that are not as low, and for shorter periods of time. An important point to note is that past literature for professionals did not deal with gay and lesbian people, but rather only with "heterosexual" mourning. Although I will talk more about male lovers, one should remember that individuals in any close relationship will grieve.

Worden outlines four major tasks which must be undertaken if mourning is to be successful: 1) Accept the reality of the loss; 2) Experience the pain of grief; 3) Adjust to an environment in which the deceased is missing; 4) Withdraw emotional energy and reinvesting in another relationship [5].

Listed below are eight categories of bereaved persons most affected by a PWA's death, with whom, as clinicians or clergy, we may be working. *These categories encompass a wide range of people and relationships and are not intended to be in any special order or all encompassing.*

People most affected in bereavement after a PWA has died:

1. Lovers or partners.
2. The deceased person's spouse, children, or ex-spouse.
3. The deceased person's biological parents, family, and friends.
4. The lover's biological parents, family, and friends.
5. The deceased person's friends.
6. Women who give birth to HIV positive children and their families.
7. The caregiving community ("second circle") for the person who died.
8. People who are affected indirectly.

The questions and concerns listed below are intended to assist one in working with clients or members of a congregation. They are not intended as a "complete checklist" but rather as a guide to explore the bereaved person's feelings and needs. For purposes of this chapter, only categories 1, 2, 3, 5, and 7 listed above will be discussed.

1. LOVER'S AND PARTNER'S CONCERNS/ISSUES

A. Age of the Bereaved Person

1. How old is the bereaved person? The younger the person, the greater the likelihood one has had little or no experience with losing a loved one.
2. Is the person older and was the relationship with someone his/her age or with someone younger?
3. Does the bereaved have his/her own children who may be the same age as the lover who died?
4. Does the person get support from a possible ex-wife or ex-husband and his/her children?
5. If the person one is counseling has children, do they know of his or her relationship with the person who died and were they involved in any of the caregiving?
6. What is the relationship like between the lover and the deceased person's children?

B. Health-Related Concerns/Issues

1. What is the bereaved lover's health like?
2. Does he or she have AIDS or is the person HIV positive?
3. If he or she has not been tested for HIV antibodies, will one now want to be and what does the person consider to be issues related to being tested?
4. How much of the individual's bereavement is fear for one's own health of contracting AIDS from the deceased lover? This fear may also exist for an individual who has not yet been tested and who had a lover from years ago recently die from AIDS.
5. Does the individual talk about the neurological problems witnessed in one's lover and about feelings toward one's own future, loss of control and body changes due to the disease?
6. Is the person run down from all the effort put into taking care of one's lover?

C. Lover's Sense of Involvement

1. Was the lover allowed involvement when the person was in the hospital, hospice unit or at home?

2. Were decisions made by the lover and a Durable Power of Attorney completed with the bereaved as the first person to make decisions?

3. What about a will and who received "possessions" when the estate is/was settled?

4. Who dealt with the death certificate, informing friends and relatives, discussions with "in-laws" and the medical bills that arrive weeks and months after the death?

5. What about life insurance? Did the deceased person have life insurance and was the lover listed as the beneficiary?

D. Funeral and Related Rituals

1. Was the survivor able to spend time with the deceased after the person died?

2. Who planned the funeral? Who paid for the funeral?

3. Was the person able to attend the funeral or memorial service? In some cases the biological family of the deceased person "bans" the lover/partner from taking part, and as a result the person does not get one's special needs met.

4. Was the individual satisfied with the rituals used if one did attend the funeral or memorial service?

5. Was the person cremated and ashes buried or scattered, or was the person buried?

6. Did the obituary list the bereaved person or was nothing mentioned of him or her and only the biological family?

7. Was anything listed in the obituary regarding donations or memorials that could be given to the AIDS movement or a gay rights, lesbian group, etc.? This question allows you to assess if "openness" about the deceased PWA existed in the biological family's world and/or also in the gay community.

8. Was the lover given time away from work for the funeral or did the person tell an employer "something else" to get off from work for the few hours, day or days. Most "widows" or "widowers" are supported by their employers and given a reasonable time off, although in almost all cases not long enough.

9. Did others know that the individual's lover died from AIDS or was the death listed as cancer, etc.?

E. What Was the Lover's/Partner's Caregiving Role?

1. Were "buddies" utilized or was the person you are counseling the sole caregiver?

2. Did the deceased person's lover/partner want any help in caregiving? What role did friends of both the deceased and the person you are counseling play with regard to caregiving?
3. How did the lover/partner balance employment and caregiving?
4. Who else was involved in the caregiving role and what perception of "help" does the bereaved person feel he or she received from these individuals? Was the deceased person's parents, spouse, ex-spouse, children, or family involved in anyway or did they abandon the PWA? If they wanted to be involved, was geographical distance a factor in the caregiving role by family?
5. What was the caregiving role like for the person you are seeing and "who is one now" if he or she is unable to be a caregiver now?
6. If the person projects into the future, who will take care of him or her should one get sick?

F. Previous Losses and What is Now Perceived Lost

1. Having them discuss past losses will provide you with the opportunity to discover if they have experienced many close deaths previously, if they are dealing with *bereavement overload* and how they have coped with the losses [6]. Most likely they will have had multiple deaths besides their lover with some experiencing the death of almost their entire social network.
2. How dependent upon the deceased was the bereaved? The larger the "piece of the pie" that has been "cut-out" the more difficult mourning will be.
3. How "important" was the deceased person in the community and what significance may this have on the bereaved person's new "status?"

G. Financial Concern

1. Is the bereaved person's financial situation a concern? Asking, "I don't want to know how much money you have, but from a financial point of view, how do you feel you will now do?" gives opportunity to discuss financial concerns.
2. Does one have any type of insurance? Did one receive money from any existing will or insurance policy from the deceased lover?
3. Where does all of this tie into one's employment situation?

H. Guilt Induction by Deceased Family and Possibly by Self

1. Has the bereaved person's lifestyle been questioned by the deceased person's family? Blaming the lover for "causing their

child to be gay" or causing the death may be mentioned. If the true relationship between the deceased and the lover is not known, it makes it difficult for the bereaved person to express his or her honest feelings. It is hard to be treated like a "widow" or "widower" if no one knows your relationship as a couple.

2. Lovers may also develop their own homophobia as they look at their lifestyle and see AIDS as an outcome. They may not seek out new partners and may abstain altogether from sexual relationships. Like "widows" or "widowers," they may ask the question, "Will I ever be happy again and have a meaningful relationship with someone?" How will the next person one encounters react if one tells them, "My partner died from AIDS?" How does the person you are counseling feel they will react if a new person they come into contact with says they also had a lover die from AIDS, or that they also now have AIDS? Would the person be willing to get involved again with someone who has AIDS or would one seek out another partner?

3. Special issues which may arouse guilt and anti-gay stigma are investigations by police, the medical examiner's office or doctors.

I. Chemical Use

1. Is the person a needle-sharing, intravenous drug user? If he or she is, what are the issues related to continued drug use and seeking support for usage? If one is an IV user, and also in a minority group, what are the feelings regarding isolation and abandonment as compared to gays and other "hidden grievers?"

2. Are they alcoholic and utilizing alcohol to get them through their bereavement?

3. Have they been through treatment previously if they are an alcoholic or IV user and will they look at treatment again as an option?

J. Depression and Self-Destructive Behavior

1. Is the person feeling self-destructive or is he or she talking about harming themselves? The individual may have a lowered self-esteem and emotional pain which can be intensified with guilt feelings leading to self-destructive behavior. Is the bereaved person having feelings of loneliness, hopelessness, and despair?

Listed below are various studies highlighting the importance of paying attention to individuals who are potentially self-destructive. **Self-destructive behavior is not to be taken lightly.**

Suicide is a concern as is impulsiveness, violent behavior, and self-destructive lifestyles concerning alcohol and drug use. Many hidden grievers often do not seek assistance until only after they are deeply depressed.

According to one report, "Three large, well-designed studies found that gay men and lesbians attempt suicide two to seven times more often than heterosexual comparison groups. Gay men and lesbians have significantly high rates of risk factors that increase suicide attempts, alcohol abuse, drug abuse, and interrupted social ties." [7, p. 1].

Similarly, "Reviewing 1985 records of the medical examiner in New York, Marzuk, et al. calculated that the suicide rate of men with AIDS who were 20- to 59-years-old was 36 times the rate of men without AIDS. Kizer et al. examined 1986 California death certificates and found the relative suicide rate of men with AIDS aged 20- to 39-years-old was 21 times the rate of men without AIDS" [8, p. 679]. A 1988 article states, "AIDS-associated suicides are not restricted to persons suffering from the disease. Fear of HIV infection and bereavement associated with AIDS can also precipitate suicidal behavior" [9, p. 227]. The article goes on to say, "Studies of suicide attempts among patients with previous depressive episodes, high levels of environmental stress, inadequate pre- and post-test counseling, and poor support networks are more likely to kill themselves." Finally, a 1988 Cornell University study found, "people with AIDS are 66 times more likely to commit suicide than the general population" [10, p. 5c]. The self-destructive behavior of the individual one is counseling needs to be addressed.

K. Replacing the Deceased and Delayed Grief

1. Many partners delay their grief as they turn to a new lover to "replace" the person who died, or move on quickly before doing their "grief work."
2. The "piling effect," or multiple deaths, can also delay the grief work as a person "does not have time" to grieve for one specific person but rather tries to deal with all of the deaths at one time. Each death needs to be looked at separately.

L. Social Support Systems

1. Guilt feelings about being gay can be intensified during bereavement and interfere moving through the grief process. What does the person perceive as one's *own* social support network and is it supportive? Is the person able to reach out to other gay individuals and get support, share feelings or loneliness, guilt, anger, and loss?

2. A key question is, "Can the person utilize church, family or work environment as a place to share honest feelings?"
3. Did the relationship with the deceased consume the bereaved person and as a result other social relationships not developed or utilized while the person was alive?
4. Individuals may physically move due to lack of social support or make major life changes during a time of transition, only adding additional stressors to the already stressful time. Whose apartment, house, etc., were they living in? Will the lover have to move out and what about all the possessions which belonged to the deceased? For every loss there will be the "small" secondary losses that all pile-up and can be overwhelming.
5. Are they still receiving support from those who supported them while their lover was dying? Often "buddies," nurses, clergy and others disappear shortly after the death.
6. What about support from their own family or are/will they be rejected? The family support system will most likely not be the first place a bereaved gay or lesbian individual will turn.
7. Have individuals whom the bereaved person cares about physically touched them or embraced them?

M. Religious Affiliations/Spirituality Issues/Faith Issues

1. In the past, what has been their involvement with the church or synagogue? The likelihood of them turning to this source now is very low if the church/synagogue has not shown support in the past. At a time when the church could help the bereaved lover explore the existential questions about spirituality and religion, the lover/partner has learned from past experiences about rejection, guilt, stigmatization, and abandonment. For some, the exact opposite can be seen. It can be a time of renewed belief and a growing experience in their faith or spirituality.
2. What is their belief in a God, afterlife, etc., and what role did that play while caring for their partners?
3. Was the deceased lover religious or spiritual or did he or she believe in a God, afterlife, etc.? How did that influence the relationship between the two of them?
4. Does the person being counseled utilize affirmation, rituals sacraments, prayer, meditation, scripture, anything special to explore their spiritual or religious state? Is God a God of compassion or judgment?
5. Has the person attended any religiously-oriented support groups in the past and would one consider utilizing them at this time?

6. In the client's "coming out of the closet" process, where did/does spirituality fit into homosexuality? Is it part of it and incorporated into his or her life, or not included at all?

N. Services Available and Being Utilized

1. What are the services offered for the bereaved person? Is the community supportive of gay and lesbian issues and do support groups exist for bereaved lovers? If not, where can support be sought? Can the person afford the services? Often if they do not have the ability to pay they will not seek out services when they really could benefit from a safe and supportive person or program.
2. Will the person lose a job if an employer knows that one's lover died and that he or she is seeking therapy/counseling?

"COMING OUT" MODELS

Individuals who have had a lover/partner die from AIDS are often not supported by the deceased person's family or their own family of origin. Often the "family," which now exists, is not blood related at all. Many gay and lesbian people are "out" and open about their homosexuality while others are still "in the closet." Knowing what phase of "coming out" the individual one is working with is at, may assist with regard to their needs during this time in their bereavement. Concerning gay men a five-step "coming out" model can be used [11]:

1. *Emergence*—exploring the beginning awareness of "difference."
2. *Acknowledgment*—individual attempts to label and cope with his homoerotic thoughts and feelings.
3. *Crashing Out*—period of "developmental adolescence" exploring gay social environments and networks.
4. *First relationships*—complicated by myths and stereotypes.
5. *Self-definition and reintegration*—establishment of a positive and proactive self-concept.

Similarities are found between gay and lesbian "coming out" models. When working with female clients, the following "coming-out" model can be considered [12]:

1. *Differentness*—awareness of being different.
2. *Dissonance*—inner turmoil acknowledging being different. Conflicting family values and expectations.
3. *Relationships*—intimate experiences with other women. Issues of separatists nonseparatists, coming out to one's family.

4. *Stable lesbian identity*—settling down, community of friends and possible ongoing committed relationship.
5. *Integration*—integrates identity into positive self-concept.

The first category, *Lovers and Partners Concerns / Issues* looked at various questions which need to be explored regarding the partner's or lover's role with the deceased. The next category will look at the roles of the deceased person's spouse, ex-spouse, or children.

2. THE DECEASED PERSON'S SPOUSE, CHILDREN, OR EX-SPOUSE'S CONCERNS/ISSUES

First of all, and perhaps most important, many lesbians and gay men marry and produce children. Studies have shown many lesbians and gay men marry heterosexual spouses and produce children [13]. In one San Francisco study, "More than 50 percent of these marriages lasted at least three years," with "at least 50 percent of (all) the marriages producing children" [14].

A national survey found homosexuality is the single most difficult subject for parents to discuss with children [15]. Concerns about fear of being censured or ridiculed by children's peers is a major problem among children of lesbian mothers or gay fathers. Additionally, "former spouses appear to be likely candidates for (service). If the reports of respondents are accurate, the heterosexual spouses were most seriously affected by the marital breakup than the gay or lesbian spouses—perhaps even more so than those whose marital breakups are not affected by homosexuality" [15, p. 548].

"There are as many styles of gay fathering as there are of heterosexual fathering. Fathers live with their wives in suburban homes, live only with their children, have split or joint custody or various other arrangements of visiting rights, and are grandfathers, stepfathers, and adoptive fathers" [15, p. 545]. Miller's study further indicated second generation homosexuals are rare and separating children from a loving father, regardless of his sexual orientation, may do more harm than good.

Children of gay and lesbian parents meet their parent's lovers and friends in many cases. In such cases a father's or mother's lover is regarded by the children as a second father or mother or as a big brother or sister. Gay men and lesbians, individuals who are bisexual, IV users, heterosexuals, hemophiliacs and others who have AIDS, can and do have spouses and children. The disease affects everyone, not just the person with AIDS. If nothing has been said by children to others about their father or mother's lifestyle, they may also have to deal with "secrets" depending on family themes and their own perception of support systems.

For individuals whose spouses have died of AIDS, many protect themselves and their children and family by sharing lies about their spouse's death. What about their own health concerns and should they be tested? What if they are pregnant? Should they continue the pregnancy? What about financial support? Similar to a lover/partner, do you tell the next person you date, "my spouse died from AIDS." Stigma about AIDS and homophobia unfortunately exists and education and discussion is imperative to help alleviate it. Some of the issues raised in the previous section about lovers may be appropriate here also, especially if the deceased person's sexual preference or IV use was not known. Factors regarding inheritance may also produce conflict.

What if it was not their husband or wife, but a long time partner? Similar to the lover/partner in category one, this person may not be recognized in any way at the funeral or memorial service or in the obituary. Additional concerns such as finances, property and possessions may be problem areas due to the nonlegal status and similar to partners/lovers described previously, "secrets" may be kept, with delayed grief resulting.

In the next category the deceased person's biological family will be looked at. A key issue is: If the person who died was gay or lesbian, or an IV drug user, did the family know it? Similar to Category 1, and 2, the concerns and questions listed are intended *only to be guides* to explore the feeling and needs of the person one is counseling.

3. THE DECEASED PERSON'S BIOLOGICAL PARENTS, FAMILY, AND FRIENDS CONCERNS/ISSUES

Often, at the same time parents discover their son has AIDS, they discover their son is gay. Most likely they knew their son was gay, but did not want to deal with it and hoped their son "would change." "Where did we go wrong?," they ask, questioning what could have "gone wrong." How could "this" have happened? He even played high school football and dated girls" [16, p.22]:

> Parents often struggle with their own guilt and a feeling they could have done something differently and their (child) being gay would not have happened, let alone contracting AIDS. The behavior that manifests itself from these feelings is usually not helpful.

Parents or other family members will sometimes rush in and try to take over every aspect of the PWA's care, pushing aside a lover of many years as if he were simply a roommate. They will dominate or attempt to control hospital visits, move into their son's home, confiscate possessions, and block the lover's contact with the doctor. Sometimes lovers will try to cut out family members for their own personal reasons. Conflicts between all parties become inevitable.

Many families don't even really know who their "child" is any longer, as they may not have had contact with the child for many years.

"Should we share the news with friends and relatives?," is a question many families deal with. For some, this is seen as a very difficult decision. Should they lie about the diagnosis of the person with AIDS so they can receive the "same support" as other individuals receive before and after a "normal death," or should they tell the truth? This may also be the first time finding out their child, sibling or partner is an IV user. Additionally, many families who do share the news of their child's or sibling's disease, are often rejected and isolated from the "caring community."

I remember being at home when I received a call from a twelve-year-old girl whose brother with AIDS had just moved back from another state to live at home again. On numerous occasions I had talked long distance with her mother to try and help with medical and health care resources, as I had with the PWA and his physician. The call from the adolescent, however, was asking what she should tell her friends. I asked her what she wanted to tell her friends and what she felt she was able to share. She quickly responded that her mother told her she had to tell everyone her brother has cancer or people in the community would "stone the house." "Hidden grievers" will at some stage have to deal with the death in real terms.

As mentioned above, for many family members, finding out their child or sibling has AIDS comes at the same time they find out they are gay. Knowing about developmental models that exist regarding a family's acceptance of a child who has a same-gender affectional preference will assist you in having a better knowledge of "where the family of origin was" at the time of the death. The premise of the model below is "coming out of the closet" is a major crisis for the family system because: 1) there are no family rules, 2) no rules for the gay person, 3) no constructive language describing the issue, 4) strong negative values, 5) unspoken rules—"taboo," and 6) family themes—what's important. This model is not absolute and each family may move through it, while others get stuck or do not even attempt to approach it [17].

Family Systems Model for Acceptance of a Child Who Has a Same-Gender Affectional Preference

1. *Subliminal Awareness*—topic avoided.
2. *Acknowledgment / Impact*—rapid disorganization, system loss.
3. *Adjustment*—external, internal coping mechanisms.
4. *Resolution*—mourning, readjusting family rules, roles, themes.
5. *Integration*—family self-actualization.

As discussed previously, many times families find out about their child's sexual preference and AIDS during the second stage or "impact" stage. It is important to note that having to confront their own feelings as a family about the sexual preference issue and remove the "stressor" adds conflict to a time when the child needs unconditional love and support. Not sharing with others what is happening to their child/family member only adds to "secrets" and enhances the chances for a more difficult mourning when the death takes place. This is also the time lovers/partners and friends of their child are also distanced and often "blamed" for what is happening to their child and influencing their child's sexual preference.

Knowing where the family was in this model before the child/family member's death can serve as a guide to how well they accepted and supported the PWA, and possibly their lover/partner and friends. While working with the family it should also be remembered that this may not be the first child in the family system who has died of AIDS or who is HIV positive.

Based upon the family's religious orientation, they may have disowned their child until they "changed their ways" or not have acknowledged their existence at all before the death and abandoned them. Guilt after the death regarding this will need to be addressed.

Often a forgotten category is that of the deceased person's friends. In the next section the impact on friends will be discussed.

5. THE DECEASED PERSON'S FRIENDS

Friends, both gay and straight, unlike lovers or partners, often receive even less support after a friend's death. They are not "widows" or "widowers" and they are not blood relatives. They are expected to stay at work because they cannot receive the time off for the funeral and they may have just buried another friend the day before.

Friends support friends through their living and their dying, and some clearly are "family" when no other family support exists. How involved in the PWA's caregiving was the person you are counseling?

Was the person involved in the funeral/memorial service plans? Were they able to attend the funeral if the person was buried in another part of the country? With more and more health and mental health services for PWAs being offered in smaller communities, more PWAs are "going home" to die and friends are being "left behind."

How many friends has the person had who have died from AIDS? What about the *bereavement overload*? If they are in a high risk group, what do they perceive their future to be? Have their friends/support system abandoned them after a friend's death?

Friends are often in the "first circle" and are deeply affected by the death of their friend. What is meant by the "first and second circles"? The next section looks at the caregiving community and the impact of a PWA's death upon us.

7. THE CAREGIVING COMMUNITY ("SECOND CIRCLE") FOR THE PERSON WHO DIED

Those of us who are not the direct grievers during impending death or during bereavement, represent the "second circle." Imagine two circles surrounding a person in the center of the inner circle. The person is the individual who is dying or who has died. The "first circle" is the person who is dealing with direct grief as we clinicians or clergy know it, whether anticipatory or after the death. The "second circle" consists of the "buddies," clinicians, clergy, health care providers, etc., who work with the person in the center of the first circle and/or who later work with persons in the "first circle." As persons in the "second circle," we too grieve. This is indirect grief which affects us internally by asking us to re-evaluate what is important in our lives, to look at our own past or current losses, our own mortality, our own relationships, our own denial system, our own religious or spiritual beliefs and our own feelings of loss if we knew the person who died.

As individuals in the "second circle," we need to be aware of our own fears and prejudices, our own conscious and unconscious thoughts, and our attitudes and responses to people we work with and their lifestyles. Our own beliefs about God, death and the afterlife need to continually be re-examined, and asking ourselves if "my feelings will interfere with providing good counseling to this client or member of the congregation" needs to be addressed? Supporting the bereaved person is the goal of our work and through it we learn from each situation.

As Clinicians, Counselors or Clergy, What Can We Do Specifically When We Work with Those Who are Bereaved?

1. *Active listening*—involves listening to both verbal and nonverbal messages. Egan suggested the helper regularly ask her/himself these four questions: 1) What is the core of what this person is trying to communicate?, 2) What is this person saying about his or her experiences?, 3) What is this person saying about his or her behaviors?, and 4) What is this person saying about his or her feelings? [18]. In her article on enabling hope, Hickey states, "active listening involves not just listening to patients, but also listening to one's own responses" [18].

2. *Probing extensively*—probing into someone's past can frighten clients and thus needs to be done carefully and appropriately. However, exploring their past and letting them re-experience the feelings that accompanied that past, is imperative. Listening to their story, finding out the various "crisis points" in their past and how they dealt with them, or did not deal with them, gives us direction.

3. *Setting personal goals*—help the person you are working with, when you perceive *them* to be ready, in setting personal goals. When setting goals, remember flexibility and attempt to obtain small hills before small mountains. Help them look ahead, make plans, and develop a social support network. What do they perceive their future to look like and how can they now move into a world where their loved one no longer is physically alive. How can they still have a "relationship" with the person who has died should be discussed. The client's personal goals need to be realistic and obtainable. Many people may already feel a loss of control and being able to provide options for the client to choose from, will be important. Bridges wrote, "Every transition is an ending that prepares the ground for a new growth and new activities," but as English novelist, John Galsworthy stated, "The beginnings . . . of all human undertakings are untidy" [19].

4. *Nutrition, hydration, exercise, and rest*—each are important during a time when the client most likely does not care, is not feeling emotionally or physically strong enough, or wants to be so busy they "don't feel the hurt." Balanced meals, lots of liquids, and fresh air are important. Providing for quiet time is also important each day.

5. *Education*—provide information on AIDS to families and safe sex practices for individuals if you feel it is necessary. Issues such as, "What can we do if we feel a client we are working with is putting other individuals at risk based on their dangerous sexual to drug-use behavior?" need to be addressed. Learning more about AIDS, IV treatment options, etc., provides the client with additional information to

assess his/her situation. As clinicians and clergy, we also need to continually update our own knowledge in all aspects of the disease. Having available for clients and others, literature, additional resources, addresses and phone numbers is also important. Consider the term "empowerment," but recognize making a phone call with the client's permission and setting up an appointment, is sometimes more important in getting them to helpful resources, then waiting for them to do it "on their own."

6. *Medication*—hopefully can be avoided, however, anti-depressants may be warranted. Is the person severely depressed and/or is he or she suicidal? Be aware many individuals are already on anti-depressants when they come to you and also note any signs of illicit drug use. Clinicians need to do more than spend a few moments with someone and provide them with more medications! At some stage the medications will stop and if the "grief work" has not been dealt with, it will begin. Utilizing a physician is important if you feel a client can benefit from medications or has concerns about his or her own health.

7. *Alcohol and other chemicals to be avoided*—try to assist the client to recognize that chemical use will most likely delay their grief work and can cause additional problems. If they have been through treatment, encourage them to utilize the resources that have assisted them up to this point, or to use new resources, so they do not regress to "old habits." Caffeine should be avoided during this time when the person is already having possibly high anxiety levels.

8. *Spiritual/religious component*—do they have a belief system? Is it one you are familiar with? Is God a "companion" in their belief or a "judge"? What are their images of God? What are the issues on top of their spiritual/religious priority list? How important are rituals/symbols for them and what issues may be increasing or decreasing their own death anxiety? Is their religious community supportive of them? Is the death related to religious beliefs in any way? A significant component in this area, is, as clinicians, we need to continue re-evaluating our own belief system and how it interacts with helping others.

9. *Note cultural differences*—individuals from different cultures have various responses to illness and death. Learn about cultures and be students to those you counsel in their process of healing and growth. Communication styles can be very different.

10. *Age of the bereaved*—are you working with adults, children, adolescents, or young adults? Learn differences in developmental levels regarding children's grief work and recognize as each of us moves on in our lives, we encounter new times when the grief work may be rekindled. It does not often take a large "forest fire" to bring back old memories and needs. Sometimes "brush fires" can do a lot of damage,

but usually with help from trusted adults or friends, the "damage" will not be extensive and only minor. How many "secrets" were kept and how large was the perceived loss, will be significant issues, regardless of the age of the bereaved.

11. *Assisting the client or member of your congregation in finding outside help*—are half-day, one-, two- or three-day intensive seminars or workshops led by professionals or others available in your area? Do drop-in centers exist where counseling or support groups, either open and/or closed, exist? We need to continue recognizing that often times one-on-one psychotherapy is too threatening, and it is advantageous to suggest "support groups" with peers or "self-help" groups. Even if one-on-one therapy is utilized, support groups are also wonderful to allow individuals to hear "they are not the only ones" and to help build a social network of concerned people. What church befriender programs exist in your area, and if they do not, what can you and others do to develop such programs? What types of education about AIDS and AIDS prevention is available? What grassroots organizations, or already established organizations, can you and/or the person you are counseling get involved with? Share other resources with those you counsel and have them share with you what resources they are aware of that you may not be. *Remember, for some "hidden grievers" you are the only individual whom they can trust, however, know your limitations, and refer to others who can better assist the individual if you feel it is appropriate.*

12. *Congratulate, understand, provide support, and enjoy* working with those who select you to assist them in their time of need [11].

As Clinicians or Clergy, What About Us?

We are in the "second circle" and we also grieve. Whether we are counselors, physicians, clergy, nurses, volunteers, funeral home personnel, or whatever our helping role may be, we have also been affected. Each person we work with takes a part of us and leaves us often vulnerable unless we, too, seek support of helpful and nurturing peers. Each of us, reaching out to find our own support, is as important as offering it. An individual cannot run a marathon race unless he or she drinks fluids along different parts of the course. Do not wait until the race is over to drink, seek nourishment as you go, and do not forget your sense of humor!

As counselors, there are two points we need to consider. First, psychologist Carl Jung said, "Know your theories as well as you can, but put them aside when you touch the miracle of the living soul" [20]. Second, in his book *How Can I Help,* Ram Dass stated, "Here, once again, our ability to remain alert to our own thoughts as they come and go serves us in our relations with others. We hear into their pain . . . they feel heard . . . we meet together inside the confusion. And yet we ourselves are able to note, perhaps even to *anticipate*, that moment when another's entrapment of mind might be starting to suck us in. We are as alert to what is happening within *us* as we are to what is happening in *them*" [21].

In conclusion, we need to continue to explore our own anxieties, our own fears and our own skills. We need to know not only our weaknesses but also our strengths. We need to provide realistic hope to those we counsel and to ourselves, to remember that even after years of counseling there will be times we may feel inadequate to "be there" for others, and to remember we cannot change the past nor can we do the "work" of those we are counseling. The gift of *our* work is knowing individuals have selected *us* to share their stories, their pain, and their dreams, and being available and able to support them needs to be our constant goal.

REFERENCES

1. R. Leliaert, Spiritual Side of "Good Grief": What Happened to Holy Saturday?, *Death Studies*, 13, 1989.
2. R. Bailey, Sr., *Biblical Perspectives on Death*, Fortress Press, Philadelphia, 1979.
3. Ira Progoff, *The Practice of Process Meditation*, Dialogue House Library, New York, 1980.
4. C. Meyer, *Surviving Death: A Practical Guide to Caring for the Dying and Bereaved*, Twenty-Third Publications, Mystic, Connecticut, 1988.
5. J. Worden, *Grief Counseling and Grief Therapy: A Handbook for the Mental Health Practitioner*, Springer, New York, 1991.
6. R. Kastenbaum, *Death, Society, and Human Experience*, 3rd Edition, The C. V. Mosby Company, St. Louis, 1986.
7. J. Saunders and S. Valente, Suicide Risk Among Gay Men and Lesbians: A Review, *Death Studies*, 11, 1987.
8. S. Perry, L. Jacobson, and B. Fishman, Suicidal Ideation and HIV Testing, *Journal of the American Medical Association*, 263, 1990.
9. R. Frierson and S. Lippmann, Suicide and AIDS, *Psychosomatics*, 299, p. 227, 1988.
10. L. Siegal, Suicide Gives Some Victims of AIDS a Sense of Final Control, *Duluth, MN New Tribune*, February 6, 1990.
11. J. Grace, *Coming Out Alive: A Positive Developmental Model of Homosexual Competence*, a paper delivered at the Sixth Biennial Professional Symposium of the National Association of Social Workers, San Antonio, Texas, November 16, 1979.

278 / DEATH AND SPIRITUALITY

12. L. Lewis, The Coming-Out Process for Lesbians: Integrating a Stable Identity, *Social Work*, September-October, pp. 464-469, 1984.
13. A. P. Bell and M. S. Weinberg, *Homosexualities: A Study of Diversities Among Men and Women*, Simon and Schuster, New York, 1978.
14. N. Wyers, Homosexuality in the Family: Lesbian and Gay Spouses, *Social Work*, pp. 143-147, 1989.
15. B. Miller, Gay Fathers and Their Children, *The Family Coordinator*, October 1979.
16. J. Johnson, *Help: Pastoral Care and AIDS*, Lutheran Social Services of Northern California, 1988.
17. J. De Vine, A Systematic Inspection of Affectional Preference Orientation and the Family of Origin, *Homosexuality and Social Work*, pp. 9-17, 1984.
18. S. Hickey, Enabling Hope, *Cancer Nursing, 9*:3, 1986.
19. W. Bridges, *Transitions*, Addison-Wesley Publishing Company, New York, 1980.
20. C. Corr, Entering into the World of Children and Adolescents, *The Forum Newsletter, 5*, p. 5, 1989.
21. R. Dass and P. Groman, *How Can I Help?*, Alfred Knopf, New York, 1986.

PART V

Death and the Human Spirit

Since spirituality is such a broad topic, it is desirable to have a section illustrating the far-reaching, interesting, and complex ramification of the interrelationship of spirituality and death. Stevenson begins this section by discussing the role of religious values in death education. Since the subject of death is inevitably intertwined with religious belief and rituals and raises serious spiritual issues, it often provides a challenge to the knowledge and sensitivities of educators as well as counselors. Educators in public schools may be especially reluctant to discuss religious beliefs. Stevenson reminds readers that there is a difference between teaching religion and teaching about religion. He suggests that the latter be done in a straight forward way or when necessary such as in discussion of AIDS or suicide in a balanced and fair approach consistent with other controversial issues. Stevenson also suggests that students and their instructor fully explore how their own values, including religious values, affect their beliefs, feelings, and behavior about dying and death.

Ellen Zinner and her group of graduate counseling psychology students consider a related issue. She and her students note that often the loss of religion as well as other losses related to spirituality can in themselves generate strong feelings of grief. And she notes these losses can often occur when students leave home for college, facing both the losses of community and culture and critical evaluation of their own beliefs and values. Not only then is Zinner's article valued for its own elucidation of a unique form of spiritual loss, it also reinforces Stevenson's point about the sensitivity required with death-related education.

Sexuality is a topic that often has strong implications for spirituality. Spiritual and religious beliefs can influence definitions of appropriate and moral behavior, including sexual behavior. In the crisis of life-threatening illness or grief, these definitions can generate conflict and grief. In addition, both patients and families may have to struggle with their own sexual needs as they face these twin crises. Finally, sexuality is often tied to two primary spiritual values, life and love. It is this latter point that Jeanne Harper's essay emphasizes. To Harper, sexuality and spirituality have no inherent conflict as they are both affirmations of the human spirit. The task for counselors, then, is to assist clients in recognizing and affirming their sexuality within their own religious or spiritual belief system as they cope with the crises of illness, dying, and death.

Neale's chapter, too, emphasizes that humor is an affirmation of the spirit in the dark moments of dying, death and grief. Neale's chapter reminds readers of the perspectives of others such as Norman Cousins who addressed the healing power of humor in his bout with cancer [1]. Klein further explains that humor gives us power to face crises, helps us cope, and provides perspective and balance [2]. He also believes that humor provides psychological benefits as well, enhancing the respiratory, cardiovascular, and perhaps even the immune systems.

Perhaps these chapters are not so disparate after all. For all affirm that value, learning and thinking, sexuality and humor are expressions of the human spirit.

REFERENCES

1. N. Cousins, *The Anatomy of an Illness*, W. W. Norton & Co., New York, 1979.
2. A. Klein, *The Healing Power of Humor*, Tarcher, Louisiana, 1989.

CHAPTER 21

Religious Values in Death Education

Robert G. Stevenson

Death education courses and individual death-related units in established courses are appearing in today's classrooms with increasing frequency. Modern death education curricula include topics such as: definitions of death, the meaning of life/death, funeral rituals, life after death, euthanasia, suicide, and coping with loss. Religion has traditionally been one means which people have used in examining these topics. Religion has also provided some students with answers to the questions which are raised by these topics.

There is little difficulty in speaking of religion when the death education takes place in the setting of a church, synagogue or in some other religious format. However, the discussion of religion has caused some concern when it takes place in a public school classroom. These concerns revolve around the place given to religious values in such lessons, and in a larger sense, in death education as a whole.

The public schools of the United States have long maintained the tradition of separation of church and state. For this reason there are some who would object to any instruction in public schools about the definition of death or the meanings of death which are based on the teachings of a particular religion.

If it is decided that there is indeed a legitimate reason to describe the teachings of different religions about death, what should such lessons include? In today's pluralistic society, there are many different beliefs about death and the meaning of death. There is an even wider variety of belief when it comes to the possibility of life after death. Which beliefs should be described and how can death educators avoid offending the beliefs of some when describing the beliefs of others?

RELIGIOUS BELIEF IN A PLURALISTIC SOCIETY

It must be clear at the start that there is a significant difference between teaching religion and teaching "about" religion. Public schools have been teaching "about" religion for years. An informal survey of several New Jersey secondary schools' curricula found that European history courses (still called "world" history in some schools), are routinely taught about the gods of ancient Egypt, Greece, and Rome, the Roman persecution of the Christians, the impact of Christian teachings on the Roman Empire, Martin Luther and the Reformation of Christianity, the Spanish Inquisition, and European emigration to America for religious freedom. In world cultures classes students learn the beliefs of Hindus, Buddhists, and Moslems in order to understand the culture of those societies which are made up of followers of those faiths. Humanities courses look at ways in which humankind has tried to describe and relate to a higher being. The Bible, Torah and Koran are studied as keys to understanding human values and beliefs.

Death education courses present death-related information from religion in much the same way. In *Dimensions of Loss and Death Education,* Patricia Zalaznik offers a unit on religious viewpoints concerning death [1]. She suggests covering a variety of beliefs through student writings, guest speakers and/or group discussion. Educators are encouraged to avoid imposing personal values on students by having the students describe their own beliefs. This also provides an opportunity for students to share their varied beliefs with their classmates. The students also play a key role in the selection of guest speakers by sponsoring the panel and by providing the guest speakers with a list of questions which they wish to have answered. Finally, students review their readings and notes and can participate in group-learning exercises by having class discussion or assignments in small groups.

In *Discussing Death: A Guide to Death Education,* Gretchen Mills and her colleagues state their observation that "many students discuss death from a religious framework." For this reason they state that there is "a need for teachers to develop learning opportunities which will stimulate examination of various religious customs and beliefs about death" [2]. They see this as helping teachers and students to gain a better understanding of and respect for the beliefs of others. There are three specific lessons devoted to the topic of religion. The first lesson is intended for children ages five and six under the concept: Causes of Death. It examines the role of religion in helping to form a child's view of death. There is no mention of religion in a specific way in the concepts aimed at students seven to fourteen years of age. The other two lessons are intended for use with secondary school students, fifteen to eighteen years of age. One explores some of the answers to the question, "Is there life after death?" The other lesson, based on a learning opportunity entitled "Organized Religion and Death" seeks to "identify the death beliefs, customs, and rituals of organized religions" as an aid to students in understanding their personal beliefs as well as any religious origins of family customs and rituals.

Students were asked by writer Mary McHugh about their views of death. The student answers showed that they use religion in two basic ways: as a way of confronting, and coping with, their fears of death and to answer the question, "What happens to you when you die?" [3]. Writers who discuss the problem of explaining death to children routinely explain how to include religious beliefs in such an explanation. Earl Grollman, in *Explaining Death to Children* included articles on various religious traditions and beliefs concerning death that make up almost one-third of that book [4]. Dale V. Hardt describes religious belief as being at the root of our death attitudes and includes an extensive number of researchers to prove his point [5]. His starting point is the belief of Sigmund Freud that "the basis of religion is an attempt by man to lessen his terror of death" [5]. It is not only children who use religion as a means of attempting to understand the world. Tellis-Nayak found that religious belief was used by elderly persons in a rural environment to render the world intelligible [6]. It seems as if the death attitudes of significant numbers of people all ages are linked to a religious framework. If we are to teach about those death attitudes or death-related behaviors in death education courses, how could religion *not* be included?

Sociology classes regularly include religion and religious institutions in high school curricula. Religion has been one way in which we humans organize our life experiences into structures which help to give them meaning. Peter Koestenbaum calls religion part of the "social expression" which validates the importance of this organization, or reorganization, of human experience [7]. One professor at a New Jersey community college consistently rejected any death education text that had a section dealing with religion. He felt that religion had no place in a secular curriculum at any level. However, for several years he had students use Glenn Vernon's *Sociology of Death*. Glenn Vernon points out a number of social behaviors that originated in attempts by religious institutions to help believers to deal with the personal and social crises which follow the death of an individual [8]. Almost all high school sociology courses study religion as an institution in society. To study, as sociology classes do, the behavior of people in groups and to understand the religious origins of some behavior, it is essential to examine religious belief as well.

There is yet another reason why teaching about religious beliefs belongs in the death education curriculum. It has been pointed out that the modern denial of death may have been a result of the decline of the belief in immortality [9]. Andrew Brennan states that the lack of strong conceptual creeds and philosophical religious views with which to transcend the crisis of bereavement greatly affects the prevailing concept of death [10]. He believes that religious belief in a hereafter can provide support to the bereaved and that the deritualization (many of these tied to religion) of grief deprives survivors of the solace these rituals may provide. Brennan describes the change in the view some have of death as a shift from a passage to eternity to a "barrier or wall . . . a bleak, abrupt cessation of life." Denial has been shown to be ineffective for adolescents in dealing with death-related issues and/or with the process of grief [11]. In attempting to prolong their use of denial in dealing with death and bereavement, many adolescents engage in "risk-taking" behavior to prove to themselves the validity of their belief in their own immortality. It is this sort of affirmation of personal belief which is replacing traditional religious belief concerning an afterlife. Both Hostler and Yalom attribute this "risk-taking" to an adolescent attempt to preserve the coping mechanism of denial [12, 13]. Each successful confrontation with death preserves the adolescent's feelings of personal immortality and the ability to continue the denial of death. To state that "learning to deal with bereavement on one's own" might be the most effective means of developing coping skills is not born out by the facts.

If death education courses are to deal with the issues raised by our transformation into a death-denying society, an examination of the role played by changes in, or the absence of, religious belief will need to be part of such courses.

The approach to teaching "about religion" in death education courses involves a straight-forward description of religious practice and/or belief. An alternate approach involves treating the topic of religion as a "controversial issue" in the school. Many schools have a policy which deals explicitly with such an issue.

THE TREATMENT OF CONTROVERSIAL ISSUES

The issue of dealing with controversial issues in the schools is not a new one. It probably reached its peak in the 1960s, during the debate which surrounded the implementation of sex education in the schools. At that time it was recognized that there were issues which could not be adequately treated by a simple presentation of "facts." With some issues, such as sex education, the values which regulated the behaviors under discussion were at least as important as physical data. However, there was a wide variety of belief over what values were "correct."

In order to deal with issues which the majority of educators and community members felt belonged in the curriculum, school systems adopted policies on dealing with issues which are regarded as "controversial." Sex education and death education are both examples of this type of controversial issue. Because of the earlier experience of the schools with implementing sex education courses, recommended policies for handling controversial issues in the curriculum have been already adopted and are now in place in many schools.

One such policy has been in place for twenty years in the River Dell Regional School System in northern New Jersey. This policy was first formulated in 1970 and was drawn up in response to community concerns over sex education, but its general wording includes all courses and applies equally well to many of the issues involving religion and death education. This policy defines a controversial issue as a question in which [14, p. 4]:

> ... one or more of the proposed answers are objectionable enough to a section of the citizenry to arouse strong reaction. The immediate cause of this reaction may be personal conviction or interest, or allegiance to an interested group. The most critically controversial questions are those characterized by current importance and by group opinion and interest.

The board, in the same document, states that the consideration of controversial questions is a legitimate function of the public schools. They contend that since young people must one day face such questions, it is valuable to deal with them in an atmosphere which will "promote consideration of all significant factors." The board directed that students should be exposed to a "many-sided study" of these questions and that students should be helped "to develop techniques" to deal with these questions.

The decision as to whether or not a particular question should be a matter for school study is to be made by the board, through approval of appropriate courses of study or, if such a question arises unexpectedly, by the classroom teacher. The decision is to be based on the answers to the following questions:

1. *Is this a question which has "timeless" importance?* The questions related to death, suffering, life after death, and the value (or "quality") of life have been asked by humankind since earliest recorded history (and perhaps for even longer than that).

Religious values have played a major role in providing answers for those questions.

2. *Are the students "mature" enough to deal with this question?* At age ten most students understand the physical reality of death. They know that its physical aspects are universal and irreversible. However, there is still a need to be sure that the topic is covered in a way that is age appropriate.

3. *Do the answers to this question help meet student needs?* It can be demonstrated that a balanced presentation of the religious values which have an impact on the beliefs and actions of students can be beneficial to the students involved.

4. *Is consideration of this question compatible with the purposes of the school?* The public schools of the United States have been charged to educate the "whole child." With the importance of religious beliefs which Freud, Jung, and other researchers see for children, it would be difficult to meet this charge if such a major factor in the lives of most students were deliberately ignored.

5. *Is the teacher prepared for the responsibility of dealing with this question?* This fifth point, concerning teacher preparation, is covered in detail. The policy contains a statement that, "The wise teacher avoids going into a controversial question which is beyond his own depth. A student would better be uninformed about a question than misinformed about it."

Finally, the River Dell policy states the rights of individuals and groups in the community. It states that, "a citizen has the right to assume that controversial questions are being presented fairly." However, no individual or group can claim the right to speak directly to students in school. If individuals or groups believe that presentations are not "fair," or do not present all sides of a question correctly, they may protest directly to the Board of Education.

It must again be pointed out that government regulations prevent the teaching "of" religion in public schools, but this does not prevent public schools from teaching "about" religion. A policy such as the one described here can be useful in easing the minds of concerned community members and heading off some difficulties related to the treatment of ethical or religious topics.

Two texts by Bender and Hagen, *Death and Dying* and *Problems of Death* complement this approach [15, 16]. They use primary source materials which present opposing sides of controversial issues. Religious spokespersons and arguments appear throughout the text as they cover topics such as: the meaning of death, when death occurs, reactions to death, life after death, euthanasia, abortion, and suicide.

To not speak of these potentially controversial topics implies that the topic is unimportant or that it is beyond the ability of the school or teacher to discuss in an objective manner. The consequence of this could be a belief by students that 1) such topics are not important enough for students to consider them or that 2) the student cannot really hope to comprehend the issues involved in examining the topic if they are too difficult to be discussed by educators and schools.

An alternate approach would be to use only secondary or tertiary sources in covering the topic. This practice threatens to strip the topic of its affective component. How can young people understand the manner in which some of these issues shape public policy and affect private lives if they are covered in a manner which is devoid of emotion. If emotionally charged topics are presented in a manner that ignores, or refers only indirectly to, the underlying emotions, the presentation must be "unbalanced" since a major component has been omitted. It must reasonably be asked how much of this desire to keep selected topics out of the classroom is due to an effort to maintain the separation of church and state and how much of it reflects the type of "anti-intellectualism" that Richard Hofstadter saw as intrinsic in the fiber of twentieth-century American life? The existence of policies regarding the treatment of controversial issues in the curriculum shows that educators and school boards believe that there are some questions for which there is not one "correct answer" and that these questions deserve to be addressed in many areas of society, including the schools.

RELIGIOUS VALUES AND SOCIETY

It is not teaching about religion alone but the transmission of religious values which causes concern for others about death education. Religious leaders have expressed concern, echoed by some parents, that if religious values are discussed in school classrooms such lessons may cause their influence to be undermined. Students may be confused by presentation of different points of view or of beliefs which contradict their own. In extreme cases this could even cause conflicts within families.

Traditionally, religion has fulfilled several functions in society. It has been a kind of "social cement" which has provided groups of people with common beliefs and *common values* to help develop a feeling of community. It helps to give people a sense that life has some meaning or purpose. Religion reinforces the most important norms of society. And, religion provides help during major life events or periods of change by assisting people to face, and to deal with, these events and the accompanying stress [17].

Religious values have had a parallel importance for individual members of those societies. These values can provide a person with a sense of belonging. They can provide a person with a sense of security when confronted with the reality of personal mortality or the death of loved ones. And, religious values have been shown to be able to give a person a sense that there is meaning to life, even to a life of suffering. This last function of religious values, is of increasing interest to educators at a time when schools are seen as playing a major role in stemming the rising tide of adolescent suicide. Schools are being asked to help educate students to place a greater value on life.

Religious values have a role to play in teaching young people to appreciate life. By drawing on the work of the American Sociological Association, one might explain the process this way [18]. We want young people to live and to embrace life. To think that life is worth living, we must value it. To learn to value life we must learn to develop a set of values. During the last twenty years, changes in the family and in organized religion have caused this learning to be left, increasingly, to the schools.

A simple goal of education is to have students accept as fact the belief that each of us is responsible for the consequences of his or her actions. The decision concerning whether an action is "right or wrong," or good/evil, is essentially a value judgment. This type of value judgment was identified by Gordon and Klass as one of the four major goals of death education [19]. They saw "defining value judgments raised by issues related to death" as this goal. They also cautioned educators that in attempting to meet this goal they would need to:

- be aware of their own values and their personal beliefs about the need for social change,
- understand the complexity of the issues involved and be able to present all sides in a clear, straight-forward manner.

To do otherwise runs the risk that the teacher may unintentionally make a biased presentation to the students. Teachers who are unaware of their own values may present personal opinion as "fact" to the detriment of students. If society decides that religious values have no place in death education, and rules that they may not be discussed, if we consciously choose to leave religious values unexamined in the schools, how can anyone really be sure of the values that educators may be using as they create and implement lesson plans? However, if we set guidelines for discussion of such values and encourage first teachers, and then students, to examine the religious values that influence us and our society, we stand a far better chance of bringing such influences into consciousness. Students should also be encouraged to discuss values and beliefs with their parents and/or guardians and with other caring adults important to them (including religious advisors, if any). The world today is too complex, too threatening a place to allow students to be forced to take sides in a school-family adversarial relationship. When all of the important adults in a student's life communicate and cooperate, a powerful force can be placed on the side of the student.

A conscious understanding of our values and those of others can help to increase our feeling of "control" over our lives. Such an understanding, to be complete, must include religious values. Ethical values are sometimes cloaked under the title of "humanistic values." Humanism fulfills many of the roles that, in the past, were assigned to religion, but humanism is under attack as a religion in itself. Its inclusion does not solve the "problem" of dealing with religious values in the classroom. It merely adds another dimension to it.

To the belief that the unexamined life is not worth living, we might reasonably add that unexamined values are not worth having. Today, a student who believes his/her life to be of no value may choose to end it, despite the positive things that all those around the student might see. This "negative illusion" has proven fatal in far too many cases. A conscious examination of religious values, as part of an overall examination of values that relate to death, loss and grief, has the potential to change those feelings. It can help a student to use an examination of values to substitute "positive illusions" for negative ones. It will mean that educators must work to develop and maintain a balanced way to examine values without bias, but if the final result is to place a greater value on life, would not that alone be worth the effort?

SUMMARY

Religion has long been discussed in public school classrooms. There is a difference between teaching religion and teaching "about" religion. It has been generally accepted that public schools are prohibited from teaching religion but that they may teach "about" religion in a number of disciplines. A policy on "controversial issues" can help insure a balanced presentation in such classes. In death education classes, students examine topics which raise questions. To answer these questions, students will have to draw on their personal values, including religious values. To explain the possible influence of these values on each of us and to do so in an unbiased way will require a great deal of effort on the part of school and community. The benefits of such a conscious examination of the impact of religious values could include diminishing the unintentional bias shown by teachers who assume they are "objective" and increasing feelings of control over those influences on the part of teachers and students alike.

REFERENCES

1. P. Zalaznik, *Dimensions of Loss and Death Education,* Ed-Pac Publishing Company, Minneapolis, Minnesota, 1979.
2. G. C. Mills, *Discussing Death: A Guide to Death Education,* ETC Publications, Palm Springs, California, 1976.
3. M. McHugh, *Young People Talk About Death,* Franklin Watts, New York, 1980.
4. A. Grollman, *Explaining Death to Children,* Beacon Press, Boston, 1967.
5. D. V. Hardt, *Death: The Final Frontier,* Prentice-Hall, Englewood Cliffs, New Jersey, 1979.
6. V. Tellis-Nayak, The Transcendent Standard: The Religious Ethos of the Rural Elderly, Gerontologist, pp. 359-363, 1982.
7. P. Koestenbaum, *Is There an Answer to Death?,* Prentice-Hall, Englewood Cliffs, New Jersey, 1976.
8. G. M. Vernon, *Sociology of Death: An Analysis of Death-Related Behavior,* The Ronald Press, New York, 1970.
9. G. Kovacs, Death and the Question of Immortality, *Death Education, 1,* pp. 15-24, 1982.
10. A. J. Brennan, Children and Death, manuscript, New York, 1983.
11. R. G. Stevenson, Curing Death Ignorance: A Death Education Course for Secondary Schools, doctoral dissertation, Teaneck, New Jersey, 1984.
12. L. Hostler, The Development of the Child's Concept of Death, in *The Child and Death,* Olle Jane Sahler (ed.), C. V. Mosby, St. Louis, 1978.
13. I. D. Yalom, *Existential Psychotherapy,* Basic Books, New York, 1980.
14. River Dell Regional Schools Board of Education, 700 Series—Instruction, adopted September 8, 1970, p. 4, (mimeographed).
15. L. Bender, *Problems of Death,* 2nd Edition, Greenhaven Press, St. Paul, Minnesota, 1981.
16. D. L. Bender and C. Hagen, *Death and Dying,* Greenhaven Press, St. Paul, Minnesota, 1980.
17. I. Robertson, *Sociology,* Worth Publishers, New York, 1977.
18. Sociological Resources for the Social Studies, *Inquiries in Sociology,* Allyn and Bacon, Boston, 1972.
19. A. K. Gordon and D. Klass, *They Need to Know: How to Teach Children about Death,* Prentice-Hall, Englewood Cliffs, New Jersey, 1979.

CHAPTER 22

The Dark Night of the Spirit: Grief Following a Loss in Religious Identity*

*Dorothy M. Barra, Erica S. Carlson,
Mark Maize, Wendy I. Murphy,
Betsy W. O'Neal, Rhonda E. Sarver, and
Ellen S. Zinner*

In the Fall of 1990, an Advanced Seminar in Loss and Grief was offered at Frostburg State University (Frostburg, MD) to focus on the understanding, assessment, and support of individuals grieving non-death losses. While numerous death and dying and grief counseling seminars have been offered at the college and graduate level throughout the country, a course focusing on intervention assessment and techniques for non-death loss survivors was considered to be relatively rare. Six graduate students in the FSU Masters of Counseling Psychology Program and their professor undertook the task to identify and explore survivorship issues often left unaddressed by mental health practitioners, and even by survivors themselves.

Several students identified the loss of religion as engendering a significant grief reaction. Through personal observation and experience, these students recognized that a break in one's religious

---

*The title of this chapter is taken from the writings of the contemplative religious, St. John of the Cross, who lived and wrote during the 16th century. In one of his contributions to Christian mysticism, St. John observed that our soul becomes "sick for the glory of God" by experiencing separation from God. We would suggest that humankind seeks, if only unconsciously, to lessen the grief of separations and to come to terms with their own spirit.

connectedness, whether in relation to traditional religious affiliation or to a more personal search for spiritual identity, frequently resulted in individuals experiencing many of the feelings associated with more "normal" loss situations. Thus, feelings of anger and resentment, emptiness and despair, sadness and isolation, and even relief could be seen in individuals struggling with the loss of previously comforting religious tenets and community identification. Here was another example of "disenfranchised grief," a situation wherein a loss is not socially recognized or sanctioned and where survivors are left to grieve alone [1]. Not only were the seminar participants interested in identifying groups of survivors experiencing religious and/or spiritual losses in general, but they were concerned and curious about the process of religious change and loss occurring at their own university. Out of this question, grew a survey research project to obtain a preliminary understanding of religious stability and change and whether these changes constituted a loss in the more conventional use of the word for students attending this small, rural-based state university.

This chapter is an outgrowth of these graduate students' efforts to prepare themselves for the many faces of loss and grief they will encounter in their careers. The chapter is broad and eclectic because the ideas of religious and spiritual loss as a grief-engendering phenomenon appears to be sparsely addressed in the literature. The topic also expanded as a direct result of increased awareness and understanding of the issues involved. Areas of exploration included anthropological, historical, and contemporary perspectives and comments on the impact of religious loss, as well as specific examples of individual and group efforts to contend with threatened and actual loss of religion, community, and spirituality. In conclusion, we present a summary and analysis of data drawn from a survey of religious attitudes and change conducted on this campus during October and November, 1990.

While religion and spirituality have been defined and understood in various ways, for our purposes we are defining "religion" as a set of beliefs and rituals related to values and to the meaning of life and death. "Organized religion" indicates a specific set of beliefs of a socially-recognized church and is of major focus here because of the Judeo-Christian predominance in religious life and activity in this country. "Spirituality" speaks to religion in its broadest understanding and pertains more to the general concerns of the psyche or "soul" [2].

BACKGROUND PERSPECTIVES

There are diverse viewpoints to consider in understanding the loss of religion, religious community, and spirituality. This section highlights anthropological, biblical, literary, and philosophical perspectives.

The study of religious practices has given anthropologists insight into humankind's development. Religious mores and practices have evolved through culturally learned and shared rituals and belief systems. Religion influences and is affected by all domains of a culture, particularly its social structure and relationships [3]. It takes its form and content from secular aspects of human experience and is considered a universal phenomenon since it exists in all cultures.

Though believers often prefer to view their own particular religion as unique, anthropologists point out strong parallels among diverse religions. For example, virtually all religions have their own creation myths, designed to explain the origins of the universe. Anthropologists further argue that religion and magic are similar in nature. Both use ritualistic expression, whether prayer, spells or incantations, as a means to summon the supernatural and to bring about some desired result.

Anthropologists have generally summarized the following as the primary benefits and functions of religion [3]:

1. Religion provides a background for moral/ethical principles and appropriate actions.
2. Religion contributes to social order by compelling people to act in a virtuous manner. Religious sanctions appear to be much more effective than secular prohibitions.
3. Religion provides motives for behavior.
4. Religion validates human existence.
5. Religion provides answers to existential concerns.
6. Religion explains the workings of the universe.
7. Religion instills hope.
8. Religion provides a sense of security/reassurance.
9. Religion allows for transcendence of mundane and psychic states.
10. Religion fosters group cohesiveness through shared rituals.

Anthropological interpretations of religion generally have assumed that the supportive effects of religion on culture outweigh any disruptive consequences.

Just as anthropology offers explanations for the human need for a religious base, so does the Bible. Several of the Old Testament's Psalms attest to human feelings of abandonment. Indeed, portions of Psalms 13, 42, and 39 express many of the feelings associated with a diminishing of the spirit: a heavy and disquieted soul, anxiety, life as nothingness, feeling forgotten, and having a "grief-filled heart." The Gospel of Matthew has Christ feeling forsaken by his Father: "My God, My God, why did you abandon me?" Many would believe that a "suffering servant" would have to burden himself with all the pain of humanity in order to be totally empathic toward those he is to save.

Twentieth century literature is also replete with similar themes of human alienation from religion. Alienation from the Supreme Being can be manifested by an emptiness such as that depicted in Camus' novel, *The Plague,* where existence appears repetitive and purposeless. "Plague is that life of a desperate loneliness, of just existing, of not celebrating life" [4].

Another example of the predicament of living within a chronic grief state due to spiritual loss can be found in Conrad's work, *Heart of Darkness* [5]. This writing exemplifies that night journey into the self, in search of the spirit and foreshadows the moral and spiritual deterioration which may occur as a result of isolating oneself from self, nature, others, and God.

Philosophers and psychologists such as Soren Kirkegaard and Carl Jung have also tackled the problematic loss of religious and spiritual content within one's life. In *Modern Man in Search of a Soul,* Jung writes that society has fostered a psychology based on experience and not on any systematic faith in a religion [6]. According to Jung, this shows a serious decline in the importance of spiritual life. As long as all goes well and there are no uncertainties or doubts, an individual can feel secure. However, when one's "river of psychic energy" is damned up, one's spiritual walk has been blocked. This results in loss of a sense of personal wholeness and in depression and hopelessness.

Kirkegaard examined the question of whether individuals grieve the loss of religion. He wrote extensively on the subject in *The Sickness Unto Death* [7]. Kirkegaard bemoans the fact that the loss of self is not considered to have the same degree of importance as losing one's possessions or part of one's body. Thus, the loss of one's self, spirit, or soul might not be particularly noticed until a person experienced a crisis. (This resulting despair is similar to that described in the works of Conrad, Camus, and others [5, 4].) Kirkegaard did praise intense despair for bringing this loss into conscious awareness and, thus, providing motivation for change. Essentially, an individual must experience the "sickness" of despair in order to grow spiritually [7]. Similarly, persons grieving a loss must work through their pain. They need to acknowledge and experience their feelings fully, allowing the grief to slowly dissipate.

The authors of this chapter sought to discern whether people responded to the loss of their religion, their religious community, or their spirituality in the same manner as those who experienced other significant losses such as the death of a loved one. Of numerous clergypersons interviewed about religious loss, most responded with feelings similar to those of persons working through a more standard grief process. One interviewee, an Episcopal priest, believes that his "spiritualness" has primarily to do with his inner thoughts, feelings, and perceptions as they relate to his sense of a higher power. This person had suffered from alcoholism, had been through a divorce, and had experienced a painful sanction from his church. Overcoming these trials, this man has equated his spiritual wholeness with his ability to let go of his feelings of loss and the need for extreme control over himself and others. Instead, he allows his faith in God to lead him.

Another clergy member talked about the commonalities among individuals who have experienced grief-engendered anger, sadness, and alienation from their own churches after suffering doubts about their faith in God. He told of two students, Roman Catholic and Jewish, who wished to marry. No clergy from either faith would marry them, resulting in this couple's alienation from their respective religions and feelings of sorrow and abandonment.

A Brethren pastor observed that a loss of spirituality, accompanied by feelings of emptiness and despair, often follows another significant loss, such as the death of a family member. Echoing that belief, another clergy person of the Lutheran faith said that ". . . in order to experience grief associated with a loss [of religion], there had to have been a relationship." It is the loss of this "relationship" with one's beliefs or religious community that may give rise to a grief response.

Anecdotes were also collected from lay persons. One graduate student wrote that she gave up believing in established regimes, including church and organized religion during the late 1960s. Along with this alienation came feelings that paralleled a grief reaction: fear, anxiety, anger, hopelessness, and even suicidal ideation. It was not until she began slowly working herself back into a more spiritually-oriented way of life that she began to attain a more peaceful acceptance of her chosen faith and identity.

Another person, a young woman in her mid-twenties, told how losing her faith in God during college resulted in her inconsistent behavior. She would act contrary to her previously held values but revert to behavior that she knew her parents would approve of when she was around them. This behavior led to feelings of emptiness, sorrow, anger, and discontent. These feelings did not abate until a friend encouraged her to seek peace through a more spiritual attitude. Others who were interviewed attested to feeling grouchy, angry, helpless, and lost as a result of severing their religious ties.

GRIEF AS A RESPONSE TO LOSS
OF RELIGIOUS COMMUNITY

Numerous examples of religious disaffiliation and resulting grief exist in society today, and yet there is a limited scope of research and clinical material available to direct counseling efforts. Because identity is culturally rooted and defined through one's social system, it seems reasonable to assume that a loss of identification with one's culture and support networks would elicit a grief reaction of significant intensity. Further, this emotional response might be expected to exist independently of the individual's willingness to leave versus being rejected by the religious group.

Former nuns have described the experience of becoming a nun as "depersonalizing." They are stripped of their possessions and isolated from family and friends. The process culminates in their resocialization and acceptance of a new identity given them by the order [8]. Leaving the convent means grieving the loss of this identity and developing once more a new sense of self.

One former nun vividly recalled the hurt and sense of rejection she experienced upon being denied permission to renew her vows, and the painful loss of social support and companionship [9]. She believed she had failed the order. During the following years, she suffered from depression, low self-esteem, and a lack of confidence. Another former nun remembered leaving the convent and changing from the habit into street clothes. "It was a sharp cutting off of my whole life" [9]. She felt like a stranger to the secular world and struggled to regain a sense of identity. She experienced feelings of anger and resentment toward her church and regretted her "wasted" years. She also mourned the loss of her life-long dream. Though Karin received psychiatric treatment to help work through her feelings, she found therapy "oppressive," and emphasized the need for support groups for ex-nuns. Such mutual help groups may facilitate grief work and ease the transition back into society [10].

The negative view of homosexuals held by many churches may result in rejection (or feelings of rejection) of gay members. There are roles such as pastor, elder, etc. that are often denied to gays. As a result, homosexuals are too often compelled to feign spirituality within the confines of a religion that does not accept them [10]. Homosexuals who have experienced a loss of spirituality frequently attribute this loss to mistreatment and prejudice encountered during involvement in traditional religion (as well as psychotherapy). Instead of receiving hoped-for acceptance, renewal, and validation, homosexuals have experienced guilt, shame, despair, isolation, and confusion [10].

Another identifiable group of individuals who may experience rejection or loss of religious identity is made up of former members of the Amish community. Religion is intrinsic to the sense of family and community among the Amish. Parental success is often measured by how many children join the church and carry on cultural traditions [11]. Approximately 12 percent of Amish youth rebel against the Amish way of life [12]. Youth who choose to further their education beyond the eighth grade face excommunication. The rationale for this is that if "they get away from the farm, they soon get away from the church . . ." [13]. The Amish adherent is forced to choose between two worlds. Leaving the community involves a complete loss of family, religion, and social support that makes this decision excruciatingly painful.

Excommunicated members are stigmatized and shunned by the community of family, friends, and business colleagues [13]. Anyone who continues to socialize with the outcasts is also ostracized. "The threat of social isolation is a powerful deterrent to disobedience in a community where everyone is linked by family ties" [13].

For some, the elusive quest for spirituality may induce an individual to enter one of the cults that can often prove harmful to the individual's spiritual well-being. When a son or daughter joins a cult, parents typically experience a grief reaction. "Anti-cult parents see their offspring's conversion as a repudiation of blood ties, career expectations, parental sacrifices, and family values" [14]. They respond with a mixture of confusion, disappointment, and rage. While some parents can do nothing but wait and hope for a change, others have the resources to hire a deprogrammer. They determine that it is necessary to intervene against their adult child's wishes as he or she is incapable of thinking clearly.

One man found his deprogramming from the Divine Light Mission "utterly devastating." "You find out that what you've based your life on is not real . . . I still doubt my ability to know my own feelings" [15]. Another woman poignantly revealed her feelings after leaving the Unification Church [15, p. 17]:

> I felt like I was in the pit of Hell . . . like I was dying . . . I lost trust and confidence in myself. I was afraid of going back to the outside world . . . I felt I couldn't relate to people . . . I was told about a support group for ex-cult members. From then on, I started dealing with my vulnerability and anger at being used, at my mind and will being taken away.

Clearly, former cult members need long-term support. Those for whom this support is lacking will find it easy to succumb to external pressure and feelings of ambivalence. They are likely to consider re-entry as a desirable option.

Another example of loss of religious culture is that of Native Americans. Certainly Native Americans have been victimized and often times stripped of their culture and spirituality. Notoriously high rates of alcoholism, suicide, and homicide among Native Americans can be understood in part as a result of religious and cultural oppression. According to Bea Shawanda, a Cree counselor, the Native American experience has been further compounded by multiple losses. These losses include: loss of native languages, family structure, elders, totems, rituals, values and traditions. Loss of spirituality touches each of these other losses deeply. She states that [16, p. 45]:

> Young people have lost their ability to dream. When you lose your ability to dream, you lose hope. We are walking around with a lot of unresolved grief.

Despite these issues, Native Americans have high rates of dropout in therapy. This illustrates the need for a "conceptual framework from which human services can be provided for the personal and emotional needs of the Indian people in a respectful manner, which is without the subtle culturally erosive effect of traditional therapy" [17]. Critics have suggested that coping skills can be utilized more productively by helping Native Americans resist the pressure to surrender their cultural and religious identity. Gene Thin Elk, a Sioux counselor, claims that "people who lose their identities by trying to force themselves into another culture are living in an unnatural world. We're teaching our people to stop bei ɔ ashamed of themselves" [18]. Effective treatment would integrate native customs and beliefs. According to Laign, "spiritual values that may seem alien to whites are deeply ingrained in the Native outlook" [18]. For example, natives can visit a Sweat Lodge to obtain instant healing through purification rituals, sharing, and support from friends and kin. The notion of spending months or years in therapy (with someone who may not be sensitive to cultural differences) is unthinkable to an American Indian who has experienced instant healing. Psychological and spiritual issues are intimately linked among Native Americans.

Not completely removed from the Native American experience of chronic alienation is the experience of children of alcoholic families. In recent years, there has been a growing awareness of issues commonly faced by Adult Children of Alcoholics (ACOAs) or anyone who has grown up within the chaotic environment of a dysfunctional family. It is important for counselors to recognize the "loss of spirituality" that may result from the contradiction of being raised by abusive or otherwise dysfunctional parents and being compelled to believe in their image of a loving and righteous God. A child may experience anger or a profound sense of helplessness upon realizing that not even God can protect him or her, and may develop a poor self-concept as a result of being told s/he is evil and deserves to be punished.

For recovering persons in general, religion/spirituality has become an increasingly controversial issue. Some crave spirituality as intrinsic to their recovery. For others, religion has nothing to do with their healing process. According to Carl Jung, addiction is the result of "spiritual bankruptcy" [6]. He advised his Catholic friend, Bill W., an alcoholic, that nothing short of a "spiritual awakening" could save him. This inspired Bill W. to organize Alcoholics Anonymous, a fellowship based on 12 steps or principles of recovery. Reliance on a "higher power" is central to this program.

Those who envision a vast gulf between religion and spirituality are frequently attracted to AA's reputation for focusing on growth through spiritual development. Such individuals are likely to be dismayed upon discovering their "spiritual" program appears biased toward Christianity. Dissatisfaction with recovery based on acceptance of a higher power has spawned a secular movement. These groups view personal healing as separate from religion/spirituality. Rather than focusing on a higher power, most members of secular recovery groups prefer to believe the greatest source of power and strength lies within the individual. Others express their faith in the collective energy of the group. Examples of secular groups include Women for Sobriety (WFS) and Secular Organization for Sobriety/Save Ourselves (SOS).

COLLEGE STUDENT RELIGIOUS AFFILIATION SURVEY

Throughout this effort, the literature that was read and anecdotal information that was gathered pointed to a loss of religion as a grief-engendering separation, with all the emotional wrenches of any other significant loss. The severity of the survivor's reactions might well depend upon the circumstances of the separation, the availability of personal and social support, etc.; but, no matter, the loss aspects always seemed to be there. As not uncommon with any initial examination of a "discovered" issue, this review left many questions unanswered and raised other questions of a more quantitative nature, such as the percent of the population who do separate from their religious roots and identifications; the number of these persons who consciously regard this separation as a loss; and the extent and severity of emotional reactions to this perceived loss. To obtain a clearer under-standing of such questions, the authors conducted a survey among college students at Frostburg State University, recognizing that this population of convenience was not representative of college students in general but might, instead, offer a preliminary glimpse into the issues raised. Further, it was also understood that there were no real time limits to the emotional manifestations of a loss, particularly a non-death loss. Although the sense of loss usually follows on the heels of the loss itself, it is not always so. With the loss of religion, the feelings of anger, sadness, and emptiness that might accompany such a letting-go may come years after the loss itself when an individual gains the emotional stability and maturity to recognize what was once held sacred as a child or young adult, what was consequently lost, and the personal ramifications of this religious change.

The purpose of this survey was to determine whether college stu-dents experience a grief reaction associated with a loss of religious identification and affiliation. Participants were college students enrolled at Frostburg State University in western Maryland. Selection was determined by voluntary participation of a number of FSU faculty who granted access to their students during class time. Each survey was accompanied by an informed consent form which each student read and signed prior to participation in the survey.

The survey inventory consisted of thirty items which addressed the following: religious affiliation and convictions of students and of their parents; any change in those convictions and affiliations; and factors which may have contributed to this change. The inventory assessed both positive and negative affective experiences related to change in religious convictions.

Three hundred and thirty-eight students participated in the survey (see Table 1). Demographic data indicated that 37.6 percent of these participants were freshmen. Not surprisingly, these individuals also comprised the most heavily surveyed age group, that of the eighteen to nineteen year olds (49.1%). Participating students were fairly evenly distributed by gender, with slightly more females surveyed (55%) than males (45%). With respect to childhood religious affiliation, almost a third of the respondents indicated that their religious affiliation as children was with the Catholic church (see Table 2). Affiliation with the Methodist faith was the second most frequently identified (19.7%), with the Baptist faith reported third most frequently (13.8%). Present religious affiliation reports paralleled these findings, although percent-age figures were lower for all three predominant religions.

Of the 338 respondents surveyed, ninety-seven (29%) reported a change in religious convictions since coming to college (see Tables 3 and

Table 1. Demographic Characteristics of Participants in
Religious Affiliation Survey (*N* = 338)

Characteristics	Totals	Percentage
Age		
18-19	167	49.4
20-21	115	34.0
22-23	33	9.8
24+	24	7.1
Gender		
Female	186	55.0
Male	152	45.0
Grade		
Freshman	128	37.9
Sophomore	60	17.8
Junior	69	20.4
Senior	66	19.5
Grad student	13	3.8
Other	2	.6

4). Of those male participants who indicated a change, slightly less than a quarter indicated that this change was a negative experience. Guilt was the most frequently reported negative emotional response, with anxiety and feelings of conflict noted by over 20 percent of male respondents. Despite endorsing negative emotional experiences to religious change, only a small minority (13.7%) of male students saw this change as a loss. Conversely, a third of the male subjects indicated a positive reaction to a self-identified religious change. Most strongly endorsed were feelings of satisfaction and relief as a result of religious changes.

Female respondents more often admitted to or disavowed emotional reactions to religious change, selecting the "neutral" response category significantly less often than male students. The majority of females who indicated that they had experienced a change in religious convictions since coming to college denied that this change constituted a loss for them. While many female students admitted to feelings of conflict and guilt, a majority denied feelings of anger, sadness, anxiety, or isolation, and expressed, instead, feelings of satisfaction and wholeness.

Table 2. Demographic Profile of Participants' Religious Affiliation
as a Child and at Present

Religion	As a Child		Now	
	N	Percent	N	Percent
Baptist	47	13.9	37	10.9
Brethren	6	1.8	3	.9
Buddhist	—	—	2	.6
Catholic	111	32.8	92	27.2
Christian/Pentecostal	19	5.6	22	6.5
Episcopalian	15	4.4	13	3.8
Jewish	9	2.6	8	2.4
Lutheran	15	4.4	13	3.8
Mennonite	1	.3	2	.6
Methodist	67	19.8	57	16.9
Mormon	2	.6	3	.9
Presbyterian	25	7.4	18	5.3
Unitarian	—	—	3	.9
Other	14	4.1	22	6.5
None	7	2.1	43	12.7

Several open-ended questions, designed to explore factors leading up to and involved with the subject's identified changes as well as concomitant emotional reactions, were included on the survey forms. Specifically, the following questions were posed: "If you have experienced a change in convictions, please describe the nature of this change"; "What factors or events led to this change?" and "How do you feel about this change?" Responses from subjects who indicated that they had indeed experienced a change in religious convictions were separated into two groups—those expressing positive emotional responses and those expressing negative emotional responses.

Six categories of responses from students who expressed positive emotional reactions to religious changes were observed. The majority of participants felt that religious change was due to maturity. This maturity was perceived as the result of exposure to different religions and philosophies as well as to the students becoming more self-reliant. Students falling into this category represented the upper range of the age groups surveyed. One 24-year-old male student stated, "I feel that it [change in religious conviction] means beginning to decide how to

Table 3. Male Participants' Reactions to a Change in
Religious Convictions (N = 51)

Reaction	Emotions Experienced (%)					
	Strongly Disagree	Disagree	Neutral	Agree	Strongly Agree	N/A
Loss	25.5	23.5	25.5	13.7	0.0	11.8
Conflict	11.8	25.5	33.3	17.7	3.9	7.8
Satisfaction	3.9	13.7	29.4	23.5	15.7	13.7
Relief	2.0	19.6	29.4	25.5	13.7	9.8
Mixed feelings	9.8	13.7	35.3	29.4	9.8	2.0
Anger	23.5	33.3	31.4	3.9	2.0	5.8
Renewal	2.0	23.5	37.3	27.5	3.9	5.8
Sadness	25.5	27.5	27.5	11.8	3.9	3.9
Guilt	17.7	23.5	17.7	25.5	7.8	7.8
Anxiety	17.7	17.7	29.4	17.7	3.9	13.7
Isolation	23.5	25.5	25.5	13.7	2.0	9.8
Sense/Wholeness	5.9	13.9	31.4	29.4	9.8	9.8

Table 4. Female Participants' Reactions to a Change in
Religious Convictions (N = 46)

Reaction	Emotions Experienced (%)					
	Strongly Disagree	Disagree	Neutral	Agree	Strongly Agree	N/A
Loss	43.5	19.6	15.2	21.7	0.0	0.0
Conflict	17.4	23.9	8.7	39.1	6.5	4.3
Satisfaction	2.2	23.9	21.7	13.0	37.0	2.2
Relief	2.2	34.8	26.1	13.0	19.6	4.3
Mixed feelings	13.0	19.6	19.6	32.6	8.7	6.5
Anger	39.1	21.7	17.4	4.3	2.2	15.2
Renewal	8.7	30.4	13.0	23.9	13.0	11.0
Sadness	28.3	34.8	11.0	19.6	0.0	6.5
Guilt	19.6	17.4	6.5	37.0	6.5	13.0
Anxiety	23.9	28.4	30.4	15.2	2.2	0.0
Isolation	34.8	32.6	15.2	15.2	2.2	0.0
Sense/Wholeness	6.5	26.1	8.7	19.6	30.4	8.7

304 / DEATH AND SPIRITUALITY

behave for myself, without parental pressure." Another student remarked, "I feel that I am more honest with myself and I know what's right for me." Others wrote, "I feel more satisfied with my life"; "I feel wonderful about this change"; and "I feel more fulfilled."

The next most common category was that of those whose religious convictions changed as a direct result of their college experience. Participants in this category indicated that college was a testing ground for their beliefs. A respondent remarked, "[The change was a result of] . . . becoming more aware of science, and having trouble in deciding which to believe." The question became one of "the heart or the mind."

The next grouping consisted of individuals who were skeptical and dissatisfied with organized religion. These students found their church affiliation no longer satisfactory due to perceived hypocrisy, and now they felt liberated as a result of letting go of former religious controls. One participant wrote, "I have a lot of problems with the way churches run things, I think a large majority of them are corrupt." Another noted, "I feel God and religion should be more personal. I feel good about it [the change in affiliation]." Another category involving positive religious change encompassed those individuals whose faith had grown as a result of increased devotional activities and church-related social functions. These people noted that they felt "more satisfied with life," and also "better about themselves and their family relationships."

A fifth group consisted of those who converted as a result of pressures stemming from interfaith relationships. These individuals generally noted the change as a favorable one. One female reported, "I feel wonderful about my new way of living [conversion]."

The final group was composed of subjects who felt isolated as a religious minority on this campus. Although these people indicated a feeling of aloneness and separation, they nonetheless stated that their minority status had resulted in a greater appreciation of their religious beliefs. One respondent wrote, "My religion is more important to me now!"

Some of the students who indicated negative reactions to their changes in religious convictions indicated that these changes were related to a clear rejection of religious dogma and perceived inconsistencies in the behaviors of those associated with their church. One student wrote, "I now feel like a hypocrite when attending church service since I do not go regularly and I do not believe half the things they say. Before I went to church because I was asked by my pastor. I also never really experienced life, I just accepted what I was told. Then I started observing and making my own opinion on things." Another student expressed feelings of guilt when she "realized that I didn't believe in everything that I did when I was younger." Yet another expressed fear of being brain-washed by her church and cited disillusionment on learning that the Shroud of Turin was not authentic. She wrote, "I feel bad that I had this change and hope to some day get faith back."

The impact of living in a college environment with competing perspectives and religious viewpoints was mentioned by a number of subjects. One student expressed uncertainty as a direct result of the "changes in environment and the mixture of cultures and backgrounds that I have been exposed to" since coming to college. However, she noted that her "convictions have not changed drastically . . . my attitudes toward certain social issues have changed in that I am more lenient." Similarly, a graduate student noted that "by being exposed to alternative ways of looking at things, I was able to examine the beliefs and lifestyle of those involved in the Catholic church. When I found a discrepancy, it sort of pulled me away from going to church, although I still recognize a God." He admits that this pull has led him to feel depressed at times. Other students have found that the change in congregations necessitated by their living away from home resulted in their feeling less comfortable and at times "upset" in a new and different church community.

External life stresses have been the cause for other students becoming dissatisfied and disaffiliated with their religious identification. Problems in life, trouble functioning, and numerous other losses were identified as leading to a falling away from previous religious supports. Yet for others, more mundane time factors appeared to limit their ability to participate fully in religious activities. Several students noted feelings of guilt in not being able to attend church regularly. Others admitted that they had not really "given it too much thought" because they were so busy with school demands. Said one student simply, "I don't have time . . . I feel bad but I can't do anything about it."

Many students appeared to equate religious conviction with church attendance—"I feel bad because I know I should attend church." Stated one freshmen male, "it bothers me, but I think to myself, if I pray more and more often, then maybe it will make up for the times I've missed [going to church]. I do know it really won't." These perspectives and rationales may reflect the youth of these respondents and their tendency to automatically respond to the "shoulds" and "musts" of their earlier training.

The results of this study indicated that fewer participants than originally expected by the researchers experienced a sense of loss due to a change in their religious convictions. There may be a number of explanations that could account for these results. Change in religious convictions can, indeed, be seen and experienced by most students as a positive event, evolving from newly-found freedoms and newly-formed perspectives. Individual choice of convictions may reinforce a student's perception of growing independence from former familial and religious ties.

On the other hand, since freshmen (and younger students) comprised such a large percentage of respondents in this college survey, it may be that a younger group lacks introspective skills to adequately explore and identify their cognitive and affective reactions to this change. Thus, students may not fully recognize all the feelings associated with change of religious convictions, nor, indeed, yet fully appreciate the extent of change taking place. This may be especially true during the hectic adjustment period associated with the beginning of college life and with being away from home for the first time. Longitudinal studies, following students' religious development while in college, might better identify the use of distancing from the immediate upset that students might employ when first experiencing a change in religious attitudes. Moreover, students may deny or minimize the unpleasant feelings associated with religious change in an attempt to reduce the incongruence with prior familial and religious loyalties. This might represent an application of cognitive dissonance in an effort to reinforce confidence in new perspectives.

Finally, one other possible theory to explain why so many students admitted to a wide range of negative feelings related to a change in their religious convictions but so few saw this change as a loss may be that this outcome represents a true indication of the lack of recognition and disenfranchisement of religious change as a grief-engendering loss. Society's inability to recognize this life crisis or transition as a valid loss denies individuals appropriate means of finding avenues of social support and expression for their feelings.

As with other situations where society appears to withhold its validation and support of a loss that "merits" grieving, the loss of religion may be seen as a disenfranchised loss most immediately addressed through the education of both mental health intervenors and the religiously bereaved themselves that, indeed, a legitimate loss has occurred. Such public recognition goes far in encouraging survivors to identify and process the emotional and behavioral consequences of any loss. Mutual support groups are especially helpful in supporting otherwise isolated ex-church members in their effort to regain their religious identity. Such groups already exist, albeit sporadically, for gays and lesbians disaffiliated from their churches, and for former nuns and priests who have left a total way of life within the Catholic church. Individual disaffiliates, those not readily identifiable as belonging to a longer group, have been less fortunate in finding any group support.

For such individuals who seek out counseling following a religious loss, the focus of support needs to be on validating the loss as a grief-engendering issue and on using a variety of Gestalt-like techniques to bring about a sense of ritual closure. "Burying the past" appears to be an important need in many non-death loss situations and may be satisfied in a creative, symbolic manner through counselor guidance. Cognitive approaches in reframing the meaning of the religious loss as an opportunity for growth and more mature religious and/or spiritual commitment may also result in steps toward grief resolution. For some anxious or depressed clients, simply discovering that religious loss may be contributing to their emotional unhappiness and feelings of disconnectedness may well be the real start of effective counseling.

In conclusion, further investigation is clearly warranted in order to gain an understanding of the issues surrounding the many aspects of religious loss. Assessing the coping styles of individuals who have adequately grieved and adjusted to their loss of religious affiliation and/or convictions may provide insight into supportive intervention strategies. Awareness and sensitivity to the impact of loss of religion constitutes the first step in enabling mental health professionals to generate appropriate counseling approaches to this relatively unrecognized loss.

REFERENCES

1. K. J. Doka, *Disenfranchised Grief*, Lexington Books, Lexington, Massachusetts, 1985.
2. L. A. Neumark, *A Perspective on Religion and Counseling*, unpublished manuscript, Frostburg State University, Department of Psychology, Frostburg, Maryland, 1984.
3. E. Norbeck, *Religion in Human Life*, Holt, Rinehart, and Winston, New York, 1974.
4. A. Camus, *The Plague*, The Modern Library, New York, 1948.
5. J. Conrad, *Heart of Darkness*, New American Library, New York, 1985.
6. C. Jung, *Modern Man in Search of a Soul*, Harvest/HBJ Books, New York, 1954.
7. S. Kierkegaard, *Sickness Unto Death*, Doubleday, New York, 1954.
8. L. San Giovanni, *Ex-Nuns: A Study of Emergent Role Passage*, Ablex Publishing House, Norwood, New Jersey, 1978.
9. R. Curb and N. Manahan (eds.), *Lesbian Nuns: Breaking Silence*, Maiad Press, Tallahassee, Florida, 1985.
10. K. Y. Ritter and C. W. O'Neill, Moving Through Loss: The Spiritual Journey of Gay Men and Lesbian Women, *Journal of Counseling and Development, 68*, pp. 9-15, 1989.

11. D. Lee, The Plain People of Pennsylvania, *National Geographic*, pp. 492-519, April, 1984.
12. D. Clayton, John Hostetler Bears Witness to Amish Culture and Calls the Movie 'Witness' a Mockery, *People Weekly*, pp. 63-64, March, 1985.
13. D. Kraybill, *The Riddle of Amish Culture*, John Hopkins University Press, Baltimore, 1989.
14. L. Streiker, Brainwashed or Converted?, *The Christian Century*, p. 2ff, March, 1989.
15. H. Mostache, *Searching*, Stravon Education Press, New York, 1989.
16. J. Laign, Looking for the Listening Tree, *Changes*, pp. 30-75, January and February, 1990.
17. T. La Fromboise and W. Rowe, Skills Training for Bicultural Competence: Rationale and Application, *Journal of Counseling Psychology, 30*, pp. 71-73, 1943.
18. J. Laign, Finding the Right Medicine, *Changes*, pp. 76-77, January and February, 1990.

CHAPTER 23

Ethical and Spiritual Concerns: Sexuality and Spirituality "A Wholistic Approach for the Living-Dying Client and the Partner"

Jeanne M. Harper

Dr. John Morgan has noted that "spirituality is found in the very nature of human thinking and human willing" [1]. I ascertain that the concept of sexuality is likewise in the very nature of human thinking and human willing. Thus, the basic premise of this chapter is simple: *spirituality is directly linked to sexuality and NOT in conflict with it.*

In exploring the issues involved, I will share examples of how each "phase" [2] of living-dying is affected by sexual/spiritual concerns, and methods I have utilized in working with the living-dying client and his/her partner. It is my hope that this will create an atmosphere for you, as caregiver, to provide "an opportunity, availability and possibility" for open communication about the sexual/spiritual issues concerning caregivers, the living-dying clients and their partners.

INTRODUCTORY EXPLORATION

> The servant of God finds meaning and purpose in the midst of suffering and conflict. (Psalm 34)

While Socrates and Plato believed in the separation of body, Ohanneson, writing on Christian sexuality, states that "[the] body and soul are meant to be friends, not enemies" [3]. If we are happily and pleasantly surprised, our body expresses that pleasure in smiles, and others can see that we are happy. Our body, then, is the mirror of our soul. It can reflect who and what we are. In like manner, our sexuality and spirituality are interrelated and to discuss one is to discuss the other. M. and K. Finley tell us that "it is our sexuality which enables us to be caring, other-centered, loving [and spiritually relating] people . . . it is impossible to be in the world except in a sexual way . . . [If we are] psychologically or emotionally alienated from our sexuality, [we are] handicapped in the pursuit of human intimacy" [4, p. 63].

Kraft proposes three levels of sexuality [5]:

primary sexuality is simply how we experience life—differently, equally and complementarily—as male and female;

affective sexuality refers to feelings, modes (moods) and emotions that move toward or incorporate intimacy. It is respectful and loving with no exploitative, manipulative, or deceptive behavior, seeing and celebrating (in chastity) the mystery—the spirit—of sex. For the living-dying client and partner, this is the area that receives new attention. This area can be primarily spiritual with affective components: touch, smile, hug, compassionate word. It does not have to be expressed through physical genital sexuality.

genital sexuality is best defined as behavior, thoughts, fantasies, desires and feelings that activate the genital organs.

In over six years of working in the areas of human growth and development, specifically sexuality and thanatology, I have acquired a number of definitions of sexuality from both the young and the old. I have found that the definitions will depend on the individual's experiences, traditions, culture or sub-culture, as well as psychological and philosophical issues. The consistent, group-approved definition of sexuality (labeled by Kraft as "primary sexuality") is *"how one, as male or female, relates in thought, word and action to the world around them."*

Being open and accepting of our sexuality can provide a "creative opportunity for personal growth"; this is the conviction with which I approached this chapter. Sexuality affects each of us *socially, physically, intellectually, emotionally and spiritually*—in other words, *wholistically.*

It is important to remember that in working with clients and their partner, we MUST accept them "where they are at" in their development (or—at whatever developmental level they currently maintain). I recommend a review of the fundamental stage theories; the basic stages/levels found in the writings of Fowler, Erikson, and Kohlberg [6-8].

Some clients' fundamental definition of sexuality was the act itself, (Kraft's "genital sexuality") and many considered it "animalistic behavior." For some, this view had been largely affected by childhood experience. Others concurred with the group-approved definition as a more global view containing spiritual qualities. From this variance, we can see that it is imperative, as caregivers, to be aware of/come to understand the potential sexual/ spiritual issues for the living-dying clients and their partners which may be involved.

From a historical perspective, discussing with them how their view of sexuality developed can be helpful in (their) redefining: observations of others, toys, secret books, "answers" from older peers or siblings, messages from the media/TV, etc. Discussing how/when they became comfortable with their own sexuality can be informative as well. A number of variables affecting their understanding of sexuality issues may include:

roles: familial, social, age, sexual (degree of assertiveness in relationship)

sexism: perception of both sexes by the other (power/control issues); words used to describe the other sex, or their body parts

sexual preference/orientation: moral, spiritual, personal issues

sexual/physical abuse

sexual expectations: married, single, elderly, dying

It is imperative to understand that the sexual/spiritual issues for the living-dying client and partner will vary according to individual and collective variables, such as personality, prior relationship situations, type of illness acquired, etc. Two factors may be particularly critical. Glaser and Strauss note that different illnesses have different trajectories [9]. By that they mean that each illness has a temporal aspect. With some diseases, the trajectory is a slow, downward slope. With others, the decline can be rapid. Still other illnesses may be characterized by recurring patterns of remission and exacerbation. In all of these cases, different issues may be raised regarding clients' sexual relationships and behaviors. Similarly, Pattison reminds clinicians that many life-threatening illnesses have three phases— acute, characterized by the crisis of diagnosis; chronic, where clients must cope with/live with the illness; and terminal, where clients face death. Again in each of these situations, clients' sexual needs, feelings and behaviors may differ [2].

Sexuality is a "relational power" [10]. There is a need to establish/reestablish what the Finleys called the "list of ingredients [involved in] the pursuit of human intimacy" [4]. The client and partner may need to redefine what it means to be "intimate," due to body changes which periodically or permanently affect or eliminate the expression of their sexuality through sexual intercourse. McCarty suggests an acronym to more fully appreciate the meaning of "intimate" [11, p. 146]:

Individual: ability to perceive and express in one's own way
Needs and sensitivity: understanding each person's own needs
Trust: trusting self and then others
Imagination: becoming creative in resolving issues
Maturity: putting off immediate gratification
Awareness: knowing personal needs, asking for them to be met
Tenderness: compassionate, responsive
Empathy: participating in the feelings and ideas of another

Lindemann, in "Reactions to One's Own Fatal Illness," shares the important aspects of the new role created by a fatal illness [12, p. 260]. He uses the example of the "uterus-deprived women" who need to question their new sexual role. Here he finds the sexual role relationship 1) threatened to be altered, 2) worked through, and 3) too often neglected, as these women attempt to work through their new role definition. Reading this paper for the expansive reactions by the living-dying clients is recommended.

Gideon and Taylor created a "Sexual Bill of Rights for Dying Person," which stated the dying person's right to [13]:[1]

1. Be a sexual person, physically, emotionally, spiritually and socially;
2. Know that intercourse and sexuality are different phenomena;
3. Receive counseling with sexual partner present and/or in absence of sexual partner;
4. Be informed about what will help one accommodate to physical changes occurring in his/her body;
5. Be in charge of one's own body;
6. State sexual needs and negotiate the meeting of those needs;
7. Maintain confidentiality;
8. Understand forms of pleasing other than intercourse;
9. Obtain information regarding the use of physical aids to enhance physical sexual activities;
10. Express sexuality regardless of hospitalization, or institutionalization;
11. Practice own sexual lifestyle, express sexual preference, express sexual needs and be respected as a person while doing so;

[1]M. Gideon and P. Taylor, Sexual Bill of Rights for Terminally Ill People, Death Education, Winter 1981, p. 303. Reprinted with permission.

12. Take a risk of "getting hurt";
13. Bear or father children within confines of full understanding between the two parents;
14. Communicate with own children regarding physical illness and sexual identity/growth;
15. Have open communication with sexual partner and to establish a communication system that would allow for the expression of physical needs that might otherwise seem to be expression of "negative feelings."

Regarding the practice of masturbation, which may enter the life of the living-dying client and partner, Bishop Mugavero "encouraged people to go continually beyond themselves in order to achieve greater sexual maturity and urged them to find peace and strength in a full sacramental life with the God who loves them" [10]. Each denomination has written a religious declaration on sexual issues, these should be explored with the client and their partner. I have found clients and their partners, regardless of denomination, to be concerned that masturbation was "sinful." We must be willing to assist them in their search for THEIR acceptable, pleasurable and peace-giving method(s) to sexually satisfy the couple's individual needs.

Working with the living-dying client calls for "the nature of love" from both caregiver and partner, no matter what phase the partner is in [11]. McCarty suggests another acronym to express the nature of love, which asks us to show "CARING" [11, p. 7]:

Concern — for each other;
Acceptance — of the situation, of the patient;
Responsibility — being responsible in our actions and responses;
Integrity — respecting each other;
Nurturing — parenting, comforting, showing compassion;
Giving — of self.

The image (both self and relational) that we conjure up when we walk into a room can make all the difference in the world. If we enter with the traditional image of counselor-client, this elicits a specific type of behavior/response. Caregivers are challenged to alter their images. Someone gave me an anonymous prayer, which I have modified to create a new image with which I am more comfortable. This is the image of two "Gifts of God," uniquely and equally pilgrimming on their journey, and for a time in unison, learning and sharing together:

Dear God,
Today on my journey, remind me that the persons I meet are Gifts from YOU to ME. They are wrapped—some loosely and some tightly enclosed. Some Gifts will open very easily, some may need

the help of others. Maybe it is because we are afraid, or have been hurt before and don't want to be hurt again. Maybe we were once opened and then discarded and now feel more like "things" than "human persons." God, you have filled each of us with a goodness that is only ours. And yet sometimes we are afraid to look inside our wrappings. Maybe out of fear of disappointment or lack of trust of even our own inner contents. Or it may be that we have never really accepted the Gift that we are. Remind me this day, that every meeting and sharing of Persons is an EXCHANGE of our GIFTS. We are Gifts to Each Other! So let us journey this day celebrating our giftedness with those we meet.

This prayer allows me to NOT have-to-have the ANSWERS to their deep sexual/spiritual issues, but rather to JOURNEY with them as they search their souls and bodies for THEIR answer. It reminds me that my patients and their families have always been a source of joy, peace, compassion, love and experience, and that through their sharing, I have become a more compassionate pilgrim for those I meet next on this journey.

As we continue to explore the sexual/spiritual issues of the living-dying client and partner, it is important to keep this introductory exploration, and the bearing it brings to the tasks of redefinition and understanding, in mind.

ACUTE CRISIS PHASE

The right time is the only time we have, which is NOW!

Henry James

In the acute crisis phase, the individual personalities, prior relationship experiences and inner child issues for both the living-dying client and partner may affect the sexuality and spirituality issues within their relationship. Parad, who studied the crisis of death as a crisis event, discussed five aspects of the study [14, p. 289]. It is the fifth aspect which we will take under consideration [14, p. 67]:

> . . .Crisis. . .reactivates unresolved problems from the near and distant past, the [crisis] provides a fresh opportunity for dealing with old problems. . .challenged to provide a "novel" solution.

I developed the "Life Loop" which is a structured learning exercise to use with clients and their partners to help them deal with these unresolved feelings from the past as well as to assist them with the new challenge of the life-threatening illness [15, 16]. When the gift of time is not present, I have verbally assisted them with the review. This exercise creates awareness of their life experiences, their responses to and feelings about them, and therapeutic renewal of faith in themselves to deal with yet another life experience—the latter one of the two ultimate spiritual experiences—birth and death.

I have found that the client who is able to find meaning in his/her life experience is better able to deal with the dying process, be that process a matter of hours, days or weeks until death. One client reviewed the sadness associated with her (early adult life) abortion; in sharing this, she realized how this episode was mentally and emotionally affecting her relationship with her husband. She felt that any/all personal spiritual issues had been resolved through participation in her church's sacramental practices. However, when faced with dying, she was discovering how concealing this information from her spouse was keeping her from being at peace with her inevitable death. She needed to explain her silence regarding this critical part of her life experience, whether or not he was able to forgive or understand.

In Berger and Luckman's *The Social Construction of Reality,* they discuss how "unsuccessful socialization may be the result of different significant others mediating different objective realities to an individual" [17]. "Every significant other," they continue, "has a different perspective on common reality simply by virtue of being a specific individual with a specific biography." This makes it clear that the client and partner must understand their OWN personal sexual and spiritual issues, and in so doing, understand their uniqueness.

CHRONIC LIVING-DYING PHASE

Fear not that your life shall come to an end; rather fear that it will never have a beginning.
St. John Cardinal Newman

In this, phase two, Pattison discusses the importance of defining and dealing with fears/feelings ONE at a time in order to enhance "self-esteem, dignity and integrity" [2]. He speaks of this as a time of "expectational hope," expecting to survive.

In 1982, *Powerline 40,* a radio talk show, shared survey results of seven fears the dying person may face in their "preparatory grief" process [15, 16]. Encompassing current research, Pattison's work and past patient experiences, I have expanded on these survey results to include:

fear of the process of dying: physical (suffering, pain, body losses, life support systems)/psychological (grief, regression, loss of spirit and identity)

fear of loss of control: dependency, burden

fear for family: loss of family/friends, not seeing them grow, loss of dreams, finances, lack of family support

fear of aloneness: loneliness

reflected fear (in their loved ones' faces): how the family will handle this

fear their life had no meaning: wouldn't be remembered, being unable to finish (unfinished) "business"

fear of unknown: life after death

Diggory and Rothman have suggested numerous fears of the unknown [18]. Those relating to the sexual/spiritual realm include:

What life experiences will I not be able to have?
What changes will occur in/to my body?
What will my emotional reactions be?

Orville Kelly, founder of Make Today Count, Inc., reflected that [19]:

. . . as time passed and the tests continued, I began to realize that the emotional problems associated with a serious illness . . . are often more difficult to cope with than the illness itself.

This living-dying phase, with its many fears, challenges the patient and family in all areas of their life.

For patients who are parents, some recognize the correlation between their sexual/spirituality and parenting issues. The ultimate gift of acting out their spirituality is the gift of life and biological immortality through their children. In a song by Deanna Edwards, "I'm Glad That I Was Here," this realization is expressed [20]:

Will you [the children] remember me? . . .
Will they know that I still love them?
Will they know I tried my best?
Is there something that I can give them
Just a thought along the way
That will help them through a trial?
That will guide them through the day . . .
I have loved you without ceasing,
And I'm glad that I was here.

For the single living-dying patient, sexuality needs are experienced as well, as "Minnie Remembers" reminds us [21]. In the poem written by Donna Sevanson, Minnie remembers how her mother held her, her first kiss, her husband's touch, how no one is touching her *now* and the loneliness involved in not being touched. Mother Theresa so poignantly reflected on this in a television interview during her last visit to the United States, when she said that "people in America were dying from the lack of touch."

Again, we are called upon to help our clients to expand beyond their limits with regard to this word "sexuality," and to come to the awareness that "spirituality" is indeed linked to "sexuality" and *not in conflict* with it. Studies have shown that healthy sexual activity continues into the eighth and ninth decades of one's life; we need to accept and encourage the living-dying patient in the affirmation of the joys of affection and sensuality [16]. The expression of touch in a caring fashion, while simplistic, has the potential for major impact on the client's (improved) psychological health. Individuals who are unable to accept or feel comfortable with their own sexuality are unable to experience the sexual/spiritual effects of an expression of affection as simple as a *hug*. One of my clients, who (with his family) had been so impressed and touched by the warmth and care of a hospice worker who hugged freely, shared with me a reading on "Hugs." It is from this reading that I would like to share the following:

> There's no such thing as a bad hug—
>   only good ones and great ones.
> They're not fattening and they don't
>   cause cancer or cavities.
> They're all-natural—with no
>   preservatives, artificial ingredients or pesticide residue.
> They're cholesterol-free, naturally sweet,
> 100% wholesome.
> And they're a completely renewable natural
> resource.
>   Author unknown

Regarding spirituality issues and the mysteries in/of our lives, Rory Foster, a patient with amyotrophic lateral sclerosis (ALS), expressed how he felt about caregivers who actively communicated/expressed their (spiritual) belief in God in relation to the patient's illness. Foster believes we should not explain why tragedies occur, but rather admits we don't know why. "Because we don't," Foster states. Foster believes it all a "mystery . . .how we got here, where we're going and why we're here" [22].

Heathcliff was a twenty-one year old who tested HIV seropositive [23]. He shared that he felt ambiguity and confusion when he was asymptomatic (experienced no symptoms of the disease), and often wondered whether or not he was really "sick." He experienced "a sense of panic" at times, and he thought it would be easier if he were sick and dying, rather than waiting for death to happen. Heathcliff described his sexual relationship as "still very intimate, very loving, and very satisfying." Intercourse had been discontinued; however, the couple continued to kiss, "a risk we could take to save our relationship."

Issues of "anticipatory grief" [24] that have been listed by family members of the dying patient include:

> fear of saying the wrong things;
> how to creatively celebrate their love;
> the need to see *time* as a precious commodity;
> knowing that little things mean a lot (favorite food,
>   cartoon, music, etc);
> fear of unfulfilled dreams.

Honesty and simplicity in caregiving by the staff are appreciated by both living-dying client and the partner; this is expected as part of the "Dying Person's Bill of Rights" [13, 25]. If sexual activity will put them at risk, they need to know this. With heart patients, I found them afraid to ask about making love; they felt they should *just* be glad they were alive and not push it.

AIDS patients and partners need accurate information so they can make rational decisions about their relationship. One such couple decided, after staff input, that they had already been exposed and no more harm could result. Therefore, as long as it was not painful to the client, they decided to continue to be sexually intimate. Many heterosexual couples with whom I work come to the same decision, with regard to sexual intimacy, after receiving information and deliberating the issue. All felt that the benefits of making love (warmth, expression of love, peace, contentment and acceptance) were much needed at this time of crisis.

This phase of chronic living-dying can be characterized in an aphorism by Francois de la Rochefoucauld, ". . . neither the sun nor death can be looked at steadily" [26, p. 861]. This is an important concept, to enjoy the good times: the times when they feel better; the times when pain, disease, the future can be forgotten, even if only for an hour, a day, or a week; the times of peace and tranquility; the times of beauty in God's natural environment; the times of warmth, support, care, love. For it is imperative—socially, physically, intellectually, emotionally and spiritually—to *not* look "steadily" at death, nor at dying.

TERMINAL PHASE

I have promises to keep, and miles to go before I sleep.
                                                    Robert Frost

"The art of dying," or "Ars Moriendi," would include the following as necessary, though not necessarily consecutive, phases in this process:

knowing you are dying;
forgiving your enemies;
making peace with (your) God;
leaving your children with a word of wisdom;
taking time to reflect on your life;
putting your affairs in order; and
saying goodbye.

Although the issues involved in sexuality are not directly stated, they are incorporated in this process. The art of dying begins, says Pattison "when the dying person begins to withdraw into him- or herself in response to internal body signals that say he or she must now conserve energies unto him- or herself" [2]. Pattison believes their hope then turns to that which is "desirable—that I might not die is a desirable hope—but no longer expected." The following is an excellent example of this phase.

A client had been discussing his inability to be sexually active (intimate) any longer with his wife [meaning, to him at this time, the inability to have sexual intercourse with her]. He admitted that he was allowing these feelings and fears to (negatively) affect his life. The homework assignment he chose was to find and read materials written on "intimacy." He happened to find an article which made a tremendous impression on him, and ultimately affected his life. The author reflected on the "making of a 'home' [the most intimate of places]," and shared how God extends the offer to us to make our home in Him, as He has made a home for Himself in us. The author explained that "home" meant a "place where it is good to be," and how fear was the "greatest enemy" of intimacy; we could either run from it, or—as a trusting child—cleave unto it. My client realized that he had been bouncing between "distance [and] closeness" with his wife, withdrawing into his own world as part of his dying process, yet not wanting to leave her (for his own personal needs/reasons, as well as feeling "responsible" to be there for her). He strongly desired to be "home" with her; however, when there, he was creating "distance" because he felt "less than a man" due to the ravages of chemotherapy and radiation on his sexual organs. By the end of our discussions, he realized the need to share his concerns with his wife, to disclose his desire to alter his definition of "intimacy," thus enabling him to hold her, lay beside her and feel the warmth, love, acceptance, joy and ecstasy in a new way for him. He now saw his past behavior as a form of (self) punishment to his body (as well as his mind and spirit) for dying on him. Choosing to cherish the time he had left caused him amazement and excitement, in that merely by changing HIS viewpoint with regard to the meaning of "intimacy," he could create the "home-coming" closeness he so strongly desired. Their relationship continued to flourish and grow throughout his final three months of life. Later, his wife was able to share how critical it was for her husband to realize that *he had the power* to be loving and intimate, merely by changing his meaning (definition) of the words. She concluded that this change did, in fact, create a greater intimacy than they had ever experienced before in all their years of marriage.

CONCLUSION

Each time anyone comes into contact with us, they must become different and better people because of having met us. We must radiate God's love.

Mother Theresa of Calcutta

As James Dunning explains, caregivers recognize that the celebration of life experiences includes "alleluias, commitment to new life, communion, expressions of genuine grief and tears, letting go of the old life, and a sense of loss" [27]. As we work with the living-dying clients and their partners, we are ministering while they are searching for meaning in their lives. With this search comes "a sense of loss, failure, loneliness, of being wrenched from their past," as well as "a need to die to self, die to rugged independence, die to own needs and surrender to another." We receive a powerful gift, an inexpressible gift, as we journey with these individuals making their pilgrimage through the living-dying experience.

In working with the dying, we can be helped by exposure to literature (articles, quotes, poems) which can truly express the greater intimacy and support a broader understanding of sexuality/ spirituality. Such a work is Walter Rinder's poem "Hands," a portion of which follows [28]:

Our hands are extensions of our heart, through their movements people know what we are, who we are, and how we feel . . . you can feel the beating of their heart, they very substance of their life . . .

hands carry episodes of your life . . . scarred, stained, calloused, scratched. Let your hands become the joining together of you and another human being, the extension of your heart, the merging of two rivers, the grafting of two branches, the birth of new life. Your hands are you.

There is an old Chinese proverb: "What I hear, I forget; what I see, I remember; and what I experience, I understand." Schuller states that "it is undeniably true that one of the fruits of experience is a more humble, more sympathetic, more understanding way of relating to human beings" [29]. I pray, then, that this chapter has given the opportunity and made available the possibility for open communication concerning sexual/spiritual issues with/for living-dying clients and their partners. May these life experiences truly become the stepping stones to a more humble, sympathetic and understanding caregiver.

REFERENCES

1. J. Morgan, Death and Bereavement: Spiritual, Ethical and Pastoral Issues, *Death Studies, 13,* pp. 85-89, 1988.
2. E. M. Pattison, The Sequence of Death, in *The Experience of Dying,* Prentice-Hall, Inc., Englewood Cliffs, New Jersey, 1977.
3. J. Ohanneson, Christian Sexuality: Body and Soul Together, *Youth Update,* Cincinnati, Ohio, 1984.
4. M. Finley and K. Finley, *Christian Families in the Real World,* Thomas More Press, Chicago, 1984.
5. W. F Kraft, *Whole & Holy Sexuality: How to Find Human and Spiritual Integrity as Sexual Person,* Abbey Press, St. Meinrad, Indiana, 1989.
6. J. W. Fowler, *Stages of Faith: The Psychology of Human Development and the Quest for Meaning,* Harper and Row, San Francisco, 1981.
7. E. H. Erikson, *Childhood and Society* 2nd Edition, Norton Publishing, New York, 1963.
8. L. Kohlberg, *The Psychology of Moral Development,* Volume 2, Harper and Row, San Francisco, 1984.
9. B. Glaser, and A. Strauss, *Time for Dying,* Aldine, Chicago, 1968.
10. Bishop F. J. Mugavero, Sexuality—God's Gift, *Catholic Update,* St. Anthony Messenger Press, Cincinnati, Ohio, 1976.
11. M. McCarty, *Loving,* William B. Brown Press, Dubuque, Iowa, 1982.
12. E. Lindemann, Reactions To One's Own Fatal Illness in *Beyond Grief: Studies in Crisis Intervention, and Death: Current Perspectives,* E. S. Schneidman (ed.), Mayfield Publishing Company, Mountainview, California, 1984.
13. M. Gideon and P. Taylor, Sexual Bill of Rights for Terminally Ill People, *Death Education,* p. 303, Winter 1981.

14. H. J. Parad (ed.), *Crisis Intervention: Selected Readings*, Family Service Association of America, New York, 1965.
15. J. Harper, Plateaus of Acceptance: Pits of Pain, *Creativity in Death Education and Counseling*, Forum for Death Education and Counseling, Lakewood, Ohio, 1983.
16. J. M. Harper, The Afternoon of A Life: Creative Avenues for Intervention, *Thanatos*, pp. 21-22, Fall, 1983.
17. P. L. Berger and T. Luckman, *Social Construction of Reality*, Doubleday and Co., Garden City, New York, 1966.
18. J. C. Diggery and D. Rothman, Values Destroyed by Death, *Journal of Abnormal and Social Psychology, 63*, pp. 205-210, 1961.
19. O. E. Kelly, *Words of Wisdom*, quote sheet produced by Make Today Count, Inc., P.O. Box 222, Osage Beach, Missouri, 65065.
20. D. Edwards, Creative Grief and Recovery, *Sharing the Gift of Love*, Rock Canyon Publishers, Provo, Utah, 1980.
21. "Minnie Remembers," written byDonna Sevanson, Williamsport, Indiana, published in *Alive Now*, September-October, 1973.
22. G. Vukelich, Dr., *The Milwaukee Journal*, September 29, 1985.
23. J. Gordon and F. C. Shontz, Living with the AIDS Virus: A Representative Case, *Journal of Counseling and Development*, by American Association for Counseling and Development, 68:3, pp. 287-292, 1990.
24. R. Fulton, A Psychological Aspect of Terminal Care: Anticipatory Grief, Symposium at Columbia University, November 6, 1970.
25. Concern for Dying, The Dying Person's Bill of Rights, New York.
26. Francois de la Rochefoucauld, Webster's Encyclopedia of Dictionaries, edited by John Gage Allee, p. 861, Ottenheimer Publishers, Inc., U.S.A., 1978.
27. J. B. Dunning, Ministries, *Sharing God's Gifts*, St. Mary's Press, Winona, Minnesota, 1985.
28. W. Rinder, Hands, *Love Is An Attitude*, Celestial Arts Publishing Co., San Francisco, California, 1970.
29. Schuller, R., *Inspired Writings*, Arrowood Press, New York, 1987.

CHAPTER 24

Joking with Death

Robert E. Neale

What if we had a joking relationship with Death? Think of us as married to Life. Life is then a spouse that has its own connections, one of the which is Death. If we are married to Life, then death is an *in-law*. So just imagine Death related to us as a mother-in-law, father-in-law, son-in-law, sister-in-law, or, as an older or younger brother-in-law or sister-in-law.

In-law relationships are fraught with dangers related to sexual attraction and family domination. So in preliterate societies, the community would establish a joking relationship. This is a kind of playful behavior involving much sexual suggestiveness and insults critiquing behavior. Anthropologists speculate that such a relationship lessens conflict, reduces hostility, releases tension, promotes community control, increases communication, adds to the strength of group identity, allows exploration of potential closeness, and, last, but not least, offers pure entertainment and drama. What more could anyone want! A relationship that is both necessary and dangerous is fashioned into a perpetual joke.

Of course, I am proposing that our relationship with death could be the same. Just think of all those benefits as applied to our relationship with death. So, which in-law would death be for us? And what would our joking relationship be like? We will "think about it" by laughing about it.

LAUGHTER IN EXTREME SITUATIONS

We are inclined to laugh most when we are at our most vulnerable or at our most victorious. Death is laughable both when it is too horrible and when the horror is overcome.

Sometimes we laugh when we do not know what else to do, actually, when we are unable to do anything else. At this extreme of vulnerability, laugher is the surmounting of shock. It is an explosion that bounces us back into life in spite of the horrible. Literary and cinematic scenes portray a corpse that wobbles in the casket or tilts while seated. We respond to such horror with laughter. This is described by Iris Murdock in a scene somewhat common at funerals [1, p. 21-22]:

> The coffin-bearers stood stiffly in a row at the back. In front of them was the huge figure of my brother, and as I turned I saw him swaying, bending forward and putting his hand to his mouth. I thought for a moment that he was ill or overcome by tears: but then I saw that he was laughing. Monstrous giggles shivered his great figure from head to foot and turned, as he tried to stifle them, into wet spluttering gurgles. 'Oh God!' said Otto audibly. He choked. Then abandoning all attempts at concealment he went off into a fit of gargantuan mirth. Tears of laughter welted his red cheeks. He laughed. He roared. The chapel echoed with it. Our communion with Lydia was at an end.

We have all experienced such "inappropriate" laughter. When it occurs, it *is* appropriate as a recognition of, and response to, terror.

Laughter occurs also at the very opposite extreme—when death is defeated. Victory is accompanied by the most unseemly whoops and hollars. Those not privy to the experience may think we are crazy, drunk, or just childish. I recall the photograph of a young African taken at the very moment he heard about the death of his father. The father had been the village chief and the son succeeded him. The man had lept high into the air with hands outstretched and mouth wide open. He was victorious over death. In the European Christian tradition, this can occur on Easter morning. The churches told jokes during the service about the Apostles, the saints, and even about the Devil. Sometimes there was a ridiculous sermon which made fun of even the most serious matters connected with the crucifixion and resurrection. This response to victory over death was called "Easter Laughter." Such laughter seems quite inappropriate to all who have not tasted of the victory. But it is most appropriate for those who believe the human tragedy to be also the divine comedy.

JOKING IN DAILY LIFE

Laughter at death *is* appropriate, especially when we are most vulnerable or most victorious. On such occasions, we are moved to laughter, just as we are moved to breathe, because the organism celebrates life in response to death. But we cannot live continually at the extremes of our relationship to death. That would make death a *drag*. We need a consciousness that can be silly with the serious relatively continually.

One who did this well in his professional life was Charlie Chaplin. Remember the person he created—the little Tramp? Recall his clothes, his walk, his relationships with people and with society, his artistry of awkwardness and perfection of bungling? Laurence Olivier said about him: "He was, perhaps, the greatest actor of all time." This is praise of silliness with death. The films about the Tramp were made before and during the Depression. The character Chaplin created reveals the brute facts of hunger, joblessness, isolation, and being an outcast. The theme is suffering. This is serious and he is silly with it. As Chaplin even said about his Tramp: "I am always aware that Charlie is playing with Death. He plays with it, mocks it, thumbs his nose at it, but it's always there. He is aware of death at every moment of his existence, and he is terribly aware of being alive . . " [2, p. 20].

The artist in Chaplin goes for horror fully and concretely. It captivates him. Some believe his finest full-length feature film to be *The Gold Rush*. He got the idea for this film by seeing pictures showing an endless stream of would-be prospectors toiling up a mountain pass. But he had trouble discovering how to motivate a possible plot. Finally he got it. He had read a book about the Donner disaster which involved men, women, and children trying to cross a mountain pass. Many died and some resorted to eating dogs, their own moccasins, and the flesh of human corpses to remain alive. No picnic! But Chaplin would turn it into one! He recalls: "Then I got into a single situation: hunger. I got that from reading about the Donner party . . . starving to death, turning to cannibalism, eating shoe strings and everything. And I thought, 'Oh yes, there's something *funny* in that'" [3, p. 94]. There was, and Chaplin showed it to us. He repeatedly stated that his basic idea with the Tramp was to get him into trouble and then out of it. The trouble was always death and getting out of it was always laughter with death.

The laughter generated by Chaplin's play with death is not the laughter of the extreme of vulnerability and victory, but of all our experiences of death that are between. It is the laughter suitable and necessary for *daily* living with the issues of death and dying.

SOME JOKES

The hope is that we can joke with death daily. My hunch is that constant solemnity about anything is really only solemnity about oneself. Only God has that privilege, and I doubt it is exercised. We can joke about death as we do about anything else. Not just on Sunday morning or Friday night, but also during coffee breaks, TV commercials, and mealtimes. Such jokes can be funny and they can be serious. At best, they can be both funny and serious. First, here is a sample of a funny joke. It is an old joke of unknown source. Consider it the one about "The Cat is On the Roof and Won't Come Down".

Joe had wanted for many years to go to Europe, but felt unable to do so because he was worried about leaving his cat—whom he loved very much. Finally his good friend, who lived fairly nearby, convinced him that it would be all right to leave the cat in his care. He promised to be very careful, feed the cat regularly, provide it with lots of affection, and be a good substitute cat-parent. So Joe got tickets and left on his long-awaited trip.

After he had been gone six days, Joe received a cable saying, "Your cat is dead."

Joe was shattered. He immediately cancelled the rest of his trip and rushed home. He confronted his friend. "How could you have been so brutal?"

The friend was astonished. "What do you mean, brutal? The cat was run over by a car and died, and I thought you would want to know."

Joe responded that there needed to be a gentle approach to the delivery of such news.

An annoyed friend queried, "Such as . . . ?"

Joe replied in detail. "Well, first of all, you could have sent a cable that said: 'Your cat climbed up on the roof and won't come down.' Then, when I've had a chance to absorb that—perhaps twenty-four hours later, you could send another cable that said: 'Have called the Fire Department. The cat has jumped from the roof to a tree, and climbed higher than they can reach.' Then, when I've had a chance to absorb that news, you could send another cable that said: 'Torrential rains expected this evening. I fear for the cat.' And then," concluded Joe, "you could send a final cable saying: 'Alas, the cat has died.' By that time, you see, I would have had a chance to prepare myself—and I would not have been so totally devastated by the news."

Several years passed. The two friends had patched up their differences. Joe thought that he would go to Europe again to finish seeing some of those things he had been unable to visit before. He left his itinerary with his friend, and they even managed a little joke about the fact that the cat wasn't a problem this time.

After he had been gone for ten days he received the following cable: "Your Mother climbed up on the roof and she won't come down."

Unless our mother has just died, this joke is quite funny for most of us. By contrast, the following is so serious that our fun is nearly quelled. Perhaps it is a joke that can only be told well, and/or only heard fully, by members of the Jewish community. But it is a joke, and there can be no doubt about that [4, p. 73]:

> In a small village in the Ukraine, a terrifying rumor was spreading: a Christian girl had been found murdered.
>
> Realizing the dire consequences of such an event, and fearing a pogrom, the Jewish community instinctively gathered in the synagogue to plan whatever defensive actions were possible under these circumstances.
>
> Just as the emergency meeting was being called to order, in ran the president of the synagogue, out of breath and all excited. 'Brothers,' he cried out, 'I have wonderful news! The murdered girl is Jewish!'

The authors who include this joke in their book on Jewish humor comment that it is in bad taste, and then observe that much of Jewish history is as well!

Now we sample some jokes from the Zen and Sufi religious traditions that are intended to be both funny and serious. They are very serious and we could spend a lifetime meditating on any one of them. Members of these traditions actually do this. But they are also very funny and are a kind of ultimate nonsense. They are spiritual jokes about death. Therefore, they are best read aloud and to someone in addition to oneself. There are a bunch of them. Ideally, a brass band would play a few bars of "Stars and Stripes Forever" between each. You might try whistling or humming a few notes—Da Daaa, Da Da Da, Da Da Daaa . . .

(a little music)

> "A student asked his master, 'What happens to the man of enlightenment and to the man of illusion after death?'
> The master answered, 'How should I know?'
> 'Why, because you are a master,' said the student.
> The master concluded, 'Yes, but no dead one!' " [5, p. 119].

(a little music)

> "A student asked his master, 'Do heaven and hell exist?'
> 'No,' replied the master instantly.
> Some others happened to be within earshot and, amazed at the answer, asked him the same question. This time, equally without hesitation, the master said, 'Yes.'
> When accused of being contradictory, the master observed,

'Well, if I tell you there's neither heaven nor hell, where would the alms come from?' " [5, p. 121].

(a little music)

"A student once asked a master, 'what is the most prized thing in the world?'
The master responded, 'A dead cat.'
The student asked, 'Why is it so prized?'
The master replied, 'Because no one thinks of its value' " [6, p. 119].

(a little music)

"A child once broke the precious heirloom teacup of his master. He was greatly upset, and while wondering what to do, he heard his teacher coming. Quickly he hid the pieces of the cup under his robe.
'Master,' he said, 'Why do things die?'
'It is perfectly natural for things to die and for the matter gathered in them to separate and disintegrate,' said the master. 'When its time has come every person and every thing must go.'
'Master,' said the child, showing the pieces, 'It was time for your cup to go' " [7, p. 28].

(a little music)

"A traveler was fleeing a tiger. He ran until he came to the edge of a cliff. There he caught hold of a thick vine and swung himself over the edge.
Above him the tiger snarled. Below him he heard another snarl. He looked down and saw a second tiger peering up at him. The vine suspended him midway between two tigers!
Two mice began to gnaw at the vine. He could see that they would eat through it very quickly. Then in front of him on the cliffside he saw a luscious bunch of grapes. Holding on to the vine with one hand, he reached over and picked a grape with the other.
How delicious!" [7, p. 61].

(a little music)

"Nasrudin was wandering in a graveyard. He stumbled and fell into an old grave. Beginning to visualize how it would feel if he were dead, he heard a noise. It flashed into his mind that the Angel of Reckoning was coming for him: though it was only a camel caravan passing by.
The Mulla jumped up and fell over a wall, stampeding several

camels. The camelteers beat him with sticks.

He ran home in a distressed state. His wife asked him what the matter was, and why he was late.

'I have been dead,' said the Mulla.

Interested in spite of herself, she asked him what it was like.

'Not bad at all, unless you disturb the camels. Then they beat you' " [8, p. 70]

(a little music)

" 'I'll have you hanged,' said a cruel and ignorant king who had heard of Nasrudin's powers, 'if you don't prove that you are a mystic.'

'I see strange things,' said Nasrudin at once; 'a golden bird in the sky, demons under the earth.'

'How can you see through solid objects? How can you see far into the sky?'

'Fear is all you need' " [8, p. 93].

(a little music)

"Nasrudin was walking along the street enveloped in a dark-blue mourning-robe. Someone stopped him and asked: 'Why are you dressed like that, Mulla—has someone died?'

'Almost certainly,' said Mulla Nasrudin. 'It could have happened, you know, without my having been informed of it' " [9, p. 214].

(a little music)

" 'When you die, Mulla,' asked a friend, 'how would you like to be buried?'

'Head downwards. If, as people believe, we are right way up in this world, I want to try being upside-down in the next' " [9, p. 215].

(a little music)

" 'When I die,' said Nasrudin, 'have me buried in an old grave.'

'Why?' asked his relatives.

'Because when Munkir and Nakir, recording angels of good and bad actions, come, I will be able to wave them on, saying that this grave has been counted and entered for punishment already' " [9, p. 218].

(a little music)

"Nasrudin's tomb was fronted by an immense wooden door, barred and padlocked. Nobody could get into it, at least through the door. As his last joke, the Mulla decreed that the tomb should have no walls around it" [10].

(a little music)

WHO IS LAUGHING AT WHOM?

The Zen Masters and Nasrudin—they are clowns who joke with death. They do not laugh just at death, or just at themselves, but at *both* themselves *and* death. Life, death, and humanity—all three are full participants in the joke of daily existence. These spiritual clowns laugh at death and hear death laughing at them. The joking relationship is reciprocal. When death is an in-law, both parties enjoy the humor. Everyone is laughing at everyone.

Much of our humor tends to be quite one-sided. We are either sadistic or masochistic. Some of us are like the practical joker who got a bridegroom drunk the night before the wedding, put his arm in a plaster cast, and sent him off after the wedding on his honeymoon without removing the illusion of a broken arm. Such humor is an attack on a victim and we laugh. Others of us are more inclined in the direction of Lou Costello of the Abbott and Costello team who is always in trouble and being punished. Such humor is an attack on oneself as the victim and everyone else laughs. Reflect on your own humor. When you laugh, *who* has slipped on the banana peel? You or someone else? Both approaches are common and quite acceptable in our society. We find sadistic comedians entertaining masochistic audiences and masochistic comedians entertaining sadistic audiences. But our suffering is more masked than overcome in these limited forms of humor. *The complete humorist is both victim and victor.* Recall the philosophic comedian Socrates' humorous presentation of himself as one who knows that he does not know. Or recall the black comic Godfrey Cambridge telling his white audiences: "I hope you notice how I rushed up here. We have to do that to change our images. No more shuffle after the revolution. We gotta be agile." For these humorists, there is no division between victim and victor. They laugh at themselves and us simultaneously. All of us are victims, so they laugh for the sake of humanity. And, *laughing together, we all become victors.* Who slips on the banana peel? If only one is perceived as slipping, there can only be concealment of pain. If all of us are so perceived, there is pain acknowledged and somehow transcended in community. So we do not just joke at death. Nor do we just joke at ourselves over death. Rather, we joke at both death and us. Yes, we are fools, but so also is death. Yes, death is a fool, but so also are we.

CONCLUSION

If we are married to Life, then Death is our in-law and a joking relationship is possible and desirable. But we know that our in-laws are not just passive recipients of our jokes. They joke about us as well. We must learn to joke *with* Death in such a manner as to witness Death joke with us. And just what jokes does Death tell?

REFERENCES

1. Iris Murdock, *The Italian Girl*, The Viking Press, New York, 1964.
2. Charles Chaplin, quoted by Robert Payne, *The Great God Pan*, Hermitage House, New York, 1952.
3. Charles Chaplin, quoted by Richard Meryman, Chaplin: Ageless Master's Anatomy of Comedy, *Life*, March 10, 1967.
4. William Novak and Moshe Waldoks (eds.), *The Big Book of Jewish Humor*, Harper and Row Publishers, New York, 1981.
5. Lucien Stryk and Takashi Ikemoto (eds. and trans.), *Zen: Poems, Prayers, Sermons, Anecdotes, Interviews*, 2nd Edition, Swallow Press, Chicago, 1981.
6. Conrad Hyers, *Zen and the Comic Spirit*, The Westminster Press, Philadelphia, 1973.
7. Retold from *Zen Buddhism*, Peter Pauper Press, Mount Vernon, 1959.
8. Idries Shah, *The Exploits of the Incomparable Mulla Nasrudin*, The Octogon Press, London, 1983.
9. Idries Shah, *The Pleasantries of the Incredible Mulla Nasrudin*, E. P. Dutton, New York, 1971.
10. Cf. Nelvin Vos, *For God's Sake Laugh!* John Knox Press, Richmond, Virginia, 1967.

PART VI

Resources

This last section attempts to provide readers with possible resources that might be useful in educating or counseling. Halporn and Pacholski provide lists of audiovisual and print resources that might be useful for counselors, clients and educators. The breadth of their lists indicates the diversity inherent in any discussion of spirituality and death. Halporn's chapter implicitly affirms the value of bibliotherapy as a counseling resource. As studies have indicated, bibliotherapy can be highly effective in assisting clients' struggles by validating their feelings and offering perspectives and behavioral models that may enhance coping [1, 2]. One caveat, though, counselors ought to be sensitive to the particular needs and belief structures of clients prior to recommending any work. For example, many clients, facing the issue of "Why has this happened to me?," may treasure Kushner's *When Bad Things Happen to Good People* [3]. Others may be deeply troubled and their faith struggle intensified by Kushner's implicit assumption that God lacks control. Such persons may find C. S. Lewis' *A Grief Observed* more helpful and comforting [4]. Pacholski's chapter offers numerous resources that might facilitate the educational process by creating opportunities that allow students to reflect upon a broad range of spiritual issues. Bouman's chapter points out that congregations may provide a critical resource for the ill, dying and bereaved. While her article emphasizes ways and resources of their religious communities and denominations. Together these chapters remind caregivers and educators that they, their students and clients do not need to struggle with spiritual crises alone.

REFERENCES

1. K. J. Doka, The Therapeutic Bookshelf, *Omega, 21,* pp. 321-325, 1990.
2. H. S. Kushner, *When Bad Things Happen to Good People,* Avon, New York, 1981.
3. C. S. Lewis, *A Grief Observed,* Bantam, New York, 1963.
4. F. Seogin, C. Jamison, and Gochneaur, Comparative Efficacy of Cognitive and Behavioral Bibliotherapy for Mildly and Moderately Depressed Adults, *Journal of Consulting and Clinical Psychology, 57,* pp. 402-407, 1989.

CHAPTER 25

Shuffling Toward Jerusalem
An Annotated Bibliography of
Books on Religion and Thanatology

Roberta Halporn

The clergyman or woman who wishes to work with the dying and bereaved may have to spend more time on preparation and self-investigation than any other helping professional. The content underlying the religious counselor's work contains the one element without which he or she might just as well be a social worker—a willingness to talk about God. This has become a marvelously embarrassing subject in our secular culture when discussed "out of place"—that is in a hospital or client's living room, instead of in a church or synagogue. An additional aspect of this potent subject which can surface when the clergy appear is a quest for answers about immortality or afterlife.

It follows then that the clergyman or woman who wishes to offer the consolation of religion to those in the terminal environment must a) be schooled in counseling techniques for this special population, b) be firmly knowledgeable about what his/her denomination's official position is on theological questions, and c) know what he or she personally believes about the answers. As a wise artist once said "Dying concentrates the mind wonderfully," and any lack of conviction or a superficial response becomes immediately suspect to the terminal patient. Finally, the clergyman or woman must d) have an ability to tolerate what sounds either like errant nonsense or total heresy.

One of the phenomena that can emerge during periods of acute anxiety is an atavistic return toward childhood religious practice and belief. Somehow this kind of pain seems to invoke early memories, wiping out decades of mature thought and evaluation. I have seen a

335

fifty-year-old businessman attending a synagogue daily, after his father's death, but refusing that right to his daughter; Orthodox Judaism forbids women to say *Kaddish* (the prayer for the dead) for their fathers. Prior to that event, he had only visited a house of worship when a wedding or bar mitzvah was taking place. I have seen a zealous convert to Vedanta pleading for help from a Catholic priest when his granddaughter died, a religion he had rejected as soon as he reached adolescence. And what philosophy student has not read the possibly apocryphal story of Nietzsche's father, shaking his fist during a thunderstorm, and proclaiming, "You do not exist." It seems to me the religious counselor could well profit by reading *Heaven: A History,* by Colleen McDonnell and Gerhard Long, published in 1988 by Yale University Press. This historically-oriented, multi-disciplinary study thoroughly investigates the myriad versions our species has created of "that immortal place," reaching back from the most primitive offering of sacrifices to the Gods to the more sophisticated concepts of modern religions. Since it seems, to me at least, as if "ontogeny repeats philogeny" in spiritual matters, as well as in the genesis of an egg, the chaplain may well find him or herself listening to what sound like very bizarre ideas from his clients. With the proper background information such a fine text can supply, one may realize that the speaker may have merely flipped back to some notion of life after death he or she may have picked up in a childhood fairy tale.

Though the reader can counter this supposition on the grounds that it is based on anecdotal evidence, there is no doubt, when one examines which thanatology books have achieved great popularity, that there is a tremendous yearning for a form of certainty about immortality. Dr. Kubler-Ross has probably done the most to bring this desire out into the open with her book for children, *Letter to a Child with Cancer* (The Dougie Letter), obtainable from the Kubler-Ross Center in Virginia, and *Remember the Secret,* from Celestial Arts Press (1982), as well as her speeches.

But other works of mystical content which promise an afterlife that have achieved huge circulation are titles such as: *The American Book of the Dead,* by E. J. Gold, (IDHHB), with rituals from an oriental perspective, and Stephen Levine's *Who Dies?* (1982), described as new Age philosophy, available from Doubleday. A cautionary text which examines the potential dangers of this aspiration to contact the "outer world," still available from Springer Publishing Corp., is pioneer, Robert Kastenbaum's *Between Life and Death,* published in 1979 when the first rash of out-of-body experience works began to surface in print.

The Future of Immortality, by psychiatrist, Robert Jay Lifton (Basic Books, 1985), presents another vision of the future in this atomic age, the hope that our spirit will live on through our descendants. Another superb work is *Guests of My Life,* by Quaker Elizabeth Watson (Celo Press, 1979). Watson found her road to recovery after the death of her daughter in the works of the great secular literature of the past, and in evocative prose, shows a reader the spirituality to be gleaned from great art.

Why then is this essay entitled "Shuffling Toward Jerusalem?" It documents the author's belief that of all the professions that have entered the search for more humane care for the dying and bereaved, only medicine has been slower than organized religion (of all denominations) to realize that century-old customs need to be reevaluated if they are to be helpful to this special population in this era. This is not to claim that individual clergymen and women did not perceive, early on, the need for new answers (or perhaps old ones); one of the pioneers of the thanatology movement, Rabbi Earl Grollman, produced a seminal text *Talking About Death, A Dialogue Between Parent and Child,* in 1970 (Beacon Press) which is still helping thousands of readers. Rev. Granger Westberg's little book, *Good Grief,* published in 1962 by Fortress Press, has added countless others in acute mourning to deal with the beginnings of acceptance. *When Bad Things Happen to Good People* by Harold Kushner, (Avon, 1981) deals with the problem of why a benign God allows suffering. An ordained Rabbi, Samuel Klagsburn, also an M.D., singlehandedly created one of the first Hospices in the early seventies. His most recent text, *Psychiatric Aspects of Terminal Illness,* (Charles Press, 1990), has much to offer the thoughtful reader trying to understand the dynamics of this most awe-ful stress. And last, but certainly not least of these few examples, the editor of this text, Kenneth Doka, has been struggling to apply the true lessons of faith to the terminal environment for decades.

However, until approximately three years age, there was only a handful of books to offer religious comfort to the grief stricken in their darkest hours, except for the standard biblical sources. Alone among the thanatology organizations, the Foundation of Thanatology managed to publish a few professionally-oriented works about the role of religion in terminal care, such as *Death and the Ministry,* (1975, now out of print) and *The Pastoral Role in Caring for the Dying & Bereaved,* Bryan P. O'Connor et al., eds., (Praeger, 1986).

If it were not for the fact that *Pastoral Bereavement Counseling* by Rabbi Jacob Goldberg was released in 1988 by Human Sciences Press, one might almost presume that the "great awakening" of religious thanatological publishing was linked to the AIDS crisis, because so many new works have recently become available, discussing the theological aspects of this new epidemic. Goldberg has been striving for over ten years to gain institutional acceptance for his ideas about religious counseling and it took almost as long to get a publisher. His new work, drawing from the wisdom of experienced thanatologic psychologists such as J. William Worden, *Grief Counseling and Grief Therapy*, (Springer Publishing Co., 1991), and Bernard Schoenberg and Austin H. Kutscher's pioneer work *Loss and Grief: Psychological Management in Medical Practice*, (Columbia University Press, 1970) has already proved extremely helpful to many sensitive pastors who felt themselves floundering before they found his book. His work was recently been supplemented by a Christian death educator, Alan Wolfelt, in his *Death and Grief: A Guide for Clergy*, (AD Publishers, 1990). Having had funeral service training, Wolfelt's book adds a perspective that can prove useful—since his rich experience of memorial ceremonies comes, as it were, from the "other side of the office."

The emergence of the AIDS crisis into world consciousness stimulated the production of a number of works from Christian religious houses, possibly because it was such a challenge to historically-bound patterns of caring for the sick. Not caring for those ill would be anathema to the average clergyman or woman, but how does one fulfill the mandate to provide solace for the life-threatened patient if one is terrified that one is on the list?

AIDS and the Spiritual Dilemma, by John E. Fortunato (Harper and Row, 1987), *AIDS: Personal Stories in a Pastoral Perspective*, by Earl S. Shelp, et al. (Paulist Press, 1986), *AIDS: Living and Dying with Hope*, by Walter J. Smith, (also Paulist, 1983), and AIDS: Sharing the Pain, by Bill Kirkpatrick (Pilgrim Press, 1990) have all emerged within three years of each other. Fortunato's book discussed how very ancient religious attitudes toward homosexuality compete with the very real demands on our compassion these patients elicit. Shelp and Smith's books were broader, after more experience was gained working with the disease.

Yet it seems to me that the two most valuable books, that should be read by every professional working with AIDS patients, are written with a secular orientation. *And the Band Played On: People, Politics and the AIDS Crisis*, by journalist Randy Wilts (St. Martin's Press, 1987), relates its spread in the United States, and the genesis and political bias of the various competing interest groups involved with the research and care of its victims. The other is *Disenfranchised Grief, Recognizing Hidden Sorrow*, Kenneth Doka, (Lexington Books, 1989). Doka's work breaks ground in discussing how to recognize and assist the stigmatized mourner, addressing itself not just to survivors of a homosexual relationship, but those of a more conventional sexual orientation as well.

Unfortunately, his work should also be useful to those working with the most heartbreaking victims of an already tragic epidemic, the children with AIDS. The spread of the disease into the heterosexual population has not only occurred by often unknowing contact with drug users but through use of blood transfusions. Thus, it has been acquired by many innocent children, and for obvious reasons, the number of these cases is still being grossly underreported.

A description of the problems related to the incidence and psycho-social environment in pediatric AIDS can be found in Mary Boland's chapter in *Perspectives on the AIDS Crisis: Thanatologic Aspects,* Robert S. Lampke, et al., eds. (Foundation of Thanatology, 1989). A first book for children from a small religious house, Multnomah, *David Has AIDS* by Doris Sanford (1989) is a picture book, suitable for reading with five year olds and up. It discusses David's isolation from his peers, after it is known that he has contracted the disease from a blood transfusion, and suggests, non-denominationally, the assistance of prayer.

Both Fortress and Paulist Presses should be highly commended for the courage to include at least one new title in each annual list relating to thanatologic subjects. *Clinical Pastoral Care for Hospitalized Children,* John B. Hesch (1986) is one of Paulist's contributions. But perhaps one of the most important background books to help us understand how children feel has just become published by a well-known psychologist, Robert Coles, *The Spiritual Life of Children,* (1991) based on years of careful research and interviewing.

This year Fortress released a particularly needed work, in a stress-producing area. The new publication from what is now Augsburg-Fortress, is *What Does the Bible Say about Suicide?,* James T. Clemons, (1990). Clemons, a scholarly professor of New Testament, presents us with what the Bible *actually* says about self-murder, analyzing how many Biblical chapters have been consistently misinterpreted to suit the bias of the interpreter. In presenting this thorough analysis, the author hopes to offer church groups a well-ground tool to analyze the complexity of this "forever decision," to prevent any further sweeping such deaths under the sophism of "temporary insanity."

Also new is Sheed and Ward's slender booklet, *Let Them Go Free. Family Prayer Service to Assist in the Withdrawal of Life Support System,* by Thomas A. Shannon and Charles N. Faso, O.F.M. This offers a dazzling aid through a terrible, thoroughly contemporary problem. This is a tool so obvious when acknowledged, that it is amazing that nothing, to my knowledge, has been published about it before.

It begins with a very calming presentation of the many issues and individuals who should be called into a discussion of the termination of technological supports, when all hope for a meaningful existence is gone. It concludes with the prayer service itself, which could easily be adapted for non-Christian use. My only problem with the book is that it does not tackle the coping strategies needed when the medical staff disagrees with the family about the necessity for this solution.

If one decides to opt for the Hospice way of death, I have found only two new titles with a religious emphasis. They are first, *A Hospice Resource Manual for Local Churches,* edited by John W. Abbott, (Pilgrim Press, 1988). Abbott was associated for many years with the Connecticut Hospice and is highly qualified to create such a manual. An even earlier veteran of the Hospice movement, Florence Wald, the prime mover in the creation of the New Haven Hospice, produced *In Quest of the Spiritual Component of Care for Terminally Ill* in 1986. This book is available only through Ms. Wald's office in the Yale University School of Nursing. For the final word on religion as integrated into a Hospice, one should read Cecily Saunders' *Hospice: The Living Idea,* (W. B. Saunders, 1981). Dr. Saunders, who founded St. Christopher's Hospice in London, has incorporated pastoral care into her work from the very beginning.

A house called Gilgal Publications in Sunriver, Oregon has issued four helpful paperback tools for the pastoral counselor: *Meditations: For Bereaved Parents, For the Widowed, For the Divorced, and For the Terminally Ill and Their Families.* Each selection contains a one page essay by representatives of the various populations, describing their own personal loss and offering the consolation they found in the Bible and other sources. These are just the right length for the short attention span of acutely distressed mourners. The pastoral counselor should, however, read each one through before recommending it to clients, to be sure each publication does not contain a denominational "time-bomb" that will create problems later. This labor really should be mandatory with all bibliographic recommendations.

Other new books that should be extremely helpful include *For the Bereaved,* Austin H. Kutscher, et al., (Charles Press, 1989), containing a huge collection of consolatory essays of varying lengths, by writers from many disciplines. Also of value because of the breadth of its contributions is *Perspectives on Death and Dying, Cross-Cultural and Multi-Disciplinary Views,* edited by Arthur Berger, et al., from the Foundation of Thanatology (Charles Press, 1989). This multi-disciplinary publication discusses viewpoints of death from many cultures, and the Eastern and Islamic religions, as well as commentaries on the issues of near death experiences and immortality. Now that our cities are filled with immigrants from so many unfamiliar countries this book should prove valuable in working with those often alien sounding clients.

Two older works have helped many of those bereaved, *Don't Take My Grief Away,* by Doug Manning, (Insight Books, 1984) and my own particular favorite, *A Grief Observed,* by English theologican, C. S. Lewis (Seabury, 1961). This publication simply describes the cyclical nature of grief, the startling mood swings that can be experienced day in and day out as one reaches to recovery. Now that a new play, *Shadowlands,* has been produced about the experience which lead to this book (Lewis' marriage at a very mature age to an American convert), there should be renewed interest in *A Grief Observed.* Readers may like to know that this play is available on video tape for training and bereavement groups, from a religiously-oriented firm, Vision Video.

What I have observed over twenty years of dealing with thanatology books is that one's first thanatology title becomes THE thanatology title one recommends, above all, to others. Such a small paperback was released when I was an adolescent, blithely ignorant of the fact that I would ever come to work in the vineyards of thanatology literature. Yet it impressed me so deeply then, that I was delighted to find it still in print. It still seems to me it can still serve as *the* primer for the clergy man or woman moving into the heartbreaking work that is the subject of this book. That book is *Peace of Mind,* by Rabbi Joshua Loth Liebman, released in 1946 (now available from Signet). At that early date he wrote, "If we are to find peace of mind today, religion must be . . . willing . . . to absorb the new insights into human motivation . . . that come from the psychological clinic. Today's cringing world needs the support of a peace-giving faith that combines the substance of the old with the light of the new" (p. 46).

CHAPTER 26

Spirituality and Death Audiovisuals

Richard A. Pacholski

Teachers, pastoral counselors and caregivers interested in audio-visuals (16mm films, videocassettes, audiocassettes, filmstrips, and the like) on any thanatological topic have literally hundreds, if not thousands, to choose from. The best sources of information about thanatological AVs produced in the last fifteen years are the following:

- Hannelore Wass, et al., editors: *Death Education: An Annotated Resource Guide.* Washington, D.C., Hemisphere Publishing Corporation, 1980. Part II, "Audiovisual Resources" (pp. 149-245) describes nearly 600 audiovisuals on a full range of thanatological topics, including "clergymen as caregivers," "life after life experiences," and "religion and death" (see the topical index).
- Hannelore Wass, et al., editors: *Death Education II: An Annotated Resource Guide.* Washington, D.C., Hemisphere Publishing Corporation, 1985. The "Audiovisual Resources" section presents information on nearly 250 more AVs.
- The journal *Death Studies* (ISSN: 0748-1187), published six times yearly. Since 1986 the present writer has published in *DS* over 200 reviews of AVs on a wide range of thanatological topics. Future issues will continue to report on AV materials in the field.

Presented is information about a carefully selected number of thanatological AVs on special topics likely to be of interest to readers of this volume. In one way these items are representative of what is generally available. Typically severely time-limited, audiovisuals tend to cover their topics in cursory fashion, focusing tightly on comparatively narrow subjects, issues or themes. However, because of their visual appeal as well as their brevity, AVs are the media of choice in school classrooms, in-service training programs, group counseling sessions, and other educational contexts. The programs described here are, each of them, well-made and informative surveys of their subjects.

In another way, the items reviewed here[1] are quite special—special in their emphases upon "spiritual" concerns broadly understood. They differ markedly from what we might call run-of-the-mill educational audiovisual programs, whose "moral" base, in those moments when they attempt to probe the "human" significance behind their subject matter, is generality, platitude, or simple common sense. The programs described here—grouped into useful categories—take definitive moral points of view as their theses and explore implications in some depth. Offering thoughtful approaches to questions of value and meaning, they are unique in their human significance.

CONFRONTING CHANGE

Before we begin to think seriously about "death," we must first consider the meanings of "change." *Begin With Goodbye* is an excellent six-film series which can help us with that task, whether change means moving to a new neighborhood, losing a job, retirement, divorce, growing old, illness, loss of a body part, the death of a loved one, or one's own death.

Distinguished actor Eli Wallach is host, and begins the series, in the program "Changes," with engaging commentary on the life transitions to be developed in other films in the series. He expresses eloquently the theme of *Begin With Goodbye:* "We must grow out of what was, so we can fully appreciate what can be. Each death is a new life. Each end, a beginning." Sadness and sorrow are profoundly human experiences, essential elements of life which must be endured attentively if we are to grow in understanding of ourselves.

The second program in the series, "Turned Loose," explores the effects of job loss and retirement. The third, "Exits and Entrances," looks at "family partings": the empty nest syndrome, divorce, and going away to school.

"Mirror, Mirror on the Wall," the fourth program, examines the connection of "body image" with our sense of personal identity and

---

[1] These reviews have appeared, in different format and style, in the journal *Death Studies*, published by Hemisphere Publishing Corporation (Washington, D.C.), and are used here with the kind permission of the editor, Professor Hannelore Wass.

approach to life generally, and then considers the impact upon us of the physical changes brought about by advancing age and disease. Two case histories are presented, those of a mastectomee and a heart attack victim. Both people have rebounded well from their experiences, and thus offer us many positive lessons.

As narrator Eli Wallach concludes, "Mirror, mirror on the wall . . .. We must all learn to accept what we see. The nicks and scars of age, the wounds of illness and the pain of loss. It is in all these little deaths that we are born again and again."

The fifth program, "A Time to Cry," studies two families experiencing the loss of a loved one. Sandy Spencer, in her thirties, has cancer and a prognosis of less than nine months to live. She and her family try to cope with the situation, try to cram "75 years of living" into one. Sandy describes her reactions, and her husband, Bob, admits to sometimes carrying his grief around "like a loaded revolver." But with faith and commitment the family managed. (Sandy died shortly after the filming was completed.)

In the next sequence Harriet Kerr, mother of three, describes the effects of the death of her minister husband upon her, her widowhood, the coping strategies which helped (*expressing* her grief and *sharing* it), and how she embarked upon a new career.

The final program in the *Begin With Goodbye* series is entitled "The Death of Ivan Ilych." In the first half, excerpts from Tolstoy's classic novella are dramatized in competent fashion by professional actors on a simply set stage. Viewers who know the story might object to the oversimplification that results from such condensation, but at least some of Tolstoy's insights into one man's dying do come through forcefully. After the performance, several terminally ill people respond in panel discussion to the dramatization which *they* have just watched, and share their feelings and fears as they now find themselves in Ivan Ilych's situation.

Each film is distributed in 16mm and videocassette format, color, 28 minutes; a 12-page "Program Guide and Bibliography" is available to purchasers of the series. Sale, 16mm format, whole series, $2220; separately, $400 each. Sale in videocassette (all formats), whole series, $299; separately, $69 each. Rental, all formats, whole series, $180; separately, $35 each. Also available from the distributor are five "Portraits of Goodbyes," excerpts from various programs in the *Begin With Goodbye* series showing individuals struggling with different "goodbyes" in their lives—divorce, separation, physical loss, and death of a loved one. These six- to twelve-minute "Portraits" are an ideal length for use in church school classes, adult discussion groups, workshops and retreats. A "Film Guide and Bibliography" is available with these programs as well. Write or call for information: Mass Media Ministries, 2116 N. Charles St., Baltimore, MD 21218; telephone 301-727-3270, or 800-828-8825.

DEALING WITH TERMINAL ILLNESS

Coming to terms with cancer is the subject of a number of films. In *You Can't Say Forget It: Profile of a Cancer Patient,* Beverly Walker discusses the 11-year course of her disease, the various treatments she has had, and her intellectual, psychological, and emotional reactions to her changing condition. She talks about what she found helpful (Reach to Recovery; visitors; being involved in treatment decisions—"having control"; concentrating on "living"; and a doctor who reminded her, "I'm available"). She talks about what caused the most difficulty (being made to feel isolated and ignored by friends; hair loss and nausea from chemotherapy; bad dreams; watching the condition of a fellow patient deteriorate). The interviews are conducted in a sensitive fashion by Peggy Michel, M.S.W., chiefly from a social-work perspective, but pastoral counselors, nurses, physicians, other health professionals, and students interested in learning about the psychosocial aspects of cancer will find this program useful and informative. (Videocassette, color, 29 minutes, 1985. Free loan from your local American Cancer Society office; telephone 800-ACS-2345.)

In *Reflections on Suffering,* Dr. Balfour M. Mount, Director of the Palliative Care Service, Royal Victoria Hospital, Montreal, conducts a series of conversations with cancer patient Jean Cameron. Before her illness, Ms. Cameron was a volunteer social worker in the Palliative Care Service. Now, after several years of suffering a particularly painful form of cancer, she still maintains professional relationships with other patients in the service. Because she has come to terms with her own condition—though, as she explains, that was a hard-won peace—"her own illness has opened up lines of communication that draw upon a common experience." Ms. Cameron shares her struggles and her profound insights into life and death in a most meaningful and moving way. Caregivers need to see this film. (16mm film and videocassette, color, 28 minutes, 1982. Sale, film, $410; videocassette $300/rental $50. National Film Board of Canada, 16th floor, 1251 Avenue of the Americas, New York, NY 10020; telephone 212-586-5131.)

John and Marcie Wienecke were an active, popular suburban couple when doctors found advanced cancer throughout Marcie's body: they gave her three weeks to live. The fact that Marcie was still alive a year later, when *No Brief Candle: A Film About Being Alive* was made, is itself the subject of the film. The main title is from George Bernard Shaw:

> I rejoice in life for its own sake.
> Life is no brief candle to me.
> It is a sort of splendid torch which
> I have got hold of for the moment,
> And I want to make it burn as brightly
> As possible before handing it on
> To future generations.

Marcie lives, apparently, because she and her husband were *determined* to live—to live each moment, to treasure it, and to commit themselves to each other and to family and friends unreservedly. In their film story they discuss the transformation of their perception of what dying—and therefore *living*—must necessarily be. The film, thus, is infused with their wisdom and optimism, and raises compelling questions about choice, freedom and will, and how these forces within our personalities shape our living and our dying.

Marcie was a fighter, oriented to life. One can "have" circumstances, or "be" them, she said. *No Brief Candle* will encourage people with serious illness and their families to build and maintain loving and satisfying relationships, and to reassert their orientation to life. For counselors and caregivers, particularly those wearied by loss and grief, the film is a source of inspiration and a validation of faith and optimism. Well produced; stimulating viewing. (Videocassette, color 27 minutes, 1988. Sale, $245/rental, $50. Fanlight Productions, 47 Halifax Street, Boston, MA 02130; telephone 617-524-0980.)

The Awakening of Nancy Kaye is a unique thanatological film, dealing with the life, dying, and death from cancer of a woman with a physical disability. Audiences as diverse as death educators and counselors, caregivers of the disabled, and general adult groups concerned with these topics should consider using this film in discussion and training sessions.

Nancy Kaye was a remarkable person. As the director of special education in the Berkeley, California, public schools, Nancy was a national pioneer in the development and implementation of the mainstreaming concept. She worked on behalf of the handicapped with all the sense of urgency, sheer will power, focused energy and—yes—occasionally abrasive pushiness that she was forced to develop in her own personal life. In a word, Nancy's was a special kind of will-to-live. It molded her character, then her professional career, and then her approach to her dying.

Nancy was born with spina bifida. Her doctor father was convinced her condition was a dislocated hip. She, and everyone else in the family, believed that for twenty years. At her father's insistence Nancy fought her condition, and fought her way in the world, with spirited determination and sometimes angry stubbornness: she resented being seen as her disability. Thus, coming to terms with her condition she made sense of her life and purpose.

Then Nancy was diagnosed with terminal cancer. Ironically enough, her kidney tumor was allowed to grow for some time because her doctor was bullheadedly convinced her poor sitting posture resulting from the spina bifida caused the pain and discomfort she was feeling. So once again, Nancy Kaye determined to make sense out of what was happening to her, and to make her dying her own. She reestablished her ties to Judaism, studied for her Bat Mitzvah, and spent time with Stephen Levine in a "Dying into Life" seminar. She rediscovered timeless truths and applied them unflinchingly to her own dying:

- Dying is different—suffer it and endure it, but hold on to life and joy.
- Open yourself to death to become open to life.
- Balance grief and joy in the moment.
- Cherish your people (Nancy reached out in new ways to her mother and daughter.)
- When the body will no longer function, control remains in the mind, and the mind can say: "This is not a body you're using any more. You don't need to hang onto it; what you are doing in every self-controlled dying moment is important."

Nancy Kaye was one impressive human being. Moved by her life and death we may more readily reaffirm our own individuality. This superbly crafted film story is a valuable and inspiring human document. (Videocassette, color, 46 minutes, 1986. Sale, $350/rental, $55. Filmakers Library, 124 East 40th St., New York, NY 10016; telephone 212-808-4980.)

CHILDREN AND DEATH

No Greater Gift explores issues of caregiving and counseling with reference to children, dying and death. Watching this film about two youngsters hospitalized with life-threatening disorders, we gain much insight into the real power of "simple" things, like friendship and sharing. Keith, on kidney dialysis awaiting a transplant, and Nick, hospitalized with a brain tumor, are both traumatized by their experience at first. But their anger and fear, loneliness and depression are gradually assuaged as their initially tentative sharing blossoms into a friendship which helps them to cope.

In this well-acted production, a number of subjects are covered in depth—children and death, parent-child tensions in life-threatening situations, organ donation, and effective caregiving. There are valuable lessons here for a wide range of audiences: school children, parents of seriously ill children, support groups, pastoral caregivers, counselors, and medical staff. (Videocassette, color, 30 minutes, discussion guide, 1986. Sale, $250/rental, $75. Coronet/MTI Film and Video, 108 Wilmot Road, Deerfield, IL 60015.)

Another film study of a seriously ill child is *You Don't Have to Die: Jason's Story*. At age eight, Jason Gaes is one of an increasingly large number of cancer victims who may expect to survive their disease. Wanting to read a book for kids about kids who live with cancer, Jason decided to write one himself: "My Book for Kids with Cancer." In his own handwriting Jason tells about "keymotharupy" that "makes your stumick hurt," but he reminds his readers, "if you get cansur don't be scared 'cause lots of people get over having cansur and grow up without dying."

Featured in this film story of Jason and his book are interviews with family members and animated scenes of Jason being treated in the hospital. Caregiving professionals, school children, young "cansur" patients and their family members all will benefit from Jason's story and its very positive message. (Videocassette, color, 40 minutes, study guide, 1989. Sale, VHS, $69.95. Ambrose Video Publishing, Inc., 381 Park Avenue South, Suite 1601, New York, New York 10016; telephone 800-526-4663; in NY call 212-696-4545.)

Sending a positive message is also the guiding purpose of another film focusing on a seriously ill child. *Encounter with Garvan Byrne* is a filmed interview with an eleven-year-old English boy with a rare and dangerous form of bone-marrow cancer. He is quite intelligent—indeed precocious—and articulate. He knows very well the nature and outcome of his incurable illness and has already experienced great pain. Yet he maintains a vigorous sense of humor and, most importantly for him, a strong and positive religious faith. Audiences close to their own faith will find the program simply inspiring. Facing his death Garvan testifies to his belief that all is from the hand of God and that after death he will experience renewed life with God.

One may wonder about the usefulness of this program for an audience of professionals, patients, or family members who have other concerns. For example, how does a dying individual deal with feelings of depression, loneliness and desperation? What caregiving techniques are especially helpful to patients? Is there anything else one can depend on when one is near death besides religious dogma? Of course for Garvan and for many others, that is enough. (Videocassette, color, 30 minutes. Sale, VHS and Beta, $34.95. Vision Video, Box 540, Worcester, PA 19490; telephone 215-584-1893.)

Thumpy's Story: A Story of Love and Grief Shared, by Thumpy, the Bunny is a story for grieving children of all ages. Thumpy shares an experience of grief when his sister, Bun, unexpectedly dies. Questions, anger, bargaining, searching for answers—the whole Bunny family reacts to their loss. Thumpy's mother and father model sharing their grief and support with their children. In time, Thumpy's hurts ease, but Thumpy does not forget Bun, and does not stop questioning.

The story of Thumpy is available in many formats, for a variety of educational and/or counseling purposes: English and Spanish language story book ($5.95), coloring book ($4.95), work book ($8.95; instructional and therapeutic, subtitled "My Story of Love and Grief by _____"; patient or student inserts her own name), audiocassette ($4.50), and videocassette.

The story can be an effective teaching and counseling tool for children who have lost siblings, no matter the cause; it can be an excellent means of opening communication within a family or in a classroom; and it can raise community awareness of a child's need to be involved, and of the real pain children experience following a death of any significant other. In the audiocassette and videocassette the text of the story is narrated by actress Wenda Shereos. The soft, lifelike, watercolor artwork of the book (1985), highly evocative in its own right, is translated faithfully to the video medium. (Videocassette, color, in English or Spanish, 9 minutes. Sale, VHS only, $125/rental $25. Prairie Lark Press, P.O. Box 699, Springfield, IL 62705.)

When Children Grieve is an important audiovisual resource on this topic, well-crafted, sensitive, and richly informative. NBC medical consultant Dr. Art Ulene supervised this film project, which involved visits to three households wherein a parent was dying, had died, or had cancer. The children were interviewed, in some cases together with their dying parent, and were encouraged to express their feelings of sadness, guilt, anger, fear, and despair.

Intercut are scenes filmed during meetings of a grief support group that these children attended, together with instructive comments offered by counselors, therapists, and other caregivers working with the families. Dr. Ulene provides effective narrative continuity.

This film stresses openness and involvement of all family members, especially the children, in such situations, and teaches in specific ways how children may be empowered to deal with and resolve their own grief, and then to contribute positively to their bereaved family group. A valuable film for medical caregiver and counselor education as well as for college level courses and adult education. (Videocassette, color, 20 minutes, discussion guide, 1987. Sale, $295. Churchill Films, 662 N. Robertson Boulevard, Los Angeles, CA 90069.)

The grieving child is the topic of another classic program, *The Death of a Friend: Helping Children Cope with Grief and Loss*. This filmed puppet show deals with the accidental death of a child from the perspective of two young friends. Audrey and Catalion have many fantasies and fears—they wonder why Allison died, where she is now, and when she will return. With the help of an understanding adult, they talk about death, about their confusion, about their sad and angry feelings, and about how they can best remember Allison.

Specially designed to enable children from preschool through early elementary grades to understand and begin to discuss these issues, *The Death of a Friend* can also be a useful learning tool for teachers, counselors, parents, parent organizations and others who work with young children. (16mm film and videocassette, color, 15 minutes, discussion guide. Sale, film, $320; videocassette, $280/rental, $32. New Dimension Films, 85895 Lorane Highway, Eugene, OR 97405; telephone 503-484-7125.)

A remarkable film about stillbirth—*Some Babies Die*—can be used effectively in any counseling situation involving perinatal and neonatal death. A medical-counseling team in Australia is filmed working with Tess—who has just lost her newborn—and her three surviving children. The conduct of the caregiving staff in these stressful circumstances teaches important lessons by example about effective counseling relationships with patients on personal levels.

Some Babies Die illustrates the effectiveness of a totally open and honest approach to the realities of death and suffering. Tess and her children are not simply allowed, but are encouraged to hold, cuddle and talk to the dead newborn. They say goodbye. Reality sinks in directly, in an atmosphere of total mutual trust. The bereaved are not told what they "should" do, but are helped to understand what they are feeling, and what particular methods they may choose to get themselves successfully through the experience. The caregiving philosophy is to trust the family members to do what is important for themselves, then support them during and after.

Pastoral counselors, medical caregivers and general adult audiences—particularly self-help and support groups of parents who know the anguish of perinatal and neonatal death—will find this film profoundly moving, deeply enriching, and inspiring. (16mm film or videocassette, color, 54 minutes, 1986. Sale, film, $850; videocassette, all formats, $450/rental (film, 3/4" U-matic, or VHS) $60. University of California, Extension Media Center, 2176 Shattuck Avenue, Berkeley, CA 94704; telephone 415-642-0460.)

HOSPICE

If I Should Die . . . tells the story of Sandy Simon who, at age forty-seven, was diagnosed as having chronic myelogenous leukemia and was given a life expectancy of three to five years. Sandy became involved in the then-fledgling hospice movement (the year was 1976). Hospice care alleviated her personal concerns with her dying, and also became her "life's" work:

> Hospice started to become my passion. It represented to me the dignity of living as well as the dignity in dying. For me, death is a transition, a rebirth and God's loving will. But how I would die was overwhelming for me to face. The knowledge that I could have hospice care set me totally free. I became so passionately involved that I couldn't even think or talk or become involved in or do anything except learn about hospice. From that day on the journey started, the hospice journey started.

Sandy Simon went on to help found the Hospice of Los Angeles, an information and referral service on hospice care, and the Hospice Program at Cedars Sinai Medical Center, a major provider of in-patient and out-patient hospice care in Los Angeles.

This film is thus a bold and vivid declaration of support and praise for hospice, its philosophy, its practice, and its many benefits. It is also a remarkable personal testament to the courage and dedication of one human being face to face with death. In 1982, Sandy's son Dan decided to make a documentary film about his mother as he saw her condition weaken:

> I did not want to see her passion for the hospice movement die when she had to die. The story of my mother's final years was so inspiring that I wanted to capture it in some way and share it with others.

Over what would be the last six months of Sandy's life, Dan Simon filmed the treatment she was receiving at Cedars Sinai. He filmed interviews with other terminally ill patients and their family members, with hospice staff, and with volunteers. He took his camera into his home as well, recording the care provided Sandy by his father, brothers, and sisters. This totally honest and frank camera work revealed the strengths of this particular family group together with the tensions and the conflicts they experienced as Sandy's death came closer.

This well-made film has won several film festival awards for its production values and for its content. Many audiences will benefit from seeing it: terminally-ill patients and their families; students in schools and colleges; caregiving and counseling staff in hospitals, hospices, and nursing homes; and any number of general community audiences interested in becoming more aware of hospice, more aware of the needs of the terminally ill and their families, and—as one reviewer put it—more aware of "how to live out the last days of a terminal illness with grace and dignity." (Videocassette, color, 47 minutes, 1986. Sale, VHS and Beta, $200; 3/4" U-Matic, $250; preview available. Daniel Arthur Simon Productions, P.O. Box 49811, Los Angeles, CA 90049.)

A fresh and forceful filmed introduction to hospice, in concept and practice, *The Heart of the New Age Hospice* is designed especially for in-service training. Basic information and insights are presented in a carefully organized fashion, by articulate speakers. Visuals, the use of color, a striking emphasis on faces, and catchy background music bridging sections and scenes are all most effective in reinforcing the program's lessons.

The full spectrum of hospice services is examined—home care, in-patient care, and bereavement—and the team approach to caring is both stressed and demonstrated. Through candid interviews with team members—physicians, nurses, social workers, chaplains, home health aides and volunteers—the film emphasizes the concept of cooperation that is the heart of effective hospice programs.

Other basic hospice principles are presented with similar force:

- Hospice is not hopelessness; to die in hospice is to die gracefully.
- The patient is in control, not staff or an institutional rule book.
- The effective hospice professional must love life, must know how to listen, must want to give, to be there.
- Hospice serves the whole patient—body, mind, spirit—and his or her whole family through the whole dying process and beyond (grief work is often long-term memory work).
- Hospice people understand that they must care for themselves and for one another.

This program earned the National Hospice Organization Award for Excellence. (Videocassette, color, 28 minutes, 1989. Sale, all formats, $295/rental, 3/4" U-matic or VHS, $65. Carle Medical Communications, 110 W. Main St., Urbana, IL 61801-2700; telephone 217-384-4838.)

SUICIDE

Among the many audiovisuals on suicide produced for use in the schools, perhaps *Suicide Prevention: A Teacher's Training Program* is the most richly informative for educational and counseling professionals interested in the topic. The first part—"A Cry For Help" (13 minutes)—examines the probable causes of the increase in teen suicides in recent years. Part two—"Hearing the Cry" (18 minutes)—offers guidelines and specific suggestions for teachers who are responding to suicidal teens.

In her survey of causal factors, Dr. Ona Robinson, a psychotherapist in Westchester County, New York, emphasizes some of the less well-known factors seen in increasing numbers of cases of adolescent depression: the diminishing influence of religious beliefs, a sense of impotence and insecurity and the resulting frustration of idealism, a fear of nuclear holocaust, and the salient characteristics of contemporary American life—violence and materialism.

Then teachers are given a set of guidelines both for intervention in particular cases, and for suicide prevention in the community in general. Emphasized are educational programs on suicide, depression and other mental health topics, for school staff, parents and students; open communication on all those issues, especially between teachers and students and among students themselves; and—in various ways—fostering values like sharing, cooperation, and volunteerism in the community. Most importantly, the program argues, let teachers be positive role models, caring and helping, demonstrating in their own lives and professional careers the sort of integrity, compassion and sense of hope we need to teach our kids, so that they want to keep on living.

The teacher's guide accompanying *Suicide Prevention* is a particularly rich resource, with content summary, filmscript, bibliography, list of 12 objectives, suggested previewing and postviewing activities for various adult and professional audiences, emergency resources checklist, list of warning signs of suicide, and specific suggestions for intervention. This program is an excellent introductory resource for school and other community groups. It is especially well designed and is highly informative. (Videocassette, color, 33 minutes, study guide, 1986. Sale (VHS) $139. Human Relations Media, 175 Tompkins Avenue, Pleasantville, NY 10570.)

Suicide among the infirm elderly is nothing new, though these days we seem to be hearing, seeing and reading more about it. In his old age, Seneca, the Roman philosopher and essayist, wrote approvingly of suicide, arguing that the wise man "lives as long as he should, not as long as he can. . . . If he encounters many vexations which disturb his tranquillity, he will release himself" (Moses Hadas translation).

Similarly, in his short story "A Summer Tragedy" (1933) Arna Bontemps vividly portrays an elderly couple's mutual choice for suicide, describing their poverty, loneliness and isolation, blindness and palsy, their mutual fear of outliving the essential other, and the threat of eviction from familiar territory to institution or back room. The situation is tragic, as the title suggests, since Jeff and Jenny make bold choices and accept their end courageously. The story is pathetic as well, illustrating the crushing power of an impersonal society.

An article in a recent issue of the *Wall Street Journal* reminds us that the elderly today "take their own lives far more often than adolescents, and their suicide rate is more than 50 percent above that of the general population." And this rate is rising steadily, due apparently to cuts in governmental support programs, rapidly ongoing technological change and urbanization, increased longevity, and the attendant frequency of chronic degenerative diseases.

An award-winning film exploring these topics, *Ernie and Rose* would be useful viewing for students, general audiences, and caregiving professionals as well, for it can help sensitize them to the *felt* concerns of the elderly. Indeed, artistic productions of all kinds— whether Senecan essay, story, music, poetry or film—have that special advantage over clinical analyses. *Ernie and Rose* uses brilliant acting, subtle character portrayal, and humor to instruct—as Aristotle would have it—with delight.

The film presents the last days of a couple of erstwhile army buddies, now sharing a house and taking care of each other in their old age and infirmities (heart trouble and cataracts among them) and lean circumstances (Ernie prepares a mean-looking cucumber stew; they celebrate a dress-up occasion with baloney sandwiches). Endearing us to them initially is their genuine unselfish friendship for each other, going back to their war years when Rose (a Black man, by the way) saved Ernie's life in combat. Ernie shoplifts a pair of pajamas for Rose, who objects both to the crime—"it's the principle of the thing"—and, more strenuously, to the style of the article—they look like "my burying pajamas." Our real delight is in their conversation, as they take stock of their situation and consider alternatives. These are ordinary men, burdened with neither formal education nor dogma, trying with only their considerable store of mother wit to come to terms with death. Ernie says,

> I used to think, when I was old enough to drink, that'd be really livin'. Then, when I was old enough to have a woman, that'd be it. It looks like death's right up there with livin' these days. . . . I don't care much about dyin' myself, but when I think about Rose I get lonesome. . . . Young guys is headin' for it just like me, blind as bats. I can't help 'em. Nobody helped me. Only thing I'd like to know is, how'd I ever get so damn old?

For his part Rose dabbles in traditional forms of consolation, sometimes dipping into *The Bible,* sometimes doing Eastern meditation and chanting. But Ernie will have none of that: "You know you gotta die. I know it. What about *our* future?" Then they come upon the Stoic philosopher: "To some, dying is a punishment, to some it is a gift; to others it is a favor." Ernie decides, "What we need is a favor."

And so they reminisce and celebrate the old times, deciding that, though "there's no lead in the pencil anymore," it was fun while it lasted. The draft an agreement and a testament, saying that life is like a picture; you add colors day by day. But when it's done a painter should know enough to step aside: "Ernie and myself, we just want to say thank you and . . . step aside."

The beauty of this film story is found in the nuances of the conversation, the subtleties of characterization, the quietly understated suffering humanity of these fellows and their equally admirable resilience, and the delightfully humorous tone of the proceedings generally, including the background music: old Edison recordings. The writer will leave undescribed the concluding action with the propane tank, the kitchen stove and Ernie's last cigarette, so inventively woven into the last lines: "Are we dead yet?" "Nope. Just outta gas." But he urges everyone who cares for the aging to see this film. (16mm film and videocassette, color, 29 minutes, 1984. Sale, 16mm film, $525; videocassette, $295/rental, $55. Filmakers Library, Inc., 124 E. 40th St., New York, NY 10016; telephone 212-808-4980.)

AIDS

AIDS: A Family Experience is a must-see film for all caregivers involved in counseling AIDS victims and their family members and for AIDS patients and family themselves. When Don Robinson learned that he had AIDS, and after his family came to terms not just with the diagnosis but with his homosexuality, they all agreed to the filming of

Don's last days. Their motivation: to help others in similar situations through their own hard times, to assure others that they are not alone. They succeed, I believe, beyond their fondest hopes.

Not only are these people intelligent and compassionate, they are forceful and articulate in relating their varied responses to Don's impending death, his sexual preference, and the complex yet steadily downhill course of Don's disease. Don's mother, father, adult siblings and in-laws—each from his or her own perspective—report their pain, their fears, their doubts. Yet the emphasis in every conversation is on the bonds of family sharing, caring and love that brought every family member together to support one another and Don. The advice they give on understanding and coping is both thoughtful and practical, as they report and analyze their responses to the changes—the maddeningly unpredictable roller-coaster ride of remission and relapse—that mark the terminal phase of AIDS.

What is so beautifully effective about this film, after all, is its uncalculated emphasis on the strength of the human spirit that suffers yet endures. Near his end, Don is grateful that he now sees life more richly; such vision, he says, must be a kind of reward for having to die. Summarizing simultaneously the course of his dying, the involvement of his family members in his caregiving, and the making of this film for the benefit of others, Don's words are right on: "It's a good story."

This award-winning film is very well made, nicely edited, and intelligently scripted. Interviews with various family members are intercut with comments by medical staff and other AIDS experts and caregivers. A well-spoken narrator provides thoughtful continuity. (Videocassette, color, 33 minutes, 1988. Sale, 3/4", Beta, VHS, $395/rental, 3/4", VHS, $75. Carle Medical Communications, 110 West Main Street, Urbana, IL 61801-2700; telephone 217-384-4838.)

Roger's Story: For Cori is a documentary about a forty-four-year-old recovering heroin addict, his struggle to go straight after a twenty-year period of heroin use, and his more recent diagnosis with AIDS. The camera shows Roger at home, with his wife and four-year-old daughter, then follows him to the hospital where he counsels other recovering addicts. We learn of his middle-class roots, the ghetto shooting gallery where he was introduced to heroin, and his subsequent chaotic relationships with drug dealers and other addicts.

Having pulled himself out of the drug addiction and having begun a new life with wife and child, Roger was to experience yet another effect of his years as an addict—he has recently discovered he has AIDS. Now he must fight for his life on yet another front.

Roger's Story focuses on the intensity of Roger's emotions as he faces this new development, and on his exceptional capacity for self-revelation—he presents brilliant insights into his wasted years, his fear of death, and his thoughts about suicide. On the other side are his love of his family, his strength of character, and his sheer perseverance. This program may inspire hope in other drug addicts and AIDS victims, and is certainly required viewing for pastoral caregivers, counselors and educators at all levels. (Videocassette, color, 28 minutes, 1989. Sale, $195/rental, $50, from Fanlight Productions, 47 Halifax St., Boston, MA 02130; telephone 617-524-0980.)

NOTE: Over the last several years the writer has published reviews of dozens of film programs on AIDS in the journal *Death Studies*. Some of these are technical or clinical in nature; *most* deal in one way or another with the human and spiritual issues central to effective AIDS counseling. The interested reader will consult the following issues of *DS*:

12(5-6), 1988, pp. 609-615 (This issue of *DS* is devoted to AIDS.)
13(2), 1989, pp. 219-220
13(3), 1989, pp. 342-343
13(5), 1989, pp. 511-512
14(1), 1990, p. 102
14(3), 1990, p. 290-291

AGING GRACEFULLY

Fool's Dance is an entertaining, insightful story for anyone professionally or personally involved with the care of the elderly, whether in their own homes or in a nursing home or other facility.

The scene is a stereotypical extended care facility wherein a bored and burned-out social activities director—badgered by a pencil-pushing manager—fails miserably in sparking the interest of a group of residents. Then one day in walks a new patient, an outspoken, Shakespeare-quoting eccentric who soon disrupts the institutional status quo while he begins to reinstill the joy of living in his fellow residents.

He is something of an Eastern "Myokonin," a man considered strange and wonderful, simple but enlightened. He soon teaches everyone in the home—patients and staff alike—to sing and dance and to think positive thoughts in the face of the painful mysteries of existence, aging, and death.

- What is the world about? There is no answer to comfort us. The world is not perfect. It is always changing. But truth and pure light are one, as a flame.

- We start to die the moment we are born. Like incense, or morning dewdrops, we are fresh and bright in the morning, and at night we return to ashes.
- Face to face with death, accept it, then forget it. Then you can truly live. This is the year you may die, so it should be the year you truly live.
- Like the face in the mirror, life and death are illusions. Life does not end with death. Life is a single moment; it is born and it dies and is born again, moment after moment after moment. . . .
- Death teaches us to celebrate life, because it is life.
- If dancing is foolish and makes us foolish, does watching the dance make us wise? If we are wise and foolish, what a pity not to dance.

All of which works a lot better in the dramatization than the words on the page might suggest. Attitudes in this community can and do change, and with them come joy and a renewed zest for living. The point is that, especially in one's old age, life and living must be celebrated.

This delightfully entertaining story will stimulate audience discussion about how to make it happen in their own homes and communities. Watching *Fools Dance*, caregiving staff and counselors, in school and in in-service programs, will come to appreciate the real power of philosophy and spirituality to enrich the lives of their patients. (16mm film and videocassette, color, 30 minutes, 1988. Sale, all formats, $385; rental, $65. Carle Medical Communications, 110 W. Main St., Urbana, IL 61801-2700; telephone 217-384-4838.)

DEATH EDUCATION

Designed for classroom use in grades 7-12, *Dying is Part of Living* provides basic information in an interesting fashion for a death education or suicide education instructional unit. The focus is on Nicole, as she grieves at the sudden death of her father, age 47, and then at the accidental death of a classmate several months later. Caring teachers, counselors, and relatives help Nicole understand her feelings in the aftermath of these deaths, the shock and pain, the fear, the guilt. They help her to come to terms with the uncaring reactions and the denial of classmates. They help her learn that death is part of the natural order of things, and that grief can heal.

These lessons are brought home in yet another way as Nicole later volunteers in a hospice and works with the elderly Mrs. Murray, dying of cancer. Learning about the "stages" of dying enables Nicole to deepen her insights into the reasons for living. She comes to appreciate the essential integrity of each individual human being, bound in families and other communities but still destined to "let go" and live her own life.

The helpful teacher's guide offers a discursive introduction to the program, a content summary, discussion questions, and a list of suggested activities. Overall, an attractive, informative teaching tool. (Three filmstrips and audiocassettes, color, teacher's guide; also available on videocassette; 1986. Sale, $165. Sunburst Communications, 101 Castleton Street, Pleasantville, NY 10570-9971; telephone 800-431-1934; in New York, 800-221-5912; in Alaska call collect, 914-769-5030.)

As We Learn to Fall: A Look at Death and Grief and Coping and Living for Children and Parents is as fine a general introduction to "death and dying" for schoolchildren (grades 4-12) as one is likely to find anywhere. The program focuses on a teenager struggling to learn about and accept the recent death of a friend. She consults with a knowledgeable school guidance counselor, who responds clearly, concisely and intelligently to her many questions.

Intercut with scenes depicting the counseling sessions are diagrams, graphics and film clips of interviews with dying children, with grieving parents, and with other students reacting to these issues. Doctors and teachers present their experience and insights into caregiving, counselling and education on a wide range of thanatological topics.

Of the several true-life cases presented in the program, perhaps that of Jeff Van Leishout, a cancer victim who died at age eleven, is the most moving. His life before and during his struggle with his disease is presented in some detail. His parents recount how they handled things. His classmates recall Jeff's courage and tenacity, speaking frankly of the Jeff they once knew and the Jeff they still remember in sorrow and tears.

These real people and their real responses to these issues are blended very professionally by the filmakers with the fine acting of the principles, the grieving schoolgirl and her counselor. Production values are all first-rate. Editing is crisp, pacing is lively yet coherent. Everyone—actors and "real people" alike—is articulate and intelligent.

The teacher's guide (available separately; see below) is well made, too. It offers many guidelines for teaching death education, including lists of both do's and don't's, explaining in some detail what to say and do when children lose a friend or relative to death; it presents an extensive outline of the developmental stages of children's awareness of death; it provides a detailed psychological portrait of the grieving child. The guide gives specific suggestions for pre- and post-viewing activities related to this program, and reprints the full production script. Included is a resources address list, and twenty-one-page bibliography of over 450 items (noting books for adults as well as fiction and non-fiction for children, kindergarten through high school).

This award-winning program (the Gold Award, from the Corporation for Public Broadcasting—it was judged best of 350 entries in its category) should become an essential audiovisual in every school's death-education curriculum. (Videocassette, color, 30 minutes, 1988. Sale, VHS, $395; 3/4", $425; rental, $60. Centre Productions, 12801 Schabarum Avenue, Irwindale, CA 91706-7878; telephone 800-234-7879. The teacher's guide costs $2. Write to Northeastern Wisconsin School of Telecommunications, Instructional Services 1110, University of Wisconsin-Green Bay, Green Bay, WI 54311.)

The Fall of Freddie the Leaf is a strikingly beautiful film version of Leo Buscaglia's well-known story for children—or rather for the child in all of us. This allegory of the wonder and the purpose of life, the cycle of the seasons, and the meaning of death is told through the voices of Freddie and Daniel, two leaves of a fine old sweet-gum tree.

Freddie wonders what is to come as the seasons advance from spring to summer and autumn, and why he and his brother leaves turn to brilliant colors and begin to fall from the tree. What is the purpose of life if one has to die with the onset of winter? As Buscaglia's spokesperson, Daniel the leaf teaches Freddie about the great cycle of life and death, about seasons and change, about the enduring parent tree whose roots go deep, about the real happiness which is found in serving others and enjoying the life we share for a time.

Sensitive narration, imaginative camera work, brilliantly colorful visuals, and background music by Mozart and Schubert are combined into a delightful and moving experience: everyone must see this film. (16mm film and videocassette, color, 16 minutes, discussion guide, 1985. Sale, 16mm film, $390; videocassette $295/rental, 16mm film only, $50. AIMS Media, 6901 Woodley Avenue, Van Nuys, CA 91406-4878. Telephone 800-367-2467; in CA, AK, HI call collect 818-785-4111; in Canada 416-265-3333.)

CHAPTER 27

Jimmy Died, Call the Church

Janet Bouman

No one episode in our lives can adequately explore or expose us to all that life holds. Nor can we know ahead of time how we will behave when tragic events in life happen/occur. What we must begin to understand and continue to develop are the mechanisms and tenets by which we will be guided. This gives us some degree of assurance that whatever happens, it/we will be alright. The more we learn about the strengths within ourselves, the more we recognize our limitations. We are/will be powerless to deal with crises alone, because there is an element of unpreparedness that accompanies sudden or critical situations. It is at this time, most of all, that we will need the strength and support to carry on, which emanates from our faith—in God, in his gift to us of one another, and in love, both given and received. The following vignettes, as well as the words of knowledge, have been recorded to help the reader toward that understanding.

ONE MOMENT IN TIME

Soaked in the pouring rain, fifty of us boarded a bus in Tiberias that would take us to one of Israel's National forests. Arriving, we huddled together, sharing umbrellas and warmth. We watched in silence as Joe stepped out of the group and uncovered a plaque which had been readied for our arrival. "I am starting a new life today," Joe said. "But before I can begin, I need to say goodbye." We joined in prayer, once again reminded of our resurrection assurance. For we were here to commemorate this new beginning for Joe; he had planted a grove of trees to honor the memory of his wife of forty-one years. After the memorial service, members of the group lined up to pay $10.00 for a certificate which marked the dedicating of a tree in honor of a loved one.

The rain continued as we reboarded the bus for Cana. When we arrived, the rain stopped and the sun shown brightly. We made our way to the tiny chapel, built in commemoration of Jesus' first public miracle at the wedding in Cana. Now we were here, gathered for a wedding as well. For Joe, resplendent in a tuxedo, and Julie, his new bride-to-be, this would be the moment of a new beginning—a new life for both of them.

After thirty-seven years of marriage, Julie had found herself a widow and thought her life had changed forever. Through her church, she began to attend a bereavement group to help her to deal with the grief and changes in her life. Julie had been devastated when she first joined the group. Now, three years later, she was here in Cana, standing before fifty teary-eyed friends and fellow travelers, making promises to Joe—and promises to God—for the rest of her life.

AND ANOTHER

Linda and Keith walked slowly down the center of the church, tears openly streaming down their faces. In their hands they carried the bread and wine to the altar. It would soon be consecrated and returned to them as His Body and Blood to give them strength to continue through the rest of this never-ending day and the days which would follow. Linda and Keith were just thankful to be doing *something*—to be occupied, and not remain still with their thoughts. They were grateful that the priest had asked all of them—Linda, Keith, their four brothers and sisters, and their parents—to help plan Steve's funeral. Steve, their fifteen-year-old baby brother . . . how could it be, when he was alive just two days earlier? But it was not fantasy or a bad dream. Steve had committed suicide, and the shock and grief had seemed unbearable. But decisions had to be made—hymns to select, lessons to read, who would do the readings or carry the Eucharistic gifts. They had to decide whom among them would carry their brother's body for the last time. They didn't want to be angry with Steve for what he had done—NOT YET. They didn't want to think about what this would do to their family—NOT YET. They didn't want to think about why they had not recognized Steve's pain—NOT YET. They wanted—they *needed*—to be busy, to concentrate on the task at hand, to share in these final preparations for Steve's funeral. The time would come for reflection, for them to work out their grief and ask "WHY?" They found the encouragement and support to work this out in their own time from their parish—the family of the church.

AND YET ANOTHER

June came to the pastor's office unannounced, hoping he would be there. "Pastor, I need to talk to you," she said when he answered the timid, yet insistent knock on his office door. Members of the parish, June and her husband George, have a five-year-old son. They had, for several years, been trying to have another child. "I was pregnant, Pastor. I was finally pregnant," she sobbed. "Our prayers had been answered. We told Sammy he was going to be a big brother. We were all so happy! But I lost the baby. I had a miscarriage two weeks ago. This is the first time that I've left my home. I am so angry. What should I tell Sammy? How can God be so cruel? A baby . . . My baby . . . God took MY baby. I already loved that child! People don't understand my grief. They tell me it was probably for the best. They tell me I am still young and I can try again. I don't want to try again. I want my baby back!"

The minister, who happens to be my husband, says that most people enter a church at least three times during their lifetime. The three times are to be baptized, to be married, and to be buried. "And," he reminds us, "for two out of these three times, the person must be carried in."

While it is true that some people only gravitate toward church at these times, there are many who consider our church, our community of believers, to be our extended family. We go there often, at least once a week, to be nourished by the words, the prayers, the community, the rituals.

The church is one of the most intergenerational organizations in existence. This is true both on the local and the national level. A pastor/priest/rabbi is expected to relate to and understand the unique problems of each and every member of the congregation. Standing before the portal of the church/synagogue and greeting the worshippers as they leave the service, he/she is on a continual roller coaster of expression and emotion. Many members of the congregation have myriad joys and heartaches they wait to share with their spiritual leader. Monday mornings often bring a flood of phone calls from those who couldn't trust the openness of the moment after service.

To provide for the wide scope of problems and concerns of a congregation, a local parish is called upon to offer a vast number and variety of programs and services. What is provided is often dependent upon the size of the congregation, the number of staff/personnel, the availability of funds, the interest and willingness of the parish to be in ministry to/with/for one another and their community, and the ability or willingness of the pastor to share the ministry.

No one pastor can be "all things to all people." I believe a congregation can and should use its diversity for strength in ministry. One program which could speak to this uniquely intergenerational fellowship would be a ministry to help people deal with death and bereavement. There is no person who is *not* touched in some way by death. And, each of us, within ourselves, will have to face the inevitability of our own death.

My friend, Doris, who was only sixty-six years old, died of cancer on Easter Sunday. We buried her yesterday (April 18, 1990). Knowing that this piece was to be delivered to the editor in a matter of a few weeks, I found myself paying particular attention to the reactions of my fellow parishioners, and to the activities performed by Doris' church family.

First, I'd like you to know something about Doris. She was lovingly devoted to her Lord, her church and her minister. Every parish is blessed with those certain individuals who form the backbone of the church. Look in your own parish. You have a Doris you recognize. You know she will be in attendance at (lend support to) every activity; in fact, she would probably be instrumental in planning it. I am tempted to tell you everything she did for our parish, but it would take the entire chapter, and this isn't really about that. This chapter is about parish ministry; therefore, I will use Doris' story to recognize some of our parish's ministries.

Doris only knew she had cancer for about two months. Three weeks before she died, she was hospitalized so that tests could be run. The test results showed no reason to give her chemotherapy; the cancer was spreading too quickly. She decided to go home to die. Doris called her closest friends and told them herself. She didn't want to go home in an ambulance. Her husband and her pastor took her home. With great difficulty, they got her up the stairs to her second floor home. It took them twenty exhausting minutes, but Doris' dignity was preserved.

Members of our congregation had signed up to bring meals to Doris and her family (which included her husband and ninety-six-year-old mother-in-law) for the entire month of April. Ironically, it was Doris who had been instrumental in starting this program, initiated by the Social Ministry Committee, for the congregation. Doris had taken a lot of covered dishes to those in need. She understood the love that was being delivered with her meals.

As Doris lay dying, she made lists of things she wanted taken from her attic and given to fellow members and to the parish at large. She made very sure that her husband delivered them, or that someone from the church came and got them. It was important to her to know this was done, to finish this piece of business.

Because we knew that Doris would never again be able to worship with us, some members decided to buy her a VCR. We would tape the church service and bring it to *her*. By contributing to the purchase of the VCR, the members felt grateful to be doing *something* for Doris. In addition, members of the parish offered to sit with Doris and/or her mother-in-law, so that her husband could get out from time to time.

Despite her illness, Doris continued to give to us; she taught us how to face death. The hospice nurse said, "You are so calm, Doris. Do you understand that you are dying?" "I understand," she said, "and I know that my Savior is waiting for me." And when she died shortly after, her husband and her pastor were at her side.

The funeral home was packed with members. The liturgy was also well attended. Several members were involved with sharing the prayers and Scripture readings at the service, or serving coffee and cake at the church following the burial. Doris had always gone to funerals, but seldom went to the cemetery. She had wanted to make sure that the coffee would be ready, and that the bereaved family would be served immediately upon their return to the church.

For now, the meals will continue while Doris' family decides how meal time will be handled, now that Doris is no longer preparing and serving those meals. Her husband will continue to know that his parish loves him as it loved his wife. He will be permitted to fill his first days alone without having to worry about meal preparation. He will be able to cry openly with people who also loved and miss his wife.

I recall hearing over and over again at the wake, "We are a family. How do people face the death of a loved one without the comfort and strength of a church family?" How we will miss our dear Doris.

The week before Doris' death, Allen died. He and his wife were faithful members who worshipped regularly. They had not been involved in the ministries of our parish, as Doris had been. No meals had been brought to their home. Some members of the congregation went to the funeral home. Some went to the funeral service; none were involved in that service. The minister brought Allen's name before us several times in prayers and in sermon references.

"When tragedy strikes people deeply involved in our community, we are aware of their pain and are quick to extend our sympathy and support. . . . Even in the smallest parish, there are those whose participation is minimal, who live almost as strangers among us. When death touches them, they turn in need to their church, perhaps for the first time, seeking the rites of burial. Too often, a funeral is all they get," says Carol Luebering, author of the wonderful little book entitled *To Comfort All Who Mourn: A Parish Handbook for Ministry to the*

Grieving.[1] Allen may not be missed as deeply by the fellowship of our parish as will Doris, who was involved in so many aspects of ministry. Her presence was felt every moment we spent trying to find people to take her place in those ministries. But Allen's wife knows she, too, has the love and support of her minister and of her fellow members.

When I began thinking about the kinds of material I would like to incorporate in this chapter, I sat down and wrote to church bodies, parishes, social ministry agencies and national organizations (like the AARP), requesting any information they could send about programs available to parishes regarding grief ministry. From the responses, I obtained a wealth of information on ministry to the dying and/or the bereaved. From this experience, I would have to say that any parish that wished to start such a ministry should have no difficulty finding helpful resource literature. The most obvious resource for a parish is its diocese or national church body. I found each contact to be extremely helpful and aware of existing programs.

I remember Eileen, a middle-aged woman with a teenage daughter still living at home, saying to me when her husband died, "I didn't know a thing I was supposed to do when Ralph died. Now I could write a book. I probably should. No one should go through what I have gone through." Well, Eileen, someone has written such a book. Mervin E. Thompson, a Lutheran minister, is the author of *What You Need To Know When Death Touches Your Life.* This book covers such topics as: funeral costs; types of caskets; decisions to make before calling a funeral director; Social Security benefits, and life insurance policies. Too often, programs in grief ministry are designed to speak of death after the fact; people don't plan for death. Hence, this book is of practical help in having to prepare oneself for all of the aspects involved immediately preceding or immediately after a death. There are, at the back of the book, several information forms, including; personal information, emergency information, a living will, and instructions for my family.

I recently attended a conference for clergy sponsored by the Division on Aging of Bergen County, New Jersey. Its purpose was to encourage churches in their ministry with older adults and to share any such relevant information. People are often unaware of the services available to/for older adults. A director of a mental health agency spoke about the high rate of depression and suicide in older adults. She said, "If every congregation offered a program concerning bereavement (for the bereaved) just once a month, the rate of depression and suicide in older adults would drop enormously." What a wonderful suggestion! I

[1] Complete addresses for books cited are on pages 376-377.

believe that a parish must be as intent on "being Christ to others" in their parish family as they are about evangelism and reaching out to others. How that care and love expresses itself differs, as it must, from congregation to congregation. It is important to remember that we should not leave the ministry of the dying and the bereaved to the minister alone to handle. Remember also that we are available in the same way and to all within the church family.

Family Life Ministries in Irvington, New Jersey, has developed a *Parish Ministry Training Program* (they would also lead program workshops, $150/person/eight-week sessions). The packet includes: a twenty-five-page outline of the actual training program; six pages of introductory group exercises; a five-page paper entitled "Grief . . . A Hopeful Journey"; a two-page paper entitled "Grief and the Family"; a page entitled "Rite of Commitment to Ministry"; a list of hymn suggestions for "Music in the Funeral Mass"; a selected bibliography; an evaluation questionnaire on the training program itself; and three pages of examples of prayers to be used (in rituals) for different types of death.

I found this material to be very clear and well done. A diocese, cluster of parishes, or an ecumenical town-wide group could use this very easily, and adapt it to their situation or faith tradition. In addition to the packet, the Archdiocese of Newark program gives two manuals to each of its trainees (purchasable by mail). The first book is entitled *Hope For Bereaved: Understanding, Coping and Growing Through Grief*, written by Theresa Schoeneck. The cover page reads, "A Handbook of Helpful Articles Written by Bereaved People for Bereaved People and Those Who Want to Help Them." This is a wonderful manual. I would suggest that any person experiencing such grief would find answers to their questions, comfort in their sorrow, or helpful information.

An example of this would be "Suggestions for Helping Yourself Through Grief" under a heading entitled *Ask For and Accept Help,* which advises:

> Don't be afraid to ask for help from those close to you when you need it. So much hurt and pain go unheeded during grief because we don't want to bother anyone else with our problems. Wouldn't you want someone close to you to ask for help if they needed it? Our family and friends can't read our minds. Some relatives and friends will not be able to handle your grief. It is very important to find someone who cares, and understands with whom you may talk freely.

I mostly agree with this suggestion. No one will ever understand exactly how the griever feels. Every relationship is different. Every loss is different. I need to know and understand that others have experienced loss, even similar loss, but no one can know how I feel, except for God Who knows all and sees into my heart. I do agree that I have to look for help from those friends who are willing to help me deal with my grief.

Irving died a year ago. A few weeks after his death, Florence, his wife, contacted his union to find out what her pension payments from his company would be. Florence was receiving Social Security payments of $450 a month and had monthly rent payments of $600. She had used her savings to pay doctors, while Irving was spending week after week in the hospital. She was desperate to know her financial future. She spent day after day, month after month, making phone calls and contacting lawyers, doctors, and social workers, as Irving's pension payments seemed to get lost deeper and deeper in bureaucratic red tape. Eleven months later, Florence finally got her answer. In the meantime, she had to rely on the generosity of her parish to pay a month's rent. She found it necessary to apply for and to receive rent subsidy. She endured questions and intrusions into her personal life, as person after person had to find out "just one more detail."

When I spoke with her the other day, she said, "I don't understand what is wrong with me. I am tired all the time and can't eat." At first, I suggested that she see her physician. Then I said to her, "Florence, the feelings you are having are natural. You are finally giving yourself a change to mourn. You have been so busy since Irving's death that you never had a chance to do that. Now all the busy work is done. You don't have a list of phone calls to make when you get up in the morning. You have time to miss Irving." She began to cry. "Thank you for understanding" was all she said. "Thank you for giving me permission to have these feelings" is what I heard.

Let me share one more example with you from this book. There is a section written by Donna Kalb entitled "How to Help Ourselves Through the Holidays." She gives a two-page, twenty-item list of ways to make the anticipation of a holiday and the celebration itself more bearable. While these suggestions may be helpful for some, others may see them as a means of denial. The importance I see in such a list is its ability to help the bereaved person to think and to plan. It could act as a discussion opener for a family. It is important to share with one another how each would like to celebrate the holiday. This kind of conversation gives one "permission" to talk about the deceased. "Remember how Dad always insisted that it wasn't Thanksgiving dinner if sweet potatoes weren't served."

Recently we put an announcement in our church newsletter and local newspaper inviting anyone experiencing a loss to attend a Sunday afternoon discussion group. The pastor began with a few opening remarks, and informed the group of the availability of resource references on the subject of grief and bereavement to be found on the side table. But the main purpose of the group was to let people share. Twenty-five people attended, with their loss having occurred as long ago as six years or, for others, only recently. All were anxious to talk and were thankful to be given the opportunity. It is unclear if the group will be ongoing, but they have decided to meet again just before Christmas, feeling the need for support before the holiday season.

While few knew each other, their instant bond was the experience of loss and the ability to speak freely and openly about that loss. The fact that a church invited them to do that also gave them the chance to witness about the strength they get from God, and to express the anger they feel toward God for their loss.

I think there is a very real need for bereavement groups, and that this is a ministry in which parishes should consider becoming involved. It does not necessarily have to involve the minister. Planning must be done. The parish council or social ministry committee needs to talk about goals for sponsorship, and qualifications for leadership. The group facilitator must have group leadership skills, compassion, knowledge of the grief process, resources for specific types of losses, and counseling skills and/or appropriate references. A needs assessment would be helpful, possibly taking the form of a questionnaire to the congregation to find out if members would be willing to or desire to participate in the bereavement group. Another could be done at group formation to help the facilitator determine the direction most helpful for the greatest number of participants. Still another might be done after the group has been together for a while and after people have both joined and left the group.

Holidays are not the only difficult times for those experiencing loss. As a case manager for older adults, I visit many homebound widows. They tell me that the worst part of their day is dinner time, when they will eat their meals in front of a television set so that there will be voices of others in the room with them. In this way, it doesn't seem so lonely. It's an escape from having to think about what meal time used to be like when it was shared with a spouse.

Anthony's wife has Alzheimer's disease. He tried to take care of her by himself. Finally, he just couldn't anymore and he had to move her into a nursing home. "Sometimes, I spend eight hours sitting at her bedside. I try to talk with her. Often she doesn't know who I am.

Sometimes she lashes out and says such mean things to me. She never talked to me that way. I am so sad. I have lost my wife, and she doesn't even realize it. It takes all my strength to go and visit her. Now I know why some people kill themselves."

Anthony is experiencing loss. He is grieving for the life he and his wife had experienced. Even though his wife has not physically died, he has already experienced her death. He would be an excellent candidate for a bereavement or support group.

The other manual the participants receive is also written by Therese Schoeneck. It is *How to Form Support Groups and Services for Grieving Persons*. The thing I like best about this book is its practicality. It asks specific questions of the reader to help in planning that person's support group. There are examples of letters to be written, schedules of meetings, ways to raise funds, and a list of *Ten Commandments for a Good Listener*.

Let me again give you two examples from this manual. The first is on page 26, written by Mark T. Scrivani, M.A., and is entitled "Support Group for Young People." His main point is that working with children presents different challenges than those of working with adults. Children attend support groups on the advice and/or insistence of others. Creativity in planning for a children's group is much more important than in planning for an adult group. He also says that the facilitator must like working with children and must have a history of good rapport with them.

The other example is on page 15 under the heading "Reasons Support Groups Dissolve." Reading these reasons before a group begins helps a parish to be aware of possible pitfalls. The main reasons for groups dissolving, according to this list, include: an unqualified facilitator or one who is not dedicated to being there, lack of commitment on the part of the congregation (financial, space availability, and continued information and invitations to parish members); and, being constantly unaccepting of and/or not open to newcomers.

While on internship for my Master's program, I was asked to lead a weekly post-stroke support group. There are so many issues of loss which can be shared in a group such as this. It is important for the facilitator to remember that grief and bereavement are experienced in more circumstances than that of death. Before our first session, I worked very hard on an agenda for our first meeting. I developed "ice breakers" and chose a topic I thought would be appropriate for our first group. When I shared my plans with my supervisor, she said, "This isn't your group. You've never had a stroke. Listen to the needs of the participants. Let them set the agenda. Don't you determine with what subjects they need to deal."

I think this could also be a reason why some bereavement groups terminate. I think a needs assessment of those participants should be the basis for the character of the group. Also, the initial assessment has to be reassessed periodically as the members of the group change.

Kristina and Alyson's father died of cancer when they were ten and twelve years old. The hospice worker suggested they attend a support group of other children who were experiencing loss. At the meetings, the girls were asked to draw pictures to describe their feelings. Alyson and Kristina only attended a few meetings. They didn't like drawing the pictures. They found the comfort they needed and the opportunity to speak of their grief with their pastor, and in the warmth and openness of their Sunday school friends. Perhaps they would have been more willing to draw pictures and talk about them had they been given an opportunity to have some input into the group structure.

The American Association of Retired Persons has a *Grief Support Training for Clergy and Congregations.* "The training is designed to be the first step in developing long-term grief support systems. It is adaptable to ecumenical/interfaith groups or to single congregations. The three sessions will prepare clergy and laypersons to recognize and understand the grief process, as well as design programs for their individual congregations and communities that will address the need for grief support" (p. 2).

This training manual also gives practical tips on preparing for a grief workshop. It makes suggestions about how the room should be set up and what equipment will be needed. The advantage of this program is the completeness of its instructions for use. The left-hand side of the page suggests to the leader how much time should be spent on each segment of the sessions. Each of the three sessions have handouts for discussion or for informational purposes, which can be copied by the trainer for her workshop. There are notes to the trainer included in the text which give helpful hints. For example, one reads: "(Note: Be sure to mention that the methods of coping vary from person to person and that some techniques are more likely to assist with grief resolution than others.)" (p. 22). Another note encourages the facilitator to let people call out their suggestions and to have someone write a list of those suggestions.

Not every parish may want, or be able to, train a facilitator for grief support groups. There are so many other services that can be done by a parish to show love and support to those who are suffering from loss.

I drove around for blocks, looking for a parking space. I was sad and nervous, and didn't want to deal with this parking hassle. Finally, blocks away, I found a spot and began to walk in the summer heat toward my destination—an old Lutheran church in Jersey City, New

Jersey. As I rounded the corner, I was overwhelmed at the line of people standing waiting to enter the church. The line formed half-way down the block. It was silent, and moved slowly. Its inhabitants were dressed elegantly, with most of the women wearing hats. What a contrast to the dirty city streets bustling with the Saturday morning activities of shopping and car-washing.

I joined the mourners at the end of the line and waited for my turn to enter the cool sanctuary. It was a relief to be out of the sun, sitting, and focusing my thoughts on the Cross at the front of the church while we waited for the service to begin.

I had come to worship God and to mourn with others the death of my friend, Mona. I had grown close to her in the two years of our friendship. She had a way of laughing that was infectious, a way of caring that was genuine and selfless. She had loved Jesus and shared this love with me, and with all these people who had gathered together in this church to say goodbye.

Mona was thirty-three when she died of AIDS. She had contracted it through her husband, who had been a drug user. Her mother had called me two days before to tell me it was "over," and to ask me to read a lesson at Mona's funeral.

Before her illness, Mona taught me about loving and caring for others. During her illness, she taught me about death. She spoke openly about her anger, her Lord, and about forgiveness.

In her church, I watched and listened as people spoke, sung songs, and read poems. I watched as her husband sat up front with her parents, and wondered about the power of God's love and the ability to forgive.

I still think about that parish and the love and support they gave to that family. What a sense of community and strength Mona's parents and husband must have derived when they saw the long line of mourners stretching down the street, waiting to join together in the comfort of prayer. The care, love and support of this parish was there for this family.

For those parishes who wish to go beyond the support shown at a funeral mass, I would suggest the Social Ministry Committee as an appropriate group to take on the responsibility of starting a grief support committee. They could devise a questionnaire to be distributed to all members of their faith community. They may want to share it with others as well. If the parish runs a school, or permit community groups to use church facilities, the questionnaire might be extended to these groups as well.

The questions to be included should come out of a committee brainstorming session, so that it properly reflects the needs and concerns of that particular parish. The questionnaire should most likely begin with a brief description of the objectives of a bereavement ministry. By sending the questionnaire to every member, an opportunity to participate in a parish ministry is offered to those who remain (for whatever reason) anonymous in the parish. This may be just the kind of ministry that will enable them to use their talents, and give them a fuller sense of belonging. The homebound members of the parish can also be made to feel part of the church family through a bereavement ministry. They can write sympathy cards or anniversary notes, make support calls, or pray for the bereaved.

A few examples from the form which would encourage members to participate in a bereavement ministry could include:

- Praying for the bereaved
- Calling the bereaved periodically for a time of at least a year
- Writing notes and sending cards
- House sitting during wake/funeral
- Picking up out-of-town relatives at the airport, etc.
- Organizing food donations
- Developing/maintaining a grief library
- Helping with the meal/reception after the burial

Open your thoughts. Dream. There are so many more ways individuals can be available to others. Make sure the choices include both a one-time only involvement as well as on-going commitment.

When sixteen-year-old Valerie suddenly fell into a coma, the doctor diagnosed it as stemming from a virus. For twelve days, she was fast asleep. Her four brothers and sisters sang to her. Her Sunday school class drew pictures for her. Her pastor and his wife held her, screamed at her, demanded that she open her eyes. The congregation asked that we, as a parish, "do something" to help bring this dear girl out of her coma. Fifty people gathered in our living room to do the best thing we could do—we held hands and we prayed. Most of all, we were comforted by the knowledge that we were a family, united in support of one another. The next day, Valerie came out of her coma. Please note that it does *not* always end this way. The focus is the support and the reminder that in life and death, God's touching love is with us.

The minister usually is, and probably should be, the first representative of a parish (and of Christ) to meet the emotional and spiritual needs of members at their moment of loss. The congregation (members) needs (need) to continue that ministering.

I have attended several wakes and heard those in mourning say, "Where would I get the strength to get through this if it weren't for my faith in my Lord and the love of my parish family!" These people will continue to need that strength after six months—a year—two years. We have that ability, to be there for them.

A FINAL MOMENT IN TIME

Vera's doctor told her that he was sending her husband, Jimmy, home the next day. It was clear now that there was no more that could be medically done to prolong his life. His cancer had won. The hospital social worker arranged for a hospice worker to be at Vera's home when the hospital released Jimmy.

When three days had passed, Vera called the pastor to inform him that Jimmy was not expected to live through the day. The pastor left for their home immediately, where he remained long enough to pray with them and to sit awhile, holding Vera's hand. He returned later in the afternoon, to see how Vera was holding up in her vigil at Jimmy's side. Susan, the hospice caregiver, was there still, sadly watching the pastor cry with Vera and hold onto to her as they watched this dearly beloved friend and husband slip away into eternity. As the evening chime struck eight o'clock, Susan, realizing what had just passed and what was to come, gently spoke to Vera, "Jimmy died—call the church."

SOME RESOURCES

Carol Luebering, *To Comfort All Who Mourn: A Parish Handbook for Ministry to the Grieving,* St. Anthony Messenger Press, 1615 Republic Street, Cincinnati, Ohio 45210, 1980.

Charles Meyer, *Surviving Death: A Practical Guide to Caring for the Dying and Bereaved,* Twenty-Third Publications, 185 Willow Street, P.O. Box 180, Mystic, Connecticut 06355 (203) 536-2611, 1988.

Therese S. Schoeneck, *Hope for Bereaved, Understanding, Coping and Growing Through Grief,* 1342 Lancaster Ave., Syracuse, New York 13210 (315) 472-HOPE, 1982.

Therese S. Schoeneck, *How to Form Support Groups and Services for Grieving People,* 1342 Lancaster Ave., Syracuse, New York 13210 (315) 472-HOPE, 1989.

Mervin E. Thompson, "What You Need to Know," in *When Death Touches Your Life,* Prince of Peace Publishing, Inc., 200 E. Nicollet Blvd., Burnsville, Minnesota 55337, 1987.

Grief Support Training for Clergy and Congregations, A Project of the Interreligious Liaison Office and the Widowed Persons Service Program Department, American Association of Retired Persons, 1909 K Street, N.W. Washington, D.C. 20049, 1989.

The Grief Helper Program, Aid Association for Lutherans, 4321 N. Ballard Road, Appleton, Wisconsin 545915-9931, 1982.

Parish Bereavement Ministry Training Program, Family Life Ministries, 100 Linden Ave., Irvington, New Jersey 07111

SOME GRIEF SUPPORT SERVICES

1. AIDS National Hot Line
   1-800-342-AIDS
   They will give you phone numbers for local AIDS Support Groups and will send you printed material.

2. *National Sudden Infant Death Syndrome Foundation*
   Two Metro Plaza, Suite 205
   8240 Professional Pl.
   Landover, Maryland 20785
   (800) 221-SIDS

3. *Parents of Murdered Children*
   100 East Eighth St., Room 1341
   Cincinnati, Ohio 45202
   (513) 721-5683

4. *Parents of Suicides*
   15 E. Brinkerhoff Ave., 2nd Fl.
   Palisades Park, New Jersey 07650
   (201) 585-7608

5. *The Compassionate Friends* (Bereaved Parents)
   P.O. Box 1347
   Oak Brook, Illinois 60521
   (312) 323-5010

6. *THEOS Foundation* (Young and Middle Age Widow/Widowers)
   410 Penn Hills Mall
   Pittsburgh, Pennsylvania 15235
   (412) 243-4299

7. *The Widowed Persons Service*
   1090 K St., N.W.
   Washington, D.C. 20049 (202) 728-4370

Conclusion

Perhaps as one concludes this volume, six observations seem to be clearly reflected.

1. Life-Threatening Illness, Dying and Loss are Spiritual Crises

These chapters clearly reinforce the concept that life-threatening illness, dying and death are not just medical, psychological and social crises, they cause profound spiritual arises as well. In fact as Becker notes, secular society is largely silent in the face of suffering and death [1]. Science may aptly explain the "how" of death, but it does not explain the "why." Here religious and philosophical systems may proffer answers. And it is both the seeking and evaluating these answers that are at the nexus of the spiritual struggle that results from an encounter with dying and death.

This encounter may be resolved in many ways. Fowler and Coles, for example, see faith often developing throughout the life cycle [2, 3]. Spiritual struggles then can be an impetus to change and growth. But this only one of many possible resolutions. Spiritual crisis can result in reaffirmation or rejuvenation of beliefs but they can also result in belief systems being deemphasized, altered or even discarded.

2. Spiritual Assessments are a Critical Part of the Counseling Process

As Joseph Campbell so eloquently states, our myths and beliefs shape our behaviors [4]. Counselors then explore the religious and spiritual beliefs of their clients. Such spiritual assessments should consider a wide variety of issues including:

- The clients' religious and spiritual background and upbringing;
- Other religious and spiritual influences within their lives;
- The clients' spiritual development, that is tracing the ways that the clients' spiritual beliefs have changed throughout the life cycle (often it can be revealing to explore the impetus for such change);
- Clients' religious and spiritual experiences including the ways that these experiences influence interpretation of and response to the current crisis;
- Clients' current religious and spiritual beliefs and values;
- Clients' current denominational and congregational affiliations;
- Clients' religious behaviors, practices and beliefs—before, during, and after the illness and loss;
- Clients' beliefs (and the roots of those beliefs) about illness, suffering, dying, death and grief;
- Factors in their faith or philosophical systems that complicate or facilitate adjustment to illness, dying, death and loss;
- Clients' experiences with rituals and traditions including facets of rituals that comforted them or troubled them;
- Rituals and traditions that they experienced at the time of the illness and loss;
- Persons, including clergy and others, that clients feel comfortable in discussing religious and spiritual issues;
- The role of their congregation and/or clergy in previous or present crises;
- Available resources such as self-help and support groups, self-help books, clergy, congregations or others.

In this assessment, counselors may also seek to understand the ways that the clients' culture and ethnicity, social roles and current place in the life course, developmental level and experiences, and historical and generational forces have influenced his/her spiritual development and perspectives.

As stated earlier, a knowledge of the person's general religious traditions may assist this exploration. But it is also important not to assume that the person's orientation or framework reflects that background. Often there is a great disparity between the official theology of a tradition, and the orientation and beliefs of members. Earlier, I had suggested that research in religious beliefs might better focus on basic faith themes such as "grace" or "judgement" perspectives rather than denominational affiliation.

3. Interventions May Need to Address Spiritual Issues

Often such interventions may even utilize religious rituals, practices and beliefs. For example, one Jewish client feeling guilty about his own treatment of his spouse when she was in the final stages of Alzheimers' disease was able to expiate his guilt by a specific act of charity. That gift, given in loving memory of his wife, was consistent with his beliefs about memory and atonement.

4. Addressing Such Concerns May be Uncomfortable to Counselors and Other Caregivers

Often such concerns may be difficult for different caregivers for disparate reasons. Clergy may be troubled by faith issues. They may be uncomfortable about addressing issues of doubt, unsure about how to deal with parishioners' beliefs when they are at odds with their own religious tradition. One clergy woman, for example, expressed a particular discomfort at dealing with what she described as "comforting hereses," or beliefs of her parishioners that she perceived as resting on a poor theological base, but that were clearly reassuring to her people. Clergy may not know how to effectively utilize the power of their own rituals. And they may be rigid in their own beliefs and rituals.

Other caregivers and counselors may feel inadequate about their own ability to assess and assist clients in their spiritual struggle. They may have unresolved spiritual issues themselves. They may feel uncomfortable in using or understanding religious language or ritual.

5. Counselors Need to Explore Their Own Religious and Spiritual Values and Beliefs

As with any other area of counseling, a counselor's ability to assist is enhanced by personal self exploration. And this exploration must address personal spiritual perspectives.

6. Counselors Must be Respectful Of and Utilize the Values, Beliefs, Framework, and Rituals of Their Clients

Counselors must begin by assisting clients in finding the strengths and utilizing the resources of their own religious and spiritual perspectives. And as with other areas of loss, these beginnings may lead to other, deeper and richer perspectives and understandings. But these remain the clients' struggles. Counselors cannot hope to impose their own belief system upon clients. For the very notion of "spiritual" struggle affirms it is ultimately an individual one.

REFERENCES

1. E. Becker, *The Denial of Death,* Free Press, New York, 1973.
2. J. Fowler, *Stages of Faith: The Psychology of Human Development and the Onset of Meaning,* Harper and Row, New York, 1981.
3. R. Coles, *The Call of Stories: Teaching and the Moral Imagination,* Houghton Mifflin, Boston, 1989.
4. Joseph Campbell, *The Mythic Image,* Princeton University Press, Princeton, New Jersey, 1974.

Contributors

CRAIG BELL, M.S., is an Associate Professor and Deputy Chairman in the Department of Health and Nutrition Sciences, Brooklyn College. He has been a member of the faculty for the past twenty-six years where, in addition to his present position, he also served as the First Coordinator of the Afro-American Institute. Professor Bell has developed and taught courses on the health problems of African-Americans, worked with the National Black Science Student Organization on campus, and served on the College Affirmative Action Committee.

JANET M. BOUMAN, Gerontologist, is currently working in the Social Work Department of an Adult Day Care Center. She has also worked as a Case Manager for older adults. She has lead retreats sponsored by her Church Body focusing on: Parish programs for bereavement ministry; Ministry to/with/for older adults; and community resources available for caregivers and older adults. She has also worked with a community organization network advocating for affordable housing for Seniors. As a Eucharistic Minister she takes the Eucharist to homebound members of her parish.

SR. ALICE CULLINAN, Ph.D. is a member of the Sisters for Christian Community. She is a New York State licensed Psychologist, certified in both Death Education and Death Counseling and has had extensive experience in counseling both traumatized and/or bereaved individuals, couples, families and groups of professional men and women. Her many publications and presentations in the area of trauma and thanatology attest to her deep care and concern for survivors of both trauma and loss, as well as for the terminally ill and dying. An additional interest she has is the teaching of Principles of Counseling the Traumatized, the Bereaved and the Dying to Health Care Professionals. These include physicians, nurses and those in allied professions, clergy, mental health professionals and hospice workers. For the past fifteen years she has taught these courses on the post-graduate and graduate level as well as to community groups.

DR. KENNETH J. DOKA is currently a professor of Gerontology and Thanatology at the Graduate School of The College of New Rochelle. Since receiving his doctorate in Sociology from St. Louis University, he has published three books, *Living With Life-Threatening Illness, Disenfranchised Grief,* and *Death and Spirituality,* and over forty articles in journals and trade magazines such as *The American Funeral Director.*

DAVID L. ECHELBARGER is a Lutheran Pastor, writer, therapist and former director of an outpatient counseling clinic. Presently he serves Immanuel Lutheran Church in Negaunee, Michigan with his wife, the Rev. Christine Thomas-Echelbarger. He is active on a national board of the Evangelical Lutheran Church in America, publishes a weekly newspaper column, "Reflections Spiritual," and has written for devotional periodicals.

RABBI DR. EARL A. GROLLMAN was the Rabbi of the Beth El Temple Center, Belmont, Massachusetts for thirty-six years before his early retirement to devote himself to writing and lecturing. He is the author of twenty-one books including the UNESCO award volume *Talking About Death: A Dialogue Between Parent and Child,* (Beacon Press, 1990).

ROBERTA HALPERN is Director of The Center for Thanatology Research. Active in the Foundation of Thanatology, she is a frequent contributor to journals and books.

JEANNE M. HARPER is Executive Director of Alpha-Omega Venture, an education and consultation firm and a psychotherapist at Lutheran Social Services. She has a B.A. in Thanatology: Death Education and Grief Counseling from University of Wisconsin and a Masters in Pastoral Studies: Family Ministry from Loyola University, Louisiana. She is contributing editor for *Thanatos*; Associate Editor of case studies for *Illness, Crisis and Loss* journal; Membership Retention Chair for the Association for Death Education and Counseling (ADEC); State Coordinator for Wisconsin Youth Suicide Prevention; co-author of *Hurting Yourself,* a book for teens who have attempted suicide; board member for Wisconsin Professional Speakers Association; trained in Clinical Pastoral Education, Youth Ministry and Critical Incident Stress Debriefing of which she is Clinical Director for her area team. She has been teaching in the area of death and dying since 1977. Her radio interview by Bill Leonoff on WIKB on "Teen Sexuality" received a Michigan State Award. She is nationally certified as a Death Educator and Grief Counselor through ADEC.

PAUL IRION is Professor Emeritus of Pastoral Theology at Lancaster Theological Seminary of the United Church of Christ in Lancaster, Pennsylvania. Educated at Elmhurst College, Eden Theological

Seminary and the University of Chicago, he has been a parish pastor and hospital chaplain prior to seminary teaching. He is author of *The Funeral and the Mourners, The Funeral: Vestige or Value?, Cremation, Hospice and Ministry,* and *Nobody's Child: A Generation Caught in the Middle.*

JEFFREY KAUFFMAN, M.A., M.S.S., L.S.W., is a psychotherapist with a specialization in Loss and Mourning. He is a consultant to clergy and congregations, hospices, funeral directors, mental retardation programs, mental health agencies, drug and alcohol programs, nursing homes and geriatric care managers, schools, and emergency services—for clinical services, program development and training. He is a clinical consultant, group facilitator and board member of Families of Murder Victims in Philadelphia, and M.A.D.D. He is founder and director of the Institute for Spirituality and Psychological Healing. He is the author of numerous articles, and editor of the forthcoming book, *Awareness of Mortality,* to be published by Baywood Publishing in the same series as this volume.

DENNIS KLASS received his Ph.D. in the psychology of religion from the University of Chicago. He is a professor and department chair at Webster University in St. Louis, Missouri. For over a decade Klass has been the professional advisor to the St. Louis chapter of the Compassionate Friends, a self-help group of parents whose children have died. He has used that role to do an ethnographic study of the group. He has written a book, *Parental Grief: Solace and Resolution* (Springer, 1988), and many journal articles on parental bereavement. In 1992, the National Board of the Compassionate Friends gave Klass their Appreciation Award. He has also published on the psychology of religious leadership and on death education and counseling. Klass maintains a small counseling/therapy practice with Resources for Crisis and Change, a group specializing in the treatment of people with complex and difficult losses.

NATHAN KOLLAR is professor of Religious Studies at St. John Fisher College and senior lecturer in the Graduate School of Education and Human Relations at the University of Rochester. He is the author of numerous books and articles, including the book *Songs of Suffering* (1982) and "Challenges to Theories of Grief," a recent article in the journal, *Human Development 11*:4 (Winter, 1990), which reviews the limits of current grief theories. He developed the National Certification Program for the Association for Death Education and Counseling and served as the chair of the program for its first four years.

DOROTHY C. H. LEY graduated in medicine from the University of Toronto in 1948 and pursued a career as an academic haematologist/oncologist. She founded the Palliative Care Foundation in Canada in 1981 and was its Executive Director until 1986. Dr. Ley's professional activities have included membership on the Boards of Directors of Casey House (a hospice for AIDS in Toronto), the National Hospice Organization (as its Canadian representative), and the International Work Group on Death, Dying and Bereavement. She is presently President and Chairman of the Board of the Dorothy Ley Hospice in Toronto and Chairman of the AIDS Committee of the Diocese of Toronto of the Anglican Church in Canada. From 1984 to 1987 she was the Chairman of the Canadian Medical Association's Committee on Health Care of the Elderly and of the Committee for implementation of its recommendations from 1988 to 1990. She is the immediate past Chairman of the Canadian Coalition on Medication Use in the Elderly and of the National Continuing Care Liaison Committee. Her distinguished career has brought many honors, including membership in the Honour Medical Fraternity Alpha Omega Alpha, Her Majesty's Jubilee Medal (1977), and a Certificate of Merit from the Canadian Cancer Society in 1963. She is a Life Member of the International Council of Women, and a past president of the Academy of Medicine in Toronto. In 1988 Dr. Ley became the first woman to receive the Canadian Medical Association's Medal of Service, and in 1989 she was created a Commander of the Military and Hospitaller Order of Saint Lazarus of Jerusalem. In 1989 the Metropolitan Toronto District of the Ontario Medical Association awarded Dr. Ley the Neville Hodson Walker Award for "Service, selflessness and sacrifice in the field of medicine and her outstanding contribution as a doctor." She is a life member of the Ontario Medical Association and a Senior Member of the Canadian Medical Association. Dr. Ley is retired from active practice. She is a Lay Reader in the Anglican Parish of Brock and Rector's Warden of St. Paul's Beaverton. She sits on a number of Diocesan committees, including the Planning Committee and the AIDS Committee and is a representative to the Provincial and Diocesan Synods. She is also on the Board of the Ontario Palliative Care Association and the Section on Palliative Care of the Ontario Medical Association.

DAVID K. MEAGHER, Ed.D., is a Professor of Health and Nutrition Sciences at Brooklyn College of CUNY where he is the coordinator of the Thanatology concentration within the Master of Arts degree program. In addition he is the President of the Association for Death Education and Counseling and the editor of The Thanatology Newsletter.

EDWARD JEREMY MILLER is a professor of religious studies at Gwynedd-Mercy College, Pennsylvania. He received the Ph.D. and S.T.D. degrees from the University of Louvain, Belgium (1975). He has also taught theology at Emory University in Atlanta, Georgia; and has published in the fields of systematic theology (ecclesiology, sacramentology, Christology) and historical theology (Aquinas, John Henry Newman). His most recent book is *John Henry Newman on the Idea of Church* (Patmos Press, 1987).

JOHN D. MORGAN is Professor of Philosophy and Director of the Center for Education about Death and Bereavement at King's College of the University of Western Ontario, London, Canada. Dr. Morgan has been teaching courses about death and bereavement since 1968 and has coordinated the King's College International Conferences on Death and Bereavement since 1982. Dr. Morgan is editor of *Thanatology: A Liberal Arts Approach; Suicide: Helping Those at Risk; Death Education in Canada; The Dying and the Bereaved Teenager;* and *Young People and Death.* Dr. Morgan is the Consulting Editor for the Death, Value and Meaning Series published through Baywood Publishing Company. Dr. Morgan's research interests focus on issues of cultural attitudes related to death and bereavement.

ROBERT E. NEALE is Emeritus Professor of Psychiatry and Religion at Union Theological Seminary. He is the author of *The Art of Dying, In Praise of Play,* and co-author of *Death and Ministry,* as well as numerous articles. Since retirement, Dr. Neale has become very interested in the "Trickster" tradition.

JANE NICHOLS is a Bereavement Consultant at Children's Hospital Medical Center of Akron (Ohio). She entered the field of Thanatology through Funeral Service where she was one of the pioneers of the adaptive funeral and of offering ongoing supportive care to bereaved persons. Since joining Children's Hospital staff in 1978, she has conducted original research regarding parental reactions to the death of newborn infants and has developed a responsive bereavement program. Author of numerous articles and contributor to several books, Ms. Nichols was the chairperson of the original workgroup on Bereavement Issues in the International Work Group on Death, Dying, and Bereavement (IWG) and has contributed to their work on the Spiritual Issues of mourners. A past officer of the Association of Death Education and Counseling (ADEC), she is a certified Death Educator and a bereaved parent.

PATRICE O'CONNOR is the Director of the Palliative Care Educational Service at St. Luke/Roosevelt Hospital Center in New York City. Ms. O'Connor was the Director of the Hospice/Palliative Care Program at St. Luke's for twelve years. She has lectured nationally and internationally on palliative care. She has done research and published in the areas of administration of hospice/palliative care and spiritual care in hospice. Ms. O'Connor is a member of the International Work Group on Death, Dying and Bereavement.

DR. RICHARD A. PACHOLSKI is Professor of English at Millikin University, Decatur, Illinois. Now in his twenty-second year at Millikin, he taught previously at Marquette University and the University of Wisconsin. He studies and teaches a variety of subjects, most recently, death and dying. Pacholski has published a number of articles, chapters and reviews in the field of death studies. He is co-author of a standard reference book for teachers, *Death Education: An Annotated Resource Guide* (1980 and 1985), and four anthologies of essays published by the Association for Death Education and Counseling. He has served as media editor of the scholarly journal, *Death Studies*.

HOWARD C. RAETHER received his Ph.B. (1937) and J.D. (1939) from Marquette University. He was granted an Honorary Doctor of Humane Letters by the Cincinnati College of Mortuary Science (Xavier University, 1986). He has spoken to funeral directors; to students in colleges of mortuary science and university classes; and at symposia on dying, death and bereavement. He edited and contributed to *Successful Funeral Service Practice* (Prentice Hall, 1971) and to *The Funeral Directors' Practice Management Handbook* (Prentice Hall, 1989). He authored or co-authored chapters in a number of books and has written numerous consumer pamphlets on pre- and post-death activities. He was a consultant to the U.S. Department of Transportation and the National Center for Health Statistics of the Department of Health and Services. He has received service awards or commendations from the Army, Air Force, Social Security Administration, and Veterans Administration. He was the Executive Secretary/Director of the National Funeral Directors Association from 1948 to 1984. He now serves that association in a consultant capacity.

DENNIS RYAN earned his Ph.D. in Comparative Religions. His doctoral thesis was on the Mahabharata, the ancient epic of the Hindus. More recently, he lived for a year in China, researching the state of traditional beliefs and practices. He teaches courses on Chinese and Indian thought and culture at the College of New Rochelle.

ROBERT STEVENSON has taught a death education course to the students of River Dell High School in Oradell, New Jersey for over twenty years and is co-chairman of the Seminar on Death at Columbia University. He is a nationally-certified death educator and grief counselor who has been widely published on topics related to loss and grief. He is active in both the International Work Group on Death, Dying and Bereavement (I.W.G.) and the Association for Death Education and Counseling (A.D.E.C.). He is a graduate of the College of the Holy Cross (B.A.) and holds master's degrees from Fairleigh Dickinson University (M.A.T.) and Montclair State College (M.A.) and a doctoral degree

(Ed.D.) from Fairleigh Dickinson. Dr. Stevenson has written curricula for health and death education courses and has been honored for his work as an educator and counselor by: The New Jersey Professional Counselors' Association, the New Jersey Governor's Office, United States Chess Federation, National Council for the Social Studies, and is listed in Who's Who Among America's Teachers and Who's Who Among Human Service Professionals.

BEN WOLFE, M.Ed., LICSW, is the developer and Program Director of St. Mary's Medical Center's Grief Support Center in Duluth, Minnesota which was established in January, 1985. He is a nationally-certified grief counselor and death educator, does life threatening illness and bereavement counseling, and currently facilitates various support groups for youngsters five through seventeen years of age, a support group for senior citizens, a support group for hospice staff and volunteers, and provides workshops, inservices and presentations on topics related to grief and loss at the local, regional, state, national and international levels. In addition to consulting with hospitals, schools, agencies and organizations throughout the United States, Canada, and overseas, he has taught a graduate course on dying and death the past twelve years at the University of Minnesota, Duluth, and the past four years a course entitled The Psychosocial-Spiritual Aspects of Life Threatening Illness for the University of Minnesota, Duluth School of Medicine. He is on the Board of Directors for the Minnesota Coalition for Death Education and Support, past board member for the Greater North AIDS Project, member of the Northeastern MN SIDS Regional Round-table, and member and co-clinical director of the Head of the Lakes Critical Incident Stress Debriefing team. Mr. Wolfe has been a member of the Association for Death Education and Counseling (ADEC) for a number of years, chairing both the ADEC National Conference Committee and the ADEC Chapter Relations Committee, and a board member for three years previous to being elected in 1992 Second Vice-President of the Association.

ELLEN ZINNER, Psy.D., is currently co-director of the Center for Loss and Grief Therapy in Kensington, Maryland. She is immediate past-president of the Association for Death Education and Counseling.

Index

Bowery, the, 75, 76
British Humanist Society, 186
Buddha Amitabha, 83, 84, 90
Buddhism, 52, 66, 75, 76, 79,
    81-84, 90, 91, 93, 116, 157,
    178
burial, 22, 24, 29, 30, 31, 62, 84, 91,
    173, 208, 209, 210, 211, 212,
    243, 244, 248, 258, 263, 272,
    273, 329, 355, 365, 366, 367,
    375
Brahman, 78, 158 282
Butts, Calvin O., 119

California, 266, 347
Calvinism, 34, 54, 62
Canada, 1, 53, 171
cancer, 66, 68, 123, 124, 125, 144,
    154, 174, 176, 221, 263, 271,
    280, 317, 336, 345, 346, 347,
    348, 349, 350, 359, 360, 366,
    373, 376
caregiving, 1, 2, 3, 9, 11-17, 30, 84,
    103, 107-112, 118, 122, 124,
    126-129, 131, 132, 133, 134,
    136, 137, 138, 139, 140, 146,
    147, 148, 156, 157, 165, 166,
    167, 168, 170, 171-179, 196,
    198, 199, 201, 204, 218, 219,
    221, 226, 230, 244, 245, 246,
    247, 248, 252, 254, 258, 259,
    260, 262, 263, 264, 272, 273,
    309, 311, 313, 317, 318, 320,
    321, 333, 343, 346, 347, 348,
    349, 350, 351, 353, 355, 356,
    357, 358, 359, 360, 376, 381
Cartesian mind/body dualism, 173,
    174, 176
casket/coffin, 23, 211, 213, 217,
    225, 324, 368
ceremonies, 19, 22, 23, 31, 85, 119,
    188, 207, 208, 209, 210, 211,
    212, 338
Chang Tsai, 84
chaplains 75, 76, 111, 171, 175,
    239, 336, 353

Chaplin, Charles, 325
Chernobyl, 177
Chevrah Kaddisha, 30
chicken pox, 40
children, 24, 30, 53, 61, 63, 101,
    122, 146, 152, 158, 162, 177,
    187, 188, 203, 217, 222, 223,
    224, 227, 228, 235, 240, 257,
    258, 260, 261, 262, 264, 265,
    269, 270, 271, 272, 282, 283,
    286, 297, 298, 299, 300, 311,
    313, 316, 319, 325, 328, 337,
    339, 348-351, 357, 360, 361,
    372, 373
children (death of), 64, 72, 125,
    145, 186, 187, 189, 236, 240,
    243-255, 348, 349, 350, 351,
    360, 365
China, 1, 75, 76, 84, 85, 86, 88, 90,
    91, 321
Chinatown (New York City), 75
Christianity, 3, 6, 25, 33-49, 51-73,
    93, 96, 110, 111, 116, 117, 147,
    148, 149, 158, 159, 161, 172,
    173, 178, 182, 209, 212, 213,
    222, 250, 251, 252, 282, 292,
    299, 309, 324, 327, 338, 340
chronicity, 11, 127, 131, 147, 170,
    211, 222, 229, 294, 298, 311,
    315, 318, 352, 355
Chuang Tzu, 86, 87, 88, 89
clergy, 2, 15, 16, 20, 59, 60, 71,
    110, 136, 138, 148, 149, 186,
    191, 192, 195, 196, 198, 199,
    204, 207, 211, 213, 214, 219,
    220, 226, 230, 231, 232, 233,
    235, 239, 240, 243, 245, 247,
    248, 249, 250, 251, 252, 253,
    254, 258, 262, 267, 273, 274,
    275, 276, 295, 335, 337, 338,
    341, 343, 368, 373, 380, 381
Cleveland, 22
*Clinical Pastoral Care for
    Hospitalized Children*, 339
"coming out" (gays and lesbians),
    268-269, 271
committal service, 212, 213, 249